Debating Gandhi

Debating Gandhi

edited by
A. Raghuramaraju

OXFORD
UNIVERSITY PRESS

OXFORD
UNIVERSITY PRESS

Oxford University Press is a department of the University of Oxford.
It furthers the University's objective of excellence in research, scholarship,
and education by publishing worldwide. Oxford is a registered trademark of
Oxford University Press in the UK and in certain other countries

Published in India by
Oxford University Press
2/11 Ground Floor, Ansari Road, Daryaganj , New Delhi 110 002, India

First Edition published in 2006
Oxford India Paperbacks 2010
Sixth impression 2018

ISBN-13: 978-0-19-807007-8
ISBN-10: 0-19-807007-1

Typeset in Times Norman on 10/12.6
by Jojy Philip, New Delhi 110 015
Printed in India by Replika Press Pvt. Ltd

Dedicated to
A. V. Afonso, who encouraged me to teach the contents of this
volume as a course; Sasheej Hegde for turning my attention
from philosophical discussion to writing; Y. S. Prahlad and
Alito Sequeira for making our stay at Goa University
a memorable one.

Contents

Introduction

A. RAGHURAMARAJU

Gandhi continues to attract the attention of scholars and social activists. Called 'Mahatma', Gandhi lived in the midst of the people, especially in difficult times such as the Indian freedom struggle and partition. He is also an author, though not in the modern sense. His writings, running into more than one hundred volumes, contain a wide range of views on different issues. Though leading a simple life and committed to moral and political values, his relentless experimentations with truth and changing contexts may not have lent his writings a propositional form. Nevertheless, works on him are both voluminous and diverse. There are works which present him from different perspectives such as Marxism, Liberalism, Feminism or Human Rights; there are also studies comparing him with other philosophers like Marx or Mill; as well as expositions of his views on themes such as moral and political philosophy, religion, women, and communalism. There are studies explicating the relevance of Gandhi to India and to the world; and studies that work out the consequences of his thoughts, provide a basis to his abstract standpoints, de-contextualize the varied contexts, and explain the meaning of his intervention, exposing the limitations and even inconsistencies in his writings.

While there is a rich variety of scholarly works on Gandhi, some of them radically different in interpretation from others, many of them run parallel to his thinking and have not resulted in a debate. There is a need to provide a platform from where different interpretations of Gandhi can be brought together in a debate, thereby elevating the understanding of Gandhi. Going beyond the comparative, expository, and even dialogical axes, this volume brings to centre stage the idea of debate. Differences are the pre-requisite to a debate, and a lively debate involves intellectual activity. Truth is not seen as given but has to be arrived at through arguments and counter-arguments.

This volume brings together essays that provide different perspectives on Gandhi. Section I brings together, for the first time, two essays on Gandhi, 'Traditional Influences on the Thought of Mahatma Gandhi' by A.L. Basham and 'Final Encounter: The Politics of the Assassination of Gandhi' by Ashis Nandy. Basham suggests that many concepts in Gandhi's thought are derived from 'Indian tradition' and were absorbed by him during his 'childhood and youth'. The contact with the West only brought to fruition these already existing traditional aspects. While maintaining that the major influence on Gandhi was tradition, Basham however concedes that 'two major planks in his platform' that are from the West and according to him 'seem to have had no prototypes in India's past'. They are: 'the dignity of manual labour and the emancipation of women' (p. 38 in this volume).

The intriguing fact is that these two aspects occupy centre stage in Nandy's brilliant interpretation explicating the politics underlying the assassination of Gandhi. In Nandy's reckoning, Gandhi's attempt is a 'part of the process of de-Brahmanization through de-intellectualization', which is 'constantly trying to pass off many aspects of the low-status, non-Brahmanic, commercial and peasant cultures in India as genuine Hinduism'. This disturbs the centre–periphery relationship, with the intellectual pursuits of the Brahmin at the centre, and manual labour at the periphery. The other aspect in Nandy's account is Gandhi's 'rediscovery of womanhood as a civilizing force in human society'. Both these, Nandy demonstrates, pose a serious threat to the 'traditional authority system in India'. What is of interest here is that these two aspects that form exceptions in Basham are the central concerns in Nandy. Further, precisely these two aspects, which are according to Basham external to what Gandhi inherited from his tradition, according to Nandy are problematic and posed serious dangers to traditional authority—which in the end cost Gandhi his life.

While Basham and Nandy draw very different conclusions (for the former, Gandhi's views on women were influenced by non-traditional sources in the West; for the latter, it is this aspect in Gandhi that subverted tradition), what must be noted here is that their primary resources are like two matching systems, and this structural feature has not been recognized by the readers of these essays. It is in this context that I think it is necessary to bring these two essays to understand Gandhi.

Here it may be of interest to note that though Basham's essay is included in a book edited by a leading Indian historian (Kumar 1971), it however hardly figures in later discussions on Gandhi. This essay is important for other reasons as well. First, it can be seen as seriously contesting attempts like that of Richard Lannoy, who, while ignoring Gandhi's childhood attempts to locate the main influences on him in his adulthood and that too during his life outside India. He recognizes no resonances of the past, as in his view Gandhi is a 'relentless explorer of immediacy'; the terrifying thing about him is the 'dimensionless *now* which he inhabits' (Lannoy 1974: 373 emphasis in original). The primary and initial influences in the formation of Gandhi are from the 'forward looking ... English liberal humanists who belonged to a tributary of the Protestant nonconformist tradition of radical dissent.' Gandhi, says Lannoy, had the 'good fortune to stumble almost somnambulistically' upon them. Spending a 'long period in the Western ambience as a pro-British Westernized Indian, coming to conscious grip with his Indian heritage' through 'Western eyes' and reading about Indian texts such as the Bhagavad Gita in English translation, Gandhi, according to Lannoy (1974: 374), 'never really got to know India at first hand,' that too not till he was well past his middle years.

While those engaging in this debate cannot perhaps deny the influence of either India or the West on Gandhi, what is contested is which of these constitutes the primary influence on him: his childhood or adulthood. For instance, Basham, almost resonating Freud, seems to emphasize the importance of childhood. On the other hand, Lannoy, as if following Descartes,[1] dismisses the domain of childhood, conceding only recalling 'childhood memories', which too are eventually 'modified' by 'Western influenced outlook'.[2]

Second, in situating the influences on Gandhi outside the fold of colonial knowledge systems and influences, it thwarts those attempts, like Partha Chatterjee's essay in this volume, which allege that the resources for dissenting colonialism are drawn from the very knowledge systems belonging to colonial societies. Third, in locating the influences on Gandhi in his 'childhood' and 'youth', Basham's essay can be seen as rejecting those interpretations like A.K. Saran's (1980: 681) that portray his 'striving towards a return to tradition' as anachronistic. Last, in conceding two important influences from the West, this essay saves Gandhi from the camp of orthodoxy, thereby distinguishing him from other religious personalities like Sankaracharya. In effect, this essay shows the availability of internal resources for dissenting colonialism within Indian tradition. Thus Basham's essay, which is conspicuously absent in the mainstream discussions on

Gandhi, is important as it exposes the limitations surrounding these other interpretations of Gandhi.

Section II focuses on a more direct relation between Gandhi and his critique of modernity. Like Section I, this section too brings together three essays. The last two of these can be seen as contesting the first one's interpretation of Gandhi, thus providing another platform to generate yet another debate. The first essay in this group is by Partha Chatterjee, titled 'The Moment of Manoeuvre: Gandhi and the Critique of Civil Society'. Chatterjee declares his task to be to read Gandhi's relation to nationalism. It is one of the major projects of modernity, that can be shown to rest on 'a total moral critique of the fundamental aspects of civil society', which falls outside the 'thematic of nationalism', whose rationalism, scientism, and historicism Gandhi rejected.

Notwithstanding his attempt to locate Gandhism outside the nationalist discourse, Chatterjee claims that 'the correct perspective for understanding the Gandhian ideology *as a whole* would be to study it in relation to the historical development of elite-nationalist thought in India.' He justifies this because, according to him, the ingenuity of Gandhism lies in facilitating the 'political appropriation of the subaltern classes by a bourgeoisie aspiring for hegemony in the new nation-state', and this uniqueness will be known only if we view it from this historical perspective. That is, though situated outside the nationalist thematic, Gandhism 'also concerned itself with the practical organizational questions of a political *movement*', which Chatterjee equates with '*national* political movement'. Thus equated, Chatterjee says that the 'unique achievement of Gandhian thought' is its attempt to 'reconcile these two contradictory aspects': namely, 'nationalism which stood upon a critique of the very idea of civil society' and 'a movement supported by the bourgeoisie which rejected the idea of progress'. Both, claims Chatterjee, 'were, at one and the same time, its integral part'. Having pointed out different ambiguities, compromises, and displeasures in Gandhi with regard to Congressmen moving towards the politics of the new nation-state and their move away from the ideals of *swaraj*, he concludes that Gandhism in its 'specific historical effectivity provided for the first time in Indian politics an ideological basis for including the *whole people* within the political nation' (emphasis in original). A nation where 'peasants are mobilised but do not participate, of a nation in which they are a part, but a national state from which they are for ever distanced' (p. 118 in this volume).

Thus, for Chatterjee, the major contribution of Gandhism (though it was itself outside the nationalist thematic) was to provide an inclusion, though not wholeheartedly and willingly, of the *whole people* within the political nation, thereby tragically getting co-opted or contributing to the growth and development of what he consistently rejected. Two important factors that contributed to this were: (i) Gandhism, unlike Tolstoy and Ruskin's romantic problematic, is also associated with 'nationalist political movement'; (ii) the powerful politics of the 'nationalist thematic', which Gandhi rejected but in a sense failed to gauge its effectiveness.

In the relation between Gandhi and modernity, Chatterjee highlighted the co-option of Gandhi by the nation-state. On the other hand, A.K. Saran —not only independent of Chatterjee but much before him[3]—in his essay, 'On the Promotion of Gandhian Studies at the University Level', sounds a cautious note suggesting the need to deflect from any attempt to introduce Gandhian studies in modern institutions like the university. Like Chatterjee, who demonstrated how Gandhism was co-opted, Saran too identifies how introducing Gandhian studies into university syllabi is a 'sure, smooth, and non-violent way to kill the spirit of Gandhian thinking'. This is because 'no total way of thinking-and-life can be understood in terms of a set of answers to questions that, in principle, belong to another world-view, another system of thought' (p. 128 in this volume). Otherwise, 'it is inevitable that it would be expected to answer questions generated from the modern Western framework of thought. This creates a dilemma: to succeed in meeting this expectation would mean damaging the form and violating the spirit of Gandhian thinking; to fail would mean exposing it as seriously inadequate on grounds that would, in reality, be logically irrelevant' (p. 128 in this volume). So Saran concludes that the 'aim of education in Gandhian thinking will most certainly be defeated, almost irreversibly, if Gandhian thinking were to be promoted through the universities' (p. 132 in this volume). Thus there is a need to save Gandhi from the necrophilic charms of the Indian universities—at any cost.[4]

Here, it may be pointed out that not only do Saran and Chatterjee both agree that there is a serious incompatibility between Gandhi and modernity; both also refer to the Nehruvian legacy in India that co-opted Gandhi. Whereas Chatterjee discusses what happened in pre-independent India to Gandhi, Saran, on the other hand, warns us against an impending danger to Gandhian thinking within the institutional prism of modernity in post-independent India. Further, while Chatterjee highlights Gandhi's critique of modernity and only marginally considers his positive programme, Saran in another essay (1980: 681) maintains that 'Gandhi's critique of the modern Western civilization ... is peripheral to his thinking.' Its real purpose is to 'participate in the transcendental Centre.' Yet another subtle difference between them is that while Chatterjee shows how Gandhism was co-opted by the nationalist thematic, for Saran the 'Gandhian world-view ... is ... a most radical one ... it [is] highly subversive to modern Western civilization' (1980: 364). For Saran there is an urgent need to 'save and nourish the radical ... spirit of Gandhian thinking' that threatened to subvert modern Western civilization. In the move by the ruling elite to promote Gandhian studies, he sees not a genuine change but their being presently 'disturbed because of the rapid deterioration of the modern Western white civilization' and their fear about the 'truly subversive potential of Gandhian thinking', which forces them to look for ways and means of co-opting and thereby containing Gandhian thinking. From the co-option in the past tense in Chatterjee to a caution against a similar possibility in the future in Saran, we can further explore the predicament of Gandhi in the present fast-changing scenario.

In Bhikhu Parekh's writing we find how Gandhi avoided relapsing into co-option. In his piece, titled 'Indianization of Autobiography', Parekh shows how Gandhi, rather than tamely imitating, instead actively Indianized a modern Western form. Parekh, away from the political terrains of contestations, focuses on 'text'. In this we have an instance which shows how Gandhi attempted to effect changes in indomitable modern Western institutions, especially in the genre of textual forms like autobiography that did not necessarily lead to co-option.

Like nation or university, autobiography too, Parekh maintains, presupposes a culture in which individuality is valued and cultivated (p. 150 in this volume), a culture which permeated 'in the late eighteenth and especially the early nineteenth century' (p. 149 in this volume). Prerequisites of autobiography were absent in India. However, during British rule, some of the cultural preconditions of autobiographical writing came into existence. For instance, British rule introduced 'modern individualism, and rationalism' and these new entries have become 'puzzles'. Access to Western literature offered the necessary intellectual tools for writing autobiographies (p. 154 in this volume). While British rule created some of the pre-conditions of autobiography, it also created others that militated against it. Situating Gandhi's autobiography against this conflicting background, that is, between modern Western and Indian, Parekh says, 'Gandhi's autobiography, written at a time when the tradition of writing one was just beginning to develop, reveals many of the doubts and anxieties ...'

While agreeing that the 'Western manner of writing the autobiography was essentially self-centred and egoistic', Gandhi, maintains Parekh, 'contended that this was not inherent in the genre' and that it was possible to write one in a 'morally innocent manner'. Gandhi overcame the 'vices' of self-assertion and self-glorification usually associated with autobiography by replacing the modern individual self with the soul or *atma*. He distinguished his *atmakatha* (the story of the soul) from autobiography (which is a description of life), and thereby claimed to achieve the 'opposite effect'. Gandhi's autobiography according to Parekh is 'free from the penitential outbursts of Augustine and the nervous exhibitionism of Rousseau, and is less brooding and introspective than either.' Summing up Gandhi's achievement, Parekh says, 'Gandhi could not Indianise the autobiography without Westernising the Indian cultural tradition ... The fact that he, a champion of traditional India, was prepared to turn his hand to a distinctively Western genre was a highly symbolic and radical act and showed to his nervous countrymen how to respond to foreign values and practices.'

This instance provides some shades which differ from the co-option thesis of Chatterjee. While these changes at the textual genre may not be suitable instances to contest political programmes, they nevertheless provide a small entry and some elbow room, within which to dodge the practice of co-option so as to lay bare the limitations of Chatterjee's thesis and in some respect even Saran's.

Likewise, it would be possible to identify aspects of Indianization in the formation of the nation or even the university. Further, Parekh's point demonstrating Gandhi as Indianizing Western forms can be said to avoid both embracing Puritanism and relapsing into essentialism. This aspect, however, eludes the attention of Saran and to some extent that of Chatterjee too. They, either explicitly or otherwise, desire Gandhi to operate outside the fold of modern Western institutional structures. Gandhi, on the other hand, seems to have willingly marched ahead, trespassing the borders of essentialism, perhaps because he assumed that in India modernity is a small, though effective, part within a large pre-modern society. Hence, for him, while there is a need to be cautious about modernity, there is no need to be extra-cautious and to become taciturn in dealing with it.

The third section also brings together three essays for a debate on Gandhi's views on modern science. The first essay, titled 'The Machine', by Sunil Sahasrabudhey maintains that Gandhi totally opposed modern science and offered a clear alternative to it. Gandhi's opposition to the modern machine is, according to Sahasrabudhey, 'total' and 'complete', and this is clearly evident both in his life and in his writings.[5] Sahasrabudhey discusses how the machine has substituted men and 'stolen their work', thus creating poverty for a large mass of people, alienating them from their traditional occupations. He identifies 'capital', 'technology', and 'time' as constituting the basic structures of the modern machine. In a section sub-titled 'The *Swadeshi* Alternative', he embarks on an elucidation of how there 'are people the world over who do not work on the machine.' There exist living aspects which 'constituted the basis of the village industries' that use 'local materials, exchange in the local market, and [have] control of the local territory as well as social community.' Their knowledge system is based on *'lokavidya'*, and the *swadeshi* alternatives believe in truth and non-violence.

Sahasrabudhey's interpretation that Gandhi totally and completely opposed modern science is challenged by Shiv Visvanathan; his other claim regarding alternatives in Gandhi is contested by Ramachandra Guha. Unlike Sahasrabudhey's somewhat literal and clear-cut rendering of Gandhi's opposition to modern science, Visvanathan, in his essay entitled 'Reinventing Gandhi', seeks to 'reinvent Gandhi using a social science format'. He maintains that Gandhi's critique of modern science cannot be taken literally, as there are some crucial points where his views converge with modern science.[6] Instead of taking Gandhi's views on modern science at face value, he, while alluding to the resources from the life of Gandhi, seeks to modernize Gandhi a bit and examines how far 'would Gandhi have modernized himself today?' (p. 192 in this volume). Moreover, he carefully reads the following postures in Gandhi: though he was a 'nationalist', he 'fought the nation-state'; though an 'anti-colonialist', he 'wished to redeem the British'; 'a Hindu who happily by-passed the *shastras*; a Congress leader who wanted to preside over the dismantling of the Indian National Congress'; similarly, he 'ranted against the colonial city, yet operated politically from it.' From these gestures constituting the Janus nature in Gandhi, Visvanathan identifies instances belonging to the other side of Sahasrabudhey's pendulum and reveal Gandhi's concern and positive gestures towards modern science. Skilfully highlighting the updated characteristic in Gandhi, he presents not merely the clear-cut pro-science statements but also an intricate and non-conventional pro-attitude towards modern science. He suggests that today Gandhi would have studied 'science rather than law', and would have joined the 'radical science group' of the anti-nuclear and ecological variety, rather than 'vegetarian and feminist groups'.

In this interpretation Gandhi cannot be seen as a puritanical anti-science type, as though he was against 'modern medicine but got his appendix removed'. Though opposed to technology, he was 'acutely sensitive to it'; moreover, he was 'ecstatic about sewing machine' and used loudspeakers.

Given this flip-side to the standard interpretations of Gandhi's opposition to modern science, Visvanathan claims that Gandhi realized that India does not have one face, either modern or anti-modern, village or city; rather it is a 'janus faced entity'. He desires an active debate between these two faces, with neither excluding the other, as this lack of reciprocity would 'become two masks confronting each other stonily'. Giving a new and heightened twist to Gandhi's preference for Nehru as his successor, Visvanathan claims that 'Gandhi did not deny the Nehru in him; he only wanted Nehru and his modernists to recognize the voice of Gandhi's India.' As if illustrating the nature of this updated Gandhi, Visvanathan claims that the situation today—when khadi and satyagraha have become 'irrevocable symbols or abstract signs' and Gandhi's 'writings into an irrevocable *shastra*'—goes against the grain of his (Gandhi's) life. On the other side, unlike his focused attention on the village, Gandhi today, claims Visvanathan, 'would have become one of the great exponents of the city,' though not the Western notion of the city. So, unlike the conventional understanding of Gandhi's opposition to 'modern science' as presented by Sahasrabudhey, Visvanathan shows its flip-side through a strategy of updating and refreshing Gandhi, thereby complicating his attitude towards modern science and thus forming a basis for a fruitful debate on this issue.

While Visvanathan's essay complicates Gandhi's critical realm, Ramachandra Guha's essay, 'Mahatma Gandhi and the Environmental Movement', refutes the positive claim made by environmentalists that Gandhi gave an 'alternative perspective' on development that also explains how the current mode of development is exploitative of man by man and nature by man. Like the environmentalists, Sahasrabudhey too makes the claim that there is a clear-cut alternative to modernity in Gandhi. Rejecting this claim, Guha maintains that re-reading *Hind Swaraj* recently, 'I found myself unable to agree with th[e] verdict [that there is an alternative].' He goes on to say that despite 'its eloquent denunciation of modern Western culture, the book has nothing to say about man's relationship with nature: still less does it offer an alternative perspective' (p. 217 in this volume). He, however, concedes that Gandhi has considerable influence on contemporary 'environmental movements' like the Chipko Andolan and the Narmada Bachao Andolan, especially in environmental activists' adoption of his technique of 'non-violent protest' and his polemics 'against heavy industrialization'. Scattered through his writings are clues to such an alternative path, such as his voluntary simplicity as a sustainable alternative to modern lifestyles. However, Guha says that through 'his immersion in village India ... [Gandhi] does not anywhere offer an alternative model of development for India—for one thing, he was not a systematic thinker.'

In addition, this essay has some interesting similarities with Visvanathan's essay in its understanding of the relationship between Gandhi and Nehru. Both repudiate the Gandhi versus Nehru formula generally maintained by many. In my understanding, this can be traced to their reading of Gandhi as not completely opposed to modern science. Guha, while accepting that 'there are profound philosophical differences' between Gandhi and Nehru, emphasizes, however, quoting statements from Gandhi, that there was also 'deep and abiding love between them'. He seems to correct environmentalists' underplaying of Nehru, which is in proportion to their overplaying of Gandhi. While Visvanathan and Guha are right in rejecting the 'Gandhi opposed modern science' thesis, this cannot be taken as completely undermining his critique of modern science.

While Sections II and III traversed a large canvas—of nationalism, the university, autobiography, modern science, machine, environmentalism—the fourth section contains two essays, one by Sumit Sarkar and another by Akeel Bilgrami, discussing Gandhi's notion of truth. Sarkar in his piece, 'Mahatma Gandhi', interprets Gandhi's truth along the lines of liberalism, according to which 'no one could ever be sure of having attained the ultimate truth, [and therefore] use of violence to enforce one's own necessarily partial understanding of it was sinful' (p. 231 in this volume).

Bilgrami, in his essay ,'Gandhi's Integrity: The Philosophy behind the Politics', terms this standard and entrenched reading of Gandhi as a 'spectacular misreading', since it 'fails to cohere with his most fundamental thinking'. Distinguishing liberals' arguments for tolerance from Gandhi's, he argues that while the liberal notion of 'modesty', which is not ever knowing the truth, would appeal to Gandhi, he 'would find something very alien in Mill's argument for it.' There is, claims Bilgrami, no echo in Gandhi of the idea that the source of this modesty is that 'however much we seek truth, we *cannot attain it,*' which is what Sarkar contends is the ground of his non-violence. Elucidating further this difference between Mill and Gandhi, Bilgrami contends that the pervasive diffidence and lack of conviction, which is the character of epistemology that Mill's argument presupposes, is entirely alien to Gandhi. Instead, he locates the source of Gandhi's notion of truth in the 'very nature of moral response and moral judgement'.

Distinguishing resistance from criticism, Bilgrami associates the former with Gandhi's morality and dissociates the latter from it. He maintains that one can resist without being critical, as the latter reflects 'an impurity of heart'. According to Gandhi, we need not be critical of those who disagree with us. Bilgrami sets this position against the 'long history in the Western tradition of moral philosophy' which maintains that to choose 'an action on moral grounds under certain circumstances is to generate a principle which we think applies as an 'ought' or an imperative to *all* others faced with relevantly similar circumstances.' An honoured slogan of that tradition claims that when 'one chooses for oneself, one chooses for everyone'. According to Bilgrami, Gandhi repudiates this entire tradition, though without necessarily relapsing into social solipsism. Pointing out the philosophy behind Gandhi's politics, Bilgrami says that 'Gandhi embraces [this] slogan too, but he understands the second half of it differently. He too wants one's act of conscience to have a universal relevance, so he too thinks one chooses for everyone, but he does not see that as meaning that one generates a principle or imperative for everyone.' In Bilgrami's interpretation, Gandhi understands this slogan as suggesting when 'one chooses for oneself, *one sets an example to everyone*'. This concept of exemplar in Gandhi provides a radical alternative to the concept of principle in moral philosophy. Further, he shows how exemplars are more effective in smaller communities than in metropolitan societies and hence Gandhi's preference for villages. The other important difference between Mill's and Gandhi's notion of truth is that, to the former this notion is cognitive, whereas for the latter, it is an 'experiential notion'. Truth, for Gandhi, like Mill, cannot be expressed in 'propositions' nor understood in 'scientific terms'; rather it is for him 'moral' (p. 252 in this volume). Through this close and complex philosophical argumentation, Bilgrami presents his opposition to Sarkar's interpretation of Gandhi's notion of truth. These two interpretations provide yet another space to debate Gandhi's notion of truth.[7]

The fifth section has two essays which discuss Gandhi's views on women. Madhu Kishwar's essay, 'Gandhi on Women', presents at length a detailed account of the role of Gandhi in bringing a large number of women into the mainstream of the freedom movement, thus effecting an influential 'break from' the tradition of nineteenth-century reformers who only saw women 'as helpless creatures deserving charitable concern' (p. 304 in this volume). Distinguishing Gandhi from these reformers, Kishwar highlights the point that for him women are 'active, self-conscious agents of social change' (p. 304 in this volume). In this context she also states that unlike these reformers, Gandhi's concern was 'not limited to bringing about change in selected areas of social life such as education and marriage ... [and he] was primarily concerned with bringing about radical social reconstruction'

(p. 304 in this volume). While Kishwar acknowledges an important limitation in Gandhi's thinking: namely, the articulation of women's concerns
only in the moral sphere and not placing any economic content in his
conception of women, she however understands differently his idea which
relates women to the sphere of 'home'. Accordingly he actively created
'conditions which could help her break the shackles of domesticity' (p. 291
in this volume).

Sujata Patel in her essay, 'Construction and Reconstruction of Woman in
Gandhi', while accepting Kishwar's claim that Gandhi's entrance into the
national arena led to mass participation of women in the national movement,
rejects Kishwar's claim that Gandhi departed from the nineteenth-century
reformers in his conception of women. She maintains that 'Gandhi not only
accepted these assumptions [nineteenth-century ideas relating women to
'home'], but extended them to fit his own perspective relating to the
participation of women in politics' (p. 321 in this volume). In this context
she points out how Kishwar's analysis leads to a 'construction of one
perception of Gandhi and his ideology, where women appear as homogeneous category, undifferentiated in terms of class, caste, religion or region'
(p. 316 in this volume). Pointing out the limitations in this construction, she
says that there is a need to understand the extent of women's participation,
going beyond the perception of any particular leader, taking into consideration the particular context that made their participation possible, and the
role played by various heterogeneous aspects such as 'caste associations,
the family, the school, the college, the peer group and especially the mother'
(p. 317 in this volume). This debate between Kishwar and Patel opens up
larger issues surrounding Gandhi, and particularly his views on women.[8]

The last essay in this volume, entitled 'Self-purification versus Self-
respect: On the Roots of the Dalit Movement,' is by D.R. Nagaraj. Unlike
the previous debates where different scholars expressed different views in
their interpretation of Gandhi, here we have an instance where the author
brings together two radically opposite views—those of Gandhi and Ambedkar
on the question of untouchability—and shows their underlying mutual
dependence. Going against present-day formulations of the Dalit movement, which rejects the Gandhian model of tackling the problem of untouchability, Nagaraj maintains that the nature of Babasaheb's political career has
to be understood along with that of Gandhi. While presenting the initial
divergent views held by both, which inevitably clashed with each other, he
demonstrates how in their engagement with each other they ultimately
emerged as transformed persons, 'deeply affected' by each other, 'internalised

each other', and though they clashed, 'quite bitterly at that, at the level of major details but are complementary at a fundamental level' (p. 370 in this volume). Ambedkar, according to Nagaraj, was instrumental in making Gandhi move away from the nineteenth-century religious radicals, who saw the problem of untouchability as basically religious and spiritual. For Gandhi, the materialistic approach to the problem of untouchability was the weakness of Ambedkar, whereas for the latter, spirituality was the weakness of Gandhi. However, in reality these apparently 'exclusivist positions concealed the simultaneous existence of both materialist and spiritualist viewpoints in both of them' (p. 365 in this volume). Looking at this whole process of confrontation, Nagaraj concludes that because of the confrontation 'Gandhiji had taken over economics from Babasaheb. Ambedkar had internalised the importance of religion' (p. 369 in this volume). Recognizing this dependency, according to Nagaraj, has a serious implication to the present-day politics of the Dalit movement. This interface brings together yet another important debate, which can throw better light on Gandhi's ideas.

Thus, this volume brings together essays that highlight the impact of tradition on Gandhi; his subversion of tradition; his being co-opted by nationalist thought which he consistently repudiated; the incompatibility between modern institutions like the university and Gandhi's thought; away from being co-opted by modernity, Gandhi's attempt at Indianizing a modern genre like autobiography; his challenge to modern science and a *swadeshi* alternative that he provided; the convergences between his thought and modern science; lack of alternatives in Gandhi; relating Gandhi's notion of truth to liberal notion; how truth in Gandhi is not the liberal notion of truth; his attempt at bringing women into the centre stage of the political movement like in the freedom struggle; the need to understand the historical intervention of Gandhi's views on women and not essentialize them; and, finally, the interdependency between Gandhi and Ambedkar. Thus the volume enhances the existing understanding of Gandhi by taking as foci of attention the notions of tradition, nation, women, and caste. The debates between Sumit Sarkar and Akeel Bilgrami as well as Madhu Kishwar and Sujata Patel are direct in the sense that Bilgrami and Patel respond directly to Kishwar and Sarkar respectively. Though this is not so in the case of the other authors, they are accepted here as participants in a debate, occupying rival positions on certain issues seminal to a critical and rewarding engagement with Gandhi as a thinker and as a phenomenon. The juxtaposition of competing standpoints for debates, which is the leitmotif of this volume, promotes a fruitful preoccupation with an original thinker whose ideas and practices deserve more than either plain adoration or dismissal.

Most of the essays in this volume are part of a course on Gandhi at Goa University where I taught earlier. I thank my students for their active participation and lively discussions. When I discussed this course with Ashis Nandy, he encouraged me to put it together as a volume. I thank him immensely for the suggestion and the continuous encouragement he has given me. Very warm thanks to Mrinal Miri, Jyotirmaya Sharma, S.G. Kulkarni, Laxmi Narayana Kadekar, D. Venkat Rao, M. Krishnaiah, Tridip Suhrud, C. Bharat Kumar, Jaya Singh, and V. Ramakrishna for their encouragement and reassurance, which helped me to stay with this project. I thank the referee for the critical comments and constructive suggestions. It helped me to revise the manuscript and in the process elaborate the introduction. Rakesh Pandey and J.V. D'cruz have carefully read the introduction and suggested important changes, for which I am extremely thankful to them. I thank all the authors for the permission to include their essay in this volume; Clarendon Press, London, for the permission to include Late A.L. Basham's essay; *Gandhi Marg* for Late A.K. Saran's article and Mrs Girija Nagraj for Late D.R. Nagraj's essay.

Notes

1. Descartes (1985: 117) dismissed childhood as the domain governed by appetite and teachers rather than by reason.

2. Yet another underlying reason for those like Lannoy (1974) and Hardiman (2003) to highlight the modern in Gandhi, thereby underplaying the impact of tradition, is not so much their attitude towards Indian tradition but in their inhabiting the modern grid where modernity in the West displays a clear hostility towards its own tradition. I am not pursuing this point here as it needs elaborate argumentation, some of which can be found in my (2005).

3. Here let me point out that the essays in each section do not necessarily adhere to chronology, as Saran's essay was published earlier than Chatterjee's, and the same is the case with Sahasrabudhey's.

4. Here let me mention that *Gandhi Marg* published a communication from A.B. Shah (1980) entitled 'A Comment on A.K. Saran's Views', which criticizes Saran's views. This communication is not included here as the main focus of the section is on derivation and not on Saran per se. For the same reason I have not included the essays by Naipaul on autobiography, as the main thrust of this section is not on this topic.

5. This view that Gandhi, rejected modern Western civilization outright, is also held by Saran. He says (1980: 681), 'For its part, Gandhi's *Hind Swaraj* is preoccupied with an uncompromising critique and rejection of modern Western civilisation. It is a devastating and uncannily contemporary critique.'

6. Shambhu Prasad's (2001) essay, entitled 'Towards an Understanding of Gandhi's Views on Science', also contests the view that Gandhi totally opposed science. The author argues that Gandhi was not anti-science and that his life defines a space for an alternative science for civil society that would operate with different methods.

7. Here it may be added that with his critique of moral principles Bilgrami turned our attention towards exemplars. This account liberates us from closure; however, there are some serious problems associated with openings suggested by Bilgrami. For instance, the problem with his account is that he considers only good exemplars, whereas about the bad he is silent. Because of this silence there is no discussion exploring how to demarcate good exemplars from bad ones, not to speak of equipping one to deal with them. In fact, Gandhi was confronted by both in his lifetime. For instance, several times he was bothered whether the message from his 'inner voice' was a 'message from God or the Devil, for both are wrestling in the human breast.' So, there is a need to make clarifications on these matters, which will throw better light on this issue.

8. The reasons for including the essay 'Gandhi on Women' by Madhu Kishwar (in two parts) from *Economic and Political Weekly*, though re-published as a book with the same title, is the fact that the very next essay by Sujata Patel is a response to them rather than to the book.

REFERENCES

Descartes. 1985. 'Discourse on Method,' in *The Philosophical Writings of Descartes*, vol. 1, trans. John Nottingham, Robert Stoothoff and Dugald Murdoch. Cambridge: Cambridge University Press.

Hardiman, David. 2003. *Gandhi and his Time and Ours*. Delhi: Permanent Black.

Kumar, Ravindra. 1971. *Essays on Gandhian Politics: The Rowlatt Satyagraha of 1919*, Oxford: Clarendon Press.

Lannoy, Richard. 1974. *The Speaking Tree: A Study of Indian Culture and Society*. London: Oxford University Press.

Prasad, Shambhu. 2001. 'Towards an understanding of Gandhi's views on science', *Economic and Political Weekly*, vol. xxxvi, no. 39, pp. 3721–32.

Raghuramaraju, A. 2005. 'West', in Vinay Lal and Ashis Nandy (eds), *The Future of Knowledge & Culture: A Dictionary for the 21st Century*. New Delhi: Viking, pp. 347–52.

Saran, A.K. 1980. 'Gandhi and the Concept of Politics: Towards a normal civilization', *Gandhi Marg*, 11 February, pp. 675–726.

Shah, A.B. 1980. 'A Comment on A.K. Saran's Views', *Gandhi Marg*, 11 February, pp. 727–35.

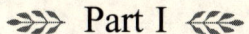 Part I

Traditional Influences on the Thought of Mahatma Gandhi[*1]

A. L. BASHAM

INTRODUCTION

It is not easy to say anything new about Mahatma Gandhi, for few men of the twentieth century have had so much written about them. I am no authority on the recent history of India in general, or on Gandhi in particular, and have read only a very small portion of the available material. Hence what I write can be only tentative, and based chiefly on my knowledge of early India.

Such knowledge is not very helpful for this task, for our problem is to assess Gandhi's debt not to ancient India in general, but to those aspects of Hindu culture which were preserved and emphasized in the Gujarat of the 1870s and 1880s, and to those ancient Indian texts which he is known to have read and admired in his earlier years. Gandhi himself in many passages of his voluminous writings admits his debt to certain Western sources, notably the Gospels (especially the Sermon on the Mount), Tolstoy, Thoreau, and Ruskin. There is no reason to minimize these influences. On the other hand, we may ask how far Gandhi accepted the doctrines of these sources in their own right, so to speak, and how far he looked on them as merely confirming and systematizing attitudes and values which he had obtained at

* A.L. Basham. 'Traditional Influences on the Thought of Mahatma Gandhi', in Ravindra Kumar (ed.), *Essays on Gandhian Politics: The Rowlatt Satyagraha of 1919,* Oxford: Clarendon Press, 1971, pp. 17–42.

home. Certain elements in the religious life of nineteenth-century Hinduism may have prepared the ground for some of Gandhi's ideas.

Gandhi's Youth

According to his autobiography, Gandhi's parents were in different degrees religious, as no doubt nearly everybody was in Porbandar and Rajkot at the time. His father, he says, had very little religious training, but he frequently visited temples and listened to pious discourses. In his last days he took to the Bhagavad Gītā, and repeated verses of it aloud every day at prayer.[2] As is commonly the case in the Hindu household, Gandhi's mother was more earnest than his father in religious observance. She prayed before every meal, and visited the temple every day. She regularly performed the annual *Caturmāsa* fast in the rainy season, with numerous works of supererogation in the form of additional fasts and vows. Yet she had 'strong common sense', and kept in touch with matters of state. Thus Gandhi grew up in an orthodox *Vaiṣṇava* home.

It would seem that the influence of his parents affected his moral rather than his mystical sense. He tells us nothing about deep religious feelings or mystical experiences and visions, such as sometimes occur to intensely pious children in India and elsewhere. He mentions being greatly inspired by religious dramas, but rather than inciting mystical awe they merely confirmed his resolution to remain devoted to his parents and to speak the truth in all circumstances. He did not remember ever having told a lie at school, either to his teachers or to his classmates.[3]

As a boy he hated sports and gymnastics, and loved to serve as nurse to his father. He would hurry home from school for this purpose.[4] His education was also interrupted by his passionate love for his child wife, Kasturbai, and he would think of her while at his lessons and long for at nightfall.[5] In his autobiography he makes no pretence that he was a good student, and one suspects that he is over-modest. He learnt a little Sanskrit, without which he would have found it difficult to take any interest in the sacred books of Hinduism.[6]

He was a timid boy, 'haunted by the fear of thieves, ghosts and serpents'. He was ashamed of the fact that Kasturbai appeared to have more courage than him. For this and other reasons he was lured by an unnamed classmate to take up meat-eating. It was widely thought at the time by the reforming youth of India that meat-eating had a psychological or physiological effect on the character of the eater, and would make him strong and brave. The young Indian could thus excuse himself if he broke the cherished taboos of his community by appeals to the patriotic desire to expel the occupying power and to make India a free nation. Gandhi took to meat-eating as a duty. In the course of a year he seems to have eaten meat half a dozen times, and to have acquired a liking for it. He gave up his secret meat-eating feasts not because he thought them intrinsically wrong, but because they involved telling lies to his mother.[7]

Later the boy Gandhi also expressed a mild revolt against parental authority by taking to smoking cigarettes. Apparently he was not allowed pocket money and stole coppers from the servants in order to buy them. After a while he and the other boy who shared this secret vice grew so exasperated at the thought of being under such tight parental control that they resolved to commit suicide. They ate one or two *dhātūrā* seeds and then decided to remain alive after all. The suicide was planned in the best Hindu tradition. The two worshipped in a temple before the attempt, and went to another one after they had given it up, in order to compose their minds. Later Gandhi confessed this and another theft to his ailing father and was freely forgiven.[8] The account of this incident, which most great men would have thought too trivial to record, shows clearly what an important effect it had on the boy.

Soon afterwards Gandhi's father died. In a memorable passage of his autobiography he tells us how, at the age of sixteen, passion for his wife took him away from his father's bedside a few minutes before the latter's death—an incident which left him with a sense of shame that he was never able to efface or forget.[9] While Gandhi's mistrust of sex evidently owes much to other sources, this traumatic event no doubt had an immense effect on his later attitude.

The Vaiṣṇava temple where his mother worshipped had no appeal for him. His old nurse, Rambha, whom he recalls with respect and affection, taught him to call on the name of Ram as an antidote to his fear of the dark. 'The good seed sown in childhood was not sown in vain', he tells us, and records that this calling on the name of God in trouble was in later life 'an infallible remedy'.[10] In fact in his last moments it was not the profound mysticism of the Bhagavad Gītā which gave him strength, far less the Sermon on the Mount, but the simple formula taught him by his nurse.

When Gandhi was thirteen, a locally famous devotee visited his father every evening to recite the Rāmāyaṇ in Tulsī Dās's Hindu version. The boy was 'enraptured at his reading', and in his maturity he regarded the Tulsī Rāmāyaṇ as 'the greatest book in all devotional literature'. However, it is not clear whether at that time he enjoyed more the religious and moral content of the poem or the poetry itself and the exciting narrative. He was then not impressed by the *Bhāgavata Purāṇa* and his reading of *Manusmṛti* made him 'incline somewhat towards atheism'. Jaina monks often visited his father and talked with him 'on subjects religious and mundane', but at that time Jainism, which is characterized by extreme *ahiṃsā*, seems to have had little or no influence on him, since he infringed this principle by eating meat, and confesses to having killed 'bugs and such other insects, regarding it as a duty'. If we are to believe his recollections, his boyhood, though not particularly religious, was characterized by intense conscientiousness and moral fervour. He quotes a Gujarati stanza by the poet Shyāmal Bhaṭṭ as having 'gripped his mind and heart' in his boyhood:

> For a bowl of water give a goodly meal;
> For a kindly greeting bow thou down with zeal;
> For a simple penny pay thou back with gold;
> If thy life be rescued, life do not withhold.
> Thus the words and actions of the wise regard;
> Every little service tenfold they reward.
> But the truly noble know all men as one,
> And return with gladness good for evil done.[11]

I am unable to obtain a better translation of these verses, which are quoted from the *Autobiography*. No doubt they are much more impressive in the original.

Thus when he first read the doctrines of the Sermon on the Mount and of Tolstoy, his mind had already been prepared by the ethical teachings which he had absorbed in his childhood.

In general, the boy seems to have favoured reform, and to have been anxious to throw off the shackles of tradition. His half-hearted attempt at suicide is evidence of the conflict, felt in some measure by all adolescent boys, between the urge towards freedom from parental restraints and love for the parents and the sense of security which they bestow. Such conflicts must have been particularly common among the educated Indian boys of Gandhi's generation. It would appear that on his father's death the rebel in him gained the upper hand, for his eagerness to go to England triumphed over his cowardice.[12] The fact that the Modh Baniyā caste council of Bombay outcasted him before his departure had no effect on him and only made him more eager to go.[13]

Gandhi's years in England were perhaps the most formative of his life. Despite his shyness and immaturity, he evidently adapted himself better to his circumstances than do many Indian students in London at the present day. He seems to have been well supplied with funds, and at first tried to become as Western as possible, taking lessons in elocution, dancing, and the violin. He even had an English girlfriend, whom he met and talked to every Sunday, only confessing that he was already married when he felt that the girl's interest in him was growing and that her guardian, an elderly widow, might be contemplating a formal engagement between the two. The exact chronology of these events is not quite clear, but it is evident that the incident took place before that meeting of his with the theosophists which turned his attention to the things of the spirit. He admits that he found the letter, confessing that he was a married man, very difficult to write, and we suspect that Gandhi's feelings for this unnamed and unidentified girl were much stronger than at first appears from the pages of his autobiography. It is only after describing this incident that he tells us of his religious life in England, which began to develop towards the end of his second year there.

It was in London that he became a convinced vegetarian, chiefly from reading English vegetarian propaganda. And here he came in touch with theosophists, through whom he was introduced to Sir Edwin Arnold's verse translation of the Bhagavad Gītā, called *The Song Celestial.* He had heard of this great Hindu text before, but previously it had made little impression on him. Arnold's then famous poem on the life of Buddha, *The Light of Asia*, also appears to have affected his outlook. From Arnold and Madam Blavatsky he turned to the Bible. The Old Testament he found dull, but the Sermon on the Mount 'went straight to his heart', and put him in mind of the Gujarati verses he had learnt as a child.[14]

This, we believe, gives the key to the influences which worked on Gandhi. The Western source of inspiration served to remind him of the verses he had heard in his childhood, which expressed roughly the same ideas, and to confirm his faith in the teaching of both. We can find partial prototypes for most of his ideas in Indian tradition, but the stimulus for their reformulation along Gandhian lines came chiefly from the West, either through personal contact or from reading.

'TRUTH'

The dominant concept of Gandhi's ideology is 'Truth', *Satya* or its derivative in all north Indian languages. It is quite clear from his use of the word in many contexts that Gandhi's Satya is not the bare logical truth of modern scientific usage, merely the function or attribute of a proposition which corresponds to an event or fact. He tells us that in his boyhood the meta-physical aspects of religion did not greatly interest him.

But one thing took deep root in me—the conviction that morality is the basis of things, and that truth is the substance of all morality. Truth became my sole objective. It began to grow in magnitude every day, and my definition of it also has been ever widening.[15]

Here he admits that he uses the word with special overtones and connota-tions. It has been suggested that we can understand Gandhi's concept of truth if we substitute the word 'Reality' for it,[16] but this evidently does not fit his sense of the term in many passages, for instance, the one quoted above. His slogans 'God is Truth' or 'Truth is God', if interpreted in this way, suggest a Spinozan or Hegelian natural monism, with no great ethical content. But Truth, for Gandhi, was the focal point of all his moral ideas.

Often he describes himself as 'a humble searcher after Truth'[17] or something similar. Self-claimed 'seekers after truth' are legion, both in the East and the West, and the term here can be taken in its literal English sense. The same is the case when Gandhi says: 'I have no policy ... save the policy of truth and *ahiṃsā*.'[18] But a statement like 'to find Truth completely is to realize oneself and one's destiny'[19] suggests that his concept approaches that of ultimate reality, the *Brahman* of *Advaita* philosophy, the single entity underlying all things. Gandhi's own definitions of Truth are often far from clear. 'What is Truth ? A difficult question, but I have solved it for myself by saying that it is what the voice within tells you.'[20] Here he seems to identify Truth with conscience. In another definition we are told:

For me truth is the sovereign principle.... This Truth is not only truthfulness in word, but truthfulness in thought also, and not only the relative truth of our conception, but the Absolute Truth, the Eternal Principle, that is God ... I worship God as Truth only. I have not yet found Him, but I am seeking after Him. Often in my progress I have had faint glimpses of the Absolute Truth, God, and daily the conviction is growing upon me that He alone is real and all else is unreal....

The world crushes the dust under its feet, but the seeker after Truth should be so humble himself that even the dust could crush him. Only then, and not until then, will he have a glimpse of Truth.[21]

Often Gandhi makes a complete identification of God and Truth:

The little fleeting glimpses ... that I have been able to have of Truth can hardly convey an idea of the indescribable lustre of Truth, a million times more intense than that of the sun.... A perfect vision of Truth can only follow a complete realization of *ahiṃsā*.[22]

To see the universal and all-pervading spirit of Truth face to face one must be able to love the meanest of creation as oneself.

But in his writings we also find references to Truth which emphasize its moral or ethical character.[23] In the introduction to his autobiography he states that his 'Experiments with Truth' include 'experiments with non-violence, celibacy and other principles of conduct believed to be distinct from truth'. But for him 'Truth is the sovereign principle, which includes numerous other principles'.

The passages which we have quoted are sufficient to show the very wide range of connotations which Truth possessed for Gandhi. We can perhaps find passages in Western literature in various languages where the word is given so many meanings, but in fact Gandhi's concept of Truth, implying not only factual truth, truthful speech, honesty, and the resolute carrying out of vows, promises, and plans, but also ultimate reality, can scarcely be paralleled outside India. On reading these quotations the mind turns to the Upaniṣads:

This Self (the Absolute *Brahman*) is obtained through Truth and penance .... Truth only conquers,[24] not falsehood. By Truth the divine road was made whereby the sages, their wishes fulfilled, ascend to the supreme abode of Truth.[25]

Here is instruction—'No No' (*Neti, neti*). There is nothing higher than that. And its name is 'The Truth of Truth', for the breaths [i.e. life] are Truth, and he is the Truth of them.[26]

In that which is so minute all things have their soul. 'That is Truth, that is the Self.' And that thou art, Śvetaketu.[27]

We have no evidence that passages such as these had made any impression on the young Gandhi when he left for London, and it is probable that at that time he had never heard or read them, for the Upaniṣads were not the usual religious literature of the Indian *vaiśya* classes of those days. But his concept of Truth did not need the Upaniṣads to inspire it. Gandhi's nurse, as we have seen, taught him to call on the name of God, in the form of Rāma. One of the commonest ejaculations of popular north Indian Vaiṣṇavism is *Rām-nām sac hai*, 'The Name of Rām is true' (or 'is Truth', since modern Indian sac, like the Sanskrit *satya*, may be either an adjective or a noun). Here we already have the possible source of the Gandhian emphasis on Truth, and of the special and un-Western usage of the word in Gandhi's speeches and writings. The implication of the phrase to the believer is not simply that God exists; it must also connote that the essence *(nām, name)* of divinity is ultimate reality, and that God carries out his promises without serving and expects his followers to do likewise. The use of the word sac with this extended connotation can also be found in the Hindi Rāmāyaṇ of Tulsī Dās, the one religious text which made a great impression on Gandhi in his childhood; for instance, Daśaratha replies to the accusations of his wicked wife Kaikeyī in the following terms:

> Don't accuse me of lying!... It has always been the custom in the clan of Raghu to keep one's word even at the cost of one's life.
> All sins together are not as bad as untruth ... for in Truth all good deeds are rooted. This the *Vedas*, the *Purāṇas* and the *Laws of Manu* all declare.[28]

Here the question is not one of simply speaking the truth. The argument revolves around whether Daśaratha shall bestow a promised boon, keeping his word at great cost to himself and his family. We have no access to a concordance of the Tulsī Rāmāyaṇ, but many similar usages of the word satya or sac must occur throughout the poem.

Unlike the English 'truth', which is related to such words as 'trust' and 'troth', satya is semantically akin to the word *sat*, 'existence', 'being', the first property of the Absolute Essence (*Sac-cid-ānanda*) or Brahman according to Vedānta philosophy. Its overtones are therefore more metaphysical than those of the corresponding English word, and in both Sanskrit and modern Indian languages its range of meaning is wider. The standard Sanskrit–English dictionary gives the following equivalents of satya as an adjective: 'true, real, actual, genuine, sincere, honest, truthful, faithful, pure, virtuous, successful effectual, valid'. As a noun it has an even wider range: 'truth, reality ... speaking the truth, sincerity, veracity, ... a solemn asseveration, vow, promise, oath, ... demonstrated conclusion, dogma, ... the quality of goodness of purity or knowledge ...'[29] Many of these meanings were carried over into modern Indian languages.

Thus the fundamental concept of Gandhi's philosophy owes nothing to Western sources. It was developed from the Hindu tradition in which he was brought up. Truth for Gandhi seems to incorporate some of the content of the pregnant Indian word dharma, especially in its Buddhist usage, as the eternal moral law by following which a man may achieve bliss. His knowledge of Buddhism does not appear to have been very profound, and he acquired whatever knowledge he had from his London days onwards. The coincidence is striking, however, for Buddhism tends to exalt dharma to the status of divinity, and in Mahāyāna Buddhism the Absolute is often called *Dharmakāya*, 'The Body of Dharma'. Another possible parallel to Gandhi's 'Truth' is the Vedic concept of *Ṛta*, the divinely ordained course of nature, which was associated in the minds of the Aryans with truth, honesty, regularity, and carrying out one's resolutions. The term is rare in classical Sanskrit, but its privative *anrta* came to possess the regular meaning of lying or dishonesty. It is hardly likely, however, that Gandhi was aware of this resemblance, or indeed of the Vedic doctrine of Ṛta itself, before his departure for England, and we can only look on it as an interesting example of the persistence and development of the concepts of Indian thought. While we have no positive evidence that the one influenced the other, the chronological sequence: Ṛta—Dharma—'Truth' is impressive.

Gandhi's frequent use of the slogan 'Truth is God' and certain passages from his speeches and writings taken out of their context might be used to suggest that he was at heart a rationalist or at least an *advaitin*, believing only in an impersonal Absolute. In one well-known passage he declares: 'I am a part and parcel of the whole and cannot find Him [i.e., God] apart from the rest of humanity.'[30] He read something of Hindu and Buddhist philosophy, and of Western humanist and rationalist literature no doubt, and with typically Indian catholicity he tried to make room for the attitudes of other schools of thought. In a remarkable passage he admitted the influence of the typically Jain doctrine of anekānta-vāda, which, in its original form, implied that a proposition might at the same time be true and false from two relative points of view:

I am advaitist and yet I can support dvaitism [dualism]. The world is changing every moment, and is therefore unreal, it has no permanent existence. But though it is constantly changing, it has a something about it which persists and it is therefore to that extent real. I have therefore no objection to calling it real and unreal, and thus being called an *anekantavadi* or *syadvadi*. But my syadvada is not the syadvada of the learned, it is peculiarly my own.[31]

This aspect of Gandhi's thought is typical of Indian philosophy, which admits relative truth and degrees of truth, without references to Aristotelian logic, according to which truth is an absolute quality and a proposition must be either true or false. The same typically Indian point of view is vividly exemplified in Ramakrishna's famous slogan, 'All Religions are True'. This proposition, from the logical point of view, is obviously false, but nevertheless it has a definite significance and validity. More than once Gandhi himself repeated this phrase, though he qualified it by declaring that all religions had 'some error in them',[32] that they had 'fundamental truth',[33] or that they were true 'more or less'.[34] At the same time he proclaimed himself in word and action a Hindu. Such an attitude seems inconsistent by strictly logical standards, but it was one which many intelligent Indians would agree with, and is thoroughly in keeping with traditional Indian ways of thought.

Whatever intellectual theories he may have had, he was emotionally a simple theistic Hindu, with absolute faith in God. 'I am surer of His existence than of the fact that you and I are sitting in this room.'[35] His faith never wavered and was evidently strengthened by mystical experience, though he made no claim to be a *jīvan-mukta*, or to any special revelation. His references to his own spiritual life are in terms of the utmost humility, and are in this respect very different from those of a certain Indian contemporary who gave up a promising career as a national leader for a very successful one as a mystical teacher. The activity which Gandhi called 'prayer' was in fact mystical communion, and he describes it as such.[36] Yet he never suggests that he is more than an imperfect seeker, rather than a finder. This attitude is possibly to some extent influenced by Western religious ideas, since for the Hindu *sannyāsī* humility in the face of his devotees is not always accounted a virtue.

Gandhi's willingness to compromise on matters which he considered inessential, and his admitted inconsistencies,[37] hardly invalidate his sincerity. He believed firmly in the doctrine of rebirth,[38] which is the hallmark of the religions which originated in India, and sharply distinguishes them from those of the West; and he even justified such difficult aspects of Hinduism as cow worship: 'It is for me a poem of pity. I worship it and I shall defend its worship against the whole world.'[39] As a Hindu he might legitimately ignore or interpret figuratively aspects of the religion which appeared irrelevant to the contemporary situation, and he might legitimately derive inspiration from the teachings of other religions. This he did in large measure, but throughout his life, at least from his student days onwards, he was impelled by an intense theistic faith, rooted in the Rāmāyan which he heard as a child, and thoroughly Hindu in character.

AHIṂSĀ

Non-violence for Gandhi was a principle second only to 'Truth' in importance. Indeed, sometimes it even appears to transcend Truth. 'Non-violence,' he wrote in 1922, 'is the first article of my faith. It is also the last article of my creed.'[40] Ahiṃsā is a common enough word in ancient Indian literature and Gandhi claimed to be following in up-to-date form an ancient Indian ideal, which he had also read in 'the teachings of all the greatest teachers of the World—Zoroaster, Mahavir [*sic*], Daniel, Jesus, Muhammad, Nanak, and a host of others'.[41]

The classical doctrine of ahiṃsā was interpreted differently in the light of varṇa and āśrama, class and stage of life. It involved not only such considerations as participation in warfare and meat-eating, but also the forcible apprehension and punishment of criminals and self-defence.

Warfare was rarely condemned in ancient India. The Bhagavad Gītā, which was one of Gandhi's chief sources of inspiration, was composed partly with a view to justifying participation in righteous war, even when the war was waged against one's own kith and kin. The kṣatriya, or member of the warrior class, had the positive duty to fight, loyally serving his king in all circumstances. Similarly the policeman or other officer of the king was justified in using force in apprehending a suspected criminal, the judge in sentencing him to mutilation or death, and the executioner in putting the sentence into effect. Only in a few Buddhist texts and in the edicts of Asoka do we find explicit condemnation of war.

Ideally, however, war was an affair of the kṣatriya class—the fighters and rulers *par excellence*. Though the members of other castes often took part in fighting or served as non-combatants, it was not their caste duty to do so. The priesthood in particular should ideally remain 'above the battle', though there are many examples of martial brahmans. The right of self-defence was generally conceded to the layman. If a learned brahman of the highest sanctity made a violent attack on a man of lower class and the latter could only save his life by killing the brahman, he incurred no sin and was not liable to punishment.[42] In the realm of politics it was generally conceded that the subjects had the moral right to rise in revolt and put a tyrannical king to death, though there was some contrary opinion.

In classical Hinduism the most significant aspect of ahiṃsā was in respect of killing animals for food and meat-eating. Many injunctions in the *Smṛti* and other literature led to the spread of vegetarianism among the higher castes. It was by no means universal, however. The low castes were never averse to eating meat. At the other end of the scale the warriors traditionally hunted, and ate the game they killed. In Bengal and some other regions fish was by convention looked on as an aquatic vegetable. The Tantrists ate meat as part of their ritual. However, the general sentiments of classical Hinduism were much in favour of vegetarianism and the preservation of animal life. The Jains were particularly emphatic in this respect.

It must be remembered that the ahiṃsā described in the foregoing paragraph refers to the ordinary layman, the *gṛhastha*. The ascetic was bound by much more stringent rules. There were many cases of hypocrisy and laxity, but the ideals set before the forest hermits and wandering ascetics, for instance in the Lawbook of Manu (Book VI), were rigid in their insistence on absolute ahiṃsā. The hermit must be a complete vegetarian and, moreover, should eat only food which he had collected from wild plants and trees, avoiding all cultivated food, presumably because this involved injury to life in the process of ploughing, reaping and so on. The wandering ascetic might only eat what was given to him, and it is not expressly stated that he should always be a vegetarian, though this seems to have been the usual case. He should be absolutely non-violent, even carefully scanning the ground on which he walks to avoid treading on insects.[43] And in the face of threatening violence he should always remain calm, unruffled, and benevolent:

> He should be patient when insulted
> nor should he insult anyone;
> nor should he feel enmity towards anyone
> for the sake of this (mortal) body.
> He should not feel anger towards one who is angry.
> He should bless the man who curses him.[44]

The ascetic ideal was even more strongly emphasized in Jainism, which so deeply influenced the life of Gujarat. The hylozoistic philosophy of Jainism resulted in regulations verging on the fantastic, calculated to avoid injury to the minute and humble forms of life in air, water, metal, and fire. Even the eating of vegetable food was looked on as an unfortunate necessity. And unconscious injury to life, such as accidentally treading on an ant, was almost as dangerous to the soul as an act of violence consciously committed. The discipline of strict ahiṃsā applied in its full force to the Jain monk, and even the layman was encouraged to follow the monks' example as far as possible, and to undertake retreats, accepting monastic discipline for limited periods. In any case no Jain layman could legitimately eat meat or kill a flea, even though the Jains in earlier times made exceptions in the case of rulers and their servants, who were permitted in this degenerate age to take part in war and to punish criminals.

The period of the Delhi Sultanate witnessed the rise of schools of popular devotional Hinduism in the Indo-Aryan-speaking regions of India. Most of these originated from teachers who composed hymns (chiefly addressed to Viṣṇu in the *avatāra*s of Kṛṣṇa or Rāma) in the current languages of the time. They much stimulated the religious life of the Hindus, especially of the non-Brahmans. The *bhakta* hymnodists taught intense devotion to a personal deity; in the realm of morals they encouraged brotherly love and integrity in thought, speech, and deed; and they deprecated ritualism. The general tendency of their message was to encourage the layman to raise his standards of behaviour, and they set something approaching the ascetic ideal before all and sundry. The Gujarati verses quoted above and the Rāmāyan of Tulsi Das, both of which Gandhi knew and loved as a boy, are products of the great bhakti movement, which encouraged non-violence towards all living things, with its corollary of vegetarianism.

Thus in nineteenth-century Gujarat, so strongly influenced both by later devotional Hinduism and by Jainism, ideas of strict non-violence and vegetarianism dominated the ethical systems of the middle classes. The boy Mohandas Gandhi rebelled against them. He ate meat secretly and only gave up his vice through his devotion to 'Truth' and his shame at having to tell lies. When he arrived in England he did not really believe in ahiṃsā, but he remained a vegetarian because he had given his word to his mother to do so. It was only after reading a now-forgotten English book on the subject that he became 'a vegetarian by choice'.[45] Later the Sermon on the Mount strengthened his belief in non-violence,[46] which was confirmed in South Africa by his study of Tolstoy.[47] Yet the foundations of Gandhi's non-violence were obviously laid in his childhood. He tells us that his first reading of certain verses of the Sermon on the Mount ('Whosoever shall smite thee on the right cheek, turn to him the other also. And if any man take away thy coat let him have thy cloak also') immediately reminded him of the Gujarati verses of Shyamal Bhatt, quoted above. These lines are echoed in the bhakti poetry of all the languages of India, and their more positive interpretation of ahiṃsā, as returning good for evil rather than refraining from definite physical violence, is to be found in much Hindu devotional literature. Thus the Sermon in St Matthew's Gospel seems to have acted as a potent stimulus in reviving and developing in his mind ideas which had been implanted in early childhood, and which were based on the religious ideology of nineteenth-century Gujarat.

Gandhi's non-violence differs from the orthodox Indian concept of ahiṃsā in that it is conceived in positive terms, and can serve as a very effective political weapon. 'The self-sacrifice of one innocent man is a million times more potent than the sacrifice of a million men who die in the act of killing others.'[48] Non-violence does not involve running away from a violent situation, or turning a blind eye to cruelty and oppression. Where there is a choice between cowardice and violence, violence is to be preferred.[49]

But far better than either is non-violence, which is the very antithesis of cowardice, 'the summit of bravery'.[50]

In many respects Gandhi's non-violence admits exceptions which the orthodox Hindu would not agree to. 'In fear and trembling, in humility and penance' he was willing to do injury to monkeys which damaged and destroyed the crops of Sabarmati āshram, 'hoping some day to find a way out'.[51] On one occasion a calf which was incurably sick and in great pain was put to death on his instructions, and he vigorously defended his action.[52] He did much to help the British in the Boer War and the First World War. And he declared that those who sincerely believe that violence is right are morally justified in using force.[53]

Thus Gandhi's non-violence is an extension of the classical Hindu principle of ahimsā, which involves merely doing as little injury to living beings as possible, in the direction firstly of 'loving one's enemy' and secondly of positively inviting injury in a non-violent spirit, as a form of resisting evil. For the first, as we have seen, there are many Indian precedents in Hindu, Jain, and Buddhist sources. For the second these are less easy to find, though they are not wholly absent. Buddhism contains several stories of pious monks who suffered persecution and torture without resentment and with complete calm. The legends of Asoka tell that he was converted by this means. A story certainly known to Gandhi in his childhood was that of Prahlāda, the son of the demon Hiranyakasipu. Prahlāda's devotion to Visṇu so enraged his father that he ordered his son's destruction. The boy endured torture and suffering of all kinds without complaint, and his spiritual power was such that steel, poison, and flames had no effect on him. He did not, however, bring about the conversion of his father, who continued in his evil courses until he was destroyed by the Narasimha incarnation of Visṇu. On at least one occasion Gandhi referred to Prahlāda in this connection, in the rules and regulations of the satyagrāha āshram at Sabarmati.[54] But in a passage repeated in more than one anthology of Gandhi's writings he mentions only Jesus Christ, Daniel, and Socrates as 'the purest form of passive resistance or soul force', and Tolstoy as 'the best and brightest modern exponent of the doctrine'. 'In India', he goes on, 'the doctrine was understood and commonly practised long before it came into vogue in Europe', but he gives no concrete examples.[55] Probably he was thinking in terms of the general ethical doctrine of ahimsā, as it was applied in classical Hinduism to the ascetic and in Jainism and medieval Hindu bhakti to the layman also.

Satyāgraha

Gandhi's boyhood experiences can have provided few precedents for his techniques of passive resistance, deliberate infringement of the law, and open invitation of arrest and imprisonment in order to bring about political or social change. Nevertheless, some practices did exist which may have inspired him in his later career. One such, which has been often noted, was *dharnā*, or in Sanskrit *prāyopaveśa*, the custom of recovering a debt through the creditor sitting doggedly, perhaps for days, at the debtor's door. This custom is very ancient, being referred to in the legal texts of Āpastamba, Manu, and several others.[56] Since a similar practice is attested in ancient Ireland the custom may go back to the days of the primitive Indo-Europeans, before their migrations.[57] Dharnā was generally accompanied by fasting on the part of the creditor, and it had a very potent effect upon the debtor. Not only was he publicly put to shame, but also, if he held the beliefs current in his time and place, he felt himself endangered by the spiritual power produced by the creditor's persistence. The performance of dharnā by a creditor might be counteracted by a similar performance on the part of the debtor. Thus there would ensue a sort of contest in the display of will power, which might result in a friendly compromise.[58]

The practice of dharnā might be put to other uses, for it was even thought possible to influence the gods by this means. A supplicant, despairing of less drastic means of obtaining a boon, might sit and fast for days at the door of a temple or shrine, and thus virtually compel the divinity to favour him. The whole idea of dharnā is closely linked with the widely held and very ancient Indian belief, not unknown elsewhere, that mental or physical concentration has a positive effect upon material things, and that self-inflicted suffering in the form of *tapas* or asceticism generates an immense power that may even shake the gods on their heavenly thrones.

Dharnā-like picketing was sometimes carried out by groups. A man performing dharnā might be accompanied by his family members. The Kashmir Chronicle contains several cases of dharnā against the ruler on the part of aggrieved subjects. Thus the wife of a dead Brahman performed a fast in order to compel King Candrāpīḍa to find her husband's murderer. The king then himself fasted for three days and nights in a temple of Viṣṇu and was rewarded by a dream which showed him the means of detecting the criminal.[59] In the tenth, eleventh, and twelfth centuries we have records of the Brahman corporations of Srinagar and its environs performing prāyopaveśa in order to achieve political ends. The most outstanding example is that whereby the Brahmans in a time of interregnum in the tenth century were able to enforce the accession of Yaśaskara, a complete non-entity. This was done by a large body of temple priests who accompanied their solemn fast with the noise of drums and cymbals.[60] Yaśaskara, and perhaps other kings also, appointed special officers who were deputed to look into all cases of prāyopaveśa throughout the kingdom.[61] Later the irreligious Harsa (1089–1101) was compelled to exempt brahmans from corvee duty as a result of a protest of this kind.[62]

In the twelfth century such practices became more frequent, as the power of the monarchy waned. The pious Uccala (1101–11) vowed that if anyone in his kingdom ever died as a result of prāyopaveśa he would take his own life.[63] In the reign of Bhikṣācara (1120–1) the corporations performed a mass fast in favour of the exiled king Sussala. Kalhaṇa gives quite a vivid description of the event, of which he may have been an eye-witness. The scene has no suggestion of solemnity about it. The Brahmans sat in the courtyard of a large temple, amid rows of sacred images brought from their various shrines, and their fasting was accompanied by the continuous playing of drums, cymbals, and other musical instruments. They were surrounded by throngs of admiring citizens, who were ready to resist with force any attack on the Brahmans, and Brahmans and lower castes alike boldly debated the politics of the day, speaking insultingly to the royal officers who tried to reason with them.[64] After the pretender had suffered a defeat, however, the Brahmans gave up their fast and ran away in fright, taking their sacred images with them.[65] The last example of prāyopaveśa recorded by Kalhaṇa took place in his own day against an oppressive minister of King Jayasiṇha (1128–49), who had unjustly raised the taxes. The fast was ineffective, and many of the Brahmans burned themselves to death as a final act of protest.[66] They succeeded, however, in so impressing another young Brahman that he vowed that he would assassinate the minister, and in fact he managed to wound him so badly that he was compelled to give up his office.[67]

The Kashmir Chronicle also records two cases of troops performing fasts of this kind in protest against their low pay.[68] In the second instance, under Sussala (1112–20), the soldiers sat with drawn swords, blocking the gates of the palace. The Brahmans also fasted at the same time, and both priests and soldiers refused the king's attempts to buy them off.[69] The situation became so difficult that Sussala was forced to quit his capital, to be succeeded by Bhikṣācara, whose brief reign, as we have seen, was also marked by similar fasts on the part of the Brahmans.

The above instances which, by no means, exhaust the references in the Kashmir Chronicle to the practice of prāyopaveśa, show that it was a regular political tool in the hands of the Brahmans of the region, and might also be practised by other classes. The performers of this early form of satyāgraha seem sometimes to have been strongly supported by the masses. Though he was himself a Brahman, the historian Kalhaṇa, an aristocrat and an advocate of strong government, generally looks on prāyopaveśa with disfavour, as one of the greatest dangers to the state.[70]

We know of no record of similar mass protests in other parts of medieval Hindu India, but this may be merely due to the fact that no detailed chronicles exist for any region but Kashmir. One remarkable incident shows that the practice of mass dharnā was known to the Brahmans of north India at a somewhat later period. Sultan Firūz Shāh decided to impose *jizyā* or poll-tax on his Brahman subjects, who hitherto had not been expected to pay it. The Brahmans of Delhi appeared before the sultan and declared that rather than pay the tax they would collect dry wood and burn themselves to death. The sultan refused to make any concession, telling them that they could burn themselves rather than expect him to let them off. They fasted outside his hunting lodge for several days, until they were near death. When the Hindu citizens of Delhi heard of their plight they offered to pay the jizyā on the Brahmans' behalf. Ultimately the sultan agreed to a compromise, and accepted jizyā from the Brahmans at the lowest of the three rates fixed, ten *tankā*s per head per annum.[71] It is to be noted that this case of mass dharnā was partially successful, even though it was directed against a ruler antagonistic to Hinduism.

In later periods, cases of mass dharnā are not known to us, though they may have taken place. Peaceful demonstrations against the re-imposition of the jizyā certainly occurred in the reign of Aurangzeb. In one of these, in 1679, the whole road between the Red Fort at Delhi and the Jama Mosque was blocked by an unarmed crowd of Hindus. They refused to disperse in order to allow the emperor to go to prayer at the mosque, and were trampled down by elephants.[72] There is thus enough evidence to show that the seeds of satyāgraha were already present in the Indian soil before Gandhi nursed them into growth.

We have found no account of anything resembling prāyopaveśa of this type in Tulsī Dās's Rāmāyaṇ, and it is not likely that Gandhi knew of the Kashmiri prototype of satyāgraha before his return from England. The *Rājataraṅgiṇī* was first fully translated into English only in 1901, five years before his first passive resistance movement in South Africa. At that time it is unlikely that it would have come to his notice. The exploits of the Kashmiri Brahman corporations must have been well known to Motilal Nehru, whose son-in-law made a complete translation of the Chronicle, but Gandhi and Nehru were not in contact at that time. It is probable that, while still a boy at school, he had read something of the protest fast of the Brahmans under Fīrūz Tughluq, but we know of no definite evidence to this effect. On the other hand, the practice of dharnā as a means of recovering debts must have been well known to a boy of a Gujarat mercantile community at that period. Similarly the Jain custom of *sallekhana*, or fasting to death by gradually reducing the daily amount of food eaten, must have been known to him. But this had little relevance to Gandhi's political techniques, for it was normally only practised by elderly Jain monks with the purpose of achieving salvation as quickly as possible.

However, certain events in the port of Surat, not very far from Gandhi's birthplace, may have had some influence in the formation of his policy of satyāgraha. The merchants of Surat had always formed a compact and wealthy community, and the well-to-do Gujarati merchant had a tradition of participation in politics going back to Hindu times. We have several records of protests of a more or less non-violent type, mounted chiefly by the mercantile population, but with considerable support from the masses. Thus, on 30 August 1844 a large gathering of 30,000 people met to protest against a rise in the salt tax. Vociferous demonstrations, accompanied by a hartal, continued for three days. At first the demonstrators were 'not disposed to commit violence', but ultimately the cry was raised—'Kill or be killed'. The demonstrators were forcibly dispersed, but their protest was not unsuccessful, for certain local duties were abolished altogether and the hated salt tax was reduced.[73]

In April 1848, Surat saw a wave of mass agitation against the introduction of Bengali weights and measures, which the East India Company wished to make standard throughout its possessions. There is no record of serious violence, but only of a hartal and a deputation to the collector. As a result of the hartal the poorer people, who had no stores of grain, were put to some difficulty, and the local merchants organized free distribution of rice to the needy. This act of mass passive resistance was completely successful, since after several days' hartal it was decided to abandon the proposal to introduce the new weights and measures.[74]

In November and December 1860 there were angry demonstrations in many cities of India, directed against the newly introduced income tax. These sometimes resulted in violence and almost invariably were accompanied by the ceremonial tearing up of income tax forms. At Surat on 29 November there was a demonstration of some 2000 people, accompanied by a hartal. Though the crowd was in 'a very excited state' there are no reports of violence. The demonstration was ultimately broken up by mounted police, and was, of course, unsuccessful.[75]

A very serious hartal occurred in Surat, for several days beginning on 1 April 1878, against a newly imposed licence tax. At that time Gandhi was eight-and-a-half years old, and news of the disturbances must have reached his family. According to the Acting Collector's Report 'representatives from almost every class and caste were adjured in the most solemn way to keep all the shops in their neighbourhood closed and to resist Government to the uttermost'. The hartal lasted for some five days, and there were numerous vociferous gatherings. However, there seems to have been no violence until 5 April, when a mob attacked the local government buildings. This was quickly stopped by armed police, and the demonstrations came to an end without achieving their objective.[76]

It is hardly likely that Gandhi was unaware of these demonstrations, and it is very probable that they, and others like them in other parts of India, had a considerable effect on his later policy. Indeed it may be said that civil disobedience, in the form of the more or less non-violent protesting crowd which refuses to disperse when ordered to do so, is traditional in Indian life.

Belief in the power of the concentrated will, especially when accompanied by fasting and penance, was common to Hindu and Jain alike, and such ideas must have been known to the young Gandhi from his early boyhood, long before he began to read in the Gospels of mountains being moved by the power of faith. We need seek for no Western prototypes for his doctrine of 'soul force', which is derived from the Indian conceptions of *puṇya* or spiritual merit, and *teja*s, the supernatural power accumulated from asceticism and meditation. The concepts have much in common with the Muslim *barkat* and, in their more primitive forms, with the widespread belief in a sort of supernatural electricity inherent in powerful beings and objects, known to anthropologists as *mana*.

It must be recognized that satyāgraha is ethically a great refinement of dharnā or prāyopaveśa. The creditors performing dharnā and the Kashmiri Brahmans performing mass prāyopaveśa evidently had no sentiments of love or compassion towards the objects of their fasts and vigils. They pinned their hope of success rather on their wills than on their moral fervour, though no doubt they were usually convinced of the justice of their cause. On at least one occasion, in 1921, Gandhi wrote against the practice, and sharply distinguished it from his own methods, calling dharnā 'barbarity' and 'a crude way of using coercion', since the practitioner of dharnā knows that he will not be injured by the object of his fast.[77] But, in fact, the relationship of dharnā and prāyopaveśa to the techniques of civil disobedience seems closer than he was willing to admit. Gandhi gave those old Indian practices a more moral content by insisting that civil disobedience volunteers should, as far as it lay in their power, cherish thoughts of love and benevolence towards their persecutors. This high ethical tone is certainly in keeping with the Sermon on the Mount but it is equally consistent with Hindu bhakti, as exemplified in the Gujarati verses quoted by Gandhi himself in his *Autobiography*. Gandhi's techniques may have been learnt in part from the West, but the practice of satyāgraha, dependent as it was on belief in the 'soul force', was in no way un-Indian. If the activities of the Irish rent-strikers and British suffragettes and the writings of Thoreau, among other 'Western' factors, stimulated Gandhi to work out the policy of satyāgraha, it must also have owed much to the influences of his boyhood.

OTHER FEATURES OF GANDHI'S THOUGHT

Gandhi's very puritanical attitude to sex no doubt also derives from his youth. The incident on the night of his father's death would be sufficient in itself to encourage any sensitive young Hindu, on reaching maturer years and producing a family, to resolve on a life of celibacy. Celibacy is prescribed for both the Christian monk and the Hindu sannyāsī, but in the two religions the motives behind the taboo on sex differ somewhat. Christian ascetic thought looks on sex with suspicion as one of the most potent sources of infatuation, and a very serious distraction of a man from his true aim, which is the worship of God; hence the Catholic priest or monk may not marry. Hinduism, Jainism, and Buddhism agree with Christianity on this point, but the two former emphasize another important reason for celibacy, which is also not unknown in Christian circles—sex is believed to sap both vital and spiritual power. India has many legends of saintly hermits who, as a result of a carnal lapse, lost all their supernatural power and were no longer able to perform miracles. Gandhi's vow of *brāhmacārya*, significantly taken just before his first South African civil disobedience campaign in 1906,[78] was largely inspired by this motive, interpreted in modern terms. His insistence on the value of celibacy owes little or nothing to the West, and his Christian disciple C.F. Andrews disagreed strongly with him on that point.[79]

Gandhi's views on class distinction may be traced to earlier Indian sources, and they began even in his childhood. When his mother told him not to touch an outcaste boy, he answered 'Why not?', and he states that his revolt against caste began from that day.[80] His interpretation of the four *varna*s of classical Hinduism, as the perversion of an originally rational division of humanity into four classes not necessarily dependent on birth and not necessarily endogamous, is substantially that of nineteenth-century reformers such as Vivekananda. And from the days of the Buddha onwards an undercurrent of equalitarianism may be traced in many parts of India. No doubt Gandhi's views on human equality were strengthened by contact with the West, but they originated, like most of his ideas, in his childhood, and are not incompatible with the doctrines of reformers of earlier ages; these doctrines were never quite forgotten in India, though they had little effect on its social structure.

One feature of Gandhi's teaching for which we can find no Indian prototype is his doctrine of the spiritual and moral value of manual labour. The idea behind the Christian proverb *Laborare est orare* seems hardly to have occurred to any Indian of older times, though there may be a few passages to that effect in early Tamil and Telugu literature. The warrior was expected to keep tough by constant exercise and hunting. The *haṭha-yogī* might perform the most difficult exercises in the hope of spiritual gain; the *brāhmacārī*, the religious student living in his teacher's home, was expected to collect firewood and perform various menial duties for his master; but the man who habitually earned his living with his hands was nearly always low in the social scale. The prejudice against manual labour was no doubt very strong among the nineteenth-century mercantile classes of Gujarat, for it would be reinforced by the Jain objection to all vigorous movement, which was believed to injure the minute invisible beings of earth and air. Gandhi explicitly admitted that he owed his belief in the dignity of labour chiefly to Ruskin's *Unto this Last*, which inspired him to establish in 1904 the first of his āshrams, the Phoenix Settlement near Durban.[81]

Also essentially non-Indian is his championship of equal rights for women. The Indian tradition gives woman an honoured place in the home and in society, but in Hinduism, Jainism, and Buddhism alike she is subordinate to man in greater or lesser degree. Earlier nineteenth-century Indian reformers had also worked for the emancipation of women, but their inspiration came mainly from Western sources, and their ideas could have had little influence on the youthful Gandhi. He admits that as late as 1898 he 'thought that the wife was the object of the husband's lust, born to do her husband's behest, rather than a helpmate, a comrade and a partner . . .'.[82] We can safely attribute his views on the place of women in society to the influence of Western feminism.

Gandhi's objection to mechanized twentieth-century life also has no counterpart in the attitudes of ancient India, which was never averse to innovations of a practical kind. The literature of statecraft abounds in references to *yantra*s, or mechanical contrivances of a simple type. As a boy Gandhi seems to have been something of a rebel against tradition, and to have had no objection to making use of all the Western inventions available to him. As a student in London he was apparently thoroughly modern in his attitudes. In 1890 he visited the Great Exhibition in Paris; his main recollections, writing over thirty years later, were of Notre Dame and the Eiffel Tower. He has little to say in favour of the latter, which was 'a good demonstration of the fact that we are all children attracted by trinkets',[83] and he refers to Tolstoy's criticism of it. But he admits that he ascended the Tower and had a meal in its restaurant, and it is quite probable that the disparaging remarks he makes about it are the effect of hindsight. His objections to mechanized life, and to urban life generally, seem to have developed after his return from England, mainly no doubt as a result of reading Ruskin, Tolstoy, and Thoreau. But in a measure they reflected the conservatism of nineteenth-century Gujarat, and feelings which must have been widespread in Gandhi's childhood. Possibly in this respect, time and maturity implanted in him the attitudes against which he had reacted in his youth—a common enough feature in the biographies of men and women the world over.

CONCLUSION

We suggest that several of Gandhi's concepts are fully in keeping with Indian tradition, and were probably developed from ideas which he absorbed in his childhood and youth, fertilized and brought to fruition by his contact with the West. Only two major planks in his platform—the dignity of manual labour and the emancipation of women—seem to have had no prototypes in India's past. He was no doubt a great innovator, but he built firmly on the foundation of his own tradition. It is possible that if he had never read the Gospels, Tolstoy, Ruskin, and much Western literature, Gandhi would not have entered politics at all, or, if he had done so, would have devised techniques and policies different from those which he actually did devise. But if he had not been brought up in a middle class Hindu–Jain environment of the type that was to be found in nineteenth-century Porbandar and Rajkot his techniques and policies would have been very different indeed. His genius was even more successful than that of earlier reformers in harmonizing non-Indian ideas with the Hindu dharma, and giving them a thoroughly Indian character; and he did this only by relating them to earlier doctrines and concepts.

NOTES AND REFERENCES

1. I am indebted to Professor J.W. de Jong, Dr S.A.A. Rizvi, and Mrs Dove, who have given me valuable references.

2. *Auto.*, I. i. The following abbreviations are used in this chapter:

   Auto., M.K. Gandhi, *An Autobiography. The Story of My Experiments with Truth.* Translated from the Gujarati by Mahadev Desai. Washington DC: Public Affairs Press, 1949. (References by part and chapter.)

   H. Harijan, Poona and Ahmedabad, 1933–42.

   MMG. R.K. Prabhar and U.R. Rao, *The Mind of Mahatma Gandhi*, Madras: Oxford University Press, 2nd edn, 1946.

   YI. Young India; Ahmedabad, 1919–32.

3. *Auto.*, I. ii.

4. Ibid., v.

5. Ibid., iv.

6. Ibid., v.

7. Ibid., vii.

8. Ibid., viii.

9. Ibid., ix.

10. Ibid., x.

11. *Auto.*, I. x.

12. Ibid., xi.

13. Ibid., xii.

14. Ibid., xx.

15. *Auto.*, I. x.

16. B.S. Sharma, *Gandhi as a Political Thinker*, Allahabad: Indian Press (Publications) Private Limited, n.d., p. 20.

17. *YI*, 12 May 1920, p. 2; *MMG*, p. i.

18. *YI*, 20 January 1927, p. 21; *MMG*, p. i.

19. *YI*, 17 November 1921, p. 377; *MMG*, p. 15.

20. *YI*, 31 December 1931, p. 428; *MMG*, p. 20.

21. *Auto.*, Introduction.

22. Ibid., Conclusion.

23. Ibid., I. x.

24. *Satyameva jayate*, the motto of the Indian Republic.

25. *Muṇḍuka Upaniṣad*, iii. I. 5–6.

26. *Bṛhadāraṇyaka Upaniṣad*, ii. 3. 6.

27. *Chāndogya Upaniṣad*, vi. 8. 7.

28. Tulsī Dās, *Srī-Rām-carit-mānas*, H. P. Poddar (ed.), Gorakhpur: Gita Press,
     V. S 2015, ii. 27. 2–3.

29. Sir M. Monier Williams, *A Sanskrit-English Dictionary*, Oxford: Oxford
     University Press, 1899, s.v. *satya*.

30. *H*, 29 August 1936, p. 226; *MMG*, p. 30.

31. *YI*, 21 January 1926; D.M. Datta, *The Philosophy of Mahatma Gandhi*,
     Madison: University of Wisconsin Press, 1953, p. 25.

32. *YI*, 19 January 1928, p. 22; *MMG*, p. 96.

33. *H*, 2 February 1934, p. 8; *MMG*, p. 97.

34. *YI*, 22 September 1927, p. 319; *MMG*, p. 94.

35. *H*, 14 May 1938, p. 109; *MMG*, p. 31.

36. Ibid., pp. 33 ff.

37. Ibid., pp. 45 ff.

38. *YI*, 5 June 1924, p. 187; *MMG*, p. 194.

39. *YI*, 1 January 1925, p. 8; *MMG*, p. 187.

40. *YI*, 23 March 1922, p. 166; *MMG*, p. 49.

41. *YI*, 9 February 1922, p. 85; *MMG*, p. 49. The choice of teachers is interesting
     —no doubt the first names to enter the writer's head at the time. Surprisingly,
     Buddha is omitted, while Zoroaster and Muhammad, not particularly rigid in
     their non-violence, are included. The appearance of Mahāvīra in the list is
     indicative of what may be gathered from other writings of Gandhi—a deep
     sympathy for the Jainism which was widespread in his native Gujarat. The
     inclusion of Daniel shows that Gandhi revised his views about, at least, parts
     of the Old Testament, which he read as a student in London 'without the least
     interest or understanding'.

42. *Manusmṛti*, viii. 349.

43. Ibid., vi. 68.

44. Ibid., vi. 47–8.

45. *Auto.*, I. xiv.

46. Ibid., xx.

47. Ibid., II. xxii, etc.

48. *YI*, 12 February 1925, p. 60; *MMG*, p. 49.

49. *YI*, 11 August 1920, p. 3; *MMG*, p. 53.

50. *YI*, 29 May 1924, p. 176; *MMG*, p. 54.

51. *YI*, 13 September 1928, p. 308; *MMG*, pp. 64–5.

52. *All Men are Brothers. Life and Thoughts of Mahatma Gandhi as Told in his Own Words*, Unesco: Melbourne University Press, 1953, pp. 41 ff. C.F. Andrews, *Mahatma Gandhi's ideas* (3rd impression, London: Allen and Unwin, 1949), pp. 132 ff.

53. *Times of India*, 8 May 1941; *MMG*, p. 57.

54. Andrews, op. cit., p. 102; *MMG*, p. 178.

55. *MMG*, p. 78; *All Men are Brothers*, p. 99.

56. For references see P.V. Kane, *History of Dharmaśāstra*, Vol. iii, Poona: Bhandarkar Oriental Research Institute, 1946, p. 438; also L. Renou, 'Le jeune du creancier dans l'Inde ancienne', *Journal Asiatique*, ccxxiv, pp. 117–24.

57. Renou, op. cit., pp. 123–4.

58. J.A., Dubois, *Hindu manners, customs and ceremonies*, 3rd edn., Oxford: Clarendon Press, 1906, p. 666.

59. *Rājataraṅgiṇī*, Stein (ed.), iv. 82–108.

60. Ibid., v. 468–77.

61. Ibid., vi. 14.

62. Ibid., vii. 1088.

63. Ibid., viii. 51.

64. Ibid., viii. 898–908.

65. Ibid., 939.

66. Ibid., 2224–6.

67. Ibid., 2227–59.

68. Ibid., vii. 1156–7; viii. 807–8.

69. Ibid., viii. 807–17.

70. Ibid., vii. 1611; viii. 110, 709.

71. 'Afīf, ed., *Tārīkh-i-Firūzshāhī*, V. 4, Calcutta, 1890, pp. 382–4; trans. S.A.A. Rizvi, *Tughluk Kālīn Bhārat*, Vol. ii, Aligarh: 1957, pp. 150–1.

72. Sir Jadunath Sarkar, *Short History of Aurangzeb*, London: Routledge, 1930, p. 158.

73. *Source material for a history of the Freedom Movement (collected from Bombay Government Records)*, Vol. i, Bombay: 1957, pp. 1–16.

74. Ibid., pp. 17–18.

75. *Source material ... Freedom Movement*, Vol. i, Bombay: 1957, pp. 19–22.

76. Ibid., p. 29.

77. *YI*, 2 September 1921.

78. *Auto.*, III. vii–viii.

79. Andrews, op. cit., pp. 111–12.
80. *H*, 24 December 1938, p. 393; *MMG*, p. 107.
81. *YI*, 4 June 1931, p. 129; *MMG*, pp. 108–9.
82. *Auto.*, IV. xviii–xix.
83. Ibid., x.

2

Final Encounter
The Politics of the Assassination of Gandhi*

ASHIS NANDY

Even in his death there was a magnificence and complete artistry. It was from every point of view a fitting climax to the man and to the life he had lived....

Jawaharlal Nehru[1]

Godse was to Gandhi what Kamsa was to Krishna. Indivisible, even if incompatible. Arjuna never understood Krishna the way Kamsa did ... hate is infinitely more symbiotic than love. Love dulls one's vision, hate sharpens it.

T.K. Mahadevan[2]

I

Every political assassination is a joint communique. It is a statement which the assassin and his victim jointly work on and co-author. Sometimes the collaboration takes time to mature, sometimes it is instantaneous and totally spontaneous. But no political assassination is ever a single-handed job. Even when the killer is mentally ill and acts alone, he in his illness represents larger historical and psychological forces which connect him to his victim.[3]

* Ashis Nandy, 'Final Encounter: The Politics of the Assassination of Gandhi', in *At the Edge of Psychology: Essays in Politics and Culture*, New Delhi: Oxford University Press, 1980, pp. 70–98.

Robert Payne's biography of Mahatma Gandhi, perhaps more than any other writing on the subject, brings out this element of collaboration in the assassination of Gandhi.[4] It was an assassination, Payne seems to suggest, in which apart from Gandhi and a motley group of dedicated but clumsy assassins, crucial indirect roles were played by Gandhi's protectors in the Indian police and its intelligence branch, by the bureaucracy, and by important parts of India's political leadership including some of Gandhi's most dedicated followers.

But why was there this joint endeavour? Where did the minds and interests of so many people converge?

To answer this question I shall first define the quintessence of Gandhi's political style and then describe the psychological and social environment in India at the time of his death in January 1948.

Gandhi was neither a conservative nor a progressive. And though he had internal contradictions, he was not a fragmented, self-alienated man driven by the need to compulsively conserve the past or protect the new. Effortlessly transcending the dichotomy of orthodoxy and iconoclasm, he forged a mode of self-expression which, by its apparently non-threatening simplicity, reconciled the common essence of the old and the new.[5] However, in spite of his synthesizing skills, the content of the social changes he suggested, and the political activism he demanded from the Indian people, were highly subversive of the main strain of Indian, particularly Hindu culture. Even though few intellectuals in his time thought so,[6] many conservatives who had a real stake in the old and the established sensed this subversion. As his conservative assassin was to later complain, 'All his experiments were at the expenses [sic] of the Hindus'.[7]

Particularly dangerous to the traditional authority system in India were two elements of the Gandhian political philosophy. The first was his continuous attempt to change the definitions of centre and periphery in Indian society; the second was his negation of the concepts of masculinity and femininity implicit in some Indian traditions and in the colonial situation. Both these attempted changes had important psychological components and the drama of Gandhi's death cannot be told without reference to them.

The first element can be crudely called a distinctive Gandhian theory of social justice. The theory rejected the role of the modernist, westernized, middle class intelligentsia as a vanguard of the proletariat. Till the advent of Gandhi, it was this gentlemanly class which dominated Indian politics and was the main voice of Indian nationalism. Gandhi, however, was always afraid that in the name of the poor and the exploited, the 'advanced-thinking', ideologically guided, middle class intellectuals would only perpetuate their own dominance. So the first thing he tried to do was to de-intellectualize Indian politics. I should not be misunderstood: Gandhi was not against intellectuals *qua* intellectuals. He was against giving importance to intellectual activities and ideologies in a culture which believed intellection to be ritually purer and more Brahmanic, and where the primacy of idea over action had a sacred sanction behind it. Therefore, anticipating Mao Tse-Tung who faced a somewhat similar literati tradition, Gandhi would not even grant the existence of progressive elements within the traditionally privileged sectors of India.

As a part of the process of de-Brahminization through de-intellectualization, Gandhi was constantly trying to pass off many aspects of the low-status, non-Brahmanic, commercial, and peasant cultures in India as genuine Hinduism. While stressing the 'syntheticism' of Gandhi, one must not ignore his attempt to make certain peripheral aspects of the Hindu culture its central core, exactly the way he tried to do with Christianity in a more limited way.

To effect this cultural restructuring Gandhi evolved what for his society was a new political technology. He began emphasizing the centrality of politics and public life in an apolitical society and mobilizing the periphery of the Hindu society, apparently for the nationalist cause so dear to the urban middle classes, but actually to remould the entire cultural stratarchy within Hinduism. It is thus that Gandhi bridged the pre-Gandhian hiatus that had arisen between mass politics and social reform movements in India.[8]

This new political technology also incidentally challenged the basis of the colonial system which rested on the assumption that the British were ruling India with the consent of the majority of Indians in the countryside, her 'martial races' and their 'natural leaders' in the Kshatriya princelings, the rajas and maharajas who owed allegiance to the British crown. Gandhi's mobilizational technique of social and political change challenged this assumption and threatened to cut the support base of the British–Indian government.

British colonialism also predicated that the only vociferous dissenters in the colonial system were the urban middle class babus, alienated from the real India and from the society's 'natural' leadership, and that colonial subjugation established the cultural inferiority of the Indians whose burden it was the white man's Christian duty willingly to carry. Having an acute sense of power, Gandhi accepted the first proposition as valid and took his fight against the Raj to India's villages. Concerned with the loss of self-esteem in

Indians, he refused to accept that it was the Indians' responsibility to model themselves on their rulers, to be self-deprecating or defensive about their society. What at first sight seems Gandhi's obscurantism was actually his attempt to disprove the civilizing role attributed to colonialism (which at the time was closely associated with modern science, industrialism, high technology, and intellectually dominant theories of progress), so that colonialism could openly become a name for racism and exploitation.

The second major element in Gandhi's philosophy was his rediscovery of womanhood as a civilizing force in human society.

Gandhi tried to give a new meaning to womanhood in a peasant culture which had lived through centuries with deep-seated conflicts and ambivalence about femininity.[9] All his life Gandhi had wanted to live down, within himself, his identification with his own outwardly powerful but essentially weak, hedonistic, semi-modernized father and to build his self-image upon his identification with his apparently weak, deeply religious, traditional but self-confident and powerful mother. Apparently his mother was the first *satyagrahi* he knew who used fasting and other forms of self-penalization to acquire and wield womanly power within the constraints of a patriarchal family. Thanks to a number of sensitive psychological studies of Gandhi, these are now reasonably well-known facts.[10] I restate them only to stress what has always been recognized in such analyses, namely, Gandhi's deep need to come to psychological terms with his mother by incorporating aspects of her femininity in his own personality.[11]

Gandhi's ambivalence towards his father was overt and his respect for his mother was total. But underlying this respect, the various studies of Gandhi's personality themselves suggest, there was—as one would expect in the case of such imputation of total goodness—a great deal of latent ambivalence towards her. And, not unpredictably, the aggressive elements of this ambivalence were associated with some degree of guilt and search for valid personal and social models of atonement.

This personal search fitted the needs of some aspects of the Indian personality too. The Indian had always feared woman as the traditional symbol of uncertain nature and unpredictable nurture, of activity, power, and aggression. In consequence, he had always feared womanhood and either abnegated femininity or defensively glorified it out of all proportion.[12] As in many such cases, here too an internal psychological problem had its counterpart in cultural divisions within the Indian society. The greater Sanskritic culture tended to give less importance to a woman and to value her less in comparison to the little cultures of India. Simultaneously, the colonial culture too derived its psychological strength from the identification of ruler-ship with male dominance and subjecthood with feminine submissiveness.

It would therefore seem that Gandhi's innovations in this area also tended to simultaneously subvert Brahmanic and Kshatriya orthodoxy and the British colonial system. He challenged the former so far as it depended upon the Indian man's fears of being polluted by woman and contaminated by her femininity; he challenged the latter in so far as it exploited man's insecurity about his masculinity and his consequent continuous potency drive.

In other words, Gandhi attacked the structure of sexual dominance as a homologue of both the colonial situation and the traditional social stratifica-tion. He rejected the British as well as the Brahmanic–Kshatriya equation between manhood and dominance, between masculinity and legitimate violence, and between femininity and passive submissiveness.[13] He wanted to extend to the male identity—in both the rulers and the ruled—the revalued, partly non-Brahmanic, equation between womanhood and non-intrusive, nurturant, non-manipulative, non-violent, self-de-emphasizing 'merger' with natural and social environments.

That is, Gandhi was trying to fight colonialism by fighting the psy-chological equation which a patriarchy makes between masculinity and aggressive social dominance and between femininity and subjugation. To fight this battle he ingeniously combined aspects of folk Hinduism and recessive elements of Christianity to mark out a new domain of public intervention. In this domain the rulers and the ruled of India could share a new moral awareness, an awareness that the meek would not only inherit the earth but could make femininity a valued aspect of man, congruent with his overall masculinity. In other words, defiant subjecthood and passive resis-tance to violence—militant non-violence, as Erik Erikson calls it—became in the Gandhian world view an indicator of moral accomplishment and superiority, in the subjects as well as in the more sensitive rulers who yielded to non-violence. Gandhi not only wanted to be a trans-sexual mahatma or saint in the Indian sense; he also wanted to be a bride of Christ—a St Francis of Assissi—in the Christian sense. His goal was to become an *alter ego* for his potency seeking rulers and to align with their super-egos too. Honour, he asserted, universally lay with the victims, not the aggressors.[14] It is evidence of how much he was in tune with some of the emerging, though marginal, strands of consciousness in the European intellectuals, that at the same time that he was establishing his primacy in Indian politics, Romain Rolland was writing to his admirer Sigmund Freud, 'Victory is always more catastrophic for the vanquishers than for the vanquished.'[15]

These two basic constructions—centrality of the periphery of Indian culture and acceptance of femininity—Gandhi pronounced not through written or spoken words, a form of dissent for which there was legitimacy in the Brahmanic culture. His means were large-scale mobilization, organizational activism, and constant demands on the Indians for conformity to an internally consistent public ethic. These means were largely alien to the Brahmanic culture which was tolerant of—and self-confident vis-à-vis—ideological dissent but became insecure when ideological dissent was supported by such low status, non-Brahmanic means as active social intervention and mass politics.

In spite of erecting this elaborate and magnificent structure of dissent, Gandhi never claimed he was a revolutionary or a reformer, someone consciously reinterpreting traditional texts to justify new modes of life, as many social reformers in India had previously done. He was convinced that he was a *sanatani* Hindu, a genuine, orthodox, full-blooded Indian, not a social reformer out to alter Hinduism and Indian culture. He was, he seemed to argue, a counter-reformist, a revivalist, and a committed traditionalist.[16] According to him, he represented continuity and the Brahmanic, educated, westernized middle classes represented change. He was, he claimed, the insider; the upper echelons of the Hindu society, the Brahmanic cognoscenti, were the interlopers. And again, not only did Gandhi indulge in this 'inner speech', he went on to give it institutional forms. He mobilized the numerically preponderant non-Brahmanic sectors of the Hindus, the lower strata of society, and the politically passive peripheries: the low castes and untouchables, the peasants, and villagers. Taking advantage of numbers, he began legitimizing a new collective ethic that threatened to challenge the traditional Indian concepts of individual salvation, responsibility, and action geared to the value of self-awareness; the concepts of private knowledge and self-knowledge; political non-participation and the belief that the political authorities were not central to life.

It was a remarkable achievement of Gandhi that so many sensitive intellectuals took him at his word. What the Mahatma was doing did not seem very revolutionary to them at first sight, and in fact, they were not entirely wrong. Gandhi's political innovations overtly did seem compatible with Hindu orthodoxy and there was nothing intrinsically non-Indian about his social and political theories. However, it must be remembered that like all major civilizations, the Indic included a plethora of cultural strains. The distinctive identifier of a major civilization is always the composite whole that it makes of its diverse, contradictory constituents, by giving different emphases or weights to the various norms and subcultures within it.

The danger that Gandhi posed to the greater Sanskritic tradition was exactly this. He introduced a different system of weightages and threatened to alter the basic characteristics of Indian society by making its cultural periphery its centre.

II

It is surely not accidental that Gandhi's assassin, Nathuram Vinayak Godse (1912–49), was a representative of the centre of the society that Gandhi was trying to turn into the periphery.

I want to concentrate on Godse among the conspirators who planned the assassination because, first of all, it was his finger which ultimately pulled the trigger on 30 January 1948. By his own choice and partly against the wishes of his collaborators, he killed Gandhi single-handed because he felt 'history showed that such revolutionary plots in which several persons were concerned had always been foiled, and it was only the effort of a single individual that succeeded.'[17]

Godse with Narayan Apte also constituted the core of the band of conspirators. The other actors in the group were minor and 'arrived late on the scene and were unknown to each other until a few weeks before the murder. There was something strangely anonymous about them, as though they had been picked up in random.'[18] It was as if two dedicated opponents of Gandhi had mobilized the larger faceless society to eliminate Gandhi from the Indian scene.

But why Godse? I shall try to give my answer as simply as possible.

First, Godse and all his associates except one came from Maharashtra, a region where Brahmanic dominance was particularly strong. He also happened to be from Poona, the unofficial capital of traditional Maharashtra and a city renowned for its old-style scholarship and for the rich, complex culture which the high-status Chitpavan or Konkanasth Brahmins had built there. Godse, himself a Chitpavan Brahmin like the other figure in the inner core of conspiracy, was by his cultural inheritance a potential opponent of Gandhi. (There had been three known unsuccessful attempts to kill Gandhi—all in Maharashtra. The first was in Poona in 1934 when Gandhi was engaged in an anti-untouchability campaign there. The second, a half-hearted one, took place in Sevagram and involved members of the Hindu

Mahasabha. That was in 1944. In 1946, once again near Poona, some unknown persons tried to derail the train in which Gandhi was travelling.)[19]

The Chitpavans, traditionally belonging to the western coast of India, were one of the rare Brahmin communities in India which had a long history of valour on the battlefield. This fact gave them, in their own eyes, a certain historical superiority over the Deshasth Brahmins belonging to the plains of Maharashtra. In the absence of martial castes like Rajputs in the region, the Chitpavans could thus combine the traditional prerogatives of the priestly Brahmins and the kingly Kshatriyas. Though a few other communities, mainly the Marathas, did claim a share of the Rajput glory in the state, the social gap between the Brahmins and the non-Brahmins was one of the widest in the region, and nowhere more so than in Poona.

The Maharashtrian Brahmanic elites also had a long history of struggle against the Muslim rulers of India in the seventeenth and eighteenth centuries. It is true that they were associated with powers that were essentially marauders and large parts of Hindu India too were victims of their aggressiveness. But by the beginning of the twentieth century, the Maharashtrian Brahmins had reinterpreted their history in terms of the needs of Hindu nationalism. They saw themselves as the upholders of a tradition of Hindu resistance against the Muslim occupation of India. It was on this reconstructed and self-created tradition that a part of the Maharashtrian elite built up their anti-British nationalism. Like the Bengali nationalists—simultaneously, their sympathizers, ego-ideals, and admirers—they did not see themselves as morally superior individuals, non-violently—and, therefore, ethically—trying to free themselves and their British rulers from a morally inferior colonial system, as Gandhi wanted them to do. They saw themselves as the previously powerful, now weakened, competitors of the British. So terrorism directed against the Raj came naturally to them. Their aim was the redemption of their lost glory.[20]

Naturally, much of Gandhi's charisma did not extend to the Chitpavans. To the extent Gandhi rejected the Kshatriya identity by his constant emphasis on pacifism and self-control, he posed a threat to the warrior cultures of India. In addition, by constantly stressing the feminine, nurturing, non-violent aspects of men's personality, he challenged the Kshatriya male identity built on fear of woman and of the cosmic feminine principles in nature, and the no less acute fears of becoming a woman and of being polluted by woman. (In other words, he posed more or less the same kind of threat to India's martial cultures as to her priestly cultures.) Thus, given the absence of Kshatriya competition, the Maharashtrian Brahmins not only

enjoyed greater status than they would have otherwise done, they incorpo-
rated—as traditional rulers, landowners, and warriors—elements of the
Kshatriya identity and lived with many of the Kshatriya fears and anxieties
relating to womanhood.

Nathuram Godse came from this background. So did most of his co-
conspirators including his younger brother Gopal.[21]

Gandhi's assassin was born in 1910, in a small village in the margin of
the Bombay–Poona conurbation. He was the eldest son and the second child
in a family of four sons and two daughters. His father was Vinayak R.
Godse, a petty government official who worked in the postal department
and had a transferable job which took him to small urban settlements over
the years. Three sons had been born to him before Nathuram and all three
had died in infancy. Both Vinayak and his wife were devoted and orthodox
Brahmins and, understandably, they sought a religious solution to the
problem of the survival of their new-born son. The result was the use of a
time-honoured technique: Nathuram was brought up as a girl. His nose was
pierced and he was made to wear a *nath* or nose-ring. It is thus that he came
to acquire the name Nathuram, even though his original name was
Ramachandra. Such experiences often go with a heightened religiosity and
a sense of being chosen. In this instance, too, the child soon enough became
a devotee of the family gods. He sang bhajans before the deities and,
according to his family, acquired the ability to occasionally go into a trance
and speak as an oracle.

Neither the burden of living a bisexual role nor the oracular religiosity,
however, stood in the way of Nathuram becoming a 'strapping young man',
given to physical culture and other 'masculine' pursuits. Perhaps in his
culture such early experiences of socially imposed bisexuality had a clear-
cut meaning and instrumentality, and it was not specially difficult to contain
the diffusion of one's gender-specific self-image. Perhaps it was given in
the situation that Nathuram would try to regain the lost clarity of his sexual
role by becoming a model of masculinity.

Whatever the inner tensions, they did not show. By all accounts, Nathuram
was a well-mannered, quiet, humble young man (unlike his flamboyant,
elegant, well-placed collaborator Apte whose father was a reputed classics
scholar and uncle a popular novelist; Apte himself was a science graduate
with a good academic record and, in spite of his Hindu nationalism, an
erstwhile holder of a king's commission in the Royal Indian Air Force and
a teacher at an American mission school). Nathuram's quiet interpersonal
style was associated with an early interest in public affairs and good works.

Biographical accounts mention the help he often gave to his neighbours and the interest he took in informal social work. However, as the span of his social interests widened, his oracular abilities declined. According to his brother, by the age of sixteen he had lost his concentration and ceased to be the medium between the family deity and the family. Nonetheless, a certain natural intellectual brightness persisted in spite of the absence of formal higher education, and so did—as a biographer puts it—a certain natural dignity. In a religious family, even a lapsed oracle cannot fail to acquire a sense of being chosen.

There is some evidence that some of these qualities became more noticeable in Nathuram after he killed Gandhi. Some who saw him in his pre-assassination days thought him poor in verbal and social skills. They were genuinely surprised by his competence and serene composure after the murder of Gandhi and the legal skill and self-confidence with which he argued his own case in English, a language he supposedly did not know well.[22] It was as if the assassination gave meaning and drive to a life which otherwise was becoming increasingly prosaic. This was perhaps the reason why Godse was eager to play out his full role as the assassin of Gandhi.[23] Until he went to the gallows, his one fear was that the Government of India, goaded by Gandhi's family and many Gandhians, might have 'pity' on him and he might have to live the rest of his life with the shame of it. He did not want an anti-climax of that kind. As he put it, 'The question of mercy is against my conscience. I have shown no mercy to the person I have killed and therefore I expect no mercy.'[24] Others who knew him in jail authenticate this attitude. 'The common feeling was that even if he were thrown out of jail and given a chance to flee, he would not have taken advantage of it.'[25]

However, there was one Brahmanic trait in him which predated his encounter with Gandhi. Though he had failed to matriculate, Godse was a self-educated man with first-hand knowledge of the traditional religious texts. He knew for instance the entire Bhagavad Gita by heart and had read texts such as *Patanjali Yogasutra*, *Gnyaneshwari*, and *Tukaram Gatha*.[26] In addition he had a good command over written and spoken Marathi and Hindi and was widely read in history, politics, sociology, and particularly in Gandhi's writings. He was also well-acquainted with the works of some of the major figures of nineteenth- and twentieth-century India, including Vivekananda, Aurobindo, Tilak, and Gokhale.

Conforming to the psychologist's concept of the authoritarian man, Godse was highly respectful towards his parents, attached to conventional ideas of social status, and afraid of losing this status. While facing death, his one fear was that his execution as Gandhi's murderer might lower the social status of his parents and, in his letters to them, he sought elaborate justification from sacred texts and the Puranas to legitimize his action. He was not worried about his parents' reaction to the loss of a son.

Well-built, soft-spoken, and like most Chitpavans fair-complexioned, Nathuram thus projected the image of a typical member of the traditional social elite. But there was a clear discrepancy between this image and his life story till the day of the assassination. The Godses may not actually have been poor, but they were haunted with the fear of it throughout Nathuram's younger days. So much so that at the early age of sixteen he had to open a cloth shop to earn his livelihood. This is less innocuous than it may at first seem: business was not merely considered highly demeaning for a Brahmin; in lower middle class Brahmin families entry into business was an almost sure indicator of academic failure. To make things worse, Nathuram's shop failed and he had to turn to tailoring, traditionally an even more lowly caste profession than business.

In sum, there was an enormous gap between Nathuram's membership of a traditionally privileged sector of the Indian society on the one hand and his actual socio-economic status and experiences in adolescence on the other.

It is from this kind of background that the cadres of violent, extremist, and revivalist political groups often come.[27] Not surprisingly, after a brief period in Gandhi's civil disobedience movement in 1929–30, Nathuram became, at about the age of twenty, an active and ardent member of the Hindu Mahasabha, a small political party, and of the Rashtriya Swayamsevak Sangh (RSS), at that time virtually a paramilitary wing of the Mahasabha with all its key posts occupied by Maharashtrian Brahmins. Overtly both groups supported the cause of Hindu revivalism and tried to articulate the Hindu search for self-esteem. Covertly however, for the Maharashtrian Brahmins who constituted their main support base, both groups had aspects of a millennial movement which promised to reinstate the hegemony of the traditional social leadership or at least contain its humiliation. The idiom of these political groups suited Nathuram's world view in other ways too. He was extremely religious, and he read into the sacred texts what one would expect a man from a traditional martial background to read into them. For instance in the case of the Gita, 'Unlike Gandhi he was convinced that Krishna was talking to Arjuna about real battles and not battles which take place in the soul.' Predictably, in the ardent politics of the Mahasabha he found a more legitimate expression of the Hindu search for political potency. Predictably too, he did well in the party, becoming, within a few years, the secretary of its Poona branch. However, he did not find the RSS militant enough, so, within a year or so, severing his links with the RSS, Godse formed a new organization, the Hindu Rashtra Dal.

In 1944, Godse purchased the newspaper *Agrani*, with the help of donations given by sympathizers, to propagate his political views. But soon the government proscribed the paper because of its fiery tone. Godse revived the paper under a new name, *Hindu Rashtra*. This time he took financial help from Narayan Apte, who became the paper's managing editor. *Hindu Rashtra* was even more violently anti-Gandhi than its predecessor and it articulated the belief popular among some sections of Indians, particularly among the Bengali and Maharashtrian middle income, upper caste elements, that Gandhism was 'emasculating' the Hindus. However, notwithstanding its shrillness, the newspaper did not give its editor any money and he continued to be a tailor. In fact, he had to start a coaching class in tailoring to supplement his income.

Whatever else *Hindu Rashtra* did or did not, it helped crystallize some of Godse's main differences with Gandhi at the level of manifest political style.

However, it is impossible to speak about these differences without stating the many manifest similarities between the two men. Both were committed and courageous nationalists; both felt that the problem of India was basically the problem of the Hindus because they constituted the majority of Indians; and both were allegiant to the idea of an undivided free India. Both felt austerity was a necessary part of political activity. Gandhi's asceticism is well-known, but Godse too lived like a hermit. He slept on a wooden plank, using occasionally a blanket and even in the severest winter wore only a shirt. Contrary to the idea fostered by a popular Hollywood film on him, *Nine Hours to Rama*, Godse neither smoked nor drank. In fact, he took Gandhi's rejection of sexuality even further; he never married and remained a strict celibate. Like Gandhi, Godse considered himself a sanatani and, in deference to his own wishes, he was cremated according to sanatani rights. Yet, and in this respect too he resembled Gandhi; he said he believed in a casteless Hindu society and in a democratic polity. He was even in favour of Gandhi's attempts to mobilize the Indian Muslims for the nationalist cause by making some concessions to the Muslim leadership. Perhaps it was not an accident that Godse began his political career as a participant in a civil disobedience movement started by Gandhi and ended his political life with a speech from the witness stand which, in spite of being an attack on Gandhi, nonetheless revealed a grudging respect for what Gandhi had done for the country.

But the differences between the two men were basic. Godse was in the tradition of the westernized upper caste elements in the tertiary sector of the Indian society who had dominated the Indian political scene in the late-nineteenth and early-twentieth century.[28] He was particularly impressed by the terrorist traditions of urban middle class Bengal, Punjab, and Maharashtra which, sharing the values of India's imperial rulers, conceptualized politics as a ruthlessly rational zero-sum game, in which the losses of the opponents must constantly be actively maximized. Like a 'normal' human being anywhere in the world, he considered totally irrational Gandhi's emphasis on political ethics, soul force, and the moral supremacy of the oppressed over the oppressor.

Godse's Hinduism too was essentially different from Gandhi's. To Gandhi Hinduism was a lifestyle and an open-ended system of universal ethics which could continuously integrate new inputs. He wanted to organize the Hindus as part of a geographically defined larger political community, not as a religious group. To semi-westernized Godse, unknowingly impressed by organized western Christianity and Islam and by the aggressive self-affirmation of the church and *ulema*, the salvation of Hindus lay in giving up their synthetism and ideological openness and in being religious in the fashion of politically successful societies. He wanted Hindus to constantly organize, compete, and 'self defend', to become a single community and a nation.

Finally, Godse looked at history as a chronological sequence of 'real' events. So he saw the one thousand years of domination of India by rulers who were Muslims or Christians as a humiliation of the Hindus which had to be redressed. Gandhi, in tune with mainstream Hinduism, never cared for chronologies of past events. History to him was a contemporary myth which had to be interpreted and reinterpreted in terms of contemporary needs. The long Muslim domination of India meant nothing to him; in any case defeat for him was a problem for the victor, not for the defeated.

These differences account for Godse's saying:

Gandhiji failed in his duty as the Father of the Nation. He had proved to be the Father of Pakistan. It was for this reason alone that I as a dutiful son of Mother India thought it my duty to put an end to the life of the so-called Father of the Nation who had played a very prominent part in bringing about vivisection of the country—our Motherland.[29]

But there were other historical reasons for Godse's antipathy towards Gandhi, behind these fantasies of a mother who becomes a victim of rapacious intruders, a weak emasculated father who fails in his paternal duty and collaborates with the aggressors, and an allegiant mother's son who tries to redeem his masculinity by protecting the mother, by defeating first aggressors in their own game and by patricide. Let us now turn to them.

Godse's humble personal history was endorsed for him by the history of his community, particularly the encroachment which the British colonial culture was making upon the traditional self-definitions of the Chitpavans. Even before he was born, the Chitpavan—and for that matter Brahmanic —domination of the Maharashtrian society had ceased to be automatic. First, they had forfeited their prerogatives as a ruling caste and they had to use their traditional Brahmanic skills to compete in the alien world of colonialism to earn a part of their social status.[30] Second, the burgeoning commercial culture of metropolitan Bombay, the capital of the state, was gradually rendering peripheral the culture of Poona, opening up the stronghold of Chitpavans to a wider world and simultaneously forcing the Chitpavans all over Maharashtra to gradually become mainly a group of lower middle class professionals and petty government officials. Third, the Chitpavans had increasingly begun to feel the growing presence and power of the upwardly mobile sectors of the Maharashtrian Hindus such as the Marathas and Mahars, the commercial success of non-Maharashtrians like the Gujarati Banias (they included the Hindu commercial castes, to one of which Gandhi belonged, and Muslim merchant communities) and Parsees.[31] In fact, the language of commerce in Bombay was Gujarati and the language of administration under the Raj was, naturally, English. Marathi, in spite of its highly developed literary and scholarly traditions, was nowhere in the picture. Even more galling must have been the growing professional dominance in Bombay of the Gujaratis and Parsees, communities largely identified in the minds of the Maharashtrians with commerce.

So the ambivalence of the Chitpavans towards the changing social environment was deep and deeply anxiety provoking. And the community was clearly split. A few did very well under the new dispensation; they saw the cultural advantages of the Chitpavans in the tertiary sector. Others saw British colonialism as an unmitigated evil which was eroding the Chitpavans' traditional self-definition. This ambivalence, too, was a part of Godse's heritage.

Gandhi, who started his political career in India in Godse's formative years in the 1920s, was a threat to his last antagonist in two ways. First,

Gandhi was trying to make the social periphery (which, as we have seen, was a periphery first of all to the Chitpavans) a part of the political centre (which was a centre first of all to the Chitpavans). Second, while Godse was one of those who competed with the British within the same frame of discourse, Gandhi never offered political competition to either the traditional system or the 'modern' colonial establishment. Truly speaking, he competed with nobody; he was always seeking complementarities.[32] Those who speak of Gandhi either as a totally atypical Indian or as a genuine son of the soil tend to miss that what he basically offered was an alternative language of public life and an alternative set of political and social values, and he tried to actualize them as if that was the most natural thing to do. This also must have been a threat to those who wanted to offer clear resistance to the colonial system on unmixed nationalist grounds.

To come to the other major theme in Gandhi's dissent which bonded him and his assassin. Consciously or not, a recent best-seller tries simplemindedly to provide a clue to this psychological link between Nathuram Vinayak Godse and Gandhi.[33] The book claims, on the basis of the authors' interviews with Gopal Godse, that Nathuram and his political mentor and father's namesake, Vinayak Damodar Savarkar, had had a homosexual experience. The book also seems to hint that by the time he participated in the assassination, Nathuram had become an ascetic misogynist. Finally, it adds that Apte, the 'brains' behind the assassination, was a womanizer.

All this may or may not be true. Gopal Godse has denied that he had ever mentioned his brother's homosexuality while being interviewed by the authors. Savarkar, some others claim, was a known womanizer. We know he had spent long stretches of time inside jails, often in solitary confinement, for his political activities.[34] His sexuality may have been distorted and found an outlet either in homosexuality or in promiscuity. But in either case he would have represented a heightened sensitivity to man–woman relationships and problems centring around masculinity and femininity. And whether he was involved in the conspiracy or not—the existing evidence tends to be in his favour legally, not morally[35]—he did serve as the assassins' ego ideal.[36] For many of them, the mighty elder revolutionary was the male prototype, vigorously protesting the reduction of the Hindus to a passive, quasi-feminine role, constantly fearing the further encroachment of femininity on their masculine self due to the 'rapaciousness' of the Muslims and the British.

The same thing applies to Nathuram Godse. Whether he had willingly joined Savarkar in a political and sexual bond or not, he articulated concerns about his sexuality, often by aggressive denial of it and by his conspicuous asceticism, often by his conflicts centring around his sexual identification and an acute sensitivity to the definitions of masculinity and femininity. If Collins and Lapierre have built a myth, they have mythologized what there was in reality. Godse's political speeches and conversations were studded with imagery which constantly reminded the sensitive listener of the equation which Godse made between Indian or Hindu subjugation and passive femininity. His writings were punctuated by references to the British and Muslims as 'rapists', and Hindus as their raped, castrated, deflowered victims.[37]

Apte, the alleged womanizer who planned the logistics of the assassination, only strengthens this interpretation. At one plane, the womanizer and the homosexual both articulate, through diametrically opposite kinds of sexuality, the same sensitivities. One tries to constantly reaffirm his masculine self and prove to himself and to others that he is a man; the other fears woman as a sex object and is uncertain about his masculinity. The main point is this: Godse belonged to a group which was deeply conflicted about sexual identity and had learnt to politicize some of these conflicts.

In sum, Godse not only represented the traditional Indian stratarchy which Gandhi was trying to break, he was sensitized by his background to this process of elite displacement. Similarly, he also sensed the other coordinate of the Gandhian 'revolution': the gradual legitimacy given to femininity as a valued aspect of Indian self-definition. This revaluation of femininity, too, threatened to deprive the traditional elite like Godse of two of their major scapegoats: the Muslims and the British, who had defeated and emasculated the Hindus and made them *nirveerya* or sterile and *napungsak* or impotent. The theory of action associated with such scapegoating was that the Hindus would have to redeem their masculinity by fighting and defeating the Muslims and the British. Now the new Gandhian culture of politics had made this theory irrelevant. This culture placed on the victims of aggression the responsibility of becoming authentic innocents, wise as the serpent to the exploitative situation, rather than pseudo-innocents colluding with the aggressors for secondary gains from the exploitative situation.[38] This self-redefinition, Gandhi seemed to argue, could not be attained by reaffirming one's masculine self—he was shrewd enough to know the might of the British empire and violence invariably associated with such reaffirmation of masculinity—but by militant non-violence, which totally refuses to recognize the defeat in violent confrontation to be defeated. No victory is complete unless the defeated accepts his defeat. The Godses had lost to the British, Gandhi seemed to argue, because they conformed to the martial values of the victors. He promised to win because he could draw upon the non-martial self of the apparent victors and create doubts about their victory in them.

So Godse was not a demented killer. Jawaharlal Nehru, soon after Gandhi's death, claimed that Godse did not know what he was doing. I contend that more than any other person Godse did know. He sensed with his entire being the threat Gandhi was to the traditional lifestyle and world view of India. K.P. Karunakaran, a political scientist who has worked on Gandhi for a number of years, once lamented that only two persons in India had correctly assessed the power of Gandhi: Godse, who killed him, and G.D. Birla, India's biggest business tycoon, who gave him unconditional financial support in pre-independence India and reaped its benefits in post-independence India. I am afraid, at least in this one instance, the political scientist is more right than the political functionary. Nehru was wrong. Godse *did* reveal a surprisingly acute sensitivity to the changing political-psychological climate in India, by killing Gandhi. I can only add that the heightened sensitivity of Godse reflected the latent awareness of dominant sections of the Indian society of what Gandhi was doing to them. In that sense, Godse's hand was forced by the real killers of Gandhi: the anxiety-ridden, insecure, traditional elite concentrated in the urbanized, educated, partly westernized, tertiary sector whose meaning of life Gandhian politics was taking away. Gandhi often talked about the heartlessness of the Indian literati. He paid with his life for that awareness.

Ten days before his assassination, on 20 January 1948, Madanlal Pahwa, one of Godse's co-conspirators, threw a bomb in a prayer meeting Gandhi was holding, and was apprehended. His intended victim pleaded with the police and the audience to have mercy on Madanlal and instead of harassing the young man, to search their own hearts.[39]

III

One final question needs to be raised: how far did Gandhi and his political heirs in the Indian government collude with the assassins?

We know Gandhi was depressed in his last days in Delhi and was fast losing interest in living.[40] The partition of India was hard on a person who had once said:

I can never be willing party to the vivisection. I would employ non-violent means to prevent it .... My whole soul rebels against the idea that Hinduism and Islam represent two antagonistic cultures and doctrines. To assent to such doctrine is for me denial of God .... If the Congress wishes to accept partition, it will be over my dead body.[41]

The primitive sadism of the pre- and post-partition Hindu–Muslim riots too had destroyed Gandhi's earlier publicly expressed wish to live for 125 years.[42] He could see the dwindling interest and attendance at his daily prayer meetings and must have also noticed that many of those who did attend the meetings did so as a daily ritual.[43] Somehow Gandhi, as if anticipating and agreeing with the accusations Godse would later make, held himself responsible for what was happening to India and felt that God after deliberately blinding him had awakened him to his mistake.[44]

He now openly yearned for a violent death while preaching pacifism. As he became fond of telling Manuben, his grand-niece and constant companion of his last days, he now only wanted to die bravely; he felt that could turn out to be his final victory. Another time he said to her that if he were to die of an illness, he would prove himself a false Mahatma.[45] But if he was felled by an assassin and could die with Rama's name on his lips, he would prove himself a true Mahatma. Thus, it is not surprising that Gandhi's last fast at Delhi, though ostensibly directed against communal violence, was by his own admission directed against everybody.[46]

His death wish found other expressions too. He now began to have forebodings of his end. He even specified, correctly as it later turned out, the religion of his future assassin and his own last words after being struck by an assassin's bullet.[47] His health, too, was fast deteriorating. In addition to ailments such as an almost chronic cough, he showed psychosomatic symptoms such as recurring giddiness and nightmares.[48]

He also became totally careless about his physical security. All his life he 'had been reckless of his own safety, and in Delhi he found abundant opportunities to place his life in danger.'[49] He was accustomed to hearing the slogan 'Death to Gandhi'.[50] Now, he seemed to be daring his detractors to act out their wish. There had been, as I have mentioned, a bomb explosion only a few days before his assassination at one of his prayer meetings, the handiwork of the same group of men who ultimately killed him. But Gandhi explicitly rejected all offers of police protection.

Those in charge of his safety too, strangely enough, did little, and this in spite of the fact that bomb-thrower Pahwa was immediately caught and was 'willing' to talk. But there was little communication between the Delhi, Bombay, and Poona police. Deliberately or not, each of these police forces sabotaged the investigation. Twenty years later, the Kapur Commission of Enquiry unearthed large-scale bureaucratic inefficiency and sheer lethargy in the police who had failed to pursue the clear clues they had to the existence of a dedicated band of conspirators.[51] To pass off the inefficiency and lethargy as the characteristics of individuals will not do.[52] One must consider these important and inherent characteristics of the culture of the modern sector of India which, in effect, colluded with the conspirators. The police officers of Delhi who later cheated and forged documents, as the Kapur Commission established, to show that the police had tried to protect Gandhi—or the police officers at Bombay and Poona, who failed to break up the conspiracy even when supplied with the names and occupations of some of the conspirators—were a part of the environment which felt menaced by Gandhi. They had worked too long for the Raj as antagonists of Gandhi, and had not been touched by his vision of a different kind of society.

The Hindu–Muslim riots which had destroyed Gandhi's will to live and turned him into a self-destructive depressive, also coloured the psychology of the investigating police, constantly exposed to the slogan of 'Let Gandhi die' during Gandhi's last 'fast unto death' to establish communal peace in Delhi. Anti-Muslim feeling was high in the predominantly Hindu police assigned to protect Gandhi. Most of them were drawn from the various Kshatriya sub-traditions or upwardly mobile social groups claiming Kshatriya status and saw Gandhi not merely as pro-Muslim but as a stereotypical model of passive Hindu submission to non-Hindu aggression. Moreover, the Indian police had already resigned from their role as secular arbiters of law. In the communal riots, the police on the subcontinent had shown itself to be particularly vulnerable to communal passions. Most policemen had supported their respective communities, and their officers had openly tolerated and colluded with the killing of people of other communities. Belonging to castes and communities which had traditionally either lived by the sword or had culturally built-in acceptance of Dionysian rules of interpersonal and public conduct, these officers must have seen in Gandhi, in the charged atmosphere of the post-Partition riots, a person identifying with a part of their feared super-ego which had been overtaken by primal impulses of violence, retribution, and fear.[53]

Finally, though to his political heirs he remained a father figure, the successful completion of India's freedom struggle ending in independence had taken its toll. Statecraft and new responsibilities took up much of the time of the leaders. The chaos and near-anarchic situation in post-independence India kept them busy. If anything, they found Gandhi's style slightly anachronistic and Gandhi somewhat unmanageable.[54] For instance, Susanne Rudolph feels 'Patel... often wished that the Mahatma would leave him alone, especially in matters where they differed greatly— as in Hindu–Muslim relations and Patel's cold-eyed *Realpolitik* orientation'.[55] But leaving him alone was the one thing Gandhi would not do. Did Home Minister Patel's failure to protect Gandhi express his unconscious rejection of the relevance of Gandhi and his interfering style, as an important first-hand witness and a major political figure of the period, Abul Kalam Azad, seems to imply?[56] One does not know, but it is not perhaps a coincidence that the last fast of Gandhi was directed as much against violent communalism as against Nehru and Patel refusing to a hostile Pakistan its share of the funds of undivided India on grounds of realpolitik.

Let us not forget that Gandhi's inability to conform to the principles of realpolitik was one of the main reasons Godse gave for killing Gandhi. Gandhian politics, Godse said in his last speech, 'was supported by old superstitious beliefs such as the power of the soul, the inner voice, the fast, the prayer, and the purity of mind.'[57]

I felt that the Indian politics in the absence of Gandhiji would surely be practical, able to retaliate, and would be powerful with the armed forces .... People may even call me and dub me as devoid of any sense or foolish, but the nation would be free to follow the course founded on reason which I consider to be necessary for sound nation-building.[58]

In the course of the same speech Godse also said that Gandhi's non-violence consisted in enduring 'the blows of the aggressor without showing any resistance either by weapon or by physical force .... I firmly believed and believe that the non-violence of the type described above will lead the nation towards ruin.' He had an example to give, too: the 'problem of the state of Hyderabad which had been unnecessarily delayed and postponed has been rightly solved by our government by the use of armed force—after the demise of Gandhi. The present government of remaining India is seen taking the course of practical politics.'[59] It is an indication of how much latent support there was for this line of thinking in the country that the Government of India prevented the publication of this speech lest it might arouse widespread sympathy for the killer of Gandhi.

Perhaps the same thread of consciousness or, if you like, unconscious-ness, ran through the inaction of B.G. Kher and Morarji Desai, chief and home ministers, respectively of the state of Bombay, where the con-spiracy to kill Gandhi was hatched. They did not follow up vigorously enough the first-hand information given to them ten days before the assassination by Jagadish Chandra Jain, a professor in a college at Bombay and father-confessor of Madanlal Pahwa. Anyone reading the tragicomic exchanges between Jain on the one hand and Kher and Desai on the other cannot but be impressed by the callous, self-righteous, and yet guilt-ridden ineptitude of the two politicians in this matter.[60]

Obviously the living Gandhi had already ceased to be a relevant figure for a large number of Indians. To some of them he had already begun to seem a threat to Hindu survival, a fanatical supporter of Muslims and, worse, one who rejected the principle of zero-sum game in politics. If not their conscious minds, their primitive selves were demanding his blood.

Godse reflected this desire. He was confident that millions in India (particularly Hindu women, subject to Muslim atrocities) would shed tears for his sacrifice; and he lived the months before his execution with the serene conviction that posterity would vindicate him. In his last letter to his parents he wrote that he had killed Gandhi for the same reasons for which Krishna had killed the evil King Sishupal.[61]

He was not wholly wrong in his estimate of public reactions. This is how, according to Justice Khosla, the public reacted to the killer of Gandhi after Nathuram had made his final plea as a defendant:

> The audience was visibly and audibly moved. There was a deep silence when he ceased speaking. Many women were in tears and men were coughing and searching for their handkerchiefs. The silence was accentuated and made deeper by the sound of an occasional subdued sniff or a muffled cough. ... I have ... no doubt that had the audience of that day been constituted into a jury and entrusted with the task of deciding Godse's appeal, they would have brought in a verdict of 'not guilty' by an overwhelming majority.[62]

IV

On 30 January 1948 Nathuram Godse fired four shots at point-blank range as Gandhi was going to his evening prayer meeting in Delhi. Before firing the shots he bowed down to Gandhi to show his respect for the services the Mahatma had rendered to the country. The killer made no attempt to run away and himself shouted for the police, even though in the stunned silence following the killing he had enough time at least to attempt an escape. As he later said, he had done his duty like Arjuna in the Mahabharata whom Krishna advised to kill his own relatives because they were evil.[63]

So Gandhi died, according to his own scenario, at the hands of one who was apparently a zealot, a religious fanatic, a typical assassin with a typical assassin's background: educated and intelligent, but an under-achiever;

relatively young; coming from the middle class and yet from a group which was a displaced elite; and with a long record of failures. Here was a man fighting a diffused sense of self-definition with the help of a false sense of mission and trying to give through political assassination some meaning to his life.[64] One might even note, for psychologists, that there was also in Godse the authoritarian man's fear of sexuality, status-seeking, idealization of parents, ideological rigidity, constriction of emotions, and even some amount of what Erich Fromm would diagnose as love of death.[65]

In other ways, too, it was an archetypal assassination. Not only the background of the assassin, but everything else too fell into place. There was the hero who became the victim; the villain, motivated by values larger than him but also, at one plane, driven by fate and maniacal; and a Greek cast of characters who invited the tragedy. There were even eloquent mourners in the Nehrus, Einsteins, and Shaws.

Finally, like many assassinations, this one too had as its immediate provocation something history had already passed by, namely, the partition of India in 1947. To both Gandhi and Godse, partition was the greatest personal tragedy. Both blamed Gandhi for it; one sought retribution, the other expiation. Partition however was irreversible and, politically, the assassination—and the martyrdom the two antagonists sought through it—was pointless. In this sense Mahadevan is right: in the confrontation between Godse and Gandhi there could be no loser and no winner; it was like two batsmen walking into the field after the stumps had been drawn.[66]

Is this, then, the whole story? At another level, was it not also a case of the dominant traditions within a society trying to contain a force which, in the name of orthodoxy, threatened to demolish its centre, to erect instead a freer society and a new authority system using the rubble of the old? Did not Godse promise to facilitate his fellowmen's escape from this freedom that Gandhi promised? If Gandhi in his depression connived at it, he also perhaps felt—being the shrewd, practical idealist he was—that he had become somewhat of an anachronism in post-partition, independent India; and in violent death he might be more relevant to the living than he could be in life. As not a few have sensed, like Socrates and Christ before him, Gandhi knew how to use human sense of guilt creatively.

Notes and References

1.   Quoted in Tapan Ghose, *The Gandhi Murder Trial*, New York: Asia, 1973, pp. 316–17.

2. T.K. Mahadevan, 'Godse versus Gandhi', *Times of India*, 12 March 1978, *Sunday Magazine*, p. 1.

3. See on this theme Ashis Nandy, 'Invitation to a Beheading: A Psychologist's Guide to Assassinations in the Third World', *Quest*, November–December 1975, pp. 69–72.

4. Robert Payne, *The Life and Death of Mahatma Gandhi,* New York: Dutton, 1968.

5. To effect this reconciliation, Gandhi frequently used his own contradictions and derived strength from his own inner battles against authoritarianism, his own masculine self and aggression. This also was, in the context of the dominant ethos of the Indian civilization, a major deviance. The tradition here was to use social experiences for purposes of self-enrichment, not to act out personal experience in social intervention.

6. It is an indicator of the strength of the subliminal revolution of Gandhi that, as late as in 1972, while reviewing Payne's and Erikson's books on Gandhi, a psychoanalyst mentioned as instances of Gandhi's irrationality, Gandhi's hostility to modern technology, mass education, industrializations, and science. H. Robert Black, 'Review of *The Life and Death of Mahatma Gandhi* by Robert Payne and *Gandhi's Truth* by Erik H. Erikson, *Psychoanalytic Quarterly*, 1972, (41), 122–9. In about 1977, in an ecologically sensitive world discussing zero growth rates and intermediate technologies, the fundamental criticisms of formal education ventured by educationists like Ivan Illich and Paulo Freire, and the deglamourization of much of modern science, Gandhi seems less backdated on these issues than the reviewer.

7. Ghose, *The Gandhi Murder Trial*, p. 218.

8. In pre-Gandhian colonial India, as is well known, one group of modernizers pleaded for the primacy of social reform, over political freedom; another insisted that the nationalist movement should have priority over reform movements. The first group, dominating the Indian political scene in the nineteenth century, gradually gave way to the second at the beginning of this century.

9. See Ashis Nandy, 'Woman versus Womanliness', in *At the Edge of Psychology*: *Essays in Politics and Culture*, New Delhi: Oxford University Press, 1980, pp. 32–46.

10. On the frequently discussed psychological dynamics of Gandhi's childhood, particularly the identification models available to him, see Lloyd and Susanne Rudolph, *The Modernity of Tradition*, Part 2, Chicago: University of Chicago Press: 1967; E.V. Wolfenstein, *The Revolutionary Personality*, Princeton: Princeton University Press: 1967, pp. 73–88; and Erik H. Erikson, *Gandhi's Truth*, New York: Norton, 1969.

11. In a recent paper Rowland Lorimer has explicitly recognized the centrality of

this aspect of Gandhi. See 'A Reconsideration of the Psychological Roots of Gandhi's Truth', *Psychoanalytic Review*, 1976, (63), 191–207. An unsophisticated but touching interpretation of Gandhi from this point of view is by his grand-niece and the constant companion of his last years, Manuben. See her *Bapu—My Mother*, Ahmedabad: Navajivan, 1962.

12. See a discussion of this in Nandy, 'Woman versus Womanliness'; and 'Sati: A Nineteenth Century Tale of Women, Violence and Protest', *At the Edge of Psychology*.

13. See on this subject the sensitive writings of Rudolph and Rudolph, *The Modernity of Tradition*; and Erikson, *Gandhi's Truth*.

14. It was this assumption of the universality of his political ethics which prompted Gandhi to give his notorious advice to the European Jews to offer non-violent, passive resistance to Hitler. But of course Gandhi was concerned with human normalities, not abnormalities. When he felt that satyagraha would work in the Europe of the 1930s and 1940s, he was showing greater respect for European civilization than those who have since correctly doubted his political acumen on this point. If the Nazis did not deserve Gandhi, Gandhi also did not deserve the Nazis.

It is interesting that the political groups which produced the assassin of Gandhi were open admirers of the Nazis and, at least in the early 1930s, wanted to treat the Muslims the way Hitler treated the Jews. In turn, Gandhi had for this very reason rejected these groups as totalitarian and attacked even their courage, nationalism, and diligence as fascist. Pyarelal, *Mahatma Gandhi—The Last Phase*, 2, Ahmedabad: Navajivan, p. 440. Evidently Gandhi's technique failed with some varieties of Indian fascism too.

15. D.J. Fisher, 'Sigmund Freud and Romain Rolland: The Terrestrial Animal and His Great Oceanic Friend', *American Imago*, 1976, (33), 1–59, quote on p. 4.

16. This is probably the explanation for his hostile comment on modern India's first social reformer, Rammohun Roy. See Stephen Hay, 'Introduction' to Rammohun Roy's *A Tract against Idolatry*, Calcutta: Firma K.L. Mukhopadhyay, 1963.

17. Statement of co-conspirator Vishnu R. Karkare, quoted in G.D. Khosla, 'The Crime of Nathuram Godse', *The Murder of the Mahatma*, London: Chatto and Windus, 1963, pp. 201–45. Quote on p. 230.

18. Payne, *Mahatma Gandhi*, p. 612.

19. J.C. Jain, *The Murder of Mahatma Gandhi: Prelude and Aftermath*, Bombay: Chetana, 1961, p. 45; Pyarelal, *Mahatma Gandhi*, pp. 750–1.

20. There was in the Maharashtrian Brahmanic elites an emphasis on cynical hard-headed pure politics which was antagonistic to the essence of Gandhism. Yet Gandhi was patently beating them at their own game. He was winning over and politically organizing the numerically preponderant non-Brahmanic sectors of Maharashtra itself. No wonder the cornered Brahmanic elites began

to regard 'Gandhi's political leadership and movement of non-violence with a strong concentrated feeling of antipathy and frustration which found expression in a sustained campaign of calumny against Gandhiji for over a quarter of a century.' Pyarelal, *Mahatma Gandhi*, 2, p. 750.

21.   There were three exceptions. One was Madanlal Pahwa, a Punjabi Hindu belonging to the Khatri or business community. He had failed the entrance examination for the Royal Indian Navy and, as a victim of the partition riots, had held a number of odd jobs and moved from place to place. He however obviously played second fiddle in the conspiracy. Other exceptions were the South Indian servant of one of the conspirators, Shankar Kistayya, ultimately acquitted as only a marginal member of the group and Digambar Badge, who turned government approver. The conspirators included a doctor, a bookshop-owner, a small-time restauranteur-cum-municipal councillor, an army store-keeper-cum-illegal arms-merchant. That is, except for Pahwa and Kistayya, all the conspirators were middle class, educated, semi-westernized professionals and job-holders.

The facts of Nathuram's early life are borrowed mainly from Manohar Malgaonkar's *The Men who Killed Gandhi*, Delhi: Macmillan, 1978, chapter 2.

22.   Payne, *Mahatma Gandhi*, p. 616.

23.   V.G. Deshpande in Ghose, *Gandhi Murder Trial*, pp. 280–1; also Gopal Godse, *Panchavanna Kotinche Bali*, Poona: Vitasta, 1971, chapter 6.

24.   Gopal Godse, *Gandhihatya ani Mee*, Poona: Asmita, 1967, p. 221; and Ghose, *Gandhi Murder*, p. 280. One of Nathuram's avowed purposes in killing Gandhi was to help the rulers of India break the Mahatma's spell and conduct statecraft on the basis of ruthless realpolitik. He thought the government's mercilessness towards him a good beginning of this. See also Nathuram's letter to G.T. Madholkar, 'Why I Shot Gandhi', *Onlooker*, 16–30 November 1978, pp. 22–4.

25.   Godse, *Gandhihatya*, p. 306.

26.   Ibid., p. 221.

27.   Harold D. Laswell and Daniel Lerner (eds), *World Revolutionary Elites*, Cambridge: MIT, 1965; and I.L. Horowitz, 'Political Terrorism and State Power', *Journal of Political and Military Sociology*, 1973, (1), 147–57.

28.   Probably the best indicator of this was Godse's intention, virtually to the end of his days, to appeal to the Privy Council, which in 1948 was still the final court of appeal for Indians. He felt that if he could somehow take this case to England, he would get an international hearing.

29.   Godse, *Gandhihatya*, p. 228.

30.   This was a situation analogous to that of the Bengali babus. Understandably, Maharashtrian Brahmans and Bengali babus were the two subcultures to which Gandhi's charisma never fully extended.

31.   The Parsees in fact had gone one better. Increasingly concentrated in metro-
       politan Bombay, they had begun to compete successfully with the Chitpavans
       in exactly those areas where the Chitpavans specialized: in the professions
       and in government service. In fact, they had already taken fantastic strides
       exploiting their faster pace of westernization, their marginality to the Indian
       society, and their almost total identification with the British rulers. E. Kulke,
       The Parsees of India, New Delhi: Vikas, 1975.

32.   That is why his declared *gurus* included liberals like B.G. Gokhale and
       Rabindranath Tagore. Even his declared political heir was the westernized
       Nehru, who differed perhaps the most from Gandhi in lifestyle and world
       view, and not Patel who had a social background similar to Gandhi and was
       more at home in the Indian village.

33.   Larry Collins and Dominique Lapierre, *Freedom at Midnight*, New Delhi:
       Vikas, 1976, chapter 16.

34.   In fact, sixty-five at the time of assassination, he had already spent nearly half
       his life in British jails and in the penal colony in the Andamans. Notwithstand-
       ing his religious fanaticism, Savarkar was a courageous self-sacrificing na-
       tionalist. He was one of the main builders of the anti-British terrorist movement
       in Maharashtra and, as such, no stranger to physical violence and conspirato-
       rial politics. He was also the mainstay of the Hindu Mahasabha, the rump of
       a party openly propagating a Hindu polity for India. See Dhananjay Keer,
       Veer Savarkar, Bombay: Popular Prakashan, 1966.

35.   A good impartial summary is in Payne, *Mahatma Gandhi*. For the opposite
       point of view, see Ghose, *Gandhi Murder Trial*; also Khosla, *Nathuram
       Godse*. Justice Khosla was one of the judges who tried the assassins.

36.   It may be of interest to the more psychologically minded that three out of half-
       a-dozen or so aliases used by the conspirators involved the first name of
       Savarkar.

37.   See Godse, *Gandhihatya*, chapter 12, to get some idea of Nathuram's idiom;
       also his letter to Madholkar.

38.   The concepts of authentic innocence and pseudo-innocence are Rollo May's.
       See his *Power and Innocence*, New York: Norton, 1972.

           The secondary gains were of two types. Those who submitted partook of
       the crumbs from the colonial table. Their incentives were firstly material and
       secondly the psychological returns of passivity and security. Those who
       defied the Raj through terrorism also made secondary gains. Even in defeat
       they got their masculinity endorsed. They were men, it seemed to them, in a
       society of eunuchs.

39.   Jain, *Mahatma Gandhi*, p. 64.

40.   Brijkrishna Chandiwalla, *At the Feet of Bapu*, Ahmedabad: Navajivan, 1954,
       quoted in Payne, *Mahatma Gandhi*, p. 573.

41. Jain, *Mahatma Gandhi*, p. 52.

42. Manuben, *Bapu—My Mother*, p. 49; Pyarelal, *Mahatma Gandhi—The Last Phase*, 2, Ahmedabad: Navajivan, p. 460.

43. N.K. Bose, My *Days with Gandhi*, Bombay: Orient Longman, p. 250.

44. Manuben, *Last Glimpses of Bapu,* Delhi: S.L. Agarwala, 1962, p. 81.

45. Ibid., pp. 81, 234, 252, 297–8.

46. Ibid., p. 114.

47. Ibid., pp. 297–8.

48. Payne, *Mahatma Gandhi*, pp. 550, 552.

49. Ibid., p. 549.

50. For example, Jain, *Mahatma Gandhi*, pp. 62–3; Pyarelal, *Mahatma Gandhi*, 2, p. 101.

51. J.L. Kapur, *Report of the Commission of Enquiry into the Conspiracy to Murder Mahatma Gandhi*, Vols 1–6, New Delhi: Government of India, 1970.

52. There is a double-bind in most antipsychologism in the arena of social interpretation. Psychological interpretation in terms of shared motives is countered by the argument that the behaviour of key individuals in a historical episode is random. Psychological interpretation in terms of individual psychodynamics is countered by the argument that the characteristics of aggregates determine all of individual behaviour.

53. No wonder that Gandhi himself was suspicious of some of the police officers in charge of communal peace. See for example his comment on Inspector General Randhawa of Delhi police in Manuben, *Last Glimpses of Bapu*, pp. 170–1.

54. To some extent, Nehru does not fit the mould. Himself never fully given to realpolitik, he also was never much impressed by the search for political *machismo*.

55. 'Gandhi's Lieutenants—Varieties of Followership', in P.F. Power (ed.), *The Meanings of Gandhi*, Honolulu: The University Press of Hawaii, 1971, pp. 41–58, see p. 55.

56. A.K. Azad, *India Wins Freedom*, Bombay: Orient Longman, 1955. It has been suggested that Patel never recovered from his sense of guilt over the whole episode and died a broken man soon afterwards. If so, he was only epitomizing the moral crisis that Gandhi wanted to precipitate in all Indians by his death. In the case of Patel, the crisis might have been further sharpened by his own alleged softness towards some of those associated with the assassination. See on this theme Gopal Godse, *Gandhihatya*, pp. 229, 237–8.

57. Quoted in Ghose, *Gandhi Murder Trial*, p. 229.

58. Quoted in Khosla, *Nathuram Godse*, p. 242.

59. Quoted in Ghose, *Gandhi Murder Trial*, pp. 228–9.

60.   Jain, *Mahatma Gandhi*, Part 2, chapters 1 and 5. Further details of such acts of carelessness all around could be found in Kapur Commission Report.

61.   Godse, *Gandhihatya ani Mee*, pp. 221–3.

62.   Khosla, *Nathuram Godse*, p. 243.

63.   Godse, *Gandhihatya ani Mee*, pp. 46, 221.

64.   See Horowitz, 'Political Terrorism and State Power', *Journal of Political and Military Sociology*; and Ashis Nandy, *Invitation to a Beheading*.

65.   See Fromm's *The Anatomy of Human Destructiveness,* New York: Holt, Rinehart and Winston, 1973. I have not dealt with them in this paper, but on Godse's search for self-esteem and meaning in death, see Godse, *Gandhihatya*, p. 222.

66.   Mahadevan, *Godse versus Gandhi.*

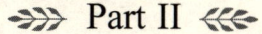 Part II

3

The Moment of Manoeuvre
Gandhi and the Critique of Civil Society*

PARTHA CHATTERJEE

> My language is aphoristic, it lacks precision. It is therefore open to
> several interpretations.
>> 'Discussion with Dharmadev', *The Collected Works
>> of Mahatma Gandhi*, Vol. 53, Appendix III, p. 485.

I

Although Gandhi's *Collected Works* will finally run into nearly ninety thick
volumes, there exist few texts in which he can be seen attempting a
systematic exposition of his ideas on state, society, and nation. One of the
first, and perhaps the fullest, is entitled *Hind Swaraj*, written in Gujarati in
1909 and published in an English translation in Johannesburg in 1910 after
the original edition was proscribed by the Government of Bombay. It
contains a statement of some of the fundamental elements of Gandhi's
politics. Romain Rolland, one of his first sympathetic but critical commentators, saw in this book a reflection of the central features of Gandhi's
thought: 'the negation of Progress and also of European science'.[1] A more
recent commentator, Raghavan Iyer, sees it as 'a severe condemnation
of modern civilzation' and '*the point d'appui* of Gandhi's moral and political

* Partha Chatterjee, 'The Moment of Manoeuvre: Gandhi and the Critique of Civil Society',
in *Nationalist Thought and the Colonial World*: *A Derivative Discourse?*, New Delhi: Oxford
University Press, 1986, pp. 85–130.

thought'.[2] I prefer to read it as a text in which Gandhi's relation to nation-alism can be shown to rest on a fundamental critique of the idea of civil society.

On the surface, it is indeed a critique of modern civilization, 'a civiliza-tion only in name'.[3] And the argument proceeds, as it does in Bankim, from a consideration of the question: Why is India a subject nation? To start with, Gandhi's answer too seems to run along the same lines. He too is concerned more with locating the sources of Indian weakness than putting the blame on British avarice or deceit. But the emphasis is not so much on the elements of culture. Gandhi points much more forcefully to the moral failure.

The English have not taken India: we have given it to them. They are not in India because of their strength, but because we keep them ... Recall the Company Bahadur. Who made it Bahadur? They had not the slightest intention at the time of establishing a kingdom. Who assisted the Company's officers? Who was tempted at the sight of their silver? Who bought their goods? History testifies that we did all this ... When our Princes fought among themselves, they sought the assistance of Company Bahadur. That corporation was versed alike in commerce and war. It was unham-pered by questions of morality ... Is it not then useless to blame the English for what we did at the time? ... it is truer to say that we gave India to the English than that India was lost.[4]

It was a moral failure on the part of Indians that led to the conquest of India. And in exploring the reasons behind this moral failure, Gandhi's answer becomes diametrically opposed to that of Bankim. It is not because Indian society lacked the necessary cultural attributes that it was unable to face up to the power of the English. It is not the backwardness or lack of modernity of India's culture that keeps it in continued subjection. And the task of achieving freedom would not be accomplished by creating a new modern culture for the nation. For Gandhi, it is precisely because Indians were seduced by the glitter of modern civilization that they became a subject people. And what keeps them in subjection is the acceptance by leading sections of Indians of the supposed benefits of civilization. Indeed, as long as Indians continue to harbour illusions about the 'progressive' qualities of modern civilization, they will remain a subject nation. Even if they succeed physically in driving out the English, they would still have 'English rule without the Englishman', because it is not the physical presence of the English which makes India a subject nation: it is civilization which subjects.

There then follows an indictment of modern civilization as it has emerged in the West and as it has been imported into India. Fundamentally, Gandhi attacks the very notions of modernity and progress and subverts the central claim made on behalf of those notions, namely, their correspondence with a new organization of society in which the productive capacities of human labour are multiplied several times, creating increased wealth and prosperity for all and hence increased leisure, comfort, health, and happiness. Gandhi argues that far from achieving these objectives, what modern civilization does is make man a prisoner of his craving for luxury and self-indulgence, release the forces of unbridled competition, and thereby bring upon society the evils of poverty, disease, war, and suffering. It is precisely because modern civilization looks at man as a limitless consumer and thus sets out to open the floodgates of industrial production that it also becomes the source of inequality, oppression, and violence on a scale hitherto unknown in human history.

Machinery, for instance, is intended to increase the productivity of labour and thus to satisfy the never-ending urge for consumption. But it only whets the appetite, it does not satisfy it. What it does instead is bring exploitation and disease to the industrial cities and unemployment and ruin to the countryside.

When I read Mr Dutt's *Economic History of India*, I wept; and as I think of it again my heart sickens. It is machinery that has impoverished India. It is difficult to measure the harm that Manchester has done to us. It is due to Manchester that Indian handicraft has all but disappeared.[5]

The driving social urge behind industrial production is the craving for excessive consumption. It is in this context that Gandhi interprets the modern spirit of scientific inquiry and technological advance; a tendency to let the mind wander uncontrolled and chase the objects of our passions.

We notice that the mind is a restless bird; the more it gets the more it wants, and still remains unsatisfied. The more we indulge our passions, the more unbridled they become. Our ancestors, therefore, set a limit to our indulgences. They saw that happiness was largely a mental condition ... Observing all this, our ancestors dissuaded us from luxuries and pleasures. We have managed with the same kind of plough as existed thousands of years ago. We have retained the same kind of cottages that we had in former times and our indigenous education remains the same as before. We have had no system of life-corroding competition ... It was not that we did not know how to invent machinery, but our forefathers knew that if we set our hearts after such things, we would become slaves and lose our moral fibres. They, therefore, after due deliberation decided that we should only do what we could with our hands and feet.[6]

Hence, his solution to the social evils of industrialism is not just to remove its defects, because he thinks these so-called defects are germane to the very fundamentals of the modern system of production. His solution is to give up industrialism altogether: 'instead of welcoming machinery as a boon, we should look upon it as an evil'.[7] It is only a complete change in moral values that will change our perception of our social needs and thus enable us once again to set deliberate limits to social consumption. Nothing short of this will succeed.

A certain degree of physical harmony and comfort is necessary, but above a certain level it becomes a hindrance instead of help. Therefore the ideal of creating an unlimited number of wants and satisfying them seems to be a delusion and a snare. The satisfaction of one's physical needs, even the intellectual needs of one's narrow self, must meet at a certain point a dead stop, before it degenerates into physical and intellectual voluptuousness.[8]

Clearly, then, Gandhi's critique of British rule in India attempted to situate it at a much more fundamental level than Bankim, or indeed any other nationalist writer of his time. Where they were criticizing merely the excesses of Western notions of patriotism and national glory which inevitably pushed those countries towards the pursuit of colonial conquests and victories in war, Gandhi has no doubt at all that the source of modern imperialism lies specifically in the system of social production which the countries of the Western world have adopted. It is the limitless desire for ever-increased production and ever-greater consumption, and the spirit of ruthless competitiveness which keeps the entire system going, that impel these countries to seek colonial possessions which can be exploited for economic purposes. Gandhi stated this position quite emphatically as early as in *Hind Swaraj* and held on to it all his life. It was, in fact, in many ways the most crucial theoretical foundation of his entire strategy of winning *svarāj* for India.

Napoleon is said to have described the English as a nation of shop-keepers. It is a fitting description. They hold whatever dominions they have for the sake of their commerce. Their army and their navy are intended to protect it. When the Transvaal offered no such attractions, the late Mr Gladstone discovered that it was not right for the English to hold it. When it became a paying proposition, resistance led to war. Mr Chamberlain soon discovered that England enjoyed a suzerainty over the Transvaal. It is related that someone asked the late President Kruger whether there was gold on the moon. He replied that it was highly unlikely because, if there were, the English would have annexed it. Many problems can be solved by remembering that money is their God ... If you accept the above statements, it is proved that the English entered India for the purposes of trade. They remain in it for the same purpose ... They wish to convert the whole world into a vast market for their goods.

That they cannot do so is true, but the blame will not be theirs. They will leave no stone unturned to reach the goal.[9]

Thus, in the case of modern imperialism, morality and politics are both subordinated to the primary consideration of economics, and this consideration is directly related to a specific organization of social production characterized not so much by the nature of ownership of the means of production but fundamentally by the purposes and the processes of production. That is to say, whereas Gandhi is in this particular historical instance talking about the capitalist system of production in Britain, his characterization of the type of economy which leads to exploitation and colonial conquest is not necessarily restricted to capitalism alone, because as long as the purpose of social production is to continually expand it in order to satisfy an endless urge for consumption and as long as the process of production is based on ever-increased mechanization, those consequences would follow inevitably. And the purposes and processes of production take on this particular form whenever production is primarily directed not towards the creation of articles of immediate *use* but towards *exchange*—exchange between town and country and between metropolis and colony. Any kind of industrialization on a large scale would have to be based on certain determinate exchange relations between town and country, with the balance inevitably tipping against the latter whenever the pace of industrialization quickens. This would lead to unemployment and poverty in the villages or, which amounts to the same thing, to the exploitation of colonial possessions.

Industrialization on a mass scale will necessarily lead to passive or active exploitation of the villagers as the problems of competition and marketing come in. Therefore we have to concentrate on the village being self-contained, manufacturing mainly for use.[10]

The mere socialization of industries would not alter this process in any way at all.

Pandit Nehru wants industrialization because he thinks that, if it is socialized, it would be free from the evils of capitalism. My own view is that evils are inherent in industrialism, and no amount of socialization can eradicate them.[11]

In fact, Gandhi's argument was that there is no feasible way in which *any* process of industrialization can avoid the creation of exploitative and inhumane relations of exchange between town and country. He states this quite clearly when he argues that khādī is the only sound economic proposition for India.

Khadi is the only true economic proposition in terms of the millions of villagers until such time, if ever, when a better system of supplying work and adequate wages for every able-bodied person above the age of sixteen, male or female, is found for his field, cottage or even factory in every one of the villages of India: or till sufficient cities are built up to displace the villages so as to give the villagers the necessary comforts and amenities that a well-regulated life demands and is entitled to. I have only to state the proposition thus fully to show that khadi must hold the field for any length of time that we can think of.[12]

It is true, of course, that in the midst of continuing controversy about the economic policies of the Congress, and especially the programme of khādī, Gandhi increasingly tended to emphasize the strict economic argument against heavy industrialization in a large agrarian economy with an abundance of underemployed labour. During the 1920s and 1930s, the period of the growth of the national movement, he would often in fact prefer to suspend the debate about the larger moral issues of mechanization *per se* in order to win his point on the infeasibility of heavy industrialization in the particular context of India. 'I have no partiality', he would say, 'for return to the primitive methods of grinding and husking for the sake of them. I suggest the return, because there is no other way of giving employment to the millions of villagers who are living in idleness.'[13] At times he even conceded that mechanization might have an economic logic in situations of labour scarcity.

Mechanization is good when the hands are too few for the work intended to be accomplished. It is an evil when there are more hands than required for the work, as is the case in India ... The problem with us is not how to find leisure for the teeming millions inhabiting our villages. The problem is how to utilize their idle hours, which are equal to the working days of six months in the year ... spinning and weaving mills have deprived the villagers of a substantial means of livelihood. It is no answer in reply to say that they turn out cheaper, better cloth, if they do so at all. For, if they have displaced thousands of workers, the cheapest mill cloth is dearer than the dearest khadi woven in the villages.[14]

But this was only a debating point, an attempt to bring round to the cause of his economic programme those who did not share his fundamental philosophical premises. Because ever so often, even as he argued about the practical economic necessity of khādī, he would remind his readers where exactly he stood with regard to the fundamental moral issues.

If I could do it, I would most assuredly destroy or radically change much that goes under the name of modern civilization. But that is an old story of life. The attempt is undoubtedly there. Its success depends upon God. But the attempt to revive and encourage the remunerative village industries is not part of such an attempt, except in so far as every one of my activities, including the propagation of non-violence, can be described as such an attempt.[15]

Even when it came to a question of the fundamental principles of organization of economic life, Gandhi would unhesitatingly state his opposition to the concept of the *homo oeconomicus*, to the supposed benefits of the social division of labour, and to the current faith in the laws of the marketplace transforming private vices into public virtues.

I am always reminded of one thing which the well-known British economist Adam Smith has said in his famous treatise *The Wealth of Nations*. In it he has described some economic laws as universal and absolute. Then he has described certain situations which may be an obstacle to the operation of these laws. These disturbing factors are the human nature, the human temperament or altruism inherent in it. Now, the economics of khadi is just the opposite of it. Benevolence which is inherent in human nature is the very foundation of the economics of khadi. What Adam Smith has described as pure economic activity based merely on the calculations of profit and loss is a selfish attitude and it is an obstacle to the development of khadi; and it is the function of a champion of khadi to counteract this tendency.[16]

And thus one comes back to Gandhi's condemnation of what he calls 'modern civilization', which in fact is a fundamental critique of the entire edifice of bourgeois society: its continually expanding and prosperous economic life, based on individual property, the social division of labour, and the impersonal laws of the market, described with clinical precision and complete moral approbation by Mandeville and Smith; its political institutions based on a dual notion of sovereignty in which the people in theory rule themselves, but are only allowed to do so through the medium of their representatives whose actions have to be ratified only once in so many years; its spirit of innovation, adventure, and scientific progress; its rationalization of philosophy and ethics and secularization of art and education. As early as in *Hind Swaraj*, Gandhi launches a thoroughgoing critique against each of these constitutive features of civil society.

Parliament, for instance, he calls 'a sterile woman and a prostitute', the first because, despite being a sovereign institution, it cannot enact a law according to its own judgement but is constantly swayed by outside pressures, and the second because it continually shifts its allegiance from one set of ministers to another depending on which is more powerful. But basically, Gandhi objects to an entire structure of politics and government in which each individual is assumed to have his own individual interest, individuals are expected to come together into parties and alliances in terms of those self-interests, these combinations of interests are then supposed to exert pressure on each other by mobilizing public opinion and manipulating the levers of the governmental machinery, and legislative enactments are then expected to emerge as choices made on behalf of the whole society.

It is generally acknowledged that the members [of Parliament) are hypocritical and selfish. Each thinks of his own little interest. It is fear that is the guiding motive ... Members vote for their party without a thought. Their so-called discipline binds them to it. If any member, by way of exception, gives an independent vote, he is considered a renegade ... The Prime Minister is more concerned about his power than about the welfare of Parliament. His energy is concentrated upon securing the success of his party. His care is not always that Parliament should do right ... If they are considered honest because they do not take what are generally known as bribes, let them be so considered, but they are open to subtler influences. In order to gain their ends, they certainly bribe people with honours. I do not hesitate to say that they have neither real honesty nor a living conscience.[17]

And the process by which support is mobilized on behalf of particular leaders, or parties, or interests is equally unworthy of moral approval.

To the English voters their newspaper is their Bible. They take their cue from their newspapers which are often dishonest. The same fact is differently interpreted by different newspapers, according to the party in whose interests they are edited ... [The] people change their views frequently ... These views swing like the pendulum of a clock and are never steadfast. The people would follow a powerful orator or a man who gives them parties, receptions, etc.[18]

Once again, Gandhi's criticism is aimed against the abrogation of moral responsibility involved in the duality of sovereignty and the mediation of complex legal-political institutions which distance the rulers of society from those they are supposed to represent. He does not accept the argument that if effective combinations are formed among individuals and groups sharing a set of common self-interests, then the institutions of representative democracy will ensure that the government will act in ways which are, on the whole, in the common interest of the entire collectivity. His argument is, in fact, that the dissociation of political values, based on self-interest, from social morality, based on certain universal ethical values shared by the whole community, leads to a structure and process of politics in which the wealthy and the powerful enjoy disproportionate opportunities to manipulate the machinery of government to their own sectional interests. Besides, the legal fiction of equality before the law and the supposed neutrality of state institutions only have the effect of perpetuating the inequalities and divisions which already exist in society: politics has no role in removing those inequalities or cementing the divisions. In fact, this very process of law and politics which thrives on conflict creates a vested interest among politicians, state officials, and legal practitioners to perpetuate social divisions and indeed to create new ones.

[The lawyers'] duty is to side with their clients and to find out ways and arguments in favour of their clients, to which they (the clients) are often strangers ... The lawyers, therefore, will, as a rule, advance quarrels instead of repressing them ... It is within my knowledge that they are glad when men have disputes. Petty pleaders actually manufacture them.[19]

Similarly, the colonial state in India, by projecting an image of neutrality with regard to social divisions within Indian society, not only upholds the rigours of those divisions, such as the ones imposed by the caste system, but actually strengthens them.[20]

By contrast, it is only when politics is *directly* subordinated to a communal morality that the minority of exploiters in society can be resisted by the people and inequalities and divisions removed. As a political ideal, therefore, Gandhi counterposes against the system of representative government an undivided concept of popular sovereignty, where the community is self-regulating and political power is dissolved into the collective moral will.

The power to control national life through national representatives is called political power. Representatives will become unnecessary if the national life becomes so perfect as to be self-controlled. It will then be a state of enlightened anarchy in which each person will become his own ruler. He will conduct himself in such a way that his behaviour will not hamper the well-being of his neighbours. In an ideal State there will be no political institution and therefore no political power.[21]

In its form, this political ideal is not meant to be a consensual democracy with complete and continual participation by every member of the polity. The Utopia is *Rāmarājya*, a patriarchy in which the ruler, by his moral quality and habitual adherence to truth, always expresses the collective will.[22] It is also a Utopia in which the economic organization of production, arranged according to a perfect fourfold varṇa scheme of specialization and a perfect system of reciprocity in the exchange of commodities and services, always ensures that there is no spirit of competition and no differences in status between different kinds of labour.[23] The ideal conception of Rāmarājya, in fact, encapsulates the critique of all that is morally reprehensible in the economic and political organization of civil society.

The argument is then extended to other aspects of civil society. The secularization of education, for instance, has made a 'fetish' of the knowledge of letters and has thereby both exaggerated and rationalized the inequalities in society. It ignores completely the ethical aspect of education and the need to integrate the individual within the collectively shared moral values of the community, and instead cultivates 'the pretension of learning many sciences'. The result is a pervasive feeling of dissatisfaction, of moral anarchy, and a license to individual self-seeking, to 'hypocrisy, tyranny, etc'.[24] It also rationalizes, by ascribing an economic logic to it, one of the fundamental aspects of the social division of labour in modern industrial society: the distinction between mental and manual work. It denies that intellectual labour is an aspect not of the creation of wealth but of human self-fulfilment and must, therefore, be made available to every human being, and this can only be done if all share equally in providing the needs of the body.

May not men earn their bread by intellectual labour? No ... Mere mental, that is, intellectual labour is for the soul and is its own satisfaction. It should never demand payment.[25]

... Bodily sustenance should come from body labour, and intellectual labour is necessary for the culture of the mind. Division of labour there will necessarily be, but it will be a division into various species of body labour and not a division into intellectual labour to be confined to one class and body labour to be confined to another class.[26]

The spirit of scientific inquiry and technological innovation too is aimed more towards physical self-indulgence and luxury than towards the discovery of truth. The science of medicine, for instance, on whose behalf the tallest claims are made by the propagators of modernity, concerns itself more with enabling people to consume more than with the removal of disease.

I overeat, I have indigestion, I go to the doctor, he gives me medicine, I am cured. I overeat again, I take his pills again. Had I not taken the pills in the first instance, I would have suffered the punishment deserved by me and I would not have overeaten again. The doctor intervened and helped me to indulge myself.[27]

And this, of course, only perpetuates the disease; it does not cure it. The modern science of medicine is satisfied by treating illnesses merely at the surface level of physical causality. The scientific spirit, divorced as it is from considerations of morality, does not feel obliged to look deeper into the true causes of diseases which must lie in the very mode of social living.

II

What appears on surface as a critique of Western civilization is, therefore, a total moral critique of the fundamental aspects of civil society. It is not, at this level, a critique of Western culture or religion,[28] nor is it an attempt to establish the superior spiritual claims of Hindu religion. In fact, the moral charge against the West is not that its religion is inferior, but that by whole-heartedly embracing the dubious virtues of modern civilization, it has forgotten the true teachings of the Christian faith. At this level of thought, therefore, Gandhi is not operating at all with the problematic of nationalism. His solution too is meant to be universal, applicable as much to the countries of the West as to nations such as India.

Not only that; what is even more striking, but equally clear, is that Gandhi does not even think within the thematic of nationalism. He seldom writes or speaks in terms of the conceptual frameworks or the modes of reasoning and inference adopted by the nationalists of his day, and quite emphatically rejects their rationalism, scientism, and historicism. As early as in *Hind Swaraj*, Gandhi dismisses all historical objections to his project of freeing India, not by the strength of arms but by the force of the soul, by saying, 'To believe that what has not occurred in history will not occur at all is to argue disbelief in the dignity of man.'[29] He does not feel it necessary to even attempt a historical demonstration of the possibilities he is trying to point out. Indeed, he objects that the historical mode of reasoning is quite unsuitable, indeed irrelevant, for his purpose. History, he says, is built upon the records not of the working of the force of the soul but of its exact opposite. It is a record of the interruptions of peace.

Two brothers quarrel; one of them repents and re-awakens the love that was lying dormant in him; the two again begin to live in peace; nobody takes note of this. But if the two brothers, through the intervention of solicitors or some other reason take up arms or go to law—which is another form of the exhibition of brute force—their doings would be immediately noticed in the Press, they would be the talk of their neighbours and would probably go down in history. And what is true of families and communities is true of nations.[30]

History therefore, does not record the Truth. Truth lies outside history; it is universal, unchanging. Truth has no history of its own.

It is instructive to compare the method Gandhi follows in his attempts to reinterpret the scriptures with those followed by practically every other nationalist reformer of the time—Bankim, or Tilak, or Dayanand, for example. Not only does he not attempt a historical examination of the authenticity of scriptural texts or of the historicity of the great characters of sacred history, he quite explicitly states that such exercises were quite irrelevant to the determination of truth. In *Anāsaktiyoga*, his commentaries on the Gītā, Gandhi does not bother at all about the history of the text itself or about the historicity of Krishna, although he was quite aware of the debates surrounding these questions. Mahadev Desai, in his introductory note to the English translation of *Anāsaktiyoga*, mentions the debate about the 'original' text of the Gītā and says,

One may however say that, even when this original is discovered, it will not make much difference to souls like Gandhiji, every moment of whose life is a conscious effort to live the message of the Gita. This does not mean that Gandhiji is indifferent to the efforts of scholars in this direction. The smallest questions of historical detail interest him intensely as I can say from personal knowledge ... But his attitude is that in the last analysis it is the message that abides, and he is sure that no textual discovery is going to affect by a jot the essence or universality of that message. The same thing may be said about questions of the historical Krishna and the genesis and history of the Krishna Vasudeva worship ... [31]

Further, Gandhi did not regard the Gītā, or even the Mahābhārata of which it appears as a part, as a historical narrative. The historical underpinnings were merely a literary device; the message had nothing to do with history.

Even in 1888–9, when I first became acquainted with the Gita, I felt that it was not a historical work, but that, under the guise of physical warfare, it described the duel that perpetually went on in the hearts of mankind, and that physical warfare was brought in merely to make the description of the internal duel more alluring. This preliminary intuition became more confirmed on a closer study of religion and the Gita. A study of the Mahabharata gave it added confirmation. I do not regard the Mahabharata as a historical work in the accepted sense. The *Adiparva* contains powerful evidence in support of my opinion. By ascribing to the chief actors superhuman or subhuman origins, the great Vyasa made short work of the history of kings and their peoples. The persons therein described may be historical, but the author of the Mahabharata has used them merely to drive home his religious theme.[32]

Indeed, whenever he was confronted with a historical argument about the great Indian epics, trying to point out, for instance, the reality of warfare and violence in human life and of the relevance of a text such as the Gītā as a practical consideration of the ethics of power politics, Gandhi would insist that the truth of the Mahābhārata or the Rāmāyaṇa was a 'poetic truth', not historical; the epics were allegories and not theoretical or historical treatises. 'That they most probably deal with historical figures does not affect my proposition. Each epic describes the eternal duel that goes on between the forces of darkness and light.'[33]

To discover the truth, one would, of course, have to interpret the text to the best of one's knowledge and belief.

Who is the best interpreter? Not learned men surely. Learning there must be. But religion does not live by it. It lives in the experiences of its saints and seers, in their lives and sayings. When all the most learned commentators of the scriptures are utterly forgotten, the accumulated experience of the sages and saints will abide and be an inspiration for ages to come.[34]

There might, of course, be conflicting interpretations of the epics and the scriptures. But such a dispute could never be resolved theoretically. Only the living practice of one's faith could show whether or not one's interpretation was correct. Gandhi mentions, for instance, the difference between his interpretation of the Gītā and the one followed by those who believed in armed violence.

The grim fact is that the terrorists have in absolute honesty, earnestness and with cogency used the *Gita*, which some of them know by heart, in defence of their doctrine and policy. Only they have no answer to my interpretation of the *Gita*, except to say that mine is wrong and theirs is right. Time alone will show whose is right. The *Gita* is not a theoretical treatise. It is a living but silent guide whose directions one has to understand by patient striving.[35]

Gandhi's argument was exactly the same when dealing with questions such as scriptural sanctions for all those social practices which he thought were unjust and immoral. He would not admit that the mere existence of scriptural texts was proof that they must be a constituent or consistent part of true religion. Nor would he agree to submit his case to a historical examination of the origins or evolution of particular social institutions. On the caste system, for instance, his position was as follows:

Caste has nothing to do with religion. It is a custom whose origin I do not know and do not need to know for the satisfaction of my spiritual hunger. But I do know that it is harmful both to spiritual and national growth.[36]

When his critics argued that caste practices were quite explicitly sanctioned by the *śāstra*, his emphatic reply was: 'Nothing in the Shastras which is manifestly contrary to universal truths and morals can stand.'[37] So also on the question of the social status of women as described in the canonical *smṛti* texts:

it is sad to think that the *Smritis* contain texts which can command no respect from
men who cherish the liberty of woman as their own and who regard her as the mother
of the race ... The question arises as to what to do with the *Smritis* that contain texts
... that are repugnant to the moral sense. I have already suggested ... that all that
is printed in the name of scriptures need not be taken as the word of God or the
inspired word.[38]

Gandhi's position, then, is that the true principles of religion or morality are
universal and unchanging. There do exist religious traditions which represent the attempts by various people through the ages to discover and
interpret these principles. But those traditions were the products of history;
they could not be taken to represent a corpus of truths.

The true dharma is unchanging, while tradition may change with time. If we were to
follow some of the tenets of *Manusmriti*, there would be moral anarchy. We have
quietly discarded them altogether.[39]

Not only did Gandhi not share the historicism of the nationalist writers, he
did not share their confidence in rationality and the scientific mode of
knowledge. He would repeatedly assert that the knowledge unearthed by the
sciences was applicable only to very limited areas of human living. If one
did not acknowledge this and pretended instead that rational inquiry and a
scientific search for truth would provide the solution for every problem in
life, one would be either led to insanity or reduced to impotence.

Nowadays, I am relying solely on my intellect. But mere intellect makes one insane
or unmanly. That is its function. In such a situation Rama is the strength of the weak.
My innermost urge is for pure non-violence. My weakness is that I do not know how
to make it work. I use my intellect to overcome that weakness. If this intellectual
cleverness loses the support of truth, it will blur my vision of non-violence, for is not
non-violence the same as truth? Mere practical sense is but a covering for truth. 'The
face of truth is hidden by a golden lid.' The reasoning faculty will raise a thousand
issues. Only one thing will save us from these and that is faith.[40]

Perhaps the most celebrated public controversy over Gandhi's preference
for instinctive faith over the claims of scientific reasoning was when he
pronounced that the devastating earthquakes in Bihar in 1934 were a 'divine
chastisement' for the sin of untouchability. Rabindranath Tagore reacted
very strongly and criticized Gandhi not only for implying that God, in
inflicting punishment upon sinners, was unable to distinguish between the
guilty and the innocent, since an earthquake is indiscriminate in its destruction, but also for strengthening the forces of unreason which fostered the
belief that cosmic phenomena had something to do with the fate of human

beings on earth.[41] Gandhi stuck to his position with characteristic firmness, but there was a somewhat unusual touch of acerbity in his reply.[42] He refused to entertain questions about the rationality of divine action.

I am not affected by posers such as 'why punishment for an age-old sin' or 'why punishment to Bihar and not to the South' or 'why an earthquake and not some other form of punishment'. My answer is: I am not God. Therefore I have but a limited knowledge of His purpose.[43]

He reiterated his belief 'that physical phenomena produce results both physical and spiritual. The converse I hold to be equally true.'[44] He admitted that his belief was 'instinctive' and that he could not prove it. 'But I would be untruthful and cowardly if, for fear of ridicule, when those that are nearest and dearest to me are suffering, I did not proclaim my belief from the house-top.'[45] In any case, there were very few things which we understood well enough to be able to prove by the use of reason. And 'where reason cannot function, it is faith that works'. Some physical phenomena were intricately related to our ways of living, and since we had only an 'infinitesimal' knowledge of the rational working of physical laws, the proper attitude would be to not remain content with this partial knowledge but to take a unified moral view of those relations.

Rain is a physical phenomenon; it is no doubt related to human happiness and unhappiness; if so, how could it fail to be related to his good and bad deeds? We know of no period in human history when countless people have not related events like earthquakes to sinful deeds of man. Even today, religious-minded people everywhere believe in such a relationship.[46]

Such faith was based on firm principles of morality. It was not, therefore, superstitious.

I beseech you not to laugh within yourself and think I want to appeal to your instinct of superstition. I don't. I am not given to making any appeal to the superstitious fears of people. I may be called superstitious, but I cannot help telling you what I feel deep down in me ... You are free to believe it or to reject it.[47]

But by believing it, one could turn a human catastrophe into a social good. It did not matter what the correct scientific explanation was for such phenomena; by taking a firm moral attitude towards it, one could strengthen one's resolution to fight all of those things which were evil in human life.

If my belief turns out to be ill-founded, it will still have done good to me and those who believe with me. For we shall have been spurred to more vigorous efforts towards self-purification, assuming, of course, that untouchability is a deadly sin.[48]

To Gandhi, then, truth did not lie in history, nor did science have any privileged access to it. Truth was moral: unified, unchanging, and transcendental. It was not an object of critical inquiry or philosophical speculation. It could only be found in the experience of one's life, by the unflinching practice of moral living. It could never be correctly expressed within the terms of rational theoretical discourse; its only true expression was lyrical and poetic.[49] The universalist religiosity of this conception is utterly inconsistent with the dominant thematic of post-Enlightenment thought.

III

From this evidence, it is tempting to characterize Gandhism as yet another example of that typical reaction of the intelligentsia in many parts of the world to the social and moral depredations of advancing capitalism: romanticism. For instance, Gandhi's descriptions of the ideal moral order and the standpoint of his moral critique of civil society suggest strong similarities with that aspect of Russian *narodnichestvo* which Lenin called 'economic romanticism'.[50] In Gandhi too, there seems to be the vision of a Utopia—'a backward-looking petty-bourgeois Utopia'—and an idealization of pre-capitalist economic and social relations. One could, of course, concede to Gandhi, as indeed Lenin did to the Populists, that despite the backwardness of his solution to the fundamental problems of a society in the throes of capitalist penetration, he nevertheless took 'a big step forward' by posing, comprehensively and in all its economic, political, and moral aspects, the democratic demand of the small producers, chiefly the peasants. But in the theoretical sense, Gandhian ideology would still be 'reactionary', since, as Lenin pointed out in the case of the Russian Populists, not only is there simply a romantic longing for a return to an idealized medieval world of security and contentment, there is also 'the attempt to measure the new society with the old patriarchal yardstick, the desire to find a model in the old order and traditions, which are totally unsuited to the changed economic institutions'.[51] In spite of conceding the 'democratic points' in Gandhi's thought, therefore, the Leninist would have to pronounce that it is based on a false, indeed reactionary, theory of the world-historical process, or else that it refuses to acknowledge a theory of history at all. In either case, it would be a variant of romanticism.

This characterization gains further weight when one considers the sources of literary influence, explicitly acknowledged by Gandhi himself, which went into the formulation of his ideas on state and society. There was, for instance, Edward Carpenter's *Civilisation: Its Cause and Cure* which greatly influenced Gandhi's ideas on the corrupting effects of science, especially modern medicine. On the social consequences of the processes of industrial production, perhaps the greatest influence was John Ruskin's *Unto This Last*, that intensely moralistic critique of 'the modern *soi-disant* science of political economy'. On the fundamentally repressive nature of the powers of the state, and on the moral duty of peaceful resistance, a strong formative influence came from the political works of Tolstoy. It is true, of course, that Gandhi was highly eclectic in his borrowings, a task made easier in his case by the fact that he was unhampered by the formal theoretical requirements of scientific disciplines and philosophical schools. But there is little doubt that he was inherently sympathetic to many of the strands of argument put forward by 19th century European romantics and critics of rationalism and industrial progress.

A detailed examination of this question of influences would take us a long way from the central argument of this chapter. But the point about Gandhi's selectiveness in picking ideas from his favourite authors can be illustrated a little more in order to lead on to my next proposition that the fundamental core of the Gandhian ideology does not lie in a romantic problematic. For instance, Gandhi liked Edward Carpenter's argument about how the limitless increase of man's powers of production, brought on by the advent of modern science and technology, draws him away '(1) from Nature, (2) from his true Self, (3) from his Fellows', and how it works 'in every way to disintegrate and corrupt man—literally to corrupt—to *break up* the unity of his nature'.[52] But Carpenter's critique of modern day civilization was also based on a somewhat idiosyncratic reading of the anthropological theories in Lewis Morgan's *Ancient Society* and Frederick Engels's *The Origin of the Family, Private Property and the State*. This, in fact, was the main theoretical foundation on which Carpenter built his argument about how civilization, by transforming the nature of 'property', destroys man's unity with nature. Yet Carpenter's theoretical efforts do not seem to have made any impression on his more illustrious reader.

So also with Ruskin: Gandhi accepted Ruskin's criticism of that 'political economy founded on self-interest' which had made 'mammon service' the new religion of society. He particularly liked the idea that although there had to be different professions, such as those of the soldier, the physician, the pastor, the lawyer, or the merchant, their incomes must only be a payment to them from society, a means of their livelihood, and 'not the objects of their life'. He approved of Ruskin's suggestion that 'that country

is richest which nourishes the greatest number of noble and happy human
beings; that man is richest who, having perfected the functions of his own
life to the utmost, has also the widest helpful influence, both personal, and
by means of his possessions, over the lives of others'.[53] But Ruskin was also
a historicist, influenced in important ways by German idealism and
particularly by Hegel. Despite the contradictoriness which he shared with all
the other critics of industrial civilization in Victorian Britain, Ruskin was, in
the fundamental elements of his thought, a 'modernist'. Collingwood points
out, for instance, that 'he cared intensely for science and progress, for
political reform, for the advancement of knowledge and for new movements
in art and letters'.[54] His critique of political economy was meant to show the
painful contradictions between the dictates of a supposedly rational science
and those of altruistic morality, and to suggest that there was something
fundamentally wrong with that 'so-called science'. It was never meant to be
a call for the abandonment of Reason. He was aware of the limits of the
intellect but never supposed 'that "conscience" or "faith" may guide us
where "intellect" breaks down'.[55]

All of these concerns were quite far removed from Gandhi's theoretical
world. The critique of civil society which appears on the pages *of Hind
Swaraj* does not emerge out of a consideration of the historical contradic-
tions of civil society *as perceived from within it.* Quite unlike any of the
European romantics, Gandhi is not torn between the conflicting demands of
Reason and Morality, Progress and Happiness, Historical Necessity and
Human Will. His idealization of a peaceful, non-competitive, just and
happy Indian society of the past could not have been 'a romantic longing
for the lost harmony of the archaic world', because unlike romanticism,
Gandhi's problem is not conceived at all within the thematic bounds of
post-Enlightenment thought. He was not, for instance, seriously troubled
by the problems of reconciling individuality with universalism, of being
oneself and at the same time feeling at one with the infinite variety of the
world. Nor was his solution one in which the individual, without merging
into the world, would want to embrace the rich diversity of the world in
himself. Indeed, these were concerns which affected many Indian
'modernists' of Gandhi's time, perhaps the most illustrious of them
being Rabindranath Tagore. Gandhi shared neither the spiritual anguish
nor indeed the aestheticism of these literary romantics of his time.
Instead, his moral beliefs never seemed to lose that almost obdurate
certitude which men like Tagore, or even Jawaharlal Nehru, found
so exasperating.

The critique of civil society which forms such a central element of Gandhi's moral and political thinking is one which arises from an epistemic standpoint situated *outside* the thematic of post-Enlightenment thought. As such, it is a standpoint which could have been adopted by any member of the traditional intelligentsia in India, sharing the modes and categories of thought of a large pre-capitalist agrarian society, and reacting to the alien economic, political, and cultural institutions imposed on it by colonial rule. But if this is all there was to Gandhism, it could hardly have acquired the tremendous power that it undoubtedly did in the history of nationalism in India and in the formation of the contemporary Indian state. It would indeed be a gross error to regard Gandhi as merely another 'peasant intellectual'; despite the inherently 'peasant-communal' character of its critique of civil society, the correct perspective for understanding the Gandhian ideology *as a whole* would be to study it in relation to the historical development of elite-nationalist thought in India. For Gandhism, like Russian populism, was not a direct expression of peasant ideology. It was an ideology conceived as an intervention in the elite-nationalist discourse of the time and was formed and shaped by the experiences of a specifically national movement. It is only by looking at it in that historical context that it becomes possible to understand the unique achievement of Gandhism: its ability to open up the possibility for achieving perhaps the most important historical task for a successful national revolution in a country like India, namely, the political appropriation of the subaltern classes by a bourgeoisie aspiring for hegemony in the new nation-state. In the Indian case, the largest popular element of the nation was the peasantry. And it was the Gandhian ideology which opened up the historical possibility for its appropriation into the evolving political structures of the Indian state.

In its critique of civil society, Gandhism adopted a standpoint that lay entirely outside the thematic of post-Enlightenment thought, and hence of nationalist thought as well. In its formulation of the problem of town–country economic exchanges, of the cultural domination of the new urban educated classes, and above all, of the legitimacy of resistance to an oppressive state apparatus, it was able to encapsulate perfectly the specific political demands as well as the modalities of thought of a peasant–communal consciousness. If one wishes to pursue the point about European influences on the formation of Gandhi's thought, it is in fact Tolstoy who emerges as the most interesting comparison. For unlike the Russian Populists, and particularly unlike N.K. Mikhailovskii, against whom Lenin directed one of his first major polemical attacks,[56] Tolstoy was a consistent anarchist in his critique of the bourgeois political order, and this from a standpoint which, as Andrzej Walicki has pointed out, was 'genuinely archaic': unlike any of the Populists, Tolstoy was 'apparently more easily able to identify himself with the world outlook of the primitive, patriarchal villagers'.[57] Tolstoy, like Gandhi, believed that 'the cause of the miserable position of the workers' was not something specific to capitalism: 'The cause must lie in that which drives them from the villages'.[58] He, too, argued against the determinism inherent in the assumptions of economic science which was 'so sure that all the peasants have inevitably to become factory operatives in towns' that it continually affirmed 'that all the country people not only are not injured by the transition from the country to the town, but themselves desire it, and strive towards it'.[59] Even more significant was Tolstoy's characterization of the entire edifice of the state as the institutionalized expression of morally unjustifiable violence. His answer to state oppression was complete and implacable resistance. One must not, he said, 'neither willingly, nor under compulsion, take any part in Governmental activity ... nor, in fact, hold any office connected with violence', nor should one 'voluntarily pay taxes to Governments' or 'appeal to Governmental violence for the protection of his possessions'.[60] This thoroughgoing anarchism in Tolstoy was not accompanied by any specific political programme. There was simply a belief that the exemplary action of a few individuals, resisting the state by the strength of their conscience, would sway the people towards a massive movement against the institutions of violence.

Men who accept a new truth when it has reached a certain degree of dissemination always do so suddenly and in a mass ... The same is true of the bulk of humanity which suddenly, not one by one but always in a mass, passes from one arrangement of life to another under the influence of a new public opinion ... And therefore the transformation of human life ... will not come about solely by all men consciously and separately assimilating a certain Christian conception of life, but will come when a Christian public opinion so definite and comprehensible as to reach everybody has arisen and subdued that whole inert mass which is not able to attain the truth by its own intuition and is therefore always swayed by public opinion.[61]

In one aspect of his thought, Gandhi shared the same standpoint; but his thought ranged far beyond this specific ideological aspect. And it is here that the comparison with Tolstoy breaks down, because Gandhism also concerned itself with the practical organizational questions of a political *movement*. And this was a *national* political movement, required to operate within the institutional processes set up and directed by a colonial state. In its latter aspect, therefore, Gandhism had perforce to reckon with the practical

realities of a bourgeois legal and political structure as indeed of the organizational issues affecting a bourgeois political movement. It was the unique
achievement of Gandhian thought to have attempted to reconcile these two
contradictory aspects which were, at one and the same time, its integral
parts: a nationalism which stood upon a critique of the very idea of civil
society, a movement supported by the bourgeoisie which rejected the idea of
progress, the ideology of a political organization fighting for the creation of
a modern national state which accepted at the same time the ideal of an
'enlightened anarchy'. Clearly there are many ambiguities in Gandhism.
And a proper understanding of its history must go into a detailed examination
of how these ambiguities created the possibility for those two great movements that form part of the story of the formation of the new Indian state: on
the one hand, the transformation, in its own distinctive way in each region
and among each strata, of the demands of the people into 'the message of the
Mahatma',[62] and on the other, the appropriation of this movement into the
structural forms of a bourgeois organizational, and later constitutional,
order. But that is the task of modern Indian historiography; for the present,
we can only indicate the elements in Gandhian thought which made possible
the coexistence of these contradictory aspects within a single ideological
unity. Here, we must turn to the celebrated concepts of ahiṃsā and satyāgraha
and their epistemic basis in a conception that can only be described, fully in
accordance with Gandhian terminology, as 'experimental'.

IV

'Truth', wrote Gandhi to Mirabehn in 1933, 'is what everyone for the
moment feels it to be.'[63] It was a decidedly personal quest, but it did not for
that reason imply a moral anarchy. A few days before, in another letter, he
had explained to her:

We know the fundamental truth we want to reach, we know also the way. The details
we do not know, we shall never know them all, because we are but very humble
instruments among millions of such, moving consciously or unconsciously towards
the divine event. We shall reach the Absolute Truth, if we will faithfully and
steadfastly work out the relative truth as each one of us knows it.[64]

More publicly, in the Introduction to the *Autobiography* in 1925, Gandhi
had written:

for me, truth is the sovereign principle, which includes numerous other principles.
This truth is not only truthfulness in word, but truthfulness in thought also, and not

only the relative truth of our conception, but the Absolute Truth, the Eternal Principle, that is God. There are innumerable definitions of God ... But I worship God as Truth only. I have not yet found Him, but I am seeking after Him ... But as long as I have not realized this Absolute Truth, so long must I hold by the relative truth as I have conceived it. That relative truth must, meanwhile, be my beacon, my shield and buckler.[65]

There did exist an Absolute Truth, absolute and transcendental; to discover it was the purpose of our lives. But one could only proceed to find it in the experience of living, through an unswerving moral and truthful practice. At every stage, one had to be firmly committed to the truth as one knew it. At the same time, one had to be prepared to learn from experience, to put one's belief to the test, to accept the consequences and revise those beliefs if they were found wanting. Only then would one have for one's moral practice an epistemic foundation that was both certain and flexible, determinate and yet adaptable, categorical as well as experiential.

So much has now been written about Gandhi's 'truths'—the Absolute Truth, which must be sought for, and the various relative truths of our conception—that it is difficult to talk about the subject without referring to various current interpretations of those concepts. But once again, this will take us away from the central line of my argument. I must, therefore, accept the risk of inviting charges of distortion and oversimplification, and without explaining its relation to the vast body of Gandhian literature, simply proceed to state my own understanding of the conception of 'truth' in the overall structure and effectivity of the Gandhian ideology. In *Hind Swaraj*, the critique of modern civilization, and the plea for a return to the simple self-sufficiency of 'traditional' village life were based on the idea that it was the very changelessness of Indian civilization, its timeless ahistoricity, which was proof of its truth. India was resistant to change because it was not necessary for it to change: its civilization had found the true principles of social organization.

It is a charge against India that her people are so uncivilized, ignorant and stolid, that it is not possible to induce them to adopt any changes. It is a charge really against our merit. What we have tested and found true on the anvil of experience, we dare not change.[66]

All that was necessary now was to find a way of protecting that social organization from the destructive consequences of colonial rule and of eliminating the poverty that had been brought upon the people. The answer was a rejection of the entire institutional edifice of civil society, uncompromising resistance to its economic, cultural, and political structures. There was no specific conception yet of a political process of struggle, of its organizational procedures, norms of practice, strategic and tactical principles. As Gandhi explained later in the *Autobiography*, 'In [*Hind Swaraj*] I took it as understood that anything that helped India to get rid of the grinding poverty of her masses would in the same process also establish swaraj.'[67] It was only in the context of the evolution of the political movement that the Gandhian ideology became something more than a Utopian doctrine. It acquired a theory of the political process within which the movement was to function; it developed its own organizational principles of political practice. In course of the full working out of Gandhian thought, the sheer tactical malleability of the 'experimental' conception of truth became the principal means by which all the seemingly irreconcilable parts of that ideology were put together.

Consider satyāgraha, that celebrated Gandhian form of mass political action. In 1917 Gandhi explained that satyāgraha was not mere passive resistance. It meant 'intense activity'—political activity—by large masses of people. It was a legitimate, moral, and truthful form of political action by the people against the injustices of the state, an active mass resistance to unjust rule. It was not aimed at the destruction of the state, nor was it—as yet—conceived as part of a political process intended to replace the functionaries of the state.

We can ... free ourselves of the unjust rule of the Government by defying the unjust rule and accepting the punishments that go with it. We do not bear malice towards the Government. When we set its fears at rest, when we do not desire to make armed assaults on the administrators, nor to unseat them from power, but only to get rid of their injustice, they will at once be subdued to our will.[68]

Satyāgraha, at this stage, was intended to articulate only a 'negative consciousness'. It is, therefore, easy to recognize why it could express so effectively the characteristic modes of peasant-communal resistance to oppressive state authority.[69] It was true, of course, that peasant resistance to injustice was not always restricted to non-violent forms: there was much historical evidence to this effect. But at this stage, Gandhi was quite dismissive of these objections.

It is said that it is a very difficult, if not an altogether impossible, task to educate ignorant peasants in satyagraha and that it is full of perils, for it is a very arduous business to transform unlettered ignorant people from one condition into another. Both the arguments are just silly. The people of India are perfectly fit to receive the

training of satyagraha. India has knowledge of dharma, and where there is knowledge of dharma, satyagraha is a very simple matter ... Some have a fear that once
people get involved in satyagraha, they may at a later stage take arms. This fear is
illusory. From the path of satyagraha, a transition to the path of *a-satyagraha* is
impossible. It is possible of course that some people who believe in armed activity
may mislead the satyagrahis by infiltrating into their ranks and later making them
take to arms. This is possible in all enterprises. But as compared to other activities,
it is less likely to happen in satyagraha, for their motives soon get exposed and when
the people are not ready to take up arms, it becomes almost impossible to lead them
on to that terrible path.[70]

Nor was the question of leadership, and of the relation between leaders and
the masses, seen as being particularly problematical in the political sense:

People in general always follow in the footsteps of the noble. There is no doubt that
it is difficult to produce a satyagrahi leader. Our experience is that a satyagrahi needs
many more virtues like self-control, fearlessness, etc., than are requisite for one who
believes in armed action ... The birth of such a man can bring about the salvation of
India in no time. Not only India but the whole world awaits the advent of such a man.
We may in the meantime prepare the ground as much as we can through satyagraha.[71]

It was this faith in the relatively spontaneous strength of popular resistance
to injustice that lay behind the call to the nation to join in the agitations in
1919 against the Rowlatt Bill. There was little concern yet about the
distinction between leader and *satyāgrahī* or the *satyāgrahī* and the masses,
or about the precise degree of maturity before the masses could be asked to
join a satyāgraha, or about the organizational and normative safeguards
against the inherent unpredictability of a negative consciousness playing
itself out in the political battleground. In March 1919, Gandhi was still able
to say to the people:

whether you are satyagrahis or not, so long as you disapprove of the Rowlatt
legislation, all can join and I hope that there will be such a response throughout the
length and breadth of India as would convince the Government that we are alive to
what is going on in our midst.[72]

All this, of course, changed after the experience of the Rowlatt satyāgraha:
'a rapier run through my body could hardly have pained me more'.[73] He had
made a massive error of judgement and there was, he admitted, some truth
in the charge that he had ignored a few obvious lessons of political history.

I think that I at least should have foreseen some of the consequences, specially in
view of the gravest warnings that were given to me by friends whose advice I have

always sought and valued. But I confess that I am dense. I am not joking. So many friends have told me that I am incapable of profiting by other people's experiences and that in every case I want to go through the fire myself and learn only after bitter experience. There is exaggeration in this charge, but there is also a substance of truth in it. This denseness in me is at once a weakness and a strength. I could not have remained a satyagrahi had I not cultivated the quality of stubborn resistance and such resistance can only come from experience and not from inference.[74]

But the experience of his first political agitation on a national scale brought in Gandhi a 'new realization'. He now became aware of the fundamental incompatibility of political action informed solely by a negative consciousness with the procedural norms of a bourgeois legal order. The ethics of resistance, if it was to be relevant to a bourgeois political movement, would have to be reconciled with a theory of political obedience. 'Unfortunately,' he said,

popular imagination has pictured satyagraha as purely and simply civil disobedience, if not in some cases even criminal disobedience ... As satyagraha is being brought into play on a large scale on the political field for the first time, it is in an experimental stage. I am therefore ever making new discoveries. And my error in trying to let civil disobedience take the people by storm appears to me to be Himalayan because of the discovery I have made, namely, that he only is able and attains the right to offer civil disobedience who has known how to offer voluntary and deliberate obedience to the laws of the State in which he is living.[75]

And from this fundamental discovery flowed a new organizational principle; as he later explained in the *Autobiography*:

I wondered how I could have failed to perceive what was so obvious. I realized that before a people could be fit for offering civil disobedience, they should thoroughly understand its deeper implications. That being so, before restarting civil disobedience on a mass scale, it would be necessary to create a band of well-tried, pure-hearted volunteers who thoroughly understood the strict conditions of satyagraha.[76]

Thus was born the *political* concept of the satyāgrahī as leader. In the course of his evidence before the Hunter Committee appointed to inquire into the Rowlatt Bill agitations, Gandhi was asked about his conception of the relation between leaders and followers.

C.H. Setalvad. I take it that your scheme, as you conceive it, involves the determination of what is the right path and the true path by people who are capable of high intellectual and moral equipment and a large number of other people following them without themselves being able to arrive at similar conclusions by reason of their lower moral and intellectual equipment?

Gandhi. I cannot subscribe to that, because I have not said that. I do not say that they are not to exercise their judgment, but I simply say that, in order that they may exercise their judgment, the same mental and moral equipment is not necessary.

C.H.S. Because they are to accept the judgment of people who are capable of exercising better judgment and equipped with better moral and intellectual standard?

G. Naturally, but I think that is in human nature, but I exact nothing more than I would exact from an ordinary human being.[77]

While mass resistance to unjust laws was the final and only certain guarantee against state oppression, the people would have to depend on their leaders for guidance.

Jagat Narayan. My point is, having regard to the circumstances, a sort of sanctity attaches to the laws of the Government of the time being?

Gandhi. Not in my estimation ...

J.N. That is not the best check on the masses?

G. Not a blind adherence to laws, no check whatsoever. It is because either they blindly adhere or they blindly commit violence. Either event is undesirable.

J.N. So as every individual is not fit to judge for himself, he would have to follow somebody?

G. Certainly, he would have to follow somebody. The masses will have to choose their leaders most decidedly.[78]

The point was further clarified when Gandhi was asked about his understanding of the reasons why the agitations had become violent. Soon after the events in Ahmedabad, Gandhi had told a mass meeting: 'It seems that the deeds I have complained of have been done in an organized manner. There seems to be a definite design about them, and I am sure that there must be some educated and clever man or men behind them ... You have been misled into doing these deeds by such people.'[79] Elaborating on what he meant by 'organized manner', Gandhi said to the Hunter Committee:

In my opinion, the thing was organised, but there it stands. There was no question whether it was a deep-laid conspiracy through the length and breadth of India or a deep-rooted organisation of which this was a part. The organisation was hastily constructed; the organisation was not in the sense in which we understand the word organisation ... If I confined that word to Ahmedabad alone, to masses of absolutely unlettered men, who would be able to make no fine distinctions—then you have got the idea of what that organisation is ... There were these poor deluded labourers whose one business was to see me released and see Anasuyabai released. That it was a wicked rumour deliberately started by somebody I have not the slightest doubt. As soon as these things happened the people thought there should be something behind it. Then there were the half-educated raw youths. This is the work of these. I am grieved to have to say. These youths possessed themselves with false ideas gathered from shows, such as the cinematograph shows that they have seen, gathered from silly novels and from the political literature of Europe ... it was an organisation of this character.[80]

The direct physical form in which the masses appeared in the political arena was always that of a mob. It had no mind of its own.[81] Its behaviour was determined entirely by the way it was led: 'nothing is so easy as to train mobs, for the simple reason that they have no mind, no premeditation. They act in a frenzy. They repent quickly.'[82] For this reason, they were as susceptible to manipulation by mischief-makers as they were open to en-lightened leadership. In order, therefore, to undertake mass political action, it was necessary first of all to create a selfless, dedicated, and enlightened group of political workers who would lead the masses and protect them from being misguided.

Before we can make real headway, we must train these masses of men who have a heart of gold, who feel for the country, who want to be taught and led. But a few intelligent, sincere, local workers are needed, and the whole nation can be organized to act intelligently, and democracy can be evolved out of mobocracy.[83]

This was the problematic which lay at the heart of what soon evolved into the other celebrated concept in the Gandhian ideology—the concept of ahiṃsā. In its application to politics, ahiṃsā was also about 'intense political activity' by large masses of people. But it was not so much about resistance as about the *modalities* of resistance, about organizational principles, rules of conduct, strategies, and tactics. Ahiṃsā was the necessary complement to the concept of satyāgraha which both limited it and, at the same time, made it something more than 'purely and simply civil disobedience'. Ahiṃsā was the rule for concretizing the 'truth' of satyāgraha. 'Truth is a positive value, while non-violence is a negative value. Truth affirms. Non-violence forbids something which is real enough.'[84] Ahiṃsā, indeed, was the concept—both ethical and epistemological because it was defined within a moral and epistemic practice that was wholly 'experimental'—which supplied Gandhism with a theory of *politics*, enabling it to become the ideology of a national political movement. It was the organizing principle for a 'science' of politics—a science wholly different from all current conceptions of politics which had only succeeded in producing the 'sciences of violence', but a science nevertheless—the 'science of non-violence', the 'science of love'. It was the moral framework for solving every practical problem of the organized political movement.

The 'science of non-violence', consequently, dealt with questions such as the requirements for being a political satyāgrahī, his rules of conduct, his relations with the political leadership as well as with the masses, questions about the structure of decision-making, lines of command, political strategies and tactics, and about the practical issues of breaking as well as obeying the laws of the state. It was as much a 'science' of political struggle, indeed as much a military science, as the 'sciences of violence', only it was superior because it was a science not of arms but of the moral force of the soul. At this level, in fact, it was not a Utopian conception at all. There was no assumption, for instance, of collective consensus in the making of decisions, for that would be wishing away the existence of a practical political problem. Decisions were to be taken by 'a few true satyagrahis'. This would provide a far more economic and efficient method of political action than that proposed by the 'sciences of violence': 'we would require a smaller army of satyagrahis than that of soldiers trained in modern warfare, and the cost will be insignificant compared to the fabulous sums devoted by nations to armaments'.[85] Second, the practice of this 'experimental science' of mass political action was not conditional upon the masses themselves understanding all its principles or their full implications.

A soldier of an army does not know the whole of the military science; so also does a satyagrahi not know the whole science of satyagraha. It is enough if he trusts his commander and honestly follows his instructions and is ready to suffer unto death without bearing malice against the so-called enemy ... [The satyagrahis] must render heart discipline to their commander. There should be no mental reservation.[86]

Third, the political employment of ahiṃsā did not depend upon everyone accepting it as a creed. It was possible for it to be regarded as a valid political theory even without its religious core. This, in fact, was the only way it could become a general guide for solving the practical problems of an organized political movement.

Ahimsa with me is a creed, the breath of life. But it is never as a creed that I placed it before India or, for that matter, before anyone except in casual or informal talks. I placed it before the Congress as a political weapon, to be employed for the solution of practical problems.[87]

And thus we come to an explicit recognition, within the overall unity of the Gandhian ideology as it took shape in the course of the evolution of the national movement, of a *disjuncture* between morality and politics, between private conscience and public responsibility, indeed between Noble Folly and realpolitik. It was a disjuncture which the 'experimental' conception of ahiṃsā was meant to bridge. And yet, it was a disjuncture the steadfast denial of whose very existence had been the foundation of the original conception of *Hind Swaraj*. Now, however, we see the spinning wheel, for instance, coming to acquire a dual significance, located on entirely different planes, and it is no longer considered politically necessary for the personal religion to be identified with a political programme.

I have never tried to make anyone regard the spinning-wheel as his *kamadhenu* or universal provider ... When in 1908 ... I declared my faith in the spinning-wheel in the pages *of Hind Swaraj*, I stood absolutely alone ... I do regard the spinning-wheel as a gateway to *my* spiritual salvation, but I recommend it to others only as a powerful weapon for the attainment of swaraj and the amelioration of the economic condition of the country.[88]

In 1930, on the eve of the Dandi March, we find Gandhi telling his colleagues that he did not know what form of democracy India should have. He was not particularly interested in the question: 'the method alone interests me, and by method I mean the agency through which the wishes of the people are reached. There are only two methods; one is that of fraud and force; the other is that of non-violence and truth.'[89] It did not matter even if the goal was beyond reach. The first responsibility of the political leader was to strictly adhere to his principles of morality.

What I want to impress on everyone is that I do not want India to reach her goal through questionable means. Whether that is possible or not is another question. It is sufficient for my present purpose if the person who thinks out the plan and leads the people is absolutely above board and has non-violence and truth in him.[90]

And once there is a recognition of the disjuncture, the failure of politics to reach Utopia could be attributed to the loftiness of the ideal, noble, truthful and inherently unreachable, or else, equally credibly, to the imperfections of the human agency. The vision of a non-violent India could be 'a mere day-dream, a childish folly'.[91] Or else, one could argue with equal validity that the problem lay not with the ideal but with one's own deficiencies.

I do not think it is right to say that the principles propounded in *Hind Swaraj* are not workable just because I cannot practise them perfectly ... not only do I refuse to excuse myself, but positively confess my shortcoming.[92]

The result, of course, was that under the moral umbrella of the quest for Utopia, the experimental conception of politics could accommodate a potentially limitless range of imperfections, adjustments, compromises, and failures. For the authority of the political leader derived not from the inherent reasonableness of his programme or the feasibility of his project, not even from the accordance of that programme or project with a collective perception of common interests or goals. It derived entirely from a moral claim—of personal courage and sacrifice and a patent adherence to truth. So much so that the supreme test of political leadership was death itself. That was the final proof of the leader's claim to the allegiance of his people. At Anand, in the middle of the Dandi March, Gandhi said,

This band of satyagrahis which has set out is not staging a play; its effect will not be merely temporary; even through death, it will prove true to its pledge—if death becomes necessary .... Nothing will be better than if this band of satyagrahis perishes. If the satyagrahis meet with death, it will put a seal upon their claim.[93]

And when Jairamdas Doulatram was injured in a police firing in Karachi during the Civil Disobedience movement, Gandhi sent a telegram to the Congress office saying:

CONSIDER JAIRAMDAS MOST FORTUNATE. BULLET WOUND THIGH BETTER THAN PRISON. WOUND HEART BETTER STILL. BAPU[94]

Gandhism finally reconciled the contradictions between the Utopian and the practical aspects of its political ideology by surrendering to the absolute truthfulness and supreme self-sacrifice of the satyāgrahī. It had gained its strength from an intensely powerful moral critique of the existing state of politics. In the end, it saved its Truth by escaping from politics.

V

And yet, as Gandhi himself put it, 'politics encircle us today like the coil of a snake'.[95] The historical impact of the Gandhian ideology on the evolution of Indian politics was of monumental significance.

The 'science of non-violence' was the form in which Gandhism addressed itself to the problematic of nationalism. That was the 'science' which was to provide answers to the problems of national politics, of concretizing the nation as an active historical subject rejecting the domination of a foreign power, of devising its political organization and the strategic and tactical principles of its struggle. In its specific historical effectivity, Gandhism provided for the first time in Indian politics an ideological basis for including the *whole people* within the political nation. In order to do this, it quite consciously sought to bridge even the most sanctified cultural barriers that divided the people in an immensely complex agrarian society. Thus, it was not simply a matter of bringing the peasantry into the national movement, but of consciously seeking the ideological means for bringing it in *as a whole*. This, for instance, is how one can interpret the strenuous efforts by Gandhi to obliterate the 'sin' of the existing jāti divisions in Indian society, and the 'deadly sin' of untouchability in particular, and to replace it by an idealized scheme based on the varṇa classification.[96] 'Do you not think', Gandhi was asked, 'that the improvement of the condition of starving peasants is more important than the service of Harijans? Will you not, therefore, form peasant organizations which will naturally include Harijans in so far as their economic condition is concerned?' 'Unfortunately,' Gandhi replied,

the betterment of the economic condition of peasants will not necessarily include the betterment of that of the Harijans. The peasant who is not a Harijan can rise as high as he likes and opportunity permits him, but not so the poor suppressed Harijan. The latter cannot own and use land as freely as the *savarna* peasant ... therefore, a special organization for the service of Harijans is a peremptory want in order to deal with the special and peculiar disabilities of Harijans. Substantial improvement of these, the lowest strata of society, must include the whole of society.[97]

Whether this idiom of solidarity necessarily referred to a cultural code that could be shown to be 'essentially Hindu', and whether that in turn alienated rather than united those sections of the people who were not 'Hindu', are of course important questions, but not strictly relevant in establishing the ideological intent behind Gandhi's efforts.

Thus, while the search was for an ideological means to unite the whole people, there was also a determinate political structure and process, specific and historically given, within which the task had to be accomplished. And here it was the 'experimental' conception of truth, combining the absolute moral legitimacy of satyāgraha with the tactical considerations of ahiṃsā, which made the Gandhian ideology into a powerful instrument in the historical task of constructing the new Indian state.

For now one could talk, within the overall unity of that ideology, of the constructive relation of the national movement to the evolving institutional structure of state power. Gandhi could say, on the one hand, 'I shall retain my disbelief in legislatures as an instrument for obtaining swaraj in terms of masses', and in the same breath go on to argue,

But I see that I have failed to wean some of the Congressmen from their faith in council-entry. The question therefore is whether they should or should not enforce their desire to enter legislature as Congress representatives. I have no doubt that they must have the recognition they want. Not to give it will be to refuse to make use of the talents we possess.[98]

Indeed, the truth of the moral conception of Utopia was for ever safe, no matter what compromises one had to make in the world of practical politics.

The parliamentary work must be left to those who are so inclined. I hope that the majority will always remain untouched by the glamour of council work. In its own place, it will be useful. But ... Swaraj can only come through an all-round conciousness of the masses.[99]

Similarly, the acceptance of ministerial office by Congressmen in 1937, an act apparently in complete contradiction with the spirit of non-cooperation enshrined in the Congress movement in 1920, now became 'not a repudiation but a fulfilment of the original, so long as the mentality behind all of them remains the same as in 1920'.[100] And if the disharmony between the act and the mentality became much too gross, the final moral act that would save the truth of the ideal was withdrawal. When the evidence became overwhelming that Congressmen as officers of the state were not exhibiting the selflessness, ability, and incorruptibility that was the justification for their being in office, Gandhi's plea to Congressmen was to make a choice:

either to apply the purge I have suggested, or, if that is not possible because of the Congress being already overmanned by those who have lost faith in its creed and its constructive programme on which depends its real strength, to secede from it for its own sake and proving his living faith in the creed and programme by practising the former and prosecuting the latter as if he had never seceded from the Congress of his ideal.[101]

Then again, the ideal of property as trust was 'true in theory only'. Like all other ideals, it would

remain an unattainable ideal, so long as we are alive, but towards which we must ceaselessly strive. Those who own money now are asked to behave like trustees holding their riches on behalf of the poor. You may say that trusteeship is a legal fiction ... Absolute trusteeship is an abstraction like Euclid's definition of a point, and is equally unattainable. But if we strive for it, we shall be able to go further in realizing a state of equality on earth than by any other method.

Q. But if you say that private possession is incompatible with non-violence, why do you put up with it?

A. That is a concession one has to make to those who earn money but who would not voluntarily use their earnings for the benefit of mankind.[102]

Sometimes the justification for this concession was crassly empirical: 'I am quite clear that if a strictly honest and unchallengeable referendum of our millions were to be taken, they would not vote for wholesale expropriation of the propertied classes.'[103] At other times, it would seem to rest on a fairly sophisticated reading of the lessons of political history: the zamindars

must regard themselves, even as the Japanese nobles did, as trustees holding their wealth for the good of their wards, the ryots ... I am convinced that the capitalist, if he follows the Samurai of Japan, has nothing really to lose and everything to gain. There is no other choice than between voluntary surrender on the part of the capitalist of superfluities and consequent acquisition of the real happiness of all on the one hand, and on the other the impending chaos into which, if the capitalist does not wake up betimes, awakened but ignorant, famishing millions will plunge the country and which not even the armed force that a powerful Government can bring into play can avert.[104]

But in considering questions of this sort, having to do with the practical organizational issues of a bourgeois political movement, Gandhism would inevitably slip into the familiar thematic of nationalist thought. It would argue in terms of categories such as capitalism, socialism, law, citizenship, private property, individual rights, and struggle to fit its formless Utopia into the conceptual grid of post-Enlightenment social-scientific thought.

Let us not be obsessed with catchwords and seductive slogans imported from the West. Have we not our own distinct Eastern traditions? Are we not capable of finding our own solution to the question of capital and labour? ... Let us study our Eastern institutions in that spirit of scientific inquiry and we shall evolve a truer socialism and a truer communism than the world has yet dreamed of. It is surely wrong to presume that Western socialism or communism is the last word on the question of mass poverty.[105]

... Class war is foreign to the essential genius of India which is capable of evolving a form of communism broad-based on the fundamental rights of all and equal justice to all.[106]

Sometimes, in trying to defend his political strategy of nationalist struggle, Gandhi would even feel forced to resort to some of the most naive cultural essentialisms of Orientlist thought:

By her very nature, India is a lover of peace ... On the other hand, Mustafa Kamal Pasha succeeded with the sword because there is strength in every nerve of a Turk. The Turks have been fighters for centuries. The people of India have followed the path of peace for thousands of years ... There is at the present time not a single country on the face of the earth which is weaker than India in point of physical strength. Even tiny Afghanistan can growl at her.[107]

These difficulties are symptomatic of the curious relationship between Gandhism and the thematic and problematic of nationalist thought. In its historical effectivity, we would be perfectly justified in characterizing the entire story of the Gandhian intervention in India's nationalist politics as the moment of manoeuvre in the 'passive revolution of capital' in India. But that is not something that can be read directly from the ideological intent expressed in Gandhian texts. Rather, we must identify the possibility of manoeuvre, the result of the struggle of social forces in the battlefield of politics, in the very tensions within Gandhism—in the fundamental ambiguity of its relation to nationalist thought, in the way in which it challenged the basic premises on which the latter was built, and yet sought at the same time to insert itself into the process of a nationalist politics.

There was, as we have seen, a fundamental incompatibility between the utopianism which shaped the moral conception of Gandhian politics and the realities of power within a bourgeois constitutional order. It is not as though Gandhism was unaware of this disjunction; it did not dogmatically deny the existence of the gap nor did it insist that it could be bridged with ease. What it suggested was a certain method of political practice—imperfect but innately truthful, flexible, and yet principled. But once the groundswell of popular upsurge had subsided and the nationalist state leadership knew that power was within its reach, it was not easy to determine what this truthful political practice was now going to be. What was the duty of the true servant of the Congress: take up the new responsibilities of running the state or stay outside it and continue the struggle towards what was known to be an unreachable goal?

Gandhi's belief was that the true satyāgrahī would always choose the latter. True non-violent svarāj would only come by pursuing the programme of rural construction; the parliamentary programme could at best bring 'political swaraj' which was not true svarāj.[108] As late as November 1945, Gandhi instructed members of the All India Spinners' Association, the central body of khādī workers, not to take part in elections or any other political activity of that sort.[109] But by 1945–6 many of his closest and most trusted associates in the constructive work programme were being asked by the Congress to enter government, and when they turned to him for advice his replies were curiously hesitant, sometimes even petulant: 'I do not want to dampen your interest. You have the aptitude for it. Nor would I consider your going into the Assembly a bad thing. After all someone has to go there. What I mean is that neither you nor anyone else can ride two horses at the same time.'[110] 'As regards the Provincial Assembly you may take it that I am not interested. But if you are inclined that way and have the ability for it, and if all others agree, please do go.'[111] In several cases he qualified his permission by a reminder about the importance of non-attachment in the life of a leader of the people:

Because all your friends want it, you may seek election to the Assembly if it can be done without any exertion on your part and on the clear understanding that it will be a bed of thorns and not of velvet ... Refrain from all arguments and discussions, observe silence, -and if even then people elect you go to the Assembly. You should not make any effort on your part to get elected.[112]

... You can give your name for the Provincial election on the condition that you would neither beg for votes from the electorate nor spend any money. If you can get elected on this condition you may enter the Assembly.[113]

Later he issued a general message for all Congressmen:

I believe that some Congressmen ought to seek election in the legislatures or other elected bodies. In the past I did not hold this view. I had hoped that the boycott of legislatures would be complete. That was not to be. Moreover times have changed. Swaraj seems to be near. Under the circumstances it is necessary that Congress should contest every seat in the legislatures. The attraction should never be the honour that a seat in a legislature is said to give ... Moreover those that are not selected by the Board should not feel hurt. On the contrary, they should feel happy that they are left there to render more useful service. But the painful fact is that those who are not selected by the Board do feel hurt.

The Congress should not have to spend money on the elections. Nominees of a popular organization should be elected without any effort on the latter's part...

Let us examine the utility value of legislatures ... He who can tell the people why they become victims of the Government ... and can teach them how to stand up against Government wrongs renders a real service. The members cannot do this essential service, for their business is to make people look to them for the redress of wrongs. [The Gujarati version of this article has a much stronger sentence: 'Councils are, have been and will be, an obstruction in this work.']

The other use of legislatures is to prevent undesirable legislation and bring in laws which are useful for the public, so that as much help as possible can be given to the constructive programme.[114]

Thus, even while conceding that many Congressmen must now enter the business of running the state machinery, Gandhi still appeared to see them in a largely oppositional role, pointing out the misdeeds of government and preventing the enactment of bad laws. The only positive role he could envisage for the national government was the support it might provide for the constructive programme. In mid-1946 he even made some specific suggestions in this regard:

The Government should notify the villagers that they will be expected to manufacture khaddar for the needs of their villages within a fixed date after which no cloth
will be supplied to them. The Governments in their turn will supply the villagers
with cotton seed or cotton wherever required, at cost price and the tools of manufacture also at cost, to be recovered in easy instalments ...

The villages will be surveyed and a list prepared of things that can be manufactured locally with little or no help and which may be required for village use or for
sale outside ... If enough care is taken, the villages, most of them as good as dead or
dying, will hum with life and exhibit the immense possibilities they have of
supplying most of their wants themselves and of the cities and towns of India.[115]

In addition to these, Gandhi suggested two other areas in which the government could help: the preservation of cattle wealth and the spread of basic
education. A few weeks later, he also proposed a modality of work: 'the
ministers', he said, 'should pick out from the bureaucracy honest and
incorruptible men' and put them under the guidance of organizations such
as the All India Spinners' Association, the All India Village Industries
Association, and the Hindustani Talimi Sangh. The official notification
regarding the stopping of mill cloth and the exclusive use of khādī in
villages should include both villagers and mill-owners as parties to the
scheme. 'The notification will show clearly that it is the people's measure,
though bearing the Government stamp.' Visualizing himself in the role of
minister in charge of the revival of villages, Gandhi posed the basic decision
problem which he thought the new national government must face: 'The
only question for me as minister is whether the AISA has the conviction and
capacity to shoulder the burden of creating and guiding a khadi scheme to
success. If it has, I would put my little barque to sea with all confidence.'[116]

Thus, even while identifying a specific role for the state in the programme
of national construction, Gandhi was not abandoning his fundamental
belief that the state could never be the appropriate machinery for carrying
out this programme. What he was suggesting in fact was that the national
state should formally use its legislative powers to *abdicate* its presumed
responsibility of promoting 'development' and thus clear the ground for
popular non-state agencies to take up the work of revitalizing the village
economies.

Was he then advocating a sort of *laissez-faire* policy? If the state was to
abandon its controlling role in the national economy, would it not leave the
field open for exploiters and powerful vested interests to take an even firmer
control over the means of economic exploitation? Now that the popular
nationalist forces had come to power, was not a certain degree of intervention,

even coercion, necessary and desirable in order to check those exploitative interests? This was the ideological argument which the increasingly dominant section of the nationalist state leadership offered against Gandhian 'visionaries'. For the national state to abandon its economic responsibilities, these leaders argued, would be a reactionary step.

Faced with this argument, Gandhi's response was to reassert the claims of his moral conception. The immediate political battle against colonial rule had been virtually won. Now the question of the relation between the nation and the state was posed more sharply than ever before. Having acceded to the political compulsions of bourgeois politics for two-and-a-half decades, Gandhi in the last years of his life resumed the struggle for Utopia.

Now he insisted with renewed conviction that mere 'political swaraj' could never be a substitute for 'true swaraj'. He reasserted the ideal of Rāmarājya and defined it concretely as 'independence—political, economic and moral':

'Political' necessarily means the removal of the control of the British army in every shape and form.

'Economic' means entire freedom from British capitalists and capital, as also their Indian counterparts ... This can take place only by capital or capitalists sharing their skill and capital with the lowliest and the least.

'Moral' means freedom from armed defence forces. My conception of Rāmarājya excludes replacement of the British army by a national army of occupation. A country that is governed by even its national army can never be morally free.[117]

While the existence of the state remained a practical reality, the true ideal of the stateless society needed to be posited with renewed emphasis, now that the immediate political battle had been won and yet the task of reconstructing the national society remained unaccomplished. The question was not whether statelessness could ever be actually achieved; the question was whether one's political practice should rest on a firm moral principle or whether the principle should be relinquished.

Would there be State power in an ideal society or would such a society be Stateless? I think the question is futile. If we continue to work towards the building of such a society, to some extent it is bound to be realized and to that extent people will benefit by it. Euclid has defined a straight line as having no breadth, but no one has yet succeeded in drawing such a line and no one ever will. Still we can progress in geometry only by postulating such a line. This is true of every ideal.

We might remember though that a Stateless society does not exist anywhere in the world. If such a society is possible it can be established first only in India. For attempts have been made in India towards bringing about such a society. We have not so far shown that supreme herosim. The only way is for those who believe in it to set the example.[118]

But no matter how relentlessly Gandhi insisted on a renewal of the moral battle, it had by then become patently obvious that the main body of the Congress leadership was now fully engaged in the task of running a modern state machinery on a national scale, using the full range of its coercive instruments. Gandhi saw this as a moral failure on the part of the political leadership, a surrender to the forces of violence. 'Congressmen think that now it is their government ... Everywhere Congressmen are thus scrambling for power and favours ... A government seems to have only military power behind it, but it cannot run on the strength of that power alone.'[119] Repeatedly in the last months of his life he spoke of his helplessness, a feeling that acquired greater poignancy in the midst of the mad violence of communal strife which marked the transfer of power.

Whatever the Congress decides will be done; nothing will be according to what I say. My writ runs no more. If it did the tragedies in the Punjab, Bihar and Noakhali would not have happened. No one listens to me any more. I am a small man. True, there was a time when mine was a big voice. Then everyone obeyed what I said; now neither the Congress nor the Hindus nor the Muslims listen to me. Where is the Congress today? It is disintegrating. I am crying in the wilderness.[120]

In sorrow not unmixed with anger Gandhi suggested that henceforth the Congress should stop talking about truth and non-violence and that it should remove the words 'peaceful and legitimate' from its constitution. 'I am convinced that so long as the army or the police continues to be used for conducting the administration we shall remain subservient to the British or some other foreign power, irrespective of whether the power is in the hands of the Congress or others.'[121] By not claiming to follow 'peaceful and legitimate' means, the Congress would at least not be hypocritical.[122]

Once again, therefore, Gandhism sought to explain the defeat of its Utopian quest by putting the blame on the moral failings of those who claimed to be leaders of the people. But, in truth, Gandhism as a political ideology had now been brought face to face with its most irreconcilable contradiction. While it insisted on the need to stay firm in the adherence to its ideal, it was no longer able to specify concretely the modalities of implementing this as a viable *political* practice. Now that there were powerful and organized interests *within* the nation which clearly did not share the belief in the Gandhian ideal, there was no way in which the Gandhian ideology could identify a social force which would carry forward the struggle and overcome this opposition in the arena of politics.

VI

Nowhere was this basic ideological problem highlighted more clearly than in Gandhi's final battle for khādī. In 1944 Gandhi, proposed a 'New Khadi Philosophy'. He had, he said, thought a great deal about khādī during his period of detention and was convinced that there was something fundamentally wrong about the way the work had been carried out for so long. 'The fault is not yours but mine' he told an assembly of khādī workers in September 1944. The main difficulty was that the programme so far had been guided exclusively by practical considerations; the principle had been lost sight of. 'I did not lay the necessary stress on the requisite outlook and the spirit which was to underlie it. I looked at it from its immediate practical aspect ... But today I cannot continue to ask people to spin in that manner.'[123]

The new khādī 'philosophy' which Gandhi kept explaining over the next two years was based on the fundamental principle that rural production must be primarily for self-consumption and not for sale. This had not been followed in the khādī programme so far, because the emphasis was more on providing a little additional employment to the rural poor and most khādī was spun in return for wages. Besides, most of the khādī cloth produced from this yarn was sold in the cities. This was not in keeping with the fundamental objective of the khādī philosophy which was to create an economic order in which the direct producer would not have to depend on anyone else for his basic necessities. If villagers continued to spin only in order to sell the yarn to khādī organizations, then despite the popularity of khādī cloth in the cities the entire programme would be founded on wrong economic principles. 'An economics which runs counter to morality cannot be called true economics.'[124]

What was this morality? The moral significance of the khādī programme lay in its relation to the true conception of svarāj. It was a mistake to regard khādī as any other industry and to work out its economics in terms of the principles of the marketplace.

If khadi is an industry it would have to be run purely on business lines. The difference between khadi and mill-cloth would then be that while a mill provides employment to a few thousand people in a city, khadi brings a crore of rupees to those scattered about in fifteen thousand villages. Both must be classified as industries, and we would hardly be justified in asking anybody to put on khadi and boycott mill-cloth. Nor can such khadi claim to be the herald of swaraj. On the other hand we have claimed that the real significance of khadi is that it is a means for uplifting the villages and thereby generating in the people the spontaneous strength for swaraj. Such a claim cannot then be sustained. It will not do to continue to help the villagers by appealing to the philanthropic sentiments of city-dwellers ... If we encouraged mills, the nation might get sufficient cloth. And if mills are nationalized cloth prices may also come down, people may not be exploited and may earn adequate wages. But our reason for putting forward khadi is that it is the only way to redeem the people from the disease of inertia and indifference, the only way to generate in them the strength of freedom.[125]

Thus Gandhi was now quite explicitly moving away from the 'practical' argument about the economic necessity of khādī with which for more than two decades he had sought to persuade those who did not share his moral presuppositions. Now he was reasserting the primacy of the moral objectives. In practical terms, the existing khādī programme had probably succeeded in providing some additional income to poor villagers. Many of his fellow workers were arguing that some 'decentralization' had also been achieved since cloth production was being carried out in village homes. But Gandhi was unwilling to accept this claim.

Even in Lancashire some cloth is made at home, not for the use of the home but for the use of the masters. It would be outrageous to call this decentralization. So also in Japan everything is made at home; but it is not for the use of the home; it is all for the Government which has centralized the whole business ... I would certainly not call this decentralization.[126]

What Gandhi suggested now was a complete change in the modus operandi of the khādī programme. An attempt should be made immediately to stop the spinning of yarn for sale. Instead khādī workers should persuade and educate people to spin for their own use. Villagers should not be encouraged to produce yarn on payment of wages and to use that income to buy mill-made cloth. It was this dependence of the small producer on the market which the khādī programme must attempt to break. The present terms of exchange between town and country must be reversed.[127] Now every village should produce the entire yarn needed to meet its cloth requirements and khādī should be put 'beyond commercial competition'.[128] Only in this way would it be possible to put an end to the growing inequality among the mass of the people, a process in which only the few who were lucky enough to find employment in industry had a chance to survive and the rest were doomed to starvation.[129] To make khādī the instrument for attaining *pūrṇa svarāj* (complete independence), it would have to be extricated from the cycle of money exchange; the only currency which could be permitted in the buying and selling of khādī was yarn.[130]

When Srikrishnadas Jaju, Secretary of the AISA, pointed out that this would mean that 300,000 spinners who were now in contact with the khādī organizations would lose their additional income and that probably not more than 30,000 could be persuaded to spin for self-sufficiency in cloth, Gandhi admitted that this might be the case at first, but 'these thirty thousand would later grow into three crores. Be it as it may, I at least will not be guilty of betraying the cause.'[131]

Even if Gandhi was able to convince his associates in khādī work that this was the right thing to do in principle, not many were sure that it was a practical or even a judicious step. The entire organizational structure of the khādī programme would be disrupted, and few believed that large numbers of rural people could be persuaded to spin all the yarn required for their own clothes. As a result, the khādī stores in the cities which were doing very well would have to close down. But Gandhi was insistent: 'Close them down', he said, 'We cannot maintain khadi bhandars [stores] to sell khadi. You will say that if khadi bhandars in the city close down we shall have to sell khadi in the villages and that khadi cannot sell in the villages as it can in the cities. I agree that khadi cannot sell in the villages and it should not. Khadi is not to be sold in the villages, it is to be worn there. It is to be spun and worn ...'[132] When his colleagues pointed out that there were not enough workers in the khādī programme who had the ability to do the new work being demanded of them, Gandhi replied: 'If that is our attitude there can be no swaraj through non-violence ... I would then go my own way even if I have to work all alone ... It is quite possible that people may not follow us ... We should then renounce the tall claim we have made ... Without hesitation, without flattering ourselves we must declare that we are weak like everybody else and that we are in no way better.'[133]

Why did Gandhi decide to demand so insistently that this drastic change be brought about in a programme built up with such care and hard work over so many years? The answer lay in the very nature of the historical conjuncture which the nationalist movement in India had reached, a conjuncture of which the predominant characteristic was a general anticipation of power. The Congress state leadership was clearly preparing to take up the reins of national power; its main concerns now were to formulate in concrete terms the economic and political details of a programme of 'national development'. The people too had anticipated a collapse of the established order and had set up during the revolt of 1942–3 a large number of localized centres of rebel authority, of varying sizes and duration, in forms characteristic of mass insurgency. Gandhi was also anticipating a transition of power, but he could not approve either the plans of development which his erstwhile Congress colleagues were chalking out in order to build a modern industrial nation or the forms of insurgent violence, disorderly and innately hateful, which was the basis of armed rebellion. In his determined, even frenetic, insistence on commencing a new programme of reconstruction aiming at an economy of self-sufficient small producers not having to enter into large-scale commodity exchange or sale of labour, Gandhi was emphasizing the historical urgency of resuming his original task, the task he had formulated in *Hind Swaraj*. The transition of power would create new possibilities. The national state leadership might decide, as Gandhi dearly wished but could not entirely believe, to abdicate its coercive authority in the field of social development and leave it to popular agencies consisting of trained and committed volunteers to carry out the work of economic reconstruction. In that case, the task of setting up those agencies and training the constructive workers would have to be taken up right away. On the other hand, the national state might decide to follow the path begun in the period of British rule, in which case the struggle would have to go on, in opposition to the state. In his discussions with khādī activists in 1944, Gandhi virtually put the problem in so many words:

We may be expected to clothe the whole country with khadi after getting political power. Should we not therefore make such an arrangement from today so that we may be able to make the country self-sufficient in clothing in case the future government of free India were to provide the requisite facilities to the A.I.S.A. and ask it, as an expert body, to do this task? But if the government of the day were to close all its mills, and to charge us with this responsibility, we are apt to fail as things are today.[134]

On the other hand, if the state did not provide this opportunity, then the battle for khādī, a means for obtaining true svarāj, must be carried out in opposition to it.

To be an instrument of swaraj, naturally [the spinning-wheel] must not flourish under Government or any other patronage. It must flourish, if need be, even in spite of the resistance from Government or the capitalist who is interested in his spinning and weaving mills. The spinning-wheel represents the millions in the villages as against the classes represented by the mill-owners and the like.[135]

Gandhi, in other words, now fully anticipated the possibility of manoeuvre. The historic battle for freedom had reached a stage where 'political swaraj' was within the reach of a nationalist leadership. It was possible that this could form a new basis for the struggle for 'real swaraj', if the political leadership was prepared to participate in the struggle. It was also possible that the state leadership would not cooperate with any degree of sincerity, in which case 'political swaraj' would itself become a major impediment in the way towards 'real swaraj' and the manoeuvre would have been accomplished. In either case, Gandhism was now called upon to resume its original quest and to clearly mark its differences with what it regarded as the narrow 'political' objectives of nationalism.

The new khādī programme was to be the spearhead of this struggle which would gradually bring within its fold a more extended plan of rural economic reconstruction encompassing the whole range of village artisanal production, animal husbandry, and basic education.[136] The object was a 'decentralization' of power in society. The very nature of industrial production, required a centralization of power in the hands of the state so that the overall conditions within which a national economy functioned could be controlled. Decentralization, on the other hand, would ideally mean that each individual producer would be entirely self-sufficient in the matter of providing his essential needs; with regard to non-essentials which too were a part of social life he would cooperate with others, not as an exchanger of commodities but in the way in which members of a family help one another.[137]

The crucial social unit in this scheme of decentralization was the village which would be self-sufficient not merely in economic matters but also in ruling and defending itself:

Independence must begin at the bottom. Thus, every village will be a republic or *panchayat* having full powers. It follows, therefore, that every village has to be self-sustained and capable of managing its affairs even to the extent of defending itself against the whole world. It will be trained and prepared to perish in the attempt to defend itself against any onslaught from without.[138]

Within the village, each individual will try to be as self-sufficient as possible and will accept cooperation from others only to the extent that it is free and voluntary, not in the false sense in which commodity exchange is described as free but in the full moral sense of collective cooperation.

Beyond the unit of the self-sufficient village, society would be organized in the form of expanding circles—a group of villages, the taluka, the district, the province, and so on, each self-reliant in its own terms, no unit having to depend on a larger unit or dominate a smaller one.[139] Towns will not disappear completely, but only a small surplus, much smaller than at present, will go out of the villages[140] and the 700,000 villages of India will dominate 'the centre with its few towns'.[141]

In this structure composed of innumerable villages, there will be ever-widening, never-ascending circles. Life will not be a pyramid with the apex sustained by the bottom. But it will be an oceanic circle ... the outermost circumference will not wield power to crush the inner circle but will give strength to all within and derive its own strength from it.[142]

Of course, this was an ideal construction, a 'picture', but, as Gandhi put it using his favourite analogy, 'like Euclid's point ... it had an imperishable value ... We must have a proper picture of what we want, before we can have something approaching it.'[143] He acknowledged that in conceiving of this system of self-sufficient village republics, he was thinking of the ancient Indian village system as described by Henry Maine.[144] 'The towns were then subservient to the villages. They were emporia for the surplus village products and beautiful manufactures.' But this was only 'the skeleton of my picture'. The ancient village system had many grave defects, most notably that of caste and probably also of the despotism of the state, and these could have no place in the ideal structure of society.[145]

But how would the struggle be carried out in leading society to the path towards this ideal state? The period of colonial rule had resulted in the entrenchment on an unprecedented scale of the forces of corruption and violence deep within the foundations of Indian society. And now after the strength of popular resistance against colonialism had been aroused and mobilized, it was tending to give birth to a new political order which, far from seeking to eliminate those entrenched forces, was building itself on the same bases. How were these overpowering forces to be resisted? Who will resist?

Gandhism's answer, as we have seen, was a moral one. The ideal must be pursued, even if it was a quest that could never end, or end only in death. Those who were convinced of the truth of the ideal must pursue it, alone if necessary. The success of the struggle depended not just crucially but entirely on the selflessness, courage, and moral will of the leaders of the people. Firm in its adherence to the principle of a truthful political practice, the Gandhian ideology asserted to the very end its faith in a moral theory of mediation. If the unswerving moral practice of a few did not appear to produce quick results in the broader arena of politics, that was no reason for giving up the quest. Echoing Tolstoy, Gandhi would say, 'History provides us with a whole series of miracles of masses of people being converted to a particular view in the twinkling of an eye.'[146]

But the theory of mediation remained an abstract theory. The success of mediation depended entirely on the morality of the mediator, not on the way his programme could be brought into conformity with a concrete set of collective ethical norms which an identifiable social force within the nation might be expected to hold. Explaining his idea of the *samagra grāmsevak*, the ideal constructive worker, Gandhi said:

He will so win over the village that they will seek and follow his advice. Supposing I go and settle down in a village with a *ghani* (village oil-press), I won't be an ordinary *ghanchi* (oil-presser) earning 15–20 rupees a month. I will be a Mahatma *ghanchi*. I have used the word Mahatma in fun but what I mean to say is that as *ghanchi* I will become a model for the villagers to follow. I will be a *ghanchi* who knows the Gita and the Koran. I will be learned enough to teach their children ... Real strength lies in knowledge. True knowledge gives a moral standing and moral strength. Everyone seeks the advice of such a man.[147]

The people, then, would *follow* the mediator because of his moral authority, which would be a consequence of his knowledge, which in turn would be obtained as a result of his unflinching moral practice. If the people were unwilling to listen to him, it would be because he had failed to attain the moral standing required of him. Seeking to launch its final battle for Utopia, the only concrete means of mediation which Gandhism could suggest was the *individual* moral will of the mediator.

When the critics laugh at [the constructive programme], what they mean is that forty crores of people will never co-operate in the effort to fulfil the programme. No doubt, there is considerable truth in the scoff. My answer is, it is still worth the attempt. Given an indomitable will on the part of a band of earnest workers, the programme is as workable as any other and more so than most. Anyway, I have no substitute for it, if it is to be based on non-violence.[148]

The inadequacy of the theory as a *political* theory of mediation soon became obvious. For instance, in 1946 when T. Prakasam's government in Madras decided that in order to promote khādī it would not permit the setting up of any new cotton mills or the expansion of existing ones, industrial interests were not unexpectedly alarmed. Responding to their vociferous criticism of Prakasam, Gandhi wrote:

It is hardly an honourable pastime to dismiss from consideration honest servants of the nation by dubbing them idealists, dreamers, fanatics and faddists.

Let not capitalists and other entrenched personages range themselves against the poor villagers and prevent them from bettering their lot by dignified labour ...

Let it be remembered that the existing Madras mills will not be touched at present. That the whole mill industry will be affected if the scheme spreads like wildfire, as I expect some day such a thing must, goes without saying. Let not the largest capitalist rue the day when and if it comes.

The only question then worth considering is whether the Madras Government are honest and competent. If they are not, everything will go wrong. If they are, the scheme must be blessed by all and must succeed.[149]

Yet mere honesty and competence could hardly ensure that such a scheme would be 'blessed by all'. There was decidedly a question of overcoming a serious political opposition. Here to attribute the likely failure of the scheme to the lack of honesty and competence of the government was to evade the fact that the scheme was not backed by a political programme which either anticipated the opposition or suggested the means of overcoming it.

In fact, whenever the contradiction between the political implications of modern industry and khādī was directly posed, as it now was with respect to the policies to be followed by the national state, the Gandhian ideology could not easily provide a political answer. It could not admit that capitalists must be coerced into surrendering their interests. Consequently, while asserting the urgency of the new khādī programme, Gandhi would immediately say: 'At the same time I believe that some key industries are necessary. I do not believe in armchair or armed socialism.'[150] On the other hand, asked how to explain how the competition between industrial manufactures and khādī was to be avoided, Gandhi's answer was that 'mill-cloth should not sell side by side with khadi. Our mills may export their manufactures.'[151] But this clearly violated a fundamental Gandhian premise about the need to eliminate competition and dependence between nations. Gandhism had no answer.

The same problem appeared when the question of suggesting a concrete structure of self-government for the village arose. Despite his fundamental disbelief in the institutions of representative government, Gandhi suggested that election by secret ballot was perhaps the only practicable step. Yet the dangers were obvious: 'While exercising centralized power over the country, the British Government has polluted the atmosphere in the villages. The petty village officials have become masters instead of being servants. So great care has to be taken to ensure that these gangster elements do not get into the panchayats.' But how was this to be ensured if they could by force or trickery elicit the required electoral support? 'They should be debarred.' How, except by a contrary coercive force? 'They should themselves keep out' was the final unconvincing reply.[152] If that was possible, the problem of power would not exist; to insist on this reply was to wish away the political problem.

Beginning its journey from the utopianism of *Hind Swaraj*, and yet picking up on the way the ideological baggage of a nationalist politics,

Gandhism succeeded in opening up the historical possibility by which the largest popular element of the nation—the peasantry—could be appropriated within the evolving political forms of the new Indian state. While it was doubtless the close correspondence of the moral conception of Gandhi's Rāmrājya with the demands and forms of political justice in the contemporary peasant–communal consciousness which was one of the ideological conditions which made it possible for those demands to be transformed into 'the message of the Mahatma', the historical consequence of the Gandhian politics of non-violence was, in fact, to give to this process of appropriation its moral justification and its own distinctive ideological form. While it was the Gandhian intervention in elite-nationalist politics in India which established for the first time that an authentic national movement could only be built upon the organized support of the whole of the peasantry, the working out of the politics of non-violence also made it abundantly clear that the object of the political mobilization of the peasantry was not at all what Gandhi claimed on its behalf, 'to train the masses in self-consciousness and attainment of power'. Rather the peasantry were meant to become willing participants in a struggle wholly conceived and directed *by others*. Champaran, Kheda, Bardoli, Borsad—those were the model peasant movements, specific, local, conducted on issues that were well within 'their own personal and felt grievances'. This, for instance, was the specific ground on which Bardoli was commended as a model movement:

The people of Bardoli could not secure justice so long as they were afraid of being punished by the Government ... They freed themselves from its fear by surrendering their hearts to their Sardar.

From this we find that the people require neither physical nor intellectual strength to secure their own freedom; moral courage is all that is needed. This latter is dependent on faith. In this case, they were required to have faith in their Sardar, and such faith cannot be artificially generated. They found in the Sardar a worthy object of such faith and like a magnet he drew the hearts of the people to himself ... This is not to say that the people had accepted non-violence as a principle or that they did not harbour anger even in their minds. But they understood the practical advantage of non-violence, understood their own interest, controlled their anger and, instead of retaliating in a violent manner, suffered the hardships inflicted on them.[153]

While the national organization of the dominant classes could proceed to consolidate itself within the institutional structure of the new Indian state, *'kisans* and labour' were never to be organized 'on an all-India basis'.[154] Thus, forced to mark its differences with a nationalist state ideology. Gandhism could only assert the superiority of its moral claim; it could not find the ideological means to turn that morality into an instrument of the *political* organization of the largest popular elements of the nation against the coercive structures of the state.

And so we get, in the historical effectivity of Gandhism as a whole, the conception of a national framework of politics in which the peasants are mobilized but do not participate, of a nation of which they are a part, but a national state from which they are for ever distanced. How this possibility, which emerged from the very tensions within Gandhism, was identified by the nationalist analytic of a mature bourgeois ideology, and the Gandhian intervention in Indian politics turned into the moment of manoeuvre in the 'passive revolution of capital', are questions we will have to discuss. But it will remain a task of modern Indian historiography to explain the historical process, in its specific regional and organizational forms, by which these political possibilities inherent in the Gandhian ideology became the ideological weapons in the hands of the Indian bourgeoisie in its attempt to create a new state structure. The 'message of the Mahatma' meant different things to different people. As recent researches are beginning to show,[155] what it meant to peasants or tribals was completely different from the way it was interpreted by the literati. Operating in a process of class struggle in which the dominance of the bourgeoisie was constantly under challenge and its moral leadership for ever fragmented, the great historical achievement of the nationalist state leadership in India was to reconcile the ambiguities of the Gandhian ideology within a single differentiated political structure, to appropriate all its meanings in the body of the same discourse.

Yet the logic of Utopia could be irreconcilably ambiguous. Thomas More has been read as the author of a text that laid the moral foundations for the political demands of a rising, but still far from victorious, bourgeoisie. He has also been regarded as the progenitor of Utopian socialism, that inchoate articulation of the spirit of resistance of the early proletariat in Europe.[156] It is not surprising, therefore, that in the unresolved class struggles within the social formation of contemporary India, oppositional movements can still claim their moral legitimacy from the message of Mahatma.

NOTES AND REFERENCES

1.   Romain Rolland, *Mahatma Gandhi: A Study in Indian Nationalism*, L.V. Ramaswami Aiyar (trs), Madras: S. Ganesan, 1923, p. 30.

2.   Raghavan N. Iyer, *The Moral and Political Thought of Mahatma Gandhi*, New York: Oxford University Press, 1973, p. 24.

3.   *Hind Swaraj* in *The Collected Works of Mahatma Gandhi*, New Delhi: Publications Division, 1958– 1991 [hereafter *CW*], Vol. 10, p. 18.

4.   *Hind Swaraj*, *CW*, Vol. 10, pp. 22–3.

5.   Ibid., p. 57.

6.   Ibid., p. 37.

7.   Ibid., p. 60.

8.   Discussion with Maurice Frydman, 25 August 1936, *CW*, Vol. 63, p. 241.

9.   *Hind Swaraj*, *CW*, Vol. 10. p. 23.

10. Discussion with Maurice Frydman, *CW*, Vol. 63. p. 241.

11. Interview to Francis G. Hickman, 17 September 1940, *CW*, Vol. 73, pp. 29–30.

12. 'Is Khadi Economically Sound?', *CW*, Vol. 63, pp. 77–8.

13. 'Why Not Labour-Saving Devices', *CW*, Vol. 59, p. 413.

14. 'Village Industries', *CW*, Vol. 59, p. 356

15. 'Its Meaning', *CW*, Vol. 60, pp. 54–5.

16. 'New Life for Khadi', *CW*, Vol. 59, pp. 205–6.

17. *Hind Swaraj*, *CW*, Vol. 10, pp. 17–18.

18. Ibid., p. 18.

19. Ibid., p. 33.

20. Letter to David B. Hart, 21 September 1934, *CW*, Vol. 59, p. 45.

21. 'Enlightened Anarchy: A Political Ideal', *CW*, Vol. 68, p. 265.

22. For example, *CW*, Vol. 35, pp. 489–90; *CW*, Vol. 45, pp. 328–9.

23. For example, *CW*, Vol. 59, pp. 61–7: *CW*, Vol. 50, pp. 226–7.

24. *Hind Swaraj*, *CW*, Vol. 10, p. 36.

25. 'Duty of Bread Labour', *CW*, Vol. 61, p. 212.

26. Discussion with Gujarat Vidyapith Teachers, *CW*, Vol. 58, p. 306.

27. *Hind Swaraj*. *CW*, Vol. 10, p. 35.

28. 'It is only a critique of the "modern philosophy of life"; it is called "Western" only because it originated in the West'. *CW*, Vol. 57, p. 498.

29. *Hind Swaraj*, *CW*, Vol. 10, p. 40.

30. Ibid., p. 48.

31. Mahadev Desai, *The Gospel of Selfless Action or the Gita According to Gandhi*, Ahmedabad: Navajivan, 1946, p. 6.

32. Ibid., pp. 123–4.

33. 'Teaching of Hinduism', *CW*, Vol. 63, p. 339.

34. 'Dr Ambedkar's Indictment-II', *CW*, Vol. 63, p. 153.

35. 'The Law of Our Being', *CW*. Vol. 63, pp. 319–20.

36. 'Dr Ambedkar's Indictment-II', *CW*, Vol. 63, p. 153.

37. 'Caste Has to Go', *CW*, Vol. 62, p. 121.

38. 'Woman in the Smritis', *CW*, Vol. 64, p. 85.

39. Letter to Ranchhodlal Patwari, 9 September 1918, *CW*, Vol. 15, p. 45. Or, again.

   Khan Abdul Ghaffar Khan derives his belief in non-violence from the Koran, and the Bishop of London derives his belief in violence from the Bible. I derive my belief in non-violence in it. But if the worst came to the worst and if I came to the conclusion that the Koran teaches violence. I would still reject violence, but I would not therefore say that the Bible is superior to the Koran or that Mahomed is inferior to Jesus. It is not my function to judge Mahomed and Jesus. It is enough that my non-violence is independent of the sanction of scriptures.

   Interview with Dr Crane, *CW*, Vol. 64, p. 399.

40. Speech at Gandhi Seva Sangh Meeting, 28 March 1938, *CW*, Vol. 66, p. 445.

41. For Tagore's statement, see Appendix I, *CW*, Vol. 57, pp. 503–4.

42. To Vallabhbhai Patel he wrote: 'You must have read the Poet's attack. I am replying to it in *Harijan*. He of course made amends afterwards. He gets excited and writes, and then corrects himself. This is what he does every time.' Letter to Vallabhbhai Patel, 13 February 1934, *CW*, Vol. 57, p. 155.

43. 'Bihar and Untouchability', *CW*, Vol. 57, p. 87.

44. 'Superstition v. Faith', *CW*, Vol. 57, pp. 164–5.

45. Ibid., p. 165.

46. 'Why Only Bihar?', *CW*, Vol. 57, p. 392.

47. Speech at Reception by Merchants, Madura, 26 January 1934, *CW*, Vol. 57, p. 51.

48. 'Superstition v. Faith', *CW*, Vol. 57, p. 165.

49. 'Ramanama to me is all-sufficing ... In the spiritual literature of the world, the *Ramayana* of Tulsidas takes a foremost place. It has charms that I miss in the *Mahabharata* and even in Valmiki's *Ramayana*.' *CW*, Vol. 58, p. 291. Also, 'Power of "Ramanama"', *CW*, Vol. 27, pp. 107–12.

50. Thanks to the historical researches of Boris Pavlovich Koz'min and Andrzej Walicki, our present understanding of the complexities of Russian Populism has made us aware of many of the polemical excesses of Bolshevik criticism of the Narodniks. But this has sharpened, rather than obscured, the central theoretical opposition between Leninism and Populism.

51. V.I. Lenin, *A Characterisation of Economic Romanticism* in *Collected Works*, Vol. 2, Moscow: Foreign Languages Publishing House, 1957, pp. 129–265, esp. p. 241.

52. Edward Carpenter, *Civilisation: Its Cause and Cure and Other Essays*, London: George Allen and Unwin, 1921; first edn, 1889, pp. 46–9.

53. John Ruskin, *Unto This Last*, London: W.B. Clive, 1931; first edn, 1862, p. 83.

54. R.G. Collingwood, *Ruskin's Philosophy*, Chichester, Sussex: Quentin Nelson, 1971; first edn, 1922, p. 20.

55. Ibid., p. 28.

56. V.I. Lenin, *What the 'Friends of the People' Are and How They Fight the Social-Democrats* in *Collected Works*, Vol. 1, pp. 129–332.

57. Andrzej Walicki, *The Controversy over Capitalism: Studies in the Social Philosophy of the Russian Populists*, Oxford: Clarendon Press, 1969, p. 66. Also, Walicki, *The Slavophile Controversy: History of a Conservative Utopia in Nineteenth Century Russian Thought*, trs. Hilda Andrews-Rusiecka, Oxford: Clarendon Press, 1975, p. 280.

58. Leo Tolstoy, *The Slavery of Our Times*, trs. Aylmer Maude, London: John Lawrence, 1972; first edn, 1900, p. 18.

59. Ibid., p. 21.

60. Ibid., p. 57.

61. Leo Tolstoy, 'The Kingdom of God is Within You' in *The Kingdom of God and Other Essays*, trs. Aylmer Maude, London: Oxford University Press, 1936; first edn, 1893, pp. 301–2.

62. For a study of this process, see Shahid Amin, 'Gandhi as Mahatma: Gorakhpur District, Eastern U.P., 1921–1922', in Ranajit Guha (ed.), *Subaltern Studies III*, Delhi: Oxford University Press, 1983, pp. 1–61.

63. Letter to Mirabehn, 20 April 1933, *CW*, Vol. 54, p. 456.

64. Letter to Mirabehn, 11 April 1933, *CW*, Vol. 54, p. 372.

65. *An Autobiography* in *CW*, Vol. 39, p. 4.

66. *Hind Swaraj*, *CW*, Vol. 10, p. 36.

67. *Autobiography*. *CW*, Vol. 39, p. 389.

68. 'Satyagraha — Not Passive Resistance', *CW*, Vol. 13, p. 523.

69. For an explanation of the concept of negative consciousness, see Ranajit Guha, *Elementary Aspects of Peasant Insurgency in Colonial India*, Delhi: Oxford University Press, 1983, pp. 18–76.

70. 'Satyagraha — Not Passive Resistance', *CW*, Vol. 13, p. 524.

71. Ibid., pp. 524–5.

72. Speech on Satyagraha Movement, Trichinopoly, 25 March 1919, *CW*, Vol. 15, p. 155.

73. Speech at Mass Meeting, Ahmedabad, 14 April 1919, *CW*, Vol. 15. p. 221.

74. Letter to Swami Shraddhanand, 17 April 1919, *CW*, Vol. 15, pp. 238–9.

75. 'The Duty of Satyagrahis', *CW*, Vol. 15, p. 436.

76. *Autobiography*, *CW*, Vol. 39, p. 374.

77. Evidence before the Disorders Inquiry Committee, *CW*, Vol. 16, p. 410.

78. Ibid., Vol. 16, p. 441.

79. Speech at Mass Meeting, Ahmedabad, 14 April 1919, *CW*. Vol. 15, pp. 221–2.

80. Evidence, *CW*, Vol. 16, pp. 391–2.

81. Alexander Herzen, often regarded as one of the progenitors of Russian Populism, wrote about the crowd: 'I looked with horror mixed with disgust at the continually moving, swarming crowd, foreseeing how it would rob me of half of my seat at the theatre and in the diligence, how it would dash like a wild beast into the railway carriages, how it would heat and pervade the air.' Quoted in Walicki, *The Controversy over Capitalism*, p. 11. Horror and disgust were the feelings which overwhelmed Gandhi too when he first encountered the Indian masses in a third class railway carriage. See *Autobiography*, *CW*, Vol. 39, p. 305.

82. 'Democracy v. Mobocracy', *CW*, Vol. 18, p. 242.

83. 'Some Illustrations', *CW*, Vol. 18, p. 275.

84. 'Meaning of the "Gita"', *CW*, Vol. 28, p. 317.

85. 'What Are Basic Assumptions?', *CW*, Vol. 67, p. 436. It is quite remarkable how frequently Gandhi uses the military metaphor when talking about the 'science of non-violence'.

86. Ibid., pp. 436–7.

87. Speech at AICC Meeting, Wardha, 15 January 1942, *CW*, vol 75, p. 220.

88. 'Cobwebs of Ignorance', *CW*, Vol. 30, pp. 450–1.

89. 'Answers to Questions', *CW*, Vol. 43, p. 41.

90. Ibid.

91. 'A Complex Problem', *CW*, Vol. 40, p. 364.

92. Letter to Labhshankar Mehta, 14 April 1926, *CW*, Vol. 30, p. 283.

93. Speech at Anand, 17 March 1930, *CW*, Vol. 43, p. 93.

94. Telegram to N.R. Malkani, 18 April 1930, *CW*, Vol. 43, p. 282.

95. 'Neither a Saint nor a Politician', *CW*, Vol. 17, p. 406.

96. Late in his life, Gandhi even seemed to suggest that the concept of *varṇāśrama* should also be dropped because it had acquired the connotation of differing privileges for different *varṇa*: ' ... in our present condition ... our dharma lies in becoming Ati-Shudras voluntarily'. Foreword to 'Varnavyavastha', *CW*, Vol. 80, p. 223.

97. 'Harijan v. Non-Harijan', *CW*, Vol. 58, pp. 80–1.

98. Speech at AICC Meeting, Patna, 19 May 1934, *CW*, Vol. 58, pp. 9–10.

99. Ibid., p. 11.

100. 'My Meaning of Office-Acceptance', *CW*, Vol. 66, p. 104.

101. 'Choice Before Congressmen', *CW*, Vol. 67, p. 306.

102. Interview to Nirmal Kumar Bose, 9 November 1934, *CW*, Vol. 59, p. 318.

103. 'Answers to Zamindars', *CW*, Vol. 58, p. 247.

104. 'Zamindars and Talukdars', *CW*, Vol. 42, pp. 239–40.

105. 'Discussion with Students', *CW*, Vol. 58, p. 219.

106. 'Answers to Zamindars', *CW*, Vol. 58, p. 248.

107. 'Divine Warning', *CW*, Vol. 22, pp. 426–7.

108. Speech at AISA Meeting, Sevagram, 24 March 1945, *CW*, Vol. 79, p. 297.

109. 'The Charkha Sangh and Politics', *CW*, Vol. 82, pp. 17–19.

110. Letter to Purnima Bannerjee, 1 January 1946, *CW*, Vol. 82, pp. 331–2. See also, Letter to Rameshwari Nehru, 15 January 1946, *CW*, Vol. 82, p. 424; and to Sucheta Kripalani, 19 January 1946, *CW*, Vol. 82, p. 440.

111. Letter to Shriman Narayan, 3 January 1946. *CW*, Vol. 82, p. 341.

112. Letter to Dada Dharmadhikari, 28 December 1945, *CW*, Vol. 82, pp. 290–1.

113. Letter to R.K.Patil, 1 January 1946, *CW*, Vol. 82, p. 322. See also, Letter to Shankarrao Deo, 1 January 1946. *CW*, Vol. 82, p. 323.

114. 'The Lure of Legislatures', *CW*, Vol. 83, pp. 95–6.

115. 'Ministers' Duty', *CW*, Vol. 84, pp. 44–5.

116. 'If I Were the Minister', *CW*, Vol. 85, pp. 210–12.

117. 'Independence', *CW*, Vol. 84, pp. 80–1.

118. 'Congress Ministries and Ahimsa', *CW*, Vol. 85, pp. 266–7.

119. Speech at Prayer Meeting, Bikram, 21 May 1947. *CW*, Vol. 87, p. 513.

120. Speech at Prayer Meeting, New Delhi, 1 April 1947. *CW*. Vol. 87, p. 187.

121. 'Congress Ministries and Ahimsa', *CW*, Vol. 85, p. 266.

122. Ibid. See also, 'Do Not Eliminate Truth and Nonviolence', *CW*, Vol. 85. pp. 351–2; and 'Answers to Questions', *CW*, Vol. 85, p. 364.

123. Speech at AISA Meeting, Sevagram, 1 September 1944. *CW*, Vol. 78, pp. 62–7.

124. Discussion with Srikrishnadas Jaju, 11 October 1944. *CW*, Vol. 78, p. 174.

125. Discussion with Srikrishnadas Jaju, 13 October 1944, *CW*, Vol. 78, pp. 192–3.

126. Ibid., p. 190.

127. 'Khadi in Towns'. *CW*, Vol. 84, pp. 438–9.

128. Speech at AISA Meeting, Sevagram, 24 March 1945, *CW*, Vol. 79, pp. 299–300.

129. 'Why Khadi for Yarn and Not for Money', *CW*, Vol. 81, pp. 56–7.

130. 'Yarn Donation', *CW*, Vol. 81, p. 137.

131. Discussion with Srikrishnadas Jaju, 13 October 1944, *CW*, Vol. 78, p. 194.

132. 'Why the Insistence on the Yarn Clause', *CW*, Vol. 82, pp. 122–3.

133. Discussion with Srikrishnadas Jaju, 13 October 1944, *CW*, Vol. 78, pp. 194–5.

134. Ibid., p. 190.

135. 'The Missing Link', *CW*, Vol. 81, p. 89.

136. 'Ministers' Duty'. *CW*, Vol. 84, p. 45.

137. 'Answers to Questions', *CW*, Vol. 81, p. 133, and Speech at Congress Workers' Conference, Sodepur, 6 January 1946, *CW*, Vol. 81, p. 369.

138. 'Independence', *CW*, Vol. 85, p. 32.

139. 'Decentralization', *CW*, Vol. 85, pp. 459–60.

140. Discussion with Shriman Narayan, 2 June 1945. *CW*, Vol. 80, p. 244.

141. Interview to P. Ramachandra Rao, before 19 June 1945. *CW*, Vol. 80, p. 353.

142. 'Independence', *CW*, Vol. 85, p. 33.

143. Ibid.

144. Henry Sumner Maine, *Ancient Law*, 1861; New York: Dutton, 1931.

145. Speech at Meeting of Deccan Princes, Poona, 28 July 1946, *CW*, Vol. 85, p. 79.

146. Discussion with Director of British Daily, before 28 October 1946. *CW*, Vol. 86, p. 50.

147. Answers to Questions at Constructive Workers' Conference, Madras, 29 January 1946, *CW*, Vol. 83, p. 46.

148. Foreword to 'Constructive Programme—Its Meaning and Place', *CW*, Vol. 82, p. 67.

149. 'Handspun v. Mill Cloth', *CW*, Vol. 85, pp. 472–4.

150. 'Alternative to Industrialism', *CW*, Vol. 85, p. 206.

151. Discussion at Hindustani Talimi Sangh Meeting, Patna, 22 April 1947. *CW*, Vol. 87, p. 330.

152. Talk with Village Representatives, Bir, 19 March 1947. *CW*, Vol. 87, pp. 121–2.

153. 'Government's Power v. People's Power', *CW*, Vol. 37, pp. 190–1.

154. 'Constructive Programme: Its Meaning and Place', *CW*, Vol. 75, pp. 159–60.

155. See, for example, Shahid Amin, 'Gandhi as Mahatma'.

156. Martin Fleisher, *Radical Reform and Political Persuasion in the Life and Writings of Thomas More*, Geneva: Librairie Droz, 1973; Karl Kautsky, *Thomas More and his Utopia*, trs. H.J. Stenning (1890), London: Lawrence and Wishart, 1979.

4

On the Promotion of Gandhian Studies at the University Level*

A.K. SARAN

The true aim of furthering the study of Gandhian ideas is to effect a metanoia: that is, to bring about a state of affairs in which more and more people are in their right minds.[1] Given this ultimate purpose, the study of Gandhi's thinking cannot be confined to Gandhi's works alone; it has to go further and deeper, endeavouring to reach the centre of Gandhi's thinking—the centre from which Gandhian thinking originates and to which it returns: the tradition in which it is rooted. Gandhian studies and education must, therefore, include a serious study of the Indian tradition and contemporary traditional thinkers like Coomaraswamy, Guenon, Weil, Dinesen, Marco Pallis, and Schuon. Gandhi's life and work has been the story of rediscovering for himself and his age a centre wholly beyond the modern Western civilization, indeed, beyond space and time, to which modern man could be firmly reoriented. This centre has usually been called the Primordial Tradition.

The Gandhian world view (and philosophy of life) is therefore a most radical one. And this makes it highly subversive to modern Western civilization as well as to non-Western contemporary societies, most of which are *de facto* its colonies or satellites.

Radical and thorough-going critiques of modern Western society and civilization and the search for 'alternative models' have been increasingly

*A.K. Saran. 'On the Promotion of Gandhian Studies at the University Level', *Gandhi Marg*, 7 October 1979, pp. 363–81.

fashionable—by now perhaps a bit commonplace. Gandhi's radical critique leading to a rejection of modern Western civilization in *Hind Swaraj* (1909) seems to belong in this line; it really goes far beyond the usual scope and purpose of all such critiques. Most contemporary critiques and even rejections of the West seek its renewal from within the framework of basic ideas constitutive of the modern age. They do not go beyond the pseudo-metaphysics on which the modern Western white civilization is founded. This is true of Roszak and Reich as well as Freire and Illich.[2] Gandhi's critique of the modern West is peripheral to his thinking: its real purpose is to prepare the ground for Gandhi's life-long striving to make it possible, once again, for man to participate in the transcendental centre. In *Hind Swaraj*, Gandhi is concerned with the destiny of man, not with the prospects of any given civilization. Hence its deeply explosive and subversive nature, hence also its radically positive and constructive stance. Once we grasp this firmly, it will be clear what the right context of Gandhian thinking is, and all efforts to relate it to the quest for an 'alternative model' will cease—hopefully once and for all. Gandhi was never concerned with models, his concern was with Truth to which he demanded absolute commitment.

Do we want to save and nourish the radical, deeply human and, in relation to the status quo, highly subversive spirit of Gandhian thinking? This is the crucial question. On the eve of India's Independence and at the inauguration of Free and Sovereign Republic of India, Nehru decided to repudiate Gandhian thinking and to accept Modern Western White Civilization: in other words, the civilization of our Imperial Masters. A quarter century later Indira Gandhi, in a sort of symbolic reaffirmation of this decision, thought it necessary to amend the Preamble to our Constitution, in order to describe the Indian Republic as secular—a concept which, after due consideration, the founding fathers had decided not to include formally in the Constitution. Today, however, the Janata Party has included Gandhism in its manifesto. A reference to Gandhian ideas is also included in the 1979 Draft National Policy on Education. Does it mean that India now realizes that it has to go back to the Gandhian way and has resolved to do so?

I wonder. For one thing, I am discouraged by the lacklustre manner in which the Gandhian way figures both in the manifesto and the National Policy on Education. Perhaps one need not attach too much importance to it. The deeper source of my anxiety is the fact that the ruling elite has yet to be effectively changed and there is reason to believe that this ruling elite is now disturbed by the rapid deterioration of the modern Western white civilization to which its destiny is indissolubly linked. As the situation further worsens, this elite, unable to love its fate, senses the truly subversive potential of Gandhian thinking and the tradition in which it is rooted, and naturally looks for ways and means of co-opting and containing Gandhian thinking—perhaps a panicky response but a most likely one.

This false support to Gandhian thinking is a most powerful force against it because it comes from the Establishment itself and the struggle against it is unusually difficult; for, it is embarrassing to fight against friends. This sort of false support constitutes, in fact, an almost irresistible internal temptation. Those who are concerned about nourishing and strengthening the Gandhian spirit in all its elemental force, have, therefore, to be ever vigilant to detect the danger of false support in its myriad forms, some subtle and others not so, but together constituting a formidable force.

One of the forms that this kind of promotional drive takes is the intellectual need many of us feel—sometimes explicit, often disguised—of making Gandhian thinking academically 'respectable'. This feeling is often expressed in the form of a demand made on Gandhian scholars to 'modernise' Gandhian thought and make it 'social-scientific'. This has intimate, though oblique, connection with the need to redeem the increasing loss of responsibility that the modern Western thought has been suffering. The threat of the 'respectability' (and 'scientific') syndrome to the Gandhian way can hardly be exaggerated: it has a great potential for far-reaching mischief and it is by no means easy to free oneself from forms of thinking that imply such pathological concerns.

However, if we want to nourish and strengthen Gandhian thinking (and the Gandhian way) as a radical and living human force, if we want to foster its growth as a new élan, the most sophisticated danger from which it has to be preserved is—the university. A sure, smooth, and 'non-violent' way to kill the spirit of Gandhian thinking is to introduce it into university syllabi. If I am serious about Gandhian thinking, I would save it from the deadly hands of our universities: maybe there are some exceptions, but most of our universities are dead and deadly places—stricken areas from which all living things have to be kept at a safe distance. I would therefore strongly urge that all efforts of the Establishment to introduce Gandhian thinking into university teaching and research should be stoutly opposed. Once Gandhian thinking becomes part of the university teaching and research, it is sure to wither away: the mighty, indomitable forces of co-option and suction will slowly and steadily maim and undermine the spirit, the meaning, and the potential élan of the Gandhian way.

I started by saying, one, that Gandhian thinking represents a world view rooted in a centre wholly outside the modern Western civilization (and beyond space and time); and, two, that the aim of fostering and strengthening Gandhian thinking and studies was to work for a metanoia at all levels. If this is accepted, it would not be difficult to see why and how the impact of the university would be fatal to Gandhian thinking. There are, I think, three ways of introducing Gandhian thought into university syllabi: (a) It may be introduced as an additional course in different academic subjects like political science, economics, sociology, philosophy, history, etc. A variant of this approach may be to introduce the Gandhian perspective as part of most of the existing courses in philosophy and the social sciences; (b) Gandhian thought may be established in the universities by way of a new and independent department under the name of Gandhian Studies; and (c) research chairs without a department may be endowed in all or selected universities. There could be only one such chair in a university: or several, each attached to a recognized academic discipline.

Now, to make Gandhian thought an additional course in different disciplines is necessarily to introduce Gandhian thinking in a fragmented and hence a seriously misleading, if not wholly distorted, form. Inevitably, it will gradually be reduced to one of the 'alternatives', one of the 'models', or 'perspectives' alongside those of the modern Western thought-system. The transcendent eccentricity of Gandhian thinking in relation to the centre of modern Western mind will thus be completely, even if implicitly, lost: Gandhi would be domesticated; and this may well be the most effective way to destroy the radical, life-giving spirit of Gandhian thinking. The principal either/or that Gandhi relentlessly presents would thus be obliterated.

It is important to see clearly the more general hermeneutic principle involved here: no total way of thinking and life can be understood in terms of a set of answers to questions that, in principle, belong to another world view, another system of thought. But in this mode of introducing Gandhian thinking into academic syllabi, it is inevitable that it would be expected to answer questions generated from the modern Western framework of thought. This creates a dilemma: to succeed in meeting this expectation would mean damaging the form and violating the spirit of Gandhian thinking; to fail would mean exposing it as seriously inadequate on grounds that would, in reality, be logically irrelevant. No, Gandhian thinking cannot be reduced to an alternative 'growth and development model' besides, say the Keynesian or the Marxian; it is not, and ought never to be another type of Utopia besides so many others, a new kind of scenario or image of society in a futurologistic context; it is not a new technique of social resistance or cultural revolution; nor another futuristic system of social engineering. But let Gandhian thinking be included in university syllabi, and nothing would save it from these fatal reductions and distortions.

The situation will not be substantially different if Gandhian thinking comes to the universities as an independent discipline. Let us see what possibilities in general the professor of Gandhian Studies has before him for going about his task. He could approach Gandhian thinking as a historian of thought, in which case he would be professing exclusively Gandhian thought not Gandhian thinking or the Gandhian way. Let us not forget the praxiological context of the present urge to promote Gandhian studies: it is, therefore, of vital importance to see that all our approaches and perspectives foster unity of theory and practice, and a dominance of history of ideas approach is not conducive to this. It is clear, of course, that the historical and the 'history of ideas' approaches are necessary and illuminating for the study of Gandhian thinking in other contexts. I have myself suggested this earlier. The point is that Gandhian thinking must not be *reduced* to the history of Gandhian thought, or to a certain type of response to a historical situation.

The other approach is that of theory. In the university situation, Gandhian studies would come to be organized along the lines of existing classification and differentiation of academic disciplines: Gandhian Economics, Gandhian Politics, Gandhian Sociology, and so on. Thus the universal and integral nature of Gandhian thinking would be systematically undermined. In fact, there would start moves on the part of the established disciplines to devalue Gandhian studies. This by itself need not be given much importance. However, the fact that in a university setting Gandhian Studies would, almost inevitably, get organized along the lines of existing disciplinary differentiations, points to a fundamental problem at the root of all modern education. The modern Western educational system is incapable of teaching a world view. (It should, in fact, be illuminating to ask whether a world view can at all be taught formally.[3]) This indeed has been the meaning of the secularization of education: its separation and independence from the Church and eventually a repudiation of theology and metaphysics. The disorientation and anomie implicit in this 'emancipation' and secularization of all knowledge and education are now too patent to be ignored by the Western thinkers: the problem of unity of knowledge and an integrated approach to teaching and research is only one of the forms in which the core incapacity of modern education has come to be acknowledged now, even if indirectly.

The problem of the unity of knowledge can no longer be ignored particularly when the modern Western civilization is passing through a crisis. Its solution must, however, elude us; for, the idea of unity of knowledge belongs to a non-modern thought-world grounded in hierarchy and creationism while modern thought is built on continuum, evolutionism, and autonomy. Any genuine movement towards unity of knowledge would therefore involve going wholly beyond the modern thought-system.

This situation suggests that it is not a question of two different or conflicting world views. The crucial question is whether it be possible to do away with the very idea of a world view. True, one often comes across the view that modernity is the story of the supplanting of 'pre-scientific' and 'unscientific' religio-mythological world views by one that is created by (modern) science. The matter is certainly far more complicated. Modern science, it is admitted on all hands, excludes a great deal of human life. It does not, in fact, investigate man, nor his God and gods; it is concerned only with Nature: the earth and the sky (and the heavenly bodies). It deliberately departs from a tradition in which man and his universe are investigated together, indeed, in their togetherness. Being concerned with only a part of human life and with certain dimensions of the physical universe, science cannot take upon itself the task of formulating a world view. The illusion of a scientific world view arises from the fact that by its theory of Nature, science can throw serious doubts on the tenability of a world view whose view of nature conflicts with that of science: it can thus lead to the decay and abandonment of a world view; but, by itself, science cannot create a new one, since a part cannot be a substitute for a whole. This inherent incapacity of science with regard to the question of world view has another source in a seemingly methodological issue, but one that, in fact, goes to the root of the matter; namely, the nature and status of theory. The great seventeenth-century schism between Church and science over the heliocentric theory was neither a conflict between Church and science, nor a dispute over the question of truth. The Church, in fact, supported in many important ways Canon Copernicus. Pope Urban VIII, who was a good friend of Galileo, did his best to support the heliocentric view and save Galileo from a trial; even after it he was not really punished. The real issue was whether the heliocentric theory represented the demonstrated truth of the matter or a new hypothesis to save the phenomena. The Church maintained the geocentric view only as a hypothesis and it was prepared to tolerate the heliocentric view as a new hypothesis, going so far as to grant that it may even be superior to the geocentric one. It was this view of theory-as-hypothesis that

Galileo rejected and wanted to resist; and this was the only point on which the Church was not prepared to compromise.[4] It is, perhaps, paradoxically, a hypothetical view of truths, that is, the stuff of which traditional world views are made. With its insistence on the exclusive and demonstrated nature of the truth of a theory, science cannot lend itself to the formation of a new world view.[5]

All modern education is based on the postulate that nothing that is not 'Scientifically' true (or 'warranted') can have any place in the educational programme except as a history of (a) ignorance and folly and (b) of survivals. (I do not know, why this exception has been made or must be made; perhaps it is some kind of a huge hangover from our 'pre-scientific' past.) A thought-system, a way of thinking and life, that is meaningful only in the context of a given world view, cannot, therefore, be taught in *any* 'modern' educational system.[6]

Thus, it is clear that Gandhian studies cannot be organized as a part of established disciplines in the Indian universities because Gandhian thinking presupposes a world view, is centrally concerned with the destiny of Man, and culminates in a total philosophy and a way of life. It cannot be introduced as an independent discipline because of the built-in incapacity of a modern university to cope with a world view as a teaching programme. In handing over Gandhian thinking to the universities we will be verily striking the devil's bargain, and a pretty poor one: Gandhian thinking may gain a certain prestige and status of doubtful value and may 'reach' the youth but at the cost of its soul, of its radical, revolutionary potential. This is the crucial point. The details—Gandhian thinking as part of existing courses, a departmental chair, or unattached chairs for Gandhian studies—do not affect the main argument. The built-in incapacities of the modern educational systems cannot be overcome from within; in any case, not by means of methodological and functional devices, however clever, or powerful, or both.

I began by saying that the true aim of furthering Gandhian thinking was to help bring about a metanoia, that is, more and more people coming to be in their right mind. In other words, our progress towards the Gandhian way or the normal society requires, first, a deconditioning of our present mentality, or our whole consciousness; and then its reconditioning or regeneration. I have used the usual terminology; however, I have not gone so far as to talk of programming and de-programming which, in fact, is the current usage. But I do want to point out that without a belief in the infra-human anthropology of modern Western thought-systems, the idioms of 'conditioning' and the more advanced one of 'programming' would not be possible at all. Gandhian thinking is a radical repudiation of all modernistic anthropology and sociology. The praxiological aim of education in Gandhian thinking is repentance (not deconditioning) and recollection (not reconditioning). Yes, I repeat: repentance and recollection: concepts which have no place at all in the modern system of education.[7] Except in some rare course in the History of Ideas, we will not find them in our university syllabi. Educating for the Gandhian way is oriented to metanoia: the total change of our mentality, a transformation of our consciousness. This aim of education in Gandhian thinking will most certainly be defeated, almost irreversibly, if Gandhian thinking were to be promoted through the universities. No, let us save Gandhi from the necrophilic charms of the Indian universities—at any cost.

So far it has been assumed that in the plans for promoting Gandhian thinking through regular university education, faculties of arts, humanities, and social sciences alone will be involved. There is, of course, good reason for this assumption, but should we accept such a circumscribed scope? What about students of commerce, business management, law, engineering, medicine? What about students of natural and exact sciences? If the idea is to transform our consciousness and lay the foundations of a Gandhian or normal society, a sane, humane civilization, then such a fragmented—almost antithetically dichotomous—approach would be seriously wrong. But how to integrate Gandhian thinking in terms of courses with the teaching and training programmes in science and various professional schools? It would be frustrating to examine here putative solutions to this problem, for there can be no genuine solution unless the root problem of science and world view is satisfactorily resolved. If Gandhian studies do not find an integral place in science and professional education but are included in social sciences and humanities schools only, we would be promoting schizophrenic forces; but that may not be the end of the matter. Science or professional education, in so far as it becomes effective in the student's life, will be a powerful corrosive influence on the Gandhian world view, for, as has just been shown, science has a great destructive power. In other words, education in (modern) science and technology and education in Gandhian thinking can co-exist only under one condition: namely, that neither really touches the student's life. It follows that if there is science education that touches the student at the deeper levels of his life, then education in Gandhian thinking, in fact, any un-scientific teaching programme will have to be altogether scrapped. Or the whole concept and nature of modern science would have to undergo radical transformation.[8]

I now turn to the promotion of Gandhian thinking at the research level. There is a large body of research and scholarly work on Gandhi and Gandhian thought. The research level is greatly important and there exists both a vital need and plenty of scope for further research. There are, of course, different kinds and levels of research and let them all flourish. There is no need to discourage any kind—certainly not directly. At the present juncture and in view of the aim of Gandhian thinking here accepted, what is needed is intellectual, creative, and holistic work in Gandhian thinking.

By intellectual research is meant work in which the whole man is involved: a man to whom the dichotomy of man and 'scientist'/ 'scholar' would be nonsense, who would not have one person as a man and another, even a contradictory one, as a 'scholar' or 'scientist'.

For the true intellectual, all thinking, scholarship, scientific activity is for the sake of truth by which he can live and not for the sake of thought, scholarship, knowledge, or science: for him scholarship-and-thinking is a vocation (*svadharma*), not merely a 'job'.

Creative and holistic research and thinking are the main supports of intellectual work. Creation, strictly speaking, is *ex nihilo*, and hence a divine attribute. At the human level, creativity refers to modes of transformation and repossession of the given. Human creativity is thus not a matter of novelty but of originality in the sense of going to the roots. Just as man gets food from sources outside his organic system, and it nourishes him only when it is made consubstantial with his body by the process of physiological assimilation, so also the creative and nourishing power of scholarly and intellectual work arises from the process of making an idea one's own through assimilation;[9] making an idea one's own does not mean that one absolutely originates it and claims proprietary rights over it. There can be no proprietary rights in ideas (and theories and principles). Man is never the sole or real originator of any idea since he always thinks in language which he inherits and never invents; and secondly, all his thinking and scholarly work take place within an inherited tradition of thought-and-life even if he may eventually reject or transcend it. An idea, therefore, is one's own when it is an idea in which one believes totally, in whose truth one lives. Creative work in Gandhian thinking would, therefore, mean that the scholar imbibes and assimilates the spirit of the Gandhian way and brings it to bear on the contemporary situation. It may, therefore, often come about that his work may bear little ostensible relation to Gandhian thought and may still be thoroughly informed by the spirit of Gandhian thinking and the Gandhian way.

By holistic research in Gandhian thinking is meant work on the Gandhian corpus in its totality with particular attention to Gandhian world view and philosophy of life. Many works on Gandhi are devoted to one or more aspects of Gandhian thought. Of course, all of them assume his philosophy of life and articulate it in different forms at more or less in length. But this is only as a background to their main purpose which remains the examination of certain aspects of Gandhian thought. It is of the utmost importance for the renewal of Gandhian thinking that attention be focused on Gandhi's world view and philosophy of life so that each aspect and sphere of Gandhian thinking could be located within it and thus be seen in its proper perspective. Completing the publication of the collected works of Gandhi is, therefore, urgent. Another important task is to collect, collate, and critically analyse the different versions of the Gandhian world view that have been formulated or presupposed in works on different aspects of Gandhian thought.

Gandhian thinking at this level needs to be greatly supported and promoted, but independently of the universities and eventually of the government too. The greatest danger here comes from the operation of Gresham's Law: Bad money drives out good. The operation of this law has been one of the main factors in defeating almost all plans for the promotion and encouragement of whatever has been considered desirable. The operation of this law seems to be particularly vigorous and especially difficult to counter in the academic sphere. Many of us, it seems, have a vulture-like sense for locating money and preferment and are also equipped with the requisite know-how for grabbing them. Gandhian thinking must be saved from this fate. No cost is too costly here—not even the risk that its promotion may go by default. Let no word go out to the academia that there is money (and career) in Gandhian thought. For this reason I want to urge that no special fellowships in 'Gandhian Thought' should at all be created nor should we devise any preferential system of scholarship awards for Ph.D. work in 'Gandhian Thought' or 'Gandhian Studies'.

I may now make a few positive suggestions: I have just said that the promotion of Gandhian thinking at the research level is a vital need, and yet I have strongly opposed any kind of fellowship programme for this. Devoted scholars and thinkers never need incentive of any kind except the good of their work, the pursuit of which is their vocation. Incentives and rewards of different kinds and at different levels have been the most insidious temptations of the life of the mind. Temptations even when socially accepted must be tempered and restrained, not fostered. Scholars and thinkers, however, need facilities for their work, and, if possible, a congenial atmosphere. What is required, therefore, on the part of funding and sponsoring bodies is that they should search out scholars who are working in Gandhian studies as well as those who may be wanting to work in this area. Their needs for the furtherance of their work should be understood and the funding bodies should respond to them not in a streamlined, bureaucratic manner but in a magnanimous, aristocratic way, tailoring their support to the specific needs and situation of the scholar. The point I wish to make is that we should not think in terms of 'attracting' scholars to Gandhian studies and that the 'incentives' approach should be wholly abandoned, generally in my opinion, but most definitely with respect to Gandhian studies. The incentives approach is unGandhian in any case, and would most likely have a corrosive influence on one's sense of vocation.

The funding bodies would still need to have a definite budget allocation for the promotion of Gandhian thinking. If the approach advocated here is sound, they must strictly observe the following two conditions. One, the total amount budgeted should be a well-guarded secret from all possible beneficiaries and, secondly, it should be allowed to accumulate up to a reasonable period, if necessary. It follows that the disbursing authorities must not be under any kind of pressure to utilize the allocation within a given period.

My second suggestion is that a small, autonomous centre should be established, preferably by non-governmental public effort, charged with the following tasks: one, promoting Gandhian thinking through creative and holistic research; two, designing and conducting an educational programme in Gandhian thinking for voluntary novices; and, three, devising and conducting a programme for training educators in Gandhian thinking. Something has already been said about the kind of research a centre of this kind is expected to engage in; a few words about the educational programme may now be in order. The centre will take on only a small number of students who evince a minimum competence and real keenness to be initiated into Gandhian thinking and the Gandhian way. Their material needs will be met during the programme, but no inducements or attractions will be offered. The method of education will be one that makes sufficient demands on the students for self-education. Dialogue, discussion, meditation, thinking, and guided reading, lectures too, if necessary, may be mentioned here as educational devices to be used at the centre. This is only by way of illustration. Different methods may be followed for individual students. The idea is to

keep the system as loosely structured as may be consistent with the discipline required for the effectiveness of any serious educational enterprise.

The aim of this educational programme will be to create a maieutic
design and a moral support-system for metanoia. The students will gradually
experience a transformation of their mind, a turning away and a turning
towards, of their consciousness, a change in the centre of their thinking. A
change in their character is bound to follow. Also, possibly some cases of
schizophrenia. In a word, the aim is conversion in the sense of a total turning
of the heart. Accordingly, all appropriate precautions will have to be taken,
as also unavoidable risks will have to be run. It should be clearly understood
that, in so far as an educational programme of this kind is at all successful,
the graduate will have no end of trouble and suffering in adjusting with
actual life-situations. But the idea is that it is through patient but active
suffering of such graduates that a Gandhian, that is, a normal, *ethos* may
slowly come to be formed.

A word about the rationale, the presuppositions—the metaphysics, if you
permit—of the approach presented above. I have been assuming that surrounded as we are by darkness and death, we can still be saved and renewed.
This could be a false hope, or again it may not be. It would, however, be a
delusion to think that this redemption and renewal can be effected wholly by
man. Indeed, this is a decisive difference between Gandhian thinking and
that of the modernistic Western thinkers. The whole approach here is based
on the idea of patience and active waiting—waiting on God. We should not
think and plan as if it were a question of cashing in on a Gandhian wave. It
would be both unrealistic and mean. Whatever crash plans we make, the
completely unGandhian character of our social, political, and economic
institutions is not going to change in the near future. We must guard against
exaggerating the revolutionary nature of the defeat of the Congress party.
Our model of development will continue to be the confused Western
modernistic one that has been since 1950; we may pack the government
with Gandhians, but that would be of no real avail. It is doubtful if India
could have accepted the Gandhian way in 1947; the loss of thirty-two years
is certainly a major, if hopefully, not a decisive one.

So those who believe in Gandhian thinking can and ought to do only this:
prepare faithfully, do their utmost and wait with patience and intensity—if
not like a Cinderella waiting for her Prince Charming, then like a young girl
waiting for her lord: so that it may not be that he came and found her
sleeping.

Epilogue[10]

It is of course an integral part of St Thomas's conception of the world, of the Christian conception of the world, that man may be placed in a position to be injured or killed for the realization of the good and that evil, considered in terms of this world, may appear as an overwhelming power. This possibility, we know, has been obliterated from the world view of enlightened liberalism.

Acknowledgement

I am indebted to Raghavan N. Iyer's excellent work on Gandhi. To Marco Pallis, my debt is beyond words. I am grateful to the Indian Council of Social Science Research, New Delhi, a fellowship from which supports the work on which this paper is based. The ICSSR, of course, is not responsible for the views expressed in this paper.

Notes and References

1.   A profound and masterly exposition of Metanoia can be found in the two essays, 'On Being in One's Right Mind', *Review of Religion*, VII, 1942 and *'Paravrtti*—Transformation, Regeneration, Anagogy', *Festschrift Morris Winternitz*, Leipzig: 1933 both by A.K Coomaraswamy.

Metanoia is, then, a transformation of one's whole being; from human thinking to divine understanding. A transformation of our being, for as Parmenides said, 'To be and to know are one and the same', Diels, *Fr*. 185, and 'We come to be of just such stuff as that on which the mind is set', *Maitri Upanisad*, VI. 34. 3. *On Being in One's Right Mind*, p. 34.

In any case, Asanga's *paravrtti*, or any other doctrine of transformation involving an attainment of analogical powers-of-the soul (*vibhuti*) or degrees-of-being (*sthana*), though it means more indeed than a rational understanding of, or intellectual assent to any dogma, does not imply a miracle: what is meant is what is also meant in the Upanisads by the constantly reiterated phrase *ya evam veda* (or *vidvan*), that is, 'Who realises and actualises this as a matter of immediate experience, and in identity'. In other words, the real transformation is a transposition of consciousness from normal faculty to a condition of identity with the principle on which the faculty depends; a coming to see 'things', not as they are or seem to be in themselves, but sub specie aeternitatis. No miracle, but a transformation of man himself, of own form and own-nature to a *svarupa* and *svabhava* in angelic, or in the last analysis transcendental being, where essence, form, and nature subsist in unity, in principio; 're-informed into her primitive and formless form' (Eckhart, *loc. cit.* I 237), *amara*—Paravrtti—Transformation, Regeneration, Anagogy, pp. 234–5.

2. See Theodore Roszak, *The Making of a Counter-Culture*, Garden City, New York: Anchor Books, Doubleday and Company, Inc., 1969; Charles Reich, *The Greening of America*, Harmondsworth: Penguin Books, 1971; and Paulo Freire, *The Pedagogy of the Oppressed*, Harmondsworth: Penguin Books, 1972.

    Ivan Illich has presented his critique in a series of short monographs on modern Western Education, Medicine, and Technology. The following books may be consulted: *Deschooling Society*, Harmondsworth: Penguin, 1973; *Limits to Medicine*, London: Marion, Boyars, 1971; *Energy and Equity*, London: Calder and Boyars, 1974; and *Tools for Conviviality*, London: Calder and Boyars, 1973.

    A more general treatment of our contemporary situation is found in his early book *Celebration of Awareness*: *A Call for Institutional Revolution*, Doubleday and Co. Inc., Garden City, N.Y.: Anchor Books, 1971.

    Peter Berger's *The Homless Mind*, New York: Vintage Books, 1974 and *Pyramids of Sacrifice,* New York: Anchor Books, 1977) may also be consulted. Berger's work differs considerably from Illich's or Roszak's. However, in its own way, it provides a good example of a 'humanistic social-scientific' radicalism that remains firmly within the basic thought-world of modern Western civilization. It should not be difficult to discover it as a subtle apology for the contemporary American way of life.

3. In a fundamental sense, a world view cannot be taught by any educational system. A world view is the total system of man's knowledge and way of life in living, integral relationship constituting a cosmos for his whole being. It is both logically and existentially prior to any educational system; all educational systems, formal as well as informal, are formed by and within the world view and they function to reflect it. The relation of man and his world view being an internal relation cannot be analysed—it is an existential mystery. The relation of a given educational system to the world view which it presupposes and reflects and radiates, refers, in the last analysis, to the same primordial mystery. Pre-modern traditional systems of education do not *teach* a world view: they only provide reminders of it. Indeed, a world view is far more than a system of knowledge and skills and habits alone; it is less a system and more a 'view', paradoxically, from a point outside space (and time)—so that a world view is neither a standpoint nor a viewpoint but a figurative Archimedean print. All the disciplines that a traditional school teaches, express—show—with varying degrees of indirection, the world view within which it (the school, the system of education) functions. Theology and metaphysics and dialectics do this in a pre-eminent way, by a sort of ultimate or absolute metonomy or

anagogy; but they too neither constitute nor teach the world view which they affirm and towards which they constantly lead the student.

The expression 'Gandhian thinking constitutes a world view' which has been sometimes used is only a stylistic convenience. What is meant is that Gandhian thinking derives from traditional metaphysics and theology which it naturally expresses and affirms in various direct and indirect ways. An educational system which does not accept that metaphysics is ipso facto incompetent to educate people in Gandhian thinking, and if it does, it cannot avoid distorting it. The unstated premise of this essay is that (i) there can be creative adaptations and recastings, but there cannot be creative distortions or perversions and (ii) that it is better to let truth suffer by default than suffer its distortion or perversion.

4.   This controversy is ably discussed by Owen Barfield in his profound and path-breaking study. *Saving the Appearances*: *A Study in Idolatry*, London: Faber and Faber, 1957 and most elaborately documented by Arthur Koestler in his famous study of the History of Man's Changing Vision of the Universe which he has entitled *The Sleepwalkers*, London: Hutchison, 1959. See especially Parts Three and Five.

5.   Though I am not sure about the central message of T.R. Kuhn's *The Structure of Scientific Revolutions*, Chicago: The University of Chicago Press, 1962, it seems to me that Kuhn's Paradigm Theory of Scientific Revolutions supports the medieval Church view of scientific theories as hypotheses to save the appearances. 'We may, to be more precise', Kuhn observes, 'have to relinquish the notion, explicit or implicit, that changes of paradigm carry scientists and those who learn from them closer and closer to the truth' (p. 169). Further, 'just because it is a transition between incommensurables the transition between competing paradigms cannot be made a step at a time, forced by logic and neutral experience. Like the gestalt switch, it must occur all at once (though not necessarily in an instant) or not at all' (p. 149). Again, 'I would argue, rather, that in these matters neither proof nor error is at issue. The transfer of allegiance from paradigm to paradigm is a *conversion experience* that cannot be forced' (p. 150, italics added). And, finally, most revealingly: 'Scientific education makes use of no equivalent for the art museum or the library of classics, and the result is sometimes a drastic distortion in the scientist's perception of his discipline's past. More than the practitioners of other creative fields, he comes to see it as leading in a straight line to the discipline's present vantage. In short, he comes to see it as progress. No alternative is available to him while he remains in the field.'

'Inevitably those remarks will suggest that the member of a mature scientific community is, like the typical character of Orwell's *1984*, the victim of a history rewritten by the powers that be. Furthermore, that suggestion is not altogether inappropriate. There are losses as well as gains in scientific revolutions, and scientists tend to be peculiarly blind to the former' (p. 166).

Now, however strong the logical argument and weighty the historiographic evidence for this philosophy of science (scientific theories as hypothesis to save the phenomena) may be, the scientific establishment is not likely to embrace any such philosophy: for it goes against its historical character. The spirit that animates modern science (as distinguished from Greek science or traditional science in general) is that of the progressive conquest of Nature and the Universe: to accept the 'theory-as-hypothesis' view would cripple this spirit. Secondly, modern science developed not as a rival metaphysics, but as the knowledge that would abolish all metaphysics—eliminating the very need for it—which is explained as a hangover from man's 'pre-scientific' past. Science cannot, therefore, accept any metaphysical theory of Truth. Accordingly, it has to exclude all those spheres of man's life and the universe which do not admit of empirically testable or theoretically demonstrable truth. With such rigidly circumscribed scope, science cannot be the basis of a world view or a total philosophy of life. (This is not necessarily to accept a theory of man-invented 'alternative' world views.) In order to see the point being made here, it is necessary to see clearly that to say that scientific theories are ultimately hypotheses (to save phenomena) is a very different thing from saying that they are indefinitely corrigible. (The latter, in fact, is the other side of the 'demonstrable truth' view of Science.)

6.   This is, of course, not to imply that a world view can be *taught* in a traditional school. This point has already been clarified in note 5 above. It may be pointed out further that education in Gandhian thinking will constantly lead towards certain implied and presupposed doctrines and ideas. And these doctrines and ideas are rejected by all 'modern' educational institutions by virtue of their 'modernity'. In consequence, if the educator takes Gandhian thinking seriously, he will be at odds with the whole educational system—in fact, with the modern age itself. This tension is bound to affect adversely his teaching, in which he can no longer engage wholeheartedly. In a word, then, Gandhian thinking is unteachable under the auspices of a modern school.

7.   For Recollection, see A.K. Coomaraswamy, 'Recollection, Indian and Platonic', Supplement to the *Journal of the American Oriental Society*, Vol. 64, (3), April–June 1944, pp. 9–10.

'So far, it is clearly implied that memory is a kind of latent knowledge, which may be either self-revealing, or may be revived by an appropriate external sign, for example, when we are "taught", or more truly "re-minded". There is a clear distinction of mere perception from recognition, whether or not evoked by the percept. Memory is recovery or re-experiencing (*pratyanubhu*, Pras Up. 4.5), and it may be observed that the other supernatural powers (*iddhi*) which can be experienced at will by the Arhat are similarly called "recoveries" (*patihara, Vprati-hr*). It is evidently not, then, the outer, aesthetic self, but an inner and immanent power, higher than that of the senses, that remembers or foreknows (*prajna*), by a "fore" knowledge that is rather "prior" with respect to all empirical means of knowing, than merely "fore" with respect to future events—*ude non* PRAE *videntia sed* PRO *videntia polius dicitur*, Boethius, De consol. 5.6.69,70. That which remembers, or rather, which is always aware of all things, must be a principle always present to (*anubhu*) all things, and therefore itself unaffected by the duration in which these events succeed one another. We are thus reduced to a Providence (*prajna*) or Providential Self or Spirit (*prajnatman*) as the ultimate source on which all memory draws, and with which whoever attains to the same uninterrupted omniscience must be identified, as in Pras Up. 4. 10.'

For Repentance see Jonathan Magonet (ed.), *Returning: Exercises in Repentance*, London: Reform Synagogues of Great Britain, 1975.

Repentance 'is the name given to the act of decision in its Ultimate intensification; it denotes the decisive turning point in a man's life, the renewing, total, reversal in the midst of the normal course of his existence. When in the midst of "sin", that is, in decisionlessness, the will to decision awakens, the cover of routine life bursts open, and primal forces break through, storming heavenward. In the man who returns, creation begins anew; in his renewal the substance of the world is renewed'. See Martin Buber, *Returning*, p. 32.

8.   It is true that there is no Gandhian physics or Gandhian bio-chemistry, etc. But the reason why modern science education cannot include Gandhian thinking is that modern science rejects the view of man and his society and culture that Gandhian thinking propagates. This may not be strictly correct—science being formally unconcerned with anthropology; the point, however, is that science cannot be integrated with Gandhian thinking and this integration is required because Gandhian thinking partakes of a tradition in which there is one science of man and nature. Today there is either no scientific theory of man, man being outside the scope of modern science, or we are waiting for a social-scientific theory of man. In either case, Gandhian thinking becomes a curiosity: Gandhi talks of man in a major way and was not waiting for a future scientific theory of man. What makes the situation absolutely incorrigible is that Gandhi talked about God in a positive and an absolutely central way, but neither science nor the social sciences can talk about God, except to debunk or at best to draw a quarantine line.

Marxian thinking too cannot be taught by modern schools, though it accepts most of the basic postulates of modernism. It, however, promises a new world view and consequently a single science of nature and man. Since the latter is rejected by modern science and this means that the very idea of world view is eliminated, Marxism too becomes unteachable by modern universities. (If

there was an attempt to develop a Marxian physics or genetics etc., as parallel
and rival disciplines to modern physics or genetics, it did not succeed.)

In the beginning, Marxian thinking had been shunned and ignored by the
universities. This has been a source of strength to it. Marxism is now included
in the syllabi of most of the universities today. This has been a considerable
factor in weakening its élan.

Nota bene that in promising a new scientific world view, Marx is making
a major departure from the basic postulates of modernism most of which are
accepted by him in principle. Unlike Comte and other 'liberal' modern
thinkers, Marx does not envisage a universal '*Social Science*' based on the
new physical sciences but a new unified science of history which will abolish
the dichotomy of natural and social sciences. *German Ideology*, Moscow:
Progress Publishers, 1976, Third revised edition, p. 34; also *Economic and
Philosophical Manuscripts of 1844*, Moscow: Foreign Languages Publishing
House, 1961, pp. 110–11). In contrast to the agnostic and anomic milieu of
much modern liberal thought, Marx rightly sees that a world view cannot be
founded on natural sciences or on a derivative social science; rejecting
tradition, however, he founds the new world view, not on metaphysics but on
the (unified) Science of History. How far can such an enterprise be tenable is
a larger—and another—question.

The modern programme for the elimination of metaphysics, theology, and
the idea of a world view has had a profound impact on philosophy which has
been at a loss to find its name and nature in the new intellectual world
dominated by science and secularism. It could not see itself as love of wisdom,
more precisely as (love of) wisdom about knowledge: the new world did not
recognize love—not in any case at the cognitive level—and had no place for
anything like wisdom which 'takes knowledge for granted and governs the
movement of the will with respect to things known'. With the decay and loss
of inherited world views, philosophy is deprived of its traditional task, namely,
the elucidation and reinforcement of a given world view. It, therefore, has to
find its task anew. This situation has been an important factor, on the one
hand: in the development of empirical (scientific) psychology largely under
the auspices of philosophical faculties, and on the other, in the predominant
place that has gradually been given in philosophy education to the history of
philosophy. 'For the very moment any one engaged in philosophizing aban-
dons the guidance of sacred tradition, two things happen to him. The first is
that he loses sight of his true subject; the real world and its structure of
meanings and finds himself instead talking about something entirely different:
philosophy and philosophers. The second is that he forfeits his legitimate hold
on the solely binding tradition and must therefore illegitimately and—it must
be said—vainly seek support in the mere facts handed down to him, in
whatever historical material happens to be at his disposal, following the "great

thinkers" whom he has encountered more or less by chance, or occupying himself industriously with the opinion of other people'. Josef Pieper, *Scholasticism*, London: Faber and Faber, 1961, p. 126. 'The purpose of the study of philosophy is not to learn what others have thought, but to learn how the truth of things stands'. St Thomas Aquinas, responding to Siger of Brabant, 1271–2. Quoted by Pieper, *Scholasticism*, p. 126. With the emergence of secularism and science and the accompanying sundering of faith and reason (and faith and knowledge) the realm of 'the truth of things' becomes increasingly out of bounds to philosophy, the 'real world and its structure of meaning' progressively remote from it. New modes of philosophizing then inevitably come into vogue. They are often seen as autonomous and autotelic and involve a radical change in the concept of philosophy itself.

One of the major movements of the philosophic spirit in modern times has nevertheless been to reassert its ageless heritage and to deal with the real world and its structure of meaning. This has, however, almost invariably been consummated in the elaboration of different philosophies of history leading to an implicit or explicit reduction of philosophy to a theory of history. Hegel, Comte, Marx, and Dilthey; each in his own way, represents this fundamental turn in philosophy which requires it eventually to assume an unprecedented task: inventing a new world view to replace the traditional world views rejected by secularism and science.

This new burden has, however, proved too heavy for philosophy which accordingly has seen itself as a critique; or as analysis of concept or words; or as hermeneutics. Roughly originating with Kant as critique of Reason and Judgement, philosophy is reduced to critique of Science (or scientific language) in Logical Empiricism (The Vienna Circle). Philosophy as analysis and clarification of concepts or as linguistic analysis tends either towards a reduction to technique or to Ideal Language or Universal Grammar: in one case this means the self-abolition of philosophy as general theory, in the second, it represents the urge of Language for self-conquest: an impossible ambition. Philosophy as hermeneutics, leaving aside its affiliations to religion-philosophy, is related to the tradition of Critique via Dilthey; in its later development in Gadamer, it endeavours once again to restore to philosophy its traditional task: Hermeneutics, claims Gadamer, is a universal mode of philosophy and not merely the methodological foundation of the so-called human sciences. The hazard of philosophy in modern times is aptly illustrated in this concern to establish hermeneutics not as a method but as philosophy (or more correctly, as a phenomenology of truth): 'Fundamentally I am *not proposing a method*, but I am describing *what is the case*. In other words, I consider the only scientific thing is *to recognise what is*, instead of starting from what ought to be or could be. Hence I am trying to go beyond the concept of method held by modern science (which retains its limited justification) and to envisage in a fundamentally universal way what *always* happens.' See Gadamer, *Truth and Method*, New York: The Seabury Press, 1975, p. 465. Gadamer's thought takes account of theology, though its place in his system is not very clear. Minus theology, however, hermeneutics, even in Gadamer's hands, may not really be safe from an implicit methodological reduction. It is, however, unnecessary to determine the true nature of Gadamer's hermeneutics. For the purposes of the present argument, it is sufficient to note the central danger from which Gadamer seeks to save it.

Phenomenology, existentialism, and pragmatism, in their own ways accept the elimination of metaphysics and theology and endeavour to develop without them. It is doubtful, however, whether any of them has really succeeded in resolving the problems of a new self-definition of philosophy. Meanwhile, in this endeavour each of them has often taken a direction that leads to the reduction of philosophy to the critique or grammar of natural science, the grammar of commonsense, psychology, theory of history or 'Social Science'. The Sartrean attempt to forge a synthesis of existentialism and Marxism is a paradigmatic illustration of the point being made here. It should, however, be stated here that there are important exceptions like Peirce, Weil, Wittgenstein, Heidegger, Chomsky, and some others, whose conceptions of both philosophy and language are quite unmodern in a number of important ways, though at the same time they cannot be said to be fully traditional either.

This is undoubtedly an extremely simplified analysis. The historical development of philosophy in modern times has certainly followed a complicated course, there being many diverging and converging trends and several currents and cross-currents. However, a comprehensive analysis is perhaps not indispensable to our argument here which is designed to show merely the precarious or, at any rate, the radically changed nature of the philosophical spirit in modern times. It is necessary to see this because it is intimately relevant to any educational programme in Gandhian thinking. The present essay has assumed throughout that a definite philosophy informs Gandhian thinking. In his opening contribution to S. Radhakrishnan and Muirhead (eds), *Contemporary Indian Philosophy*, London: Allen and Unwin, 1958; first edn, 1936, Gandhi says:

'I HAVE been asked by Sir S. Radhakrishnan to answer the following three questions:
(1) What is your Religion?
(2) How are you led to it?
(3) What is its bearing on social life?

My religion is Hinduism which, for me, is Religion of humanity and includes the best of all the religions known to me.

I take it that the present tense in the second question has been purposely used instead of the past. I am being led to my religion through Truth and Nonviolence, i.e., love in the broadest sense. I often describe my religion as Religion of Truth. Of late, instead of saying God is Truth I have been saying Truth is God, in order more fully to define my Religion. I used, at one time, to know by heart the thousand names of God which a booklet in Hinduism gives in verse form and which perhaps tens of thousands recite every morning. But nowadays nothing so completely describes my God as Truth. Denial of God we have known. Denial of Truth we have not known. The most ignorant among mankind have some truth in them. We are all sparks of Truth. The sum total of these sparks is indescribable, as-yet-Unknown-Truth, which is God. I am being daily led nearer to It by constant prayer' (p. 21).

This philosophy, centred in God (as-yet-Unknown-Truth) and prayer, has close kinship with traditional concepts of philosophy and is incompatible with almost all the forms of modern philosophy. To make Gandhian thinking teachable *within* the modern system of education, one would need to rid it of its philosophy: that is, literally to undermine it.

Ultimately this assimilation is to be accomplished at the psychological level, psychology being understood in the traditional sense: 'The traditional and sacred psychology takes for granted that life (*bhava*) is a means to an end beyond itself, not to be lived at all costs. The traditional psychology is not, in fact, based on observation; it is a science of subjective experience. Its truth is not of the kind that is susceptible of statistical demonstration; it is one that can only be verified by the expert contemplative. In other words, its truth can only be verified by those who adopt the procedure prescribed by its proponents, and that is called a "Way".' See A. K. Coomaraswamy, 'On the Indian and Traditional Psychology, or Rather Pneumatology,' Roger Lipsey (ed.), *Coomaraswamy 2*, Princeton, New Jersey: Princeton University Press, 1977, p. 334.

9. 'Waiting on God' is one of the basic ideas of Simone Weil. 'God has provided that when his grace penetrates to the very centre of a man and from there illuminates all his being, he is able to walk on the water without violating any of the laws of nature. When, however, a man turns away from God, he simply gives himself up to the law of gravity. Then he thinks he can decide and choose, but he is only a thing, a stone that falls.' Simone Weil, *Waiting on God*, London: Collins, Fontana Books, 1959, p. 86.

Gandhi's thinking-and-life is almost a paradigm of relentless political action wholly based on a God-centred personal life and a divine, metaphysical theory of history.

The self-contradiction of man-centred philosophy of History and revolutionary political action based on it, is repeatedly rejected in Gandhian thinking.

Peter Berger has put the matter most succinctly (though he is unwilling to see the full meaning of what he says and misunderstands the traditional metaphysics of history):

'There is an underlying paradox in all ideologies that seek to control or contain modernity, a paradox closely related to the phenomenon that we have called cognitive contamination: if one wishes to control modernization, one must assume one has an option and the ability to manipulate. Thus one may opt against modernity. Thus one will seek to manipulate the processes of modernization. These very ideas, however, are modern—indeed, modernizing —*in themselves*. Nothing could be more modern than the idea that man has a choice between different paths of social development. One of the most pervasive characteristics of traditional societies is the notion that there is no choice; that the structures of the given society are inevitable, rooted in human nature, or indeed in the very constitution of the cosmos. Similarly, the notion that the course of human events can be deliberately manipulated and controlled as a specifically modern notion, which is alien to the thinking of most people in traditional societies. Therefore, at least in this one fundamental theme, modern consciousness is a well-nigh irresistible force, and it imposes the theme of option and manipulability even on those who most strenuously resist it.' Peter L. Berger, Brigitte Berger, and Hansfried Kellner, *The Homeless Mind*, Harmondsworth: Penguin Books, 1974, pp. 157–8.

It is a pity that Berger, (and the overwhelming majority of social scientists and philosophers of India and the Third World countries) does not see the almost idiotic self-contradiction blatantly implied in his proud demonstration: 'Therefore, at least in this one fundamental theme, modern consciousness is a well-nigh irresistible force, and it imposes the theme of option and manipulation even on those who most strenuously resist it.' It is obvious that modern man has 'to 'choose' and 'manipulate' *willy-nilly*. Does he not then cease to be a *freely* choosing, unexploited agent and creative subject? If modern man just cannot help manipulating, will not this manipulation include manipulation of man by man? What then sets him apart from and superior to Berger's conception of traditional man?

The modification of 'irresistible force' by 'well-nigh' reflects an inability to decide between the logical or historical nature of the necessity implied in 'irresistible force': the device can neither save the self-contradiction nor weaken the counter argument; in fact, it strengthens it dialectically.

10.   The source of the passage that constitutes the Epilogue is Josef Pieper's *Fortitude and Temperance*, London: Faber and Faber, 1955, p. 32.

5

Indianization of Autobiography*

BHIKHU PAREKH

But for men like me you have to measure them not by the rare moments of greatness in their lives but by the amount of dust which they collect on their feel in the course of life's journey.[1]

I

Autobiography is a complex genre of writing. In the broad sense of men writing about themselves, it goes back several thousand years. In the strict and narrow sense of what Auden called 'serious and truthful self-study' directed at self-understanding, it is relatively recent and goes back no further than the eighteenth century.

As long as five thousand years ago, Egyptian kings left behind descriptions of their achievements to be inscribed on their carefully planned tombs. Solon's elegiacs and iambics referred to the great reforms in which 'I made free men' and to the way he resisted temptations that would have 'destroyed a lesser man'.[2] Plato's Seventh Epistle described an important period in his life. Lutatius Catulus, Scarus, Rutilius, Rufus, Sulla, Caesar, and other Roman statesmen left behind accounts of what they regarded as their great achievements in order to create among their contemporaries and especially posterity a 'favourable opinion' of themselves. Epictetus, Marcus Aurelius, and other Roman philosophers and philosophically inclined statesmen wrote

* Bhikhu Parekh, 'Indianisation of Autobiography', in *Colonialism, Tradition and Reform: An Analysis of Gandhi's Political Discourse*, New Delhi: Sage Publications, 1989, pp. 247–66.

about their deepest thoughts on life with only minimal references to themselves and their achievements.

The practice of writing about one's life rather than achievements was begun by the early converts to Christianity. St Augustine's appropriately entitled *Confessions* (written in AD 397–8) is the best known but not the only one. It was preceded by dozens of similar works by such men as Justin the Martyr, Hilarius, the Bishop of Poitiers, and Gregory of Nazianzus. Bishop Synesius of Cyrene was probably one of the first to call his book *Dio or my own Bios*. Most of these works had a common structure and orientation largely derived from their novel content. Under the impact of Christianity, their authors had undergone intense and unusual experiences involving a sense of dramatic transition from ignorance to truth, from fall to grace, from a life of sin to one of virtue. Since their ruptured and transformed lives could not be told as coherent stories gradually unfolding in time, their accounts took the form of passionate and emotionally charged confessions suffused with the spirit of self-discovery and self-pity. Having embarked upon an exciting spiritual journey, they were anxious to share its joys and agonies with others and to urge them to undertake it themselves. They saw their lives as metaphors with a universal significance. Not surprisingly, their confessions had a didactic and evangelical orientation and concentrated on a general message rather than the details of their lives.

St Augustine spoke for most when he said that his *Confessions* was intended to be a 'lengthy record' to be laid before God, not because there was anything in it He did not know but in order to 'confess my miserable state' and to 'fire my own heart and the hearts of my readers with love of you'. His deeply moving book contains the barest personal details. He condemned his carnal life without mentioning any of the women involved. With the exception of Faustus of Mileva, he made only passing references to people who had influenced him. And he did not even refer to his domestic surroundings until the ninth chapter.

Once Christianity became an established religion and lost its earlier novelty, confessional writing underwent important changes and became more reflective and detached. During the late middle ages and especially during the Renaissance, non-confessional and secularly oriented accounts of life began to appear. Diaries, memoirs, chronicles, journals, and other forms of writing became popular and paved the way for autobiography in the modern and narrow sense. The term autobiography itself seems to have been first used in Germany in 1796. Commenting on the new kind of writing that was then beginning to appear, Herder distinguished between

Confessionen and *Lebensbeschreibungen* (life-stories). It is striking that he should have called autobiography life-story and distinguished it from confession. His contrast between autobiography and confession was intended to suggest that the former was a new and autonomous form of writing not to be confused with its more familiar predecessor. He divided confessions into religious and 'humanly philosophical', the former referring to the early Christian and the latter to late medieval writing, and insisted that autobiographies or life-stories should only be written by 'remarkable men'.

At Herder's suggestion, Seybold published in 1796 a collection of writings entitled *Selbstbiographieen berubmler Manner* (self-biographies of famous men). Like Herder, Seybold thought that famous and remarkable men alone were entitled to write about themselves. The term self-biography implied that the autobiographical genre was subsumed under the much older biographical form of writing and deemed to be basically of the same kind. Instead of others writing about them, famous men wrote about themselves. From Germany the term autobiography travelled to Britain where it was first used by Robert Southey in 1809. In the course of reviewing contemporary Portuguese literature, he referred to a book by a Portuguese painter as a 'very amusing and unique specimen of auto-biography'. Southey's remark is triply striking. He hyphenated the term autobiography thereby implying that for him, too, it was a form of biography, considered it a novel and unusual form of writing, and found it amusing to read about the details of its author's life.

Over time, autobiography developed into a unique and autonomous genre of writing governed by its own distinct requirements. It was expected to provide not only the details of its author's life, which any good biography of him could do, but also, and more importantly, a privileged form of self-understanding. Dilthey put the point well when he observed that the 'new' autobiographical form of writing represented the 'highest and most instructive form in which the understanding of life comes before us'. It was both historical and 'meditative', both narrative and reflective, a history of a life recollected, interpreted, and reflected upon from the calm vantage point of the present. As a reflective personal history, an autobiography was a way of appropriating and making sense of one's life. It is interesting that unlike Herder, Dilthey contrasted autobiography not with confession but with memoir. Unlike the latter, in which the author merely described the events of his life as an external observer, the autobiography represented an attempt to comprehend them from within and to give them a coherent personal meaning.

It was not an accident that the modern form of autobiographical writing first appeared in the late eighteenth and especially the early nineteenth century. Like other literary forms such as the epic, narrative poetry, drama, and the novel, autobiography presupposes specific cultural conditions in the absence of which it cannot emerge, acquire a firm structure and become socially respectable. We might mention four by way of illustration. First, as the story of a unique self, autobiography presupposes a culture in which individuality is valued and cultivated. Unless a culture encourages men and women to make their own choices, form their own views, take risks, look upon life as a journey and, in general to fashion their lives as they please, one man's life is no different from another's. It is not distinct and interesting enough to constitute the subject matter of a story, and there is no obvious reason why anyone should wish to write about himself or others should wish to read about it.

Second, autobiography rests on the assumption that the self is a product of its past choices and decisions, that it has a history, and is only intelligible in historical terms. As a form of reflective personal history in which the author traces and seeks to understand himself in terms of his gradual development in time rather than some transcendental source or naturally endowed properties, the autobiography is only possible in a society with a well-developed historical manner of thinking.

Third, unlike a diary which one writes primarily for oneself and which has a deeply subjective orientation, and unlike a chronicle or even a memoir which are primarily written for others, an autobiography is written for *both* oneself and others. As a pursuit of self-understanding by means of a silent and constant dialogue with oneself, it springs from a desire to make sense of oneself. There is, however, no obvious reason why anyone should wish to write down let alone publish his self-reflections unless he has others in mind. An autobiography is the story of a social being sharing his thoughts about himself with others and seeking to explain his life both to himself and to them. As such, it presupposes both a body of commonly shared meanings and values, and a unique individual definition and articulation of them. Insofar as it has *others* in mind, it is vulnerable to self-glorification and even exhibitionism and liable to miss out the crucial element of self-reflection. Insofar as it is written for *oneself*, it is prone to self-obsessed brooding and likely to lack the capacity to render the self intelligible to others. An autobiography properly so called must hold the self and society together, seeing each in relation to and emphasizing neither at the expense of the other.

Fourth, as a reflective and reasonably detached account of a life, an autobiography presupposes a self at peace with itself and its environment. A person at war with his past, as was the case with the early Christian converts, or with society, as was the case with Rousseau and many eighteenth century romantic writers, lacks the stability and detachment necessary for self-examination and reflection. He is too nervous to face himself and suppresses or distorts large areas of his life. Or he is too combative to look at the world around him with a measure of disinterestedness. He is no more able to compose a coherent and reflective narrative of his life than is a historian able to write with detachment about a subject matter he deeply hates or with which he is passionately involved. His strong feelings and restlessness can only find an adequate expression in a moving but unstructured confession, a personal testament or a manifesto.

II

Some of these and other preconditions of autobiography did not obtain in India as, indeed, in many other civilizations. The dominant Hindu metaphysic does not grant ontological dignity to individuality or uniqueness. The body is subject to change and dissolution, and the mind is little more than an unending stream of uniform and basically trivial desires and passions. Since the *ātman* alone is real and identical in all men, Hindu philosophers argue that all men are ultimately one. Individuality, selfhood, ego-consciousness, or particularity, the terms used interchangeably by them, are therefore *māyā* or inconsequential. All forms of self-assertion, including the desire to perpetuate one's name after death and to claim originality for one's thoughts are generally frowned upon. Almost every great Indian thinker, including the Buddha, linked himself to a series of real and sometimes imaginary predecessors and presented his view as an extension or reinterpretation of an established tradition. Given the fact that men occupy distinct bodies and are centres of distinct physiological and psychological processes, it is natural for them to think that they are irreducible and indivisible wholes. *Vidyā* or *jnāna* consists in overcoming such false consciousness. Moksha, the ultimate goal of human life, consists in liberating oneself from all sense of selfhood, including that of self-conscious agency.

Like the dominant Hindu metaphysic, Hindu social structure too places little value on individuality. The socially prescribed *varnāshrama-dharma* lays down the duties of each individual at each of the four stages of his life. From his birth onwards, he is cast in the mould of a specific caste and sees himself largely as a player of roles and a bearer of obligations. The range of his choices is severely circumscribed. His caste specifies what it is proper for him to do or not to do, and many of his important decisions such as the choice of a marriage partner are generally made for him. Though different castes and ethnic groups follow different lifestyles, there is little diversity *within* each of them. Not individuality but plurality, not individual but group diversity, is the central feature of Hindu society.

As we saw elsewhere, the modern historical manner of thinking did not develop in India either. Since transience or change was equated with illusion, historical details were dismissed as mere gossip devoid of value and significance. Historical truth was important only as an exemplification of universally valid moral truths. Historical understanding, therefore, never occupied an important place in Hindu epistemology. This meant that the details of an individual's life, his habits, idiosyncrasies, moods, feelings, and responses to events—in short, the raw material of autobiography, were deemed to be trivial and unworthy of being recorded or written about. The Hindus, of course, do have a strong sense of the past and believe that an individual is a product of his choices and decisions in his previous lives. Since the previous lives are unrecorded and unremembered, they do not and cannot form the basis of historical self-understanding. The doctrine of rebirth *prepared* the Hindu for, but did not itself represent, historical thinking.

Since some of the preconditions of autobiographical writing were absent in India, it is conspicuous by its absence. Ananda Coomaraswamy put the point well:[3]

Hinduism justifies no cult of ego-expression, but aims consistently at spiritual freedom. Those who are conscious of a sufficient inner life become the more indifferent to outward expression of their own or any changing personality. The ultimate purposes of Hindu social discipline are that men should unify their individuality with a wider and deeper [*sic*] than individual life, should fulfil appointed tasks regardless of failure or success, distinguish the timeless from its shifting forms, and escape the all-too-narrow prison of the 'I and mine'.

Anonymity is thus in accordance with the truth; and it is one of the proudest distinctions of the Hindu culture. The names of the 'authors' of the epics are but shadows, and in later ages it was a constant practice of writers to suppress their own names and ascribe their work to a mythical or famous poet, thereby to gain a better attention for the truth that they would rather claim to have 'heard' than to have 'made'. Similarly, scarcely a single Hindu painter or sculptor is known by name; and the entire range of Sanskrit literature cannot exhibit a single autobiography and but little history.

Unlike the autobiography, biography was common in India and is perhaps older than in the West. In its oldest form, it consists of quasi-historical writings about the lives of divine incarnations, the Vedic *rishi*s and such men as Veda Vyāsa, the Buddha, and Mahavira Jain. A little later, the *Carita* literature began to appear giving rise to such works as Bana's *Harshacarita* and Bilhana's *Vikramānk-deva-carita*. These were largely *prashasti*s or eulogies commissioned by kings and generally published after their death. They were not primarily concerned with historical facts and aimed to glorify their subjects' deeds, legitimate their status and to trace their real or fictitious geneologies. From about the eleventh century AD, those copying the manuscripts of the Purānas and the *Dharmashāstra*s began to write their own, their ancestors' and gurus' names, and to provide basic details about themselves, occasionally referring to some important events in their lives. From about the thirteenth century onwards, quasi-autobiographical works began to appear. In a somewhat similar manner to early Christianity, the *bhakti* movement triggered off profound changes in the religious lives of its adherents. Not surprisingly, a long line of such saint-poets as Basava, Akkama, Chaitanya, Mira, Kabir, Tulsidas, Tukaram, Akho, and Narasinha Mehta wrote quasi-autobiographical poetry, providing details about their parents, brothers, relatives, wives, domestic quarrels, and personal frustrations, but little directly about themselves. A few of them did describe some of their traumatic experiences, but largely with a view to drawing out important moral lessons. Almost every one of them saw his or her life as an illustration of human life in general, and his or her trials and travails as those of all men and women everywhere. For the most part, their writings were didactic sermons illustrated and enlivened by occasional and freely interpreted personal examples. Unlike the early Christian writings, these were not confessions or passionate outbursts of self-pity but devotional works laced with touches of self-mocking irony and self-deprecating humour. Since they were socially meaningful, they became immensely popular and were widely memorized, recited, and used as a common currency of moral intercourse.

   Islam came to India through Persia and brought with it the Persian penchant for historical details. It encouraged a tradition of writing history, memoirs, diaries, and records of royal achievements. Court poets and official record-keepers were engaged to write royal biographies and histories of their periods. It would seem that the Muslim tradition had only a limited influence on Hindu India, for there are only a few instances of such writing by or about Hindu kings and eminent personages. Nana Phadnis, an astute administrator during the last decades of Peshwa rule, Dada Pandurang, and a few others left behind diaries and memoirs containing fascinating personal and political information. However, these were too selective, patchy, and impersonal to be called autobiographies in any sense of the term.

During British rule, some of the cultural preconditions of autobiographical writing came into existence. Thanks to the work of British and Indian archaeologists and historians, a chronologically coherent picture of pre-Muslim India was constructed and history as an autonomous and distinct mode of inquiry became respectable. In the early years, history was widely feared and resented. British historians presented an unflattering and distorted picture of India's past, and Indians had little difficulty noticing that history was used to legitimize and to brainwash them into accepting British rule. They were also worried that the new discipline challenged not only the authenticity of the epics, the Puranas, and the myths but also their traditional and largely pragmatic mode of dealing with the past. But over time, Indian attitude to history underwent a radical change. Indians realized that the only way to counter a bad history was to write a good history themselves. They saw, too, that even as science need not threaten religion, there were ways of safeguarding traditions and myths from the invasion of history. More importantly, they saw that history was a *political* discipline capable of contributing to the growth of their sense of nationhood and fostering patriotism. Once history was accepted as a legitimate and indispensable discipline, such ideas as historical truth, autonomy of the past and explaining the present in terms of it began to strike roots in India.

British rule also introduced modern individualism and rationalism. Indians began to question traditional values and practices and to experiment with new forms of life and thought. Unwilling to fully embrace the new and unable to break with the tradition, they became puzzles to themselves. This heightened their self-consciousness and stimulated self-reflection. They were anxious to share with others the excitement of their newly found freedom and the problems it had brought in its train. Since Hindu society was generally hostile to them, they sought each other's approval and good opinion. For these and other reasons, there grew up a new subculture conducive to autobiographical writing. A group of people were anxious to write about themselves; a well-developed constituency was interested in reading them; and the newly acquired access to Western literature offered the necessary intellectual tools for writing autobiographies.

While British rule created some of the preconditions of autobiography, it also created others that militated against it. Thanks to British political and cultural domination and the sense of racial inferiority it inspired, those writing autobiographies found it difficult to resist the temptation to please and impress their masters. The result was often a good deal of unauthenticity, play-acting, and exaggeration. Furthermore, Westernized Indians enjoyed an ambiguous existence. Though critical of their society, they were, also heavily dependent on it for social, moral, and emotional support. They had only a limited understanding of the Western ways of life and thought and retained far more of the traditional Indian habits and values than they realized or cared to admit. Not surprisingly, their lives lacked coherence and consistency, and their self-perceptions were often at odds with who and what they really were.[4] Nervous about the continuing presence of the past they thought they had overcome, they were afraid to look at themselves closely lest that shattered their comfortable illusions. Not many of them, therefore, had the courage to write about themselves. Such autobiographies as did appear often lacked structure and displayed an unstable mixture of self-pity and self-assertion, of despair and defiance.[5]

Once British culture lost its novelty and became integrated into the Indian ways of life and thought, and once the Indians, no longer awed by their masters, began to write for each other, autobiographical writing began to acquire a coherent character.[6] It was still an exotic and alien genre and aroused considerable curiosity and a measure of hostility. Authors were not clear either about their reasons for writing autobiographies or about their audience. Thanks to the Hindu disapproval of self-assertion, they felt uneasy and nervous talking about themselves and searched for an impersonal entity around which to weave the stories of their lives. They were not certain about what they should include in or exclude from it, or how much they should reveal about their dead ancestors, parents, brothers, wives, children, friends and, above all, their innermost thoughts and feelings. Since many of them had grown up and continued to live in joint families, their lives substantially overlapped with their other members raising delicate questions about the morality of talking about them. Conventional Hindu notions of modesty, propriety, and privacy also raised disturbing questions concerning how to be interesting and informative without appearing self-indulgent, boastful, or exhibitionist. Each writer made his own judgement and took the risk.

Let us take two autobiographies by way of illustration.[7] Damodar Hari Chapekar, a terrorist freedom fighter and a Hindu fundamentalist, wrote an interesting autobiographical fragment. In the preface, he observed that only a person worthy enough to have a biography written about him had a right to write an autobiography, and that it should only include either 'fascinating episodes' likely to interest others or righteous deeds likely to guide and 'save' mankind. Chapekar conceded that he was an obscure Indian with no claim to fame and no right to write about himself. However, he was about to engage in a 'great deed'—shooting a British officer—and wanted to write about it so that the 'patriotic friends who will come after me will take care to avoid the mistakes I may have committed'. Since he was a traditionalist opposed to 'importing' foreign practices including writing an autobiography, he wondered what his ancestors would have thought of his attempt to write one. He solved the problem by arguing that the autobiography was not really new to India and that Vyāsa, Vālmiki, Parashara, and Manu had written 'their own histories'. He did not provide a single reference and invented a non-existent tradition to legitimate what he was determined to do anyway. Although he talked about himself, he was rarely at ease and made his deeds, not his life, the centre of his autobiography. It avoided all unflattering details and was largely a story of his terrorist activities punctuated by general statements of his views on India.

In the preface to his autobiography, Sir Surendra Nath Banerjee tackled the question differently.[8] As we saw elsewhere, he was deeply worried about the fact that since Indians had no tradition of writing history books, they never remembered or cherished the struggles and sacrifices of their ancestors. His autobiography was intended to rectify the situation. Inevitably, as its very title indicates, it took the form of reminiscences of the great Indians he had encountered. As he said: the 'need for reminiscences such as these has become all the more pressing in view of recent developments in our public life when unfortunately there is a marked, and perhaps a growing, tendency among a certain section of our people to forget the services of our early nation-builders'. Names of these great men had remained buried in newspapers, and no historian had bothered to write immortal accounts of their deeds. Banerjee wanted 'to do some justice to their honoured memories', and hoped that his reminiscences 'will not have been written in vain if I am able even in part to accomplish this object'. Not surprisingly, he dedicated the book to those 'whose achievements the present generation is apt to forget.' For Banerjee, the autobiography had no other purpose than to remember, cherish, and express gratitude to the illustrious contemporaries one was privileged to know. It was an act of both grateful remembrance and pious homage. Whether he would have taken this view if Indians had been in the habit of writing history is difficult to say. His autobiography contained a wealth of personal details but these remained marginal to the narrative.

Not he but modern India was its subject and provided the principle of coherence and continuity. It was really the biography of modern India as reflected in the life of one of its most distinguished citizens. Like Chapekar, Banerjee felt uneasy talking about himself and could only do so in the name and under the protective shelter of an impersonal entity.

III

Gandhi's autobiography, written at a time when the tradition of writing one was just beginning to develop, reveals many of the doubts and anxieties of his predecessors. He said in the preface that the idea of writing it was not his, but pressed upon him by some of his colleagues. He did not immediately accede to their proposal and decided to think further. When he was in prison and had considerable free time, they renewed the request. When he eventually agreed to comply, a close friend raised two objections which made sense in the Hindu cultural context sketched earlier.[9]

First, writing autobiographies was a Western practice and no one in pre-modern India was known to have written one. This was not an accident because it was a form of self-assertion and involved self-display and self-glorification. The West admired these qualities whereas India had always condemned them. Gandhi's colleague asked to know why he, a fervent champion of Indian civilization, wished to 'borrow' and legitimize an alien and apparently immoral genre of writing.

Second, autobiography was fraught with grave dangers. Indian culture disapproved of people writing about themselves and gave the adhikār to do so only to those who had attained great moral and spiritual heights and had something wise and worthwhile to say. Such men only expressed their mature and well-considered views which were widely accepted as authoritative. Since Gandhi was a Mahātma, his autobiography was bound to be taken as a morally definitive text. That was bad enough. To make matters worse, he was also a scientist constantly experimenting with truth and revising his ideas. His readers were therefore bound to feel confused and even likely to be misled. His colleague observed:[10]

What if you stop believing in what you take to be true today? Or what if you later interpret your principles differently and reconsider your earlier actions? Many men take your writings to be authoritative and conduct themselves accordingly. Will they not be misled? Would it not therefore be better to be cautious and for the time being at least refrain from writing something like an autobiography?

Gandhi was 'impressed' by these objections, but thought that they could be met by suitably revising the Western method of writing an autobiography. As for the first objection, he rejoined that unless they were patently evil, there was no harm in adopting and indigenizing foreign institutions and practices. He agreed that the Western manner of writing the autobiography was essentially self-centred and egoistic. Even when its author was self-effacing and self-critical, his very preoccupation with his transient thoughts, feelings, moods, and achievements involved self-assertion and heightened his self-consciousness and sense of particularity. However, Gandhi contended that this was not inherent in the genre and that it was possible to write one in a 'morally innocent manner'. The Western autobiography was vulnerable to the 'vices' of self-assertion and self-glorification because it took the *self* as its subject matter. There was no reason why the *soul* could not be made its centre. As a spiritual aspirant, he had devoted his life to realizing Truth or God and conducted all manner of experiments. If he were to describe these, the difficulties he had faced, the lapses he had suffered, the way he had overcome them, and the lessons he had painfully learnt, he could easily avoid the characteristic vices of the autobiography. It was true that he could not describe his experiments without mentioning the relevant details of his life. However, since his primary purpose was not to tell the story of his life and write an autobiography in the Western sense, he could legitimately exclude all personal details which did not bear upon his experiments and describe those that did solely from the standpoint of the experiments. The 'I' was not to be the subject of his autobiography and would enter it only as the agent or bearer of experiments. His autobiography would thus be concerned not with him but with his experiments; not with his psychological feelings and moods but with his spiritual struggles; not with the transient trivia of his life but with the abiding discoveries he had made in the laboratory of life; not with his self but with his soul.

Gandhi argued that since the kind of autobiography he intended to write was very different from its dominant Western form, the term autobiography was misleading and gave rise to wrong expectations. Accordingly, he distinguished between *jivanvritānta* (description of a life) and *ātmakathā* (the story of a soul) and insisted that his autobiography belonged to the second category. In order to make his point clearer, he sometimes said that he was not 'really' writing an autobiography but a history of his experiments 'in the name of' or 'under the pretext of' an autobiography. On yet other occasions he said that he was writing an 'autobiography confined to his experiments with truth' (*satyanā proyogo purti ātmakathā*) or an 'autobiography of experiments with truth' (*Satyanā proyogoni ātmakathā*).[11] At several places in the preface and in the text, Gandhi used the term *kathā* to describe what he was doing. This old and evocative term connotes a story told with a view to drawing out and emphasizing important moral lessons.

Gandhi contended that far from strengthening egoism and self-assertion, an autobiography written along these lines was bound to have the opposite effect. Moral and spiritual achievements were inherently fragile and both secured and shadowed by humiliating lapses. He could not describe them without confessing his limitations and recognizing the vast moral distance still waiting to be traversed. To write about them it was to 'grow in humility' and to see the self as nothing more than a mere vehicle for the discovery of truth. Gandhi asked his readers to read his autobiography *only* in order to learn from his experiments and to ignore and 'condemn' him for every intrusion of egoism.

Since Gandhi intended to write an 'autobiography of his experiments', he said that his reasons for doing so and the constituency he had in mind were very different from those generally associated with Western autobiography.[12] He did not write it to come to terms with his past, for that was of no concern to others; nor to tell the story of his life, for that only titillated idle curiosity and had no moral meaning for them; nor to justify himself to others and earn their good opinion, for the only opinion that mattered to him was the approval of his own conscience. He wrote it in order to share with others his moral and spiritual aspirations, struggles, lapses, and discoveries, and thereby to offer them 'some useful material' for their spiritual journey. His autobiography was a scientist's manual and intended to offer to the world the supreme gift of inevitably partial and tentative truths. He wanted to encourage others to conduct similar experiments, in the hope that such experimentally based and reflective autobiographies would contribute to the creation of a collective pool of moral and spiritual knowledge. One lamp lit others, and together they generated the light needed to illuminate the journey of life. Gandhi said that he had therefore written his autobiography for the benefit of his fellow-seekers 'who form my world'. As an advanced explorer himself, he owed it to them to write about his journey. And his fellow-explorers would know how to read his autobiography with requisite care and sensitivity.

Gandhi had so far dealt with his colleague's first objection. He now briefly turned to the second, namely, that his autobiography ran the risk of being regarded as morally authoritative. He said that he was writing it for his fellow-seekers who, being themselves engaged in experiments, could not possibly treat it as definitive. Furthermore, since his autobiography was a story of his experiments, he was bound to say that some had proved abortive, that some others had unexpected consequences, and that yet others were inconclusive. No one reading it could therefore conclude that it was anything but tentative and exploratory. Indeed, he hoped that his readers would go away charged with the scientific spirit of experimentation and humility.

Having discussed how he proposed to 'purge' Western autobiography of egoism and self-assertion and adopt it to the central values of Indian civilization, Gandhi went on to explain how he intended to write it. Like the scientific experiments, moral and spiritual experiments had to be conducted with clinical precision and described with utmost accuracy. He therefore hoped to write his autobiography in a simple, lucid, and measured language, a spicy and ornate language being 'as foreign to truth as hot chillies to a healthy stomach'. He also intended to write at a slow pace, lingering on every important experiment and carefully describing all its relevant features. Gandhi knew that the story of his experiments did not coincide with the chronology of his life. Since most of his experiments were incomplete and threw up unsuspected problems, he kept returning to them at different periods of his life. They had therefore their own chronology and a distinctly circular time structure. As a result his autobiography had two separate but criss-crossing chronologies. The narration of his life was brisk and unilinear, whereas that of his experiments was circular and had an air of timelessness about it.

Since Gandhi intended to write the story of his experiments, his autobiography was expected to be a kathā and not an *itihās*, a didactic discussion of selected experiments rather than their complete and impartial account. The two, however, could not be easily separated. The experiments did not take place in a social vacuum. They involved others either directly, as in the case of his wife, children, and close friends, or indirectly, as in the case of his colleagues and associates. As such, they could not be discussed without detailed references to their nature and degree of involvement in them, the way they interpreted and reacted to them, the lessons they learned, and so on. Gandhi said that he necessarily saw his experiments from his own point of view and that his description of them was bound to remain biased and one-sided unless accompanied by detailed statements of the views of those involved. He only wanted to write a kathā but found that it also involved an itihās and that, the two were subject to different, even conflicting, criteria. A kathā could be selective and subjective whereas an itihās was necessarily objective and many-sided. Gandhi was in a 'moral quandary'. It was interesting that he faced no such dilemma when discussing his wife and children. Apparently he thought that he was at liberty to be brutally frank about them and that he could offer an objective and truthful account of their involvement in his experiments. It was his relations with his European friends that worried him, so much so that he even changed the title of the relevant chapter. Gandhi observed:[13]

I understand better today the meaning of what I had earlier read about the imperfections and difficulties of autobiography as history. I know that I am not even offering all I remember in the autobiography of the experiments with truth. Who knows how much I should offer in order to present the truth of the matter? And what is the value of the one-sided and incomplete evidence in a court of law? If someone with plenty of free time were to cross-examine me on the previous chapters, would he not throw a flood of new light on their content? And if he were to examine them as a critic, would he not entertain the world by gleefully exposing the hollowness of my account? When sometimes I think like this I cannot help asking myself whether it would not be more proper to stop writing these chapters?

Gandhi did not resolve the dilemma and was tempted to abandon his autobiography. Since writing it was itself 'perhaps a dubious activity', he said that he could afford not to be too finicky about historical accuracy and objectivity. Trying truthfully to describe his experiments was itself one of these experiments, and he would let his readers form their own judgement.

Given his conception of a morally innocent autobiography, it is hardly surprising that Gandhi's autobiography should be intensely moralistic and display an unusual structure. As we saw elsewhere, he conducted different types of experiments in his personal, social, professional, and political life. After a prolonged moral struggle, he succeeded in becoming a noble soul, a Mahātma. As he himself said, it was these experiments and what he gained from them that earned him that tide. His autobiography is thus really a story of how he evolved into a Mahātma. With serene detachment, the Mahātma narrates the way Mohandas Gandhi had tried to live his life according to certain principles. He describes Gandhi's moments of achievement and failure and how he had felt about these at the time. The Mahātma then reflects on Gandhi's reflections, and the hero and the narrator, the subject and the object, become one. The Mahātma finds Mohandas Gandhi both familiar and unfamiliar. He recognizes himself in him, for the moral struggle is not yet over and the experiments with the soul are not yet complete. The Mahātma has also, however, overcome many of Gandhi's limitations and even outgrown him and retains only a non-emotive memory of him. Being a story of the fascinating and extremely complex encounter between Gandhi and the Mahātma, Gandhi's *Autobiography* does not remain an autobiography in the Western sense. It is basically a biography of Gandhi written by the Mahātma. As an intriguing combination of the related but logically distinct biographical and autobiographical genres of writing, it should perhaps be called an autobiographical biography.

Gandhi presents his life as a coherent and constantly evolving whole. Although marked by several painful experiences each of which gave a new turn to his life, he sees in it no radical ruptures or discontinuities. He suffered many lapses but learned his lessons and came out the better on each occasion. His *Autobiography* is therefore free from the penitential outbursts of Augustine and the nervous exhibitionism of Rousseau, and is less brooding and introspective than either. It shows neither self-pity nor moral conceit and is suffused with the spirit of self-confidence and self-reconciliation. The emotionally charged memories of an early and lustful marriage still unsettle him, largely because his sexual self-discipline is still incomplete, and his references to it show an abiding feeling of guilt and remorse. By contrast, he has come to terms with his ill-treatment of his wife, childhood theft, hot temper, and early attempts at playing an English gentleman, and his descriptions of them are remarkably non-emotive and tinged with self-mocking irony.

Since Gandhi was primarily concerned to describe his experiments, his life fell into two broad stages. His early life was marked by a constant struggle to fashion a satisfactory form of life and involved a series of experiments. His later life was largely devoted to living according to the truths he had already discovered and involved few new experiments. This is clearly reflected in the structure of his autobiography. The early parts which describe his years of struggle and the eventual attainment of Mahātmahood are more personal, reflective, and self-critical and read like a kathā; the later parts which deal with his mature public life are largely descriptive and read like an itihās.

Gandhi had hoped to write a morally innocent autobiography, one exclusively concerned with his moral experiments and free of egoism. He was not wholly successful. As the autobiography progressed, he tended to get carried away by its momentum and introduced several details that had no bearing on the experiments. He also began to describe his moods, fears, feelings, hopes, and anxieties, and his autobiography was sometimes little different from its Western counterpart. On occasions he even 'fell prey' to egoism. Compare, for example, his description of his years in South Africa in *Autobiography* with that given in his *History of Satyagraha in South Africa*.[14] His account of his reasons for deciding to stay on there is nearly five times as long in the *Autobiography;* he uses the first person singular three times as often; and he places much greater emphasis on his apparent indispensability in the struggle against racial discrimination. Even the determined Mahātma found it beyond his powers to completely overcome the inherent logic of autobiographical writing.

Gandhi could not Indianize the autobiography without Westernizing the Indian cultural tradition. The very fact that he wrote it and the manner in which he wrote it had important consequences. The fact that he, a champion of traditional India, was prepared to turn his hand to a distinctively Western genre was a highly symbolic and radical act and showed to his nervous countrymen how to respond to foreign values and practices. In writing an autobiography, further, he lent his considerable moral authority to the growing practice of talking and writing about oneself in public and helped weaken the traditional hostility to self-disclosure and self-assertion. By describing in detail how he, a timid young man who had once eaten eggs in order to be as strong as an Englishman, eventually overcame his colonial sense of inferiority and regained his racial self-respect and pride, Gandhi showed his countrymen how to come to terms with the menacing reality of colonial domination. In the contemporary context, his autobiography had a great therapeutic and inspirational value and was a profoundly political act. Again, unlike almost all Indian autobiographers before him, Gandhi discussed his personal limitations, failures, and moral lapses with remarkable frankness. By revealing that even a saint had a regrettable past and still a long way to go, he introduced the badly needed elements of honesty, moral humility, and social courage in Indian life. Not that he said things his countrymen did not know. A culture whose epics and Puranas are replete with tantalizing references to the moral foibles of gods and goddesses is well-insulated against claims of moral perfection. Gandhi's contribution lay in encouraging a frank and honest discussion of moral issues, including sexuality. As he once put it: 'A person who has realised his or her own error has changed into a new body. Why should he or she feel ashamed of talking about the old one?'[15] For a constantly evolving self, an error or a lapse once recognized and corrected was no longer a living part of him. It belonged to his dead self which he should be able to criticize without emotional involvement. This was an important and relatively novel view in the Indian context.

Although Gandhi chose to write about his experiments rather than himself, the two were not as distinct as he imagined and his autobiography had the opposite implications to those that he intended. It showed that life was not a diligent discharge of inherited roles and obligations but a romance in self-creation; not a journey along a prescribed route but an adventure in self-enactment. Compared to the great spiritual explorations of the Buddha, Mahavira, and other Indian sages, some of Gandhi's experiments were dull and conservative. However, his refusal to accept traditional values without first trying them out and his insistence on seeing life as a laboratory in which the restless individual explores new ideas in his unending quest for self-knowledge introduced an essentially modern, though suitably Indianized, conception of the self in Indian culture. Once experimentation with life became an acceptable practice, the door was opened to different and unconventional experiments.

Compared to many of his predecessors and contemporaries, Gandhi's autobiography had wholeness and integrity. While the autobiographies of Damodar Chapekar, Surendra Nath Banerjee, Subhas Bose, Narmada Shankar, and others began as descriptions of their lives but soon turned into commentaries on political events, Hindu society, contemporary India or on life in general, Gandhi's autobiography never ceased to be one until the end. By and large, he never lost sight of the fact that he was writing about himself and his experiments, and that he had an *adhikār* and indeed a dharma only to talk about his struggles and discoveries. Since he had a clear conception of what he intended to do and was determined to remain within its bounds, his autobiography contained very few digressions and had a remarkably economical structure.

This had its price. Gandhi's gaze remained fixed on his inner world and nothing was allowed to disturb his intense introspection. He had therefore little to say about the wider social and political world he dominated for just under three decades. Unlike Banerjee, Bose, Nehru, and others, he nowhere outlined his views on the larger issues of the day, entered into a debate with his colleagues and opponents, analysed their triumphs and failures, commented on their physical appearances, mannerisms, and political styles and skills or even described the physical surroundings in which he worked. In this respect Nehru's autobiography presents a remarkable contrast.[16] He located and attempted to understand himself in the context of the wider world; he said so in the introduction and remained faithful to it until the end. He analysed his social background, bourgeois upbringing, conflicting influences of India and Europe, his desperate and unsuccessful struggle to integrate the two, his habits of thought and ways of looking at the world, and his hopes and fears for his country. He described in detail his surroundings and the places he had visited, offered insightful analyses of his colleagues, including Gandhi, discussed his differences and disagreements with them and outlined his vision of independent India. Gandhi could never have written the following paragraph:[17]

I have become a queer mixture of the East and West, out of place everywhere, at home nowhere. Perhaps my thoughts and approach to life are more akin to what is called Western than Eastern, but India clings to me, as she does to all her children, in innumerable ways; and behind me lie, somewhere in the subconscious, racial memories of a hundred, or whatever the number may be, generations of Brahmans. I cannot get rid of either that past inheritance or my recent acquisitions. They are both part of me, and, though they help me in both the East and the West, they also create in me a feeling of spiritual loneliness not only in public activities but in life itself. I am a stranger and alien in the West. I cannot be of it. But in my own country also, sometimes, I have an exile's feeling.

But Gandhi's and Nehru's autobiographies represented serious attempts at self-understanding. While Gandhi hoped to arrive at it by means of an intense and introspective self-analysis, Nehru sought it in the larger social and political forces that had structured and moulded his personality. Like a yogi, Gandhi sat still and immovable with his gaze turned inward; Nehru saw himself from the outside and kept stepping back and forth to find an appropriate vantage point. We might say that Gandhi was concerned to *analyse* and Nehru to *explain* himself, and that Gandhi's autobiography was *introspective* whereas Nehru's was *reflective*. In any case, they were informed by different modes of self-analysis and offered different *forms* of self-understanding. Of the two, Gandhi's had a distinctively Indian orientation and flavour.

Notes and References

1.   Gandhi to N.K. Bose, cited in M.P. Sinha, *Contemporary Relevance of Gandhi*, Bombay: Nachiketa Publication, 1970, p. 45.

2.   George Misch, *A History of Autobiography in Antiquity*, London: Routledge, 1951, Vols I and II.

3.   Ananda Coomarswamy, *The Dance of Siva*, Delhi: Munshiram Manoharlal, 1982, p. 119.

4.   See G.N. Devy, 'Romantic, Post-Romantic and Neo Romantic Autobiography in Indian English Literature', in Dioranne MacDermott (ed.), *Autobiography*

and Biography in the Commonwealth, Barcelona: University of Barcelona Press, 1985, and the Preface to *CW*, Vol. 36, pp. ix f.

5. For example, Gujarati autobiographies by Narmada Shankar and Hemachandra. The former finds it difficult to decide what to say about himself and ends up writing a series of notes. Vishwanath Bhatt remarks that Narmada's autobiography lacks 'coherence, order and a sense of discrimination about what to write'; cited in Raman Modi, *Gandhijinun Sahitya,* Ahmedabad: Navajivan, 1971, p. 175. See also Devy, op. cit., p. 64.

6. Dozens of autobiographies by Indian writers began to appear from about the middle of the nineteenth century. Most of the early authors were social reformers. Only at the turn of the century did political leaders begin to write about themselves. The novelty of the genre was evident in the fact that their titles showed little variety. For example, Narmada Shankar's autobiography was called *Mari-Hakikat* (My life or statement); Narayan Hemchandra's *Hoon Pote* (I myself); Rajnarayan Basu's *Atmajivani* (My life); Dadoba Pandurang's *Atmacharitra* (My life); and Dwarkanath Tagore's *Autobiography*. Most of them said in the preface that they wanted to popularize this 'useful' and 'instructive' genre. Narmada Shankar said that his purpose in writing it was 'not so much introspection as the desire to provide a model so that like the West, Gujarat too could start the practice of writing autobiography.' (*Mari-Hakikat*, p. 2, cited in Modi, op. cit., p. 174).

7. Chapekar's *Autobiography* is included in *A History of the Freedom Movement in India*, Bombay: Government of Bombay Publication Division, 1958, Vol. II.

8. S.N. Banerjee, *A Nation in the Making*, Delhi: Oxford University Press, 1925.

9. See his 'Introduction' to *An Autobiography*: *The Story of My Experiments with Truth*, London: Jonathan Cape, 1949. The translation is mine. In Gujarat, Narmada Shankar and Hemchandra were the only ones to have written autobiographies before Gandhi. For good discussions of Gandhi's autobiography, see preface to *CW*, Vol. 36; C.N. Patel, *Mahatma Gandhi in his Gujarati Writings*, Delhi: Sahitya Akademi, 1981, pp. 63 ff; and Hyman Muslin and Prakash Desai, 'The Transformation of the Self in Mahatma Gandhi', in C.B. Strozier and D. Offer (eds), *The Leader*, Chicago: Plenum Publishing Corporation, 1985. For a dramatic rendering of Gandhi's Autobiography, see Asif Currimbhoy's three-act play called *An Experiment With Truth*, Calcutta: Writers Workshop Publication, 1972.

10. Ibid., p. XI.

11. Ibid., p. xi f. The English translation misses Gandhi's distinction. Even as late as 1946, he insisted that he had 'certainly not written an autobiography' and promised to update his *Autobiography* if he found the time; see *Harijanbandhu*, 1946. Gandhi had a fairly clear idea of how a good biography should be written. See *CW*, Vol. 32, pp. 3 f, where his reminiscences of Raichandbhai are an interesting mixture of biography and autobiography.

12.   Ibid. The Gujarati 'Introduction' is much clearer on this point. See also p. 234.

13.   Ibid., p. 234.

14.   Compare Part II, Chapter 17 *of Autobiography* with Chapter VI of his *Satyagraha in South Africa*, Ahmedabad: Navajivan, 1928. There are also other interesting differences.

      In his *Autobiography*, Gandhi is preoccupied with himself and says little about his surroundings. *Satyagraha in South Africa* is different.

15.   Raghavan Iyer, op. cit., Vol. II, p. 197.

16.   See his *An Autobiography*, London: Bodley Head, 1958, pp. xi f and, especially, 595 f.

17.   Ibid., p. 596.

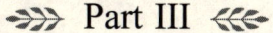 Part III

6

The Machine*

SUNIL SAHASRABUDHEY

What comes to pass resists debate. So with the machine. It is a *fait accompli* so nothing can be done about it. And one must adapt to it. What is more, one should do it happily, discovering sources of joy in it. What was seen—at its advent—as the chief source of alienation, is now considered the chief source of human activity. A story which has known little else than dehumanization, exploitation, destruction, and devastation has come to be considered a unique and unprecedented success of the human species. The palpable results of modern science from the steam engine to the computer have come to define the machine age.

Gandhi stood in total opposition to this machine. His life embodied this opposition. His writings are full of extensive and all-round criticism of the machine. He argued in detail about how the machine emasculates man both spiritually and materially. He even tried to build his challenge to imperialism around the *charkha*. In fact, Gandhi's opposition to the machine is so complete that it looks like a challenge also to modern science, to its claims of veracity, universality, enlightenment, and material well-being. The attempt in this chapter is to reconstruct this challenge through a reconstruction of the critique of the modern machine.

The term 'machine' is a general term meaning technology and its ostensive constructs. Processes and software are not external to it. Contraptions processing information are included too. As we shall see in the course of this

* Sunil Sahasrabudhey, 'The Machine', in *Gandhi's Challenge to Modern Science*, Goa: Other India Press, 2002, pp. 41–67.

chapter, developments from the steam engine to the computer, even though they are separated as they are so far in time, still constitute a unity. It is this unity which is called the machine. What this machine has done to man and nature is discussed under the title of denotation, relating to the conse-quences, the extrinsic parameters, as it were, of the machine. This has involved discussion of the concept of power and its science and how the substitution of man by the machine constitutes part of the meaning of the machine. The third section deals with the inconsistencies and essential falsehood in the backdrop of the claims associated with the machine. At the end there is a discussion of the Indian phenomenon of non-modern machines like the spinning wheel and the potter's wheel and their theoretical and practical consequences for humankind.

THE DENOTATION

The palpable consequences constitute the denotation. The idling millions and their abject poverty are as much consequences of the machine as its busy managers and their windfall super-profits. So is the case with the disorganization of entire societies, forced migration of millions and the loss of the forest cover on the one hand and the intricate and logical organization of computers and communication systems on the other. The machine alien-ates those who do not work on it as much as, or even more than, the 'worker'. This alienation becomes the source of great changes in the fields of art and science, in fact in all departments of human life. The economic, physical, and even human consequences can be seen everywhere. The Third World today constitutes the 'sight'. A vivid narrative may bring the point home more effectively. But what concerns us here is something different. It is the logic of the machine. So my attempt here is not to list the conse-quences of the machine, but to try to capture the essence of what it denotes. Therefore, the discussion in this section is divided into four conceptually identifiable areas of labour, capital, technology, and time.

LABOUR

Perhaps the most far-reaching consequence of the machine is the coming into existence of wage labour. Man's labour, transformed into wage labour, does not belong to him, it belongs to those on whose properties he works. Karl Marx's analysis of this phenomenon in the *Economic and Philosophic Manuscripts of 1844* still remains unsurpassed. His design of relating private property and all other categories of modern political economy finally to estrangement of labour is like a perfect painting which touches the heart, something that, philosophically speaking, analyses are not intended to do. With the advent of the steam engine, man was reduced in stature as never before and it may not be an exaggeration to say that the height of Marx's achievement owes much to his sensitivity to the degradation of man inaugurated by the modern machine. Much has been written and understood in this respect since then. However, what I wish to draw attention to is the labour of those who do not work on the machine.

Talking about the economic drain as a sequel to Dadabhai Naoroji's formulation, Mahatma Gandhi had said that the biggest drain of all was that we were turned into a nation of idlers. Idling should not be confused with unemployment: they are two entirely different things. On the one hand was the new speed and the assembly line turning man himself into a machine and on the other, was this idling where even the concept of time was irrelevant.

The idler's condition in life is not reproducible in a picture. It must be *seen*. The idler is not even a wage worker. He must work in order to live. But he does not get the wages of his work and he lives without eating. He is not a slave for he does not fight for his master; he does not fight at all. He is nobody for he does not count in a human assembly and yet he is everywhere. He is said to preserve a cultural tradition ironically only by flesh. It is he who has taken an endless beating *with* the spread of the machine. He does not struggle, for he has lost all the battles before they were fought. This was his self-image till Gandhi changed it.

An idler, however, is like an iceberg. When we look at the knowledge he has about men and of materials around him, about nature and its activities around him, and when we look at the details of the skills he possesses—both irrelevant to the modern machine—we may discover the existence of the nine-tenths not seen covered by the tenth part related to the machine and therefore the subject of all hitherto analysis and discursive thought. The peasant, the artisan, the tribals, and women across the length and breadth of nations possess more knowledge and are more scientific in their work, yet not related to the machine. The machine, as an instrument of destruction of the people, of transformation of man into a wage worker, of human activity into labour for the 'other', of self-transcendence into self-seeking, of the fraternities into the economic classes, etc., constitutes a success story only until the other nine-tenths of the idler remains submerged.

Gandhi's challenge to the machine is the first attempt to open ways for the submerged to surface.

CAPITAL

The machine is an expensive affair. It requires raw materials from distant places and seeks markets all over the world. The story of plunder, exploitation, accumulation, genocide, and wars put into the service of this enterprise has been told over and over again. The historical course as narrated always appears as an unstoppable sequence of events. The necessity and the inevitability of these forces owe their existence to a new factor that appeared with the advent of the machine: capital.

Gandhi pointed out time and again that the machine should never be a substitute for man: it should only assist man, that is, be man's tool. The character of the modern machine which makes it a substitute for man gives rise in society to a power apart from man. This power is capital. With it, objectivity, universality, value independence, etc., become legitimate qualities. Man's reason can now face him standing outside him in the form of modern science and the modern state.

The machine as capital has already enslaved Western man. It has taken several generations, in fact a few centuries, to effect this enslavement. The colonized, although enslaved by the same powers, have been saved a similar ordeal. Therefore, they do not grant legitimacy to either science or the modern state however much they may be exploited or pushed around by the latter. Peasants and artisans, therefore, keep alive forms of knowledge which are not 'objective', 'universal', or 'value-free', they keep alive forms of power, namely satyagraha etc., which do not confront man standing outside of him.

Although neither possessing the machine nor enslaved by it, the peasants and the artisans do live in this machine age dominated by capital. Therefore they need money if they want to do anything. This need opens the way for monetizing their social formations and the new forms of exploitation through the market. On the one hand they do not have the money; on the other, they do not know how to handle it, for the logic of the machine and the market is the logic of capital, the logic of an alien and objective power which they have not internalized. So a world free of capital can be a world free of the machine and this world can be built again and afresh only by people not yet enslaved by the machine.

TECHNOLOGY

The machine embodies a technology which is part of modern science. Speed, scale, noise, and glitter are its characteristics one observes at first glance. The machine organizes men, materials, energy, and information on a scale unknown before and at an ever-increasing speed. So does it disorganize societies and destroy their knowledge bases elsewhere on a colossal scale with equal speed. It has produced wealth and glitter for a few, and poverty, darkness, and 'noise' for the rest. Underlying both creation and destruction, organization and disorganization, lies a common characteristic of modern technology: violence. Modern technology is violent for all. This uncompromisingly violent nature of the machine seems to be the immediate cause for Gandhi's position on non-violence.

The nation's power today is measured by the strategic weaponry it commands; its progress is measured by the amount of steel, power, and chemical fertilizer it produces; and by its possession of the latest technologies including computers and telecommunications. Food, clothing, and shelter available to the people do not even count in the measurement of material progress achieved. Technology has tended to assume the status of a criterion for everything. A hospital is good if it has the latest equipment, a school is good if its laboratories are well equipped, even a college of arts gets recognition only if it commands the latest infrastructure and facilities. Households are no exception either; electrical appliances and electronic gadgetry have already stolen the show which once belonged to the aesthetic sense of man, a sense derived from nature by being one with its rhythm. But all this has involved large-scale destruction of nature—forests, minerals, and agriculture—and large-scale destruction of human societies all over the world. Technology, and therefore violence, has thus penetrated our idea of ourselves; conceptions of force, aggression, and power have occupied centre-stage in the modern conceptions of man, society, history, etc. The moral and the aesthetic have given way to the mechanical and the pleasure-seeking activities of man. Gandhi had once told us in *Hind Swaraj* that in buying cloth from Manchester we paid only in terms of money but by installing the machine on our soil we would have to pay in terms of our blood.

But there are still people in India and in other parts of the non-European world who are neither violent, nor aggressive. They do not believe in the use of force as the principal means of survival. These are the people whose lives have been brutalized by the complete disorganization of their social formations by modern technology. They include the peasants, artisans, tribals and women in general. Their knowledge systems, methods of work, organization of production, work ethic, and social and moral values, everything is in disrepute. The desecration of their epistemic and technical traditions continues through the ideology and practice of modern technology and development.

And yet it is these very people who, as if by the sheer force of their existence, keep alive the possibility of a future without modern technology.

It is a misconception spread by modern education and the state that modern technology is superior to and more efficient and competitive than traditional technologies. Neither modern science nor modern technology has ever entered into any competition with other forms of knowledge and doing things. The traditional sciences and technologies were always first made unviable by the economic, political, and legal processes unleashed by the state backed by military power. In the spaces thus created walked in modern science and technology. This process still continues and so do the latest technologies thrive in the imperial nexus supported by sheer force. But this means that this technology itself must embody the logic of force and violence.

Thus technology robs man of his activity. Genuine human activity knows no violence. So the first victims of modern technology are the politicians, the scientists, and the capitalists. It takes them from one choiceless situation to another and with them the whole society. Therefore, it seems that the peasants and the artisans shall have the last laugh, going through this battle which is waged on them by the machine. So in tune with Gandhi's opposition to the machine, opposition to modern technology is of equal theoretical and practical significance. However, it is necessary for this opposition to be real, that it be rooted in non-violence.

TIME

The machine has robbed man of his leisure. This has not only degraded the quality of his life, it has in fact taken life away from him and left him on the prowl for ever. The machine-age has brought a concept of time not known to man before: the supra-terrestrial monotonic concept of time.

The machine keeps ticking day and night, round the year, everywhere on the globe. This concept of time is reflected by the clock and it knows no seasons, no colours, no emotions. The clock and the calendar are tuned to be in consonance with the period of the revolution of the earth around the sun, mechanically divided. They do not relate with events on the earth and therefore this 'time' is supra-terrestrial and supra-human (to the extent that man is a terrestrial being). This unearthly 'time' is strange for man, to say the least. We measure it all the time and yet do not understand it. The theory of the modern machine has, however, tried to put a boundary condition on it, namely, that it is monotonic.

The Second Law of Thermodynamics gives rise to a dynamic physical variable called 'entropy' which is in general a measure of disorder. Strict statements of the law are highly technical but for our purposes we may note that according to this law the entropy of an isolated system always increases. That is, if we observe a physical system which is not involved in any give-and-take with its surroundings, then the entropy of this system will not reduce at a later time. This entropy is a well-defined, dynamic, physical variable whose values can be measured. Thus comes into existence the idea of 'the arrow of time'. Time cannot go back because entropy cannot decrease in a spontaneous process.

Thus, although machine time is supra-terrestrial and although we do not understand it (the Theory of Relativity notwithstanding), we know this much about it—it is monotonic. When the criminal does not have an alibi and when an acquittal has already been ordered, it is necessary that the crime situation be non-visitable. For the machine to be born, and for it to go on to live, it was necessary that hundreds of millions of people be killed all over the world. So they were. What is surprising then if the theory of this machine proclaims it is impossible for anyone to revisit those space-time sites where these crimes were committed?

Those who survived have been robbed of their leisure physically. Idling now is not distinguished from leisure: machine time has only one slot available for those not working. Leisure is that form of human activity which breeds creativity, excellence, finesse, and sensitivity. The great Indian tradition of industrial excellence and finesse owed itself in no small measure to the leisure at the command of the craftsman. It is in leisure that man lives, imagining, playing with himself, thinking effortlessly, having time to care for others and their problems. One who does not work on the machine, that is, one who is not an industrial worker, nor a policeman, clerk, or teacher in the modern state apparatus, may still have an idea of what is leisure and therefore may be the one who will recover for man this one-time priceless possession of his.

The Connotation

By the 'machine' we generally mean a mechanical contraption designed to make man's work easier and quicker. It is often used to perform tasks which cannot be performed otherwise. For example, a bicycle is a machine which makes human transport over small distances easier and quicker. Likewise, a sewing machine makes stitching easier and quicker. An axe may be used to cut logs which would be difficult to cut otherwise. Similarly, a furnace may melt metals which are difficult to melt otherwise, and a bullock-driven plough is used to prepare fields in a way which is difficult to replicate with merely the use of a spade or similar tools. Another set of examples is constituted by contraptions using a lever or pulley systems. One may be familiar with chain-pulley systems used to lift heavy weights. The same principle is involved in a simple lever whose fulcrum divides a beam unequally so that large weights placed at the end of the smaller side can be easily lifted by the application of a small force. All these are examples of machines or tools which make man's work easier, and quicker. If this is the meaning of the 'machine' and these are the examples, then Gandhi was not opposed to it. Gandhi's opposition was to the modern machine whose very meaning had now changed over time.

The machine today in fact is a form of capital. Wage-labour is a great consequence of it. But neither 'capital' nor 'labour' are part of the meaning of 'machine'. These are contingent facts which may or may not be associated with machines in different societies. Socialists did image a future society with this very machine and yet without capital or wage labour. They created the imagery of a society in which men and women would have the leisure to pursue higher goals which they would set for themselves. Technology keeps changing and no specific technology can be part of the meaning of the word 'machine'. So all that we have discussed under 'denotation' may be highly intertwined with whatever has happened ostensibly with the development of the modern machine and yet it is not part of the meaning of the word 'machine'. It may be true that the machine has acquired a new meaning as a result of all this and yet this new meaning may not be dependent on it either.

From its earlier feature of making human tasks easier the machine today has become a substitute for man. And from its earlier status of doing work quicker and faster, the machine in today's world means 'power'. The cause of this lies in social structure, property relationships, nature of the organization of political power, and in modern science. The part related to science concerns us here and we shall discuss it after we have had a closer look at the transformation of meaning suggested above.

SUBSTITUTING MAN

Ask anybody outside the metropoles and they will tell you how the machine has stolen their work. Potter, weaver, blacksmith, carpenter—all have been substituted by the machine. The women have lost their work across the board. The idling millions in the rural areas, all have lost their work. The men in the cities have also lost their work, but they do not complain, for they are paid for their parasitism. The growing tertiary sector in the metropoles and the widespread unemployment in the Third World are two sides of the same coin. The modern machine substitutes man irrespective of where he is.

This is the transformation from charkha to the spinning mill, from bicycle to motorcar, from wood-stove to the gas-flame or electric heater. Man used to be called the toolmaker. He earlier made and used tools as he and his mates decided. But now the machine casts the die. Not just this but it literally substitutes man and thereby fundamentally violates the natural life of man. Man is no more. It is not just an economic phenomenon, nor is it just a culture shock. It is a fatal blow. Millions have died in the wake of this substitution.

Developments in the latter half of the twentieth century have deepened the meaning of this substitution. Advancements in the areas of computers and telecommunications have lent a new meaning to storage organization, processing, and transfer, over long distances of information by machines. These are unconventional modern machines in the sense that their working neither requires large power-inputs nor are they environmentally hazardous. Such elements are no doubt involved in the processes of making these machines, but as they are not in the front all the time, they stay in a sense hidden and do not affect the psyche. However, the situation is now worse because it removes certain obstacles to the substitution of men by such machines. This substitution is particularly ugly because it is accompanied by a well-propagated claim that these machines are capable of doing aspects of man's 'mental' work. There are even areas of research called 'computer intelligence'. So now there is—or there is an attempt at—a theory which would justify in absolute scientific terms the substitution of man by machines. This is what deepens the meaning of this substitution.

Violation of truth is not just a consequence of this substitution, it is part of the meaning of this substitution. Therefore, violation of truth is part of the connotation of 'machine'. So in the metropoles where the machine substitutes man a science grows which is essentially false and in the hinterlands where the machine displaces man and disorganizes his life, traditions of true knowledge are steadily falsified and their bases eroded. Thus, in the sphere of *vidya*, substitution of man by machine leads to the creation of two worlds. The organized knowledge systems taught and grown in the universities turn cannibalistic against their unorganized brethren who survive in the name of *lokavidya*.

Lokavidya as we know it is inseparably intertwined with dharma. So dharma of ordinary man takes a severe beating too. The violation of truth by the machine takes away from it its central function namely, regulation of life in tune with the rhythm of nature and truth as such. Thus the power of dharma is eroded and this power is appropriated by the machine, only, as if, to lend it a satanic incarnation.

POWER

Power is the blood of the modern machine. So industry generating power is the heart of the world of machines. This is what gives importance to the engines and the mechanics of generating electricity. The identification with electricity is now so complete that the factory producing electricity is simply called a power plant and the word 'electricity' is used interchangeably with 'power'. What is this power without which the modern machine is not even conceivable?

In science, power is defined as the rate at which work is done. So power equals work done per unit time. Work also has a well-defined technical meaning which equates it to the product of force and distance traversed under the application of that force (actually the displacement vector). Work actually represents organization of motion. Random motion is least organized and is equal to no work at all since the displacement vector is zero for random motion. Better and better organization of motion represents more and more work. We may say that the rate at which motion is organized is the rate at which work is done. So power is the rate at which motion is organized. This is the same as the rate at which energy is organized or delivered.

This is the primary sense in which modern energy forms are distinguished from traditional forms of energy. Whereas men and women, bullocks, horses, and wood (as fuel) are traditional sources of energy, modern sources are mainly fossil fuels, coal, petrol, diesel, naphtha, etc. It is these fuels that are used in the engines of automobiles, it is these fuels which are burnt to produce electricity. The fundamental process in all these involves conversion of heat energy obtained by burning the fuel into the motion of a piston and then a rotor. The entire branch of physics called thermodynamics deals with the science of this conversion. The rotor is then used to run automobiles or produce electricity, etc. So these fossil fuels constitute modern sources of energy precisely because their heat is convertible into organized motion at a high rate. That is, these fuels constitute sources of power.

It is this power which is the source of the modern machine's capacity to do a great amount of work in a very small time. Not just this, but to do a number of such tasks whose performance is unimaginable if we were to rely only on traditional sources of energy. Railways, aeroplanes, and blast furnaces are the obvious cases, but hundreds of others abound all round us. The modern machine is the embodiment of power. It was no coincidence therefore that the huge factories, the large dams, and the big power plants were once called the 'temples' of modern India. It was in the sense of being omnipotent. But the progress towards being omniscient has been remarkable too.

Computers and telecommunications represent the omniscient phase. When Francis Bacon said long ago that knowledge was power, he could have hardly foreseen the meaning this dictum has assumed today when the rate of organization of information has become the chief ally of power. When machine substitutes man, knowledge becomes information and the rate of doing work becomes a function of the rate of organization of information.

This electromechanical organization of information through computers, telephones, email, fax, and what not has developed as a necessary aid to the continuation of imperialism whose social basis has constantly been shrinking. If very few people in the world want to control everything—finance, technologies, markets, and people—then they must have at their command methods which organize, process, store, and transfer to great distances information at a very high speed. There should be no confusion, however, that the information technology is in the service of the modern machine which ultimately delivers goods and whose blood is power. Thus having looked into the nature and function of 'power' we should now have some understanding of the science of this 'power'.

SCIENCE OF POWER

This is the science of tapping large potentials in small amounts of time. The steam engine, car engine, thermal power plants, hydel power plants, nuclear energy stations all work on the principle of tapping large potentials in small amounts of time.

Steam engines and thermal power plants exploit the thermal potential in coal. When coal burns, a great amount of heat is given out which is used to heat water in large boilers to produce superheated steam. Jets of this steam are then used to push a piston, rotate a rotor or a turbine and we have highly

organized motion at our command for locomotion or production of electricity as the case may be. Nuclear reactors use nuclear energy to produce the
same effect, namely heating of water to obtain high-speed jets of superheated steam.

Automobiles use the chemical potential of fossil fuels. Petrol, diesel,
kerosene, etc., are simply hydrocarbons, that is compounds consisting of
very large molecules made up only of carbon and hydrogen. These are
highly inflammable liquids which release a lot of heat and undergo substantial expansion when burnt. The latter property is used by the internal
combustion engines to move a piston which in turn moves a rotor. Sudden
expansion on burning and the rise in the temperature of the gases
are—although not the same—mutually related phenomena. One can also
say that these engines tap the thermal potential of petrol, etc.

The point to note is that large thermal or chemical potentials are suddenly
tapped into organized motion. Chemical or thermal energy stored in fossil
fuels through processes lasting over tens of thousands and millions of years
is tapped in a very small time to produce highly organized motion. This is
the same as saying that large amounts of potential energy are converted into
lot of useful work per unit time. It could be any kind of potential. For
example, even gravitational potential is used precisely in the same fashion.
This is what hydel plants do. Rivers are dammed to raise the level of water
reservoir to great heights and then made to fall on the blades of turbines
below. Thus the gravitational potential of water is first converted into
kinetic energy and then into the rotation of the turbine which in turn when
placed in a magnetic field generates electricity.

Industries generating electricity are called power plants. Power, as we
stated in the previous section, is the rate of organization of motion, which is
the rate at which useful work is performed. So electricity is the means of
transport of this power instantaneously and on a large scale. Electricity is
used for heating and lighting purposes and for running of machines. This is
just the reverse of what happens at the power plant. At the power plant,
thermal, chemical, or gravitational potential is used up to produce organized
motion which in turn is used to produce electricity. At the user's end the
reverse happens, electricity is used to produce motion in the machine, heat
in the oven and hot plates, light by heating the tungsten filament, etc. So
electricity makes great sense in societies in which power is produced at one
place and consumed at other distant places.

But this entire activity of tapping large potentials in small time-periods is
highly unnatural. In nature we do not find large temperature gradients, nor

do we find water falling through hundreds of feet without obstruction, nor are mass particles destroyed to produce suddenly absolutely large amounts of energy. Nature in general acts across small gradients. Most processes of the living world take place at ambient temperatures. So in natural processes, energy converts from one form to another and work is done at a pace at which there is no waste and the efficiency of conversion is very close to one, even by scientific calculations. In total opposition to all this the science of power fuels an industry which has very low efficiency and which is very wasteful.

The concept of waste is born with modern industry. Fly ash from thermal plants, slag from steel-mills, plastic fallen into disuse, and effluents from the chemical industry (not to mention nuclear waste) are inevitabilities of modern industry. Inefficiency and wastefulness are built into the sudden tapping of large gradients to produce high rates of organization of motion.

But waste cannot be considered only a dead load on nature. The more wasteful an industry is, the more environmentally degrading it is. If corpses do not go back into the soil, they become ghosts. Fly ash, slag, exhaust gases, plastics, and what flows out of the drains of the chemical industry are not acceptable to nature. The order in nature cannot assimilate them. They are the physical correlate of disorder (entropy) created by the modern machine by its very operation. The toxicity of the gases in the atmosphere, the presence of dangerous bacteria and microbes in drinking water, the pollution of edibles by chemical inputs in agriculture, and the noise level in the cities do not merely disturb ecology, they violate the underlying principle of life. It is here that the science of power—modern science—violates human chastity.

But chastity is no more a consideration. Purity and morality are no more constitutive of public criteria. The world and everything in it stands divided on considerations of power—Europe and the Other. The machine and the theory of the machine are no exception.

THE EUROCENTRIC THEORY

The machine leads to a division not known until it arrived. It divides the society or the human world extensionally and man and his essence, intentionally. Nineteenth century onwards the world is divided into those who wield power and those against whom it is wielded. On the one side are those who possess capital and on the other those who have not even seen the machine. There are those who employ others and there are the hungry millions who do not have any employment. The masters of modern technology stand aloof from those who cannot comprehend the logic of modern science or the market. So there are people who are busy all the time and there are those who are forced to idle away entire lives.

Corresponding to this division in society, and in unity with it, man finds his essence split into two parts, each opposed to the other. This split expresses itself in a great many ways. It is this split which is underlined by the treatment of estranged labour by Karl Marx in the *Economic and Philosophic Manuscripts of 1844*. It is to overcome this that Marx conceives of the idea of sensuous human activity in the First Thesis on Feurbach. It is this split that keeps the idler busy with acts of inconsequence and gives him all the time in the world without leisure.

In and through this division the machine and the machine-man appropriate everything, literally everything. As if to compensate for the loss of that pride of place which the earth had enjoyed in Europe long before Copernicus, Europe becomes the centre of the world. The anthropomorphisms of the Christian tradition, in this process, turn into Eurocentric conceptions. From now on culture becomes the hand-maiden of the European ruling classes, European history becomes the history of man, European science becomes the only science, and the modern European state and society start representing that pinnacle of human progress toward which all societies and people must gravitate. As a result, the European theory of the machine is beset with inconsistencies and falsehoods. It is to a discussion of these that we turn our attention now.

The theory of machines, strictly speaking, is not separable from the science developing in Europe in the nineteenth century. Nor is this science separable from the development of general theories—social, biological, mathematical—during that period. Even a cursory look reveals the common underlying paradigms, categories, logic, economic and cultural biases, etc. However, we are concerned with the machine, that is, energetics in general or thermodynamics in particular. This is the theory of conversion of thermal energy into mechanical energy or in other words, the conversion of heat into useful work. We shall in the following section discuss two pivotal concepts of this theory—useful work and isolated systems—and demonstrate the Eurocentric nature of these concepts.

USEFUL WORK

The concept of useful work is central to machine-theory. Natural science for the first time encountered an explicit anthropomorphism. For the Christians everything was made by God for the use of man. Science had thought that it had liberated itself from Christian anthropomorphism, so when it reappeared in thermodynamics in the form of useful work there was great resistance to its acceptance. If science had retained a human touch the concept should have been accepted and the meaning of anthropomorphism redefined according to contemporary times. But that did not happen and instead an attempt was made to conceptualize useful work as a universal concept. Organized motion was contrasted to random motion where there was heat. The concept of usefulness was replaced by the concept of organization making it appear independent of human need and context.

Let us take as an illustrative example the railways, a target of Gandhi's criticism in *Hind Swaraj*. It may appear obvious to most of us that the steam engine which converted the energy available in coal into the rapid trains did a great amount of very useful work. It transported coal, minerals, and wood to long distances. It carried armies quickly to long distances. It quickly carried finished goods to distant markets and it provided a means for the people to go to distant places in relatively short periods of time. We may think that such service by the railways was necessary and useful for the purposes of modern industry, national defence/imperial governance, trade and lucrative employment, etc. But this is no different from how an Englishman must have thought about India during British rule and perhaps even later. But there is necessarily the other side to each one of these 'useful' acts performed with the help of the steam engine. When raw materials and resources are lifted away on a large scale, life around those places is disorganized completely. Witness tribal life today. The movement of armies which was once the tool of imperial governance is still the tool of imperial governance although it now appears under the label of national integrity or national defence. The task is no different, only the names have changed. When things are sold at great distances from the site of production, trade grows and what follows is the deprivation of labour-intensive areas, growth in the financial strength of the capitalized and tertiary sectors of the economy. Witness the state of agriculture vis-à-vis industry and the family budgets of the unorganized sector vis-à-vis the overflowing riches of the metropoles.

It is easy to see that starting from the steam engine, through the aeroplane, the motor car, electric power, and to the computer and information technology, useful work has a very definite meaning in terms of 'useful for whom'. The useful work done by these machines has been useful only for the Europeans and their allies elsewhere. Just take a look at who travels in the aeroplanes, who owns a car or a two-wheeler, who uses electric power, and who makes use of computers, telephones, email, and so on. If we imagine a use-scale on which the poor Indian masses are on 1, then those in Delhi, Mumbai, and other large cities may be around 1000 and the Europeans and the Americans may be somewhere near the million mark.

'Useful work' with the anthropomorphism in it is a meaningful concept. A lot of useful work is done when food is cooked. An incomparable amount of useful work is done in cloud formation and rain. The amount of useful work that the sun's rays do every day is incomparably more than all the work done by the entire modern industry till date. Parochialism and inconsistency creeps in precisely when the attempt is made to transform 'useful work' into 'organized motion'. The universal appearance of this concept becomes a smokescreen to hide the Eurocentric bias in the whole phenomenon. In fact, the disregard of others—namely non-Europeans—the suppliers of raw materials, the processes of fuel formation, the destructive consequences of modern industry, etc., are rooted theoretically in a certain trend in nineteenth century European theory which can be well illustrated through a discussion of the idea of an 'isolated system'.

ISOLATED SYSTEMS

While discussing the mechanics and economics of thermal power plants, we do not discuss the processes of the formation of coal. While discussing a spinning mill, the cotton growers, the displaced spinners, or the manner of production of electricity are not seen as issues to be taken into consideration. Efficiencies of steel mills do not take into account the disorganization caused by large-scale mining. The study of industrial processes in general does not bother about the consequences which are very often destructive for nature and man. But this is the dominant trend. The mechanics and the economics of the machine in general do not take into account either the sphere of raw materials or the consequences of processes. *The machine is always treated in isolation.* And this has its rationale ultimately in the theory of machines, namely the Second Law of Thermodynamics.

The Second Law formulates the concepts of entropy, useful work, available and unavailable energy, efficiency, energy-quality, etc. It is the basis of Energetics and of the Theory of Machines. The formulation of the Second Law makes use of the concept of isolated systems. An isolated system means a system which neither takes anything from the surroundings nor gives anything to the surroundings. According to the law, the entropy of an isolated system never decreases. It is through postulation of such a system that the energetics of the machine are worked out. For example, the calculations of efficiency of a petrol engine have nothing to do either with the processes of formation of oil or with the manner and rate at which the exhaust gases pollute the atmosphere or are fixed by the vegetable kingdom. Comparisons of the efficiencies of the electric stove and the wood stove (*chulha*) do not take into consideration the economic and social costs and the labour and energy efficiencies of related phenomena.

It is the unrealizability of an isolated system which has given space for serious suspicion that the Theory of Energetics may after all be false. It is obvious that an isolated system does not exist in practice. When one talks about an isolated system, it is only as a limiting case or as an idealization. What if it is a wrong kind of idealization, that is, if it is not a limiting case at all? If even in thought, that is, even in principle, it is not possible to reduce all the exchange of a system with its surroundings to zero, then it is a wrong kind of idealization. Then, it is not the limiting case of any series of actual systems arranged in a particular order. It is this kind of doubt that lends support to the suspicion that the Theory of Energetics is after all false. For it is difficult to believe how truth could so blatantly have an economic or European bias.

Thermodynamics is a scientific theory formulated during the unprecedented industrial upsurge of nineteenth-century Europe. The isolated system syndrome seems to have been the general paradigmatic trap of contemporary European theory. It seems to be best illustrated in the theories of economic progress. Europe was witnessing along with the Industrial Revolution an upsurge in the wealth of nations. European theory attributed the source of this wealth to science and industry or to the worker's labour (depending upon the doctrinal inclinations of the theoreticians). However, both the bourgeois theorists and the socialists saw the source of this wealth as located within Europe, namely, European science or the labour of the European worker. The feed from the colonies was not supposed to be even a part of the principal source. Where is the discussion on the relation between the efficiency of the Manchester mill and the *zamindari* system in India? Europe stood aloof like an isolated system and all its relations with the outside world—America, Africa, Asia, Australia—were nothing more than perturbations on the central phenomenon. Europe was not isolable and any manner of understanding based on the isolated system syndrome should have led to false theory. And we now know that this indeed was the case.

Thus the Theory of Machines too fits itself into a Eurocentric paradigm of social and economic theory. Whether this makes the theory false can be debated but what necessarily follows from this is that the Theory of Machines serves the same order of men and things which the machine serves. But then isn't that a trivial thing to say?

THE *SWADESHI* ALTERNATIVE

There are people the world over who do not work on the machine and therefore do not belong to any publicly functioning orders. Much has been said about the subordinate, reduced, alienated, and exploited state they are in. But it is now time to talk about what they do have. Weavers, spinners, printers, potters, blacksmiths, metal workers, carpenters, and hundreds of other small and local communities are masters of a great variety of industrial arts. There is much discussion in the literature about the great tradition of these industrial arts but not enough on their contemporary status and the possibilities associated with them. Without denying the ruptured state they are to be found in, we may recall that it is the living aspect of this tradition that constituted the basis of the village industries movement inaugurated by Gandhi. In utter contrast to the modern machine, these industrial arts do not derive their strength either from capital or from wage labour and yet have a widespread existence even today sufficient for a swadeshi alternative.

In the sphere of machines, swadeshi means use of local raw materials, exchange in the local market, and control of the local territory as well as social community. The knowledge basis also ought to be local which means that lokavidya ought to have primacy over the organized universal knowledge systems. Further, the technical practice and its conception belong to a world view whose inseparable other parts are the rituals, forms of worship and beliefs of the practicing community, and the bigger world to which it belongs. All this and much more constitute the universe of public interaction in which lies the basis of correction, improvement, innovation, and even rejection. The swadeshi movement is not just a technical alternative: it involves a belief that truth and non-violence shall be the ultimate victors. It is not a belief in some distant goal. It is a regulative belief, a basis for the incorporation of human values within the body of science and technical practice. To save our discussion from unbridled speculation, let us proceed further through discussion of a few important examples.

THE CHARKHA

During the Indian independence struggle the charkha (or spinning wheel) symbolized opposition to the power-driven machine. For Gandhi, the return of the charkha meant a return of the dynamism of the Indian people. Gandhi wrote and talked about the charkha and organized around it for more than two decades. The charkha was seen by him as a means to ameliorate the economic condition of his people and also as a source of spiritual regeneration. The message was simple. A machine is not related only to the material life of man, it is an equal instrument in shaping his spiritual life too. The charkha work was designed so that it was based on the cooperation of the villagers. Cooperation between individuals was a necessary aspect; without it the techno-material contraption would not even qualify as a charkha for him.

Today cotton is produced only in certain areas of the country and it goes to the places where it is used only through the large *mandis*. The charkha, to whatever extent it is in use, has been reduced to the status of a mere tool. It can come back to life and give life to much more, provided cotton is grown everywhere. The lifestyle and the oneness with the rhythm of nature for which the charkha stands is well illustrated equally by the *chak* of the *kuumhar*.

THE CHAK

Much praise has been showered in the literature on the potter for his skill and finesse, for the way his fingers work through the mud on the wheel (the chak) to produce unimaginably beautiful objects. This deceptively simple technology has served mankind for millennia. It is in neglect today due to the large-scale production of metals, plastic, and changes in lifestyle.

The chak is peculiarly representative of a swadeshi way of life and organization of production. The mud from the local pond is first cleaned removing the pebbles, grass, etc. This mud is left for a few days wet or under water so that it becomes sticky. It is then beaten sufficiently to homogenize. Then it is put on the chafe and the craftsman makes pitchers, toys, and whatever he wants. The making of these objects itself involves several stages. They are then allowed to dry, then fired in a furnace. These furnaces are open air structures of cowdung cakes arranged in pits as large as 20 × 15 ft dimensions.

The dried mud products are laid in various layers—horizontally and vertically—for firing. The raw material is local, the market is local, the knowledge and the skills belong exclusively to the community, and there are practically no capital needs. The entire process is literally earthly.

The community of potters is generally recognized as peaceful, as if partaking with the rhythm of nature induces in them the quality of nature. The chak it seems will survive as long as nature does. The odds are heavy. But there are others like it, groaning under perhaps heavier odds.

The practice of smelting iron ore locally is not yet dead. It will perhaps never die. The Agariyas still seem to know the art of producing the kind of steel from which the legendary Damascus blade was made.

Agariyas are a tribe that has specialized knowledge about the smelting of iron ore. Their economy and society, in spite of external aggression and disruption suffered for more than two hundred years, continue still to be organized chiefly around ironworks. Their social values, beliefs, and history all have iron at their centre. The tribe is a genuine *loha-jati* which, in the course of millennia, appears to have developed a special relationship with nature, iron-smelting being its forte. The whole operation is organized around the bhatthi which remains an enigma to the modern metallurgist.

Simple tree branches are used to make charcoal. The bhatthi is made of mud. It is of vertical cylindrical shape, the base having a diameter of about 50 cm and the height equalling approximately 75 cm. Erected on a small pit the bhatthi has a vertical hole of 10–15 cm diameter. It is in this hole that the ore mixed with the charcoal is charged from above. At the bottom there are two holes, one for the slag to flow out and the other to allow air to be blown into the furnace. It is from the second hole that the reduced metal bloom is taken out. The whole operation including the pumping of the air through the simple, manually operated bhatthi and tube system, slagging and the correctives applied by the craftsman is an enchanting combination of science and art for which there is no name or equivalent in the modern knowledge system. An operation lasting for about two-and-a-half hours yields some 3–5 kg. of metal.

The bhatthi renders a unique challenge to the modern machine. It is swadeshi in every respect and performs a task considered most advanced by modern technology. *It is by force that it is kept out of the mainstream.* Its inner logic has a compulsive strength comparable to that of a saint in social life. This logic is entirely different, as it is in the case of the chak and the charkha. So these obviously practical alternatives appear to constitute the basis of a theoretical challenge. They seem to stand for a different way of thinking, a different logic of science and life.

7

*Reinventing Gandhi**

SHIV VISVANATHAN

I

Myself Mohan Gangadhar Ambedkar. Yes, you wog bastards, you would
have loved a beginning like that. It brands me as being separate from you
effete intellectuals, wearing your English like corsets, ready to snigger at
every mistake. Yet, think of it. The word 'myself' is a far better introduction
than the word 'I'. 'I' sounds like a certificate. There is a certainty to the
claim. It pins a person like a dead beetle but the introduction myself is not
a scientist's label; it is in invitation, an offering, a tentative listing. Myself
like my garden, or my stamp album; the self not as an integral unitary 'I' but
as a mosaic, a collage or a crossword puzzle. Myself, a word asking, inviting
you to discover me.

My three names might puzzle you. It frightens me. I see it as a sentence,
a burden of the national movement. Ambedkar was a lawyer and unlike
most elite Indians of his time, those fussy Oxbridge dons, he studied at
Columbia University. Gangadhar was Tilak, archetypal Maharashtrian Brahmin, the real lion of the nationalist movement, before the advent of Gandhi.
And my first name Mohan derives from the Mahatma.

Only in India would a man carry three crosses, the burden of three
hallowed names. Only in India would a dalit father give his son such a name
combining three rough varnas—*Bania*, Dalit, and Brahmin.

Dalit I might be but Hindu I also am. Fortunately my father didn't engage
in any neo-Buddhist nonsense. Like all Hindus I was a reincarnation and

* Shiv Visvanathan, 'Reinventing Gandhi', *Information Unit on Militarization & Demili-
tarization in Asia News Letter*, 5, 1992, pp. 34–64.

that is where my sorrows begin. I was Mohandas Gandhi in my last life. When Godse shot me—remember he was one of the few Indian assassins who did not miss—I went to what is popularly called heaven. While India was free of the British, heaven was not. God was still Victorian and heaven was run by the East India Company. All those stuffed figures, with cruel eyes, those greedy barons, the clerks, the jaundiced surveyors, and the lords who resided in grimy portraits, were all there. And the Lord god decided I would be born again for my sins. In heaven as below, it is the bureaucrat who decides and the Lord's secretary was the old war horse, Sir J.H. Hutton.

J.H. Hutton was the last great census commissioner of India, enshrined in every sociologist's memory as the director of the 1931 Census, the last census in which caste was listed as an official category. Hutton, with a mind like a gazetteer and a heart like one, was one big filing cabinet of a man. It was Hutton who decided in what form Hindus should be reborn. It was he who decided with that genocidal twinkle that I would be reborn a Dalit.

He confessed to me he was in two minds. He first thought I should be a Muslim. But Gandhi, he explained had already borne the Muslim cross, first through that mad secularist, Jinnah, still pining for his Parsi wife and then through his son Harilal, who to spite an authoritarian father became Mohammed Abdallah Gandhi. Poor alcoholic Harilal died soon after of rage and tuberculosis. Sir Hutton decreed that I was to be reborn a Dalit.

I was reborn an LDC clerk's son, condemned to a Poona father who was a mouse at office, lion at home. Religious as hell and a wife beater, my new father was also terribly ambitious for his sons. And I, the eldest, was his pride and my mother's too. Mediocre at school, I still passed with flying colours, thanks to an advance copy of the question papers, my father's proudest achievement. Through that happy lottery, the reservation system, I managed to escape home to the chawls of Bombay, and worked my way to a state government scholarship to Ohio State University.

There is a sadness to this. Elite India is Ivy League or Oxbridge. If you claim to be a mere pass, a happy drone from these institutions, you acquire a halo; but with a social science degree from Ohio, Idaho, or Georgia State you are as welcome as AIDS. But one thing mediocre state universities do, they let everyone be; expect so little and provide so much, especially anonymity, money, and a library where an Indian can read his heart out. The libraries were heaven; 'cornucopias' as my Sunday crosswords tell me.

Sadly once an Indian, you are always an Indian. Everyone in America expects an Indian to be a mathematician, a Marxist, or an accountant, and as predictable. There is also an irony about a whole generation of Indian social scientists who came to America to study India. Third rate characters these, they lack the crossness of the American ethnographers or the confident orientalism of the British. Too meek to study America, they write commentaries on India. At least I was second rate and bored, desperate enough to invent anything, with an imagination stuffed full of American best-sellers from Perry Mason to Garp, *Catch 22* to Saul Alinsky. I was one mad salad of Americana, desperate to look at India through Indo-American eyes.

My stupid supervisor, meek and fortyish, who had served time in India on a Fulbright years ago, insisted I study the relevance of Gandhi. I was in despair, I, raised on Pynchon, Barthes, Mailer, Asimov, I study Gandhi. There is no despair like not being able to escape your own history.

I fell asleep over *Experiments with Truth*. *Hind Swaraj* bored me. It seemed drivel, its words crystalline, regimented, and boring. It read like a dull Charles Lamb to a lost Shakespearean text. I thought I would review studies on Gandhi's sexuality by N.K. Bose, Ved Mehta, and Bhikhu Parekh. But sexuality, as Masters and Johnson proved, can be dull and duller still as social science. Sex can titillate as pornography but the Mahatma wrote his sexual experiments as if he were describing a titration, pipette in hand. English, like sex, came easy to me and this man sounded like a dull grammar book.

Yet, through reincarnation, this man was me and was not. He was both myself and a distant horrible other. He was me fifty years ago and yet he was all that I despised now. There was something magical in this; this man, me and not me. Gandhi was the first Hindu who laughed at fear and did not boast about it. He looked normal but was surreal. So matter of fact and yet he appeared like a happy self-assured Artaud ready to turn India into a large experimental theatre. He anticipated Grotowski by turning politics in India into a poor man's theatre. Utterly good, yet someone absolutely confident before evil. I remember what he said when he reviewed Mussolini's crack troops, hundreds of fascists, marching crisply un-Italian in line. 'You all look healthy to me.' Woody Allen would have loved it, Groucho Marx would have stolen the line.

It was then that I read Robert Payne's biography of Gandhi. It moved me in a way Louis Fischer's didn't. Fischer's was an authentic, exact, accurate study. Payne, like many Americans, wrote with an eye to Hollywood. His *Gandhi* read like a monumental filmscript. It was alive, real, dramatic. More fruitful than the Tendulkar's and the Pyarelals. His words are visual and you can feel yourself being dragged along to Champaran and Dandi. When you read Payne describing Jalianwala, when you watch as he describes the Salt

March your blood boils and your mind races and you feel proud, proud to be an Indian. If I were Roland Barthes I would have done a semiotics of satyagraha, shown how a pinch of salt dissolved the symbolism of Empire. Semiotics, like yeast, adds fizz to social science while statistics and survey dull the subject. What I needed was a halfway house, something distant from number crunching, but something less frighteningly esoteric than deconstructing Gandhi *a la* Derrida or something potboilerly subaltern.

I was convinced that the tragedy lay in the fact that Gandhi as a Luddite had not read science fiction. I don't mean serious books on Utopia. I mean literature, that great act of story telling from H.G. Wells and Jules Verne to Ray Bradbury. I felt *Hind Swaraj* would have been more successful as a science fiction story. Imagine if Ray Bradbury or Karl Capek had written it. I decided Robert Heinlein, Isaac Asimov, or an Arthur C. Clarke couldn't do a Gandhi. They were too technophilic, somewhat like adolescents who invented technological marvels as a substitute for ideas. That was inadequate. You see, miracles, even technological ones, don't make a religion. One needs ideas and the smell and taste of people. I was convinced I could rewrite Gandhi, at least recast him. But social scientists are not authors. They cannot invent. They conform to George Steiner's description of the critic, that when 'they look behind they see a eunuch's shadow'. At best, as futurists we write scenarios. As a saving grace, we avoid catechisms. That much the sociology of knowledge has taught us to do. Anyway a social scientist could at least use the science fiction 'as if' as a heuristic to ask a question. If Gandhi were to return today, how would he redo his book, particularly *Hind Swaraj*.

I was more confident of this exercise. I knew that if Gandhi were to go abroad today, it would not be to Oxford, London, or redbrick Manchester but to a large American state university like mine. He could easily be my dorm-mate across the corridor, cooking food separately.

I decided to reinvent Gandhi using a social science format. I realized that a social science format was flatter than a short story but I felt intuitively it would be more legitimate. A fictional Gandhi frightens no one, a social science Gandhi even if duller, might. It was a choice between Heinlein and Alvin Toffler.

I realized the wisdom of this when I saw the Attenborough video of *Gandhi*. There is an old tribal taboo about photographing anyone. They say filming a man robs him of his self, his soul. Attenborough did just that. When one sees Gandhi today, one sees the actor Ben Kingsley. Gandhi is more athletic in the film, more sensual. One misses the toothless imp with jug ears, his head as bald as a bulb. Attenborough's Gandhi was an athlete but the real Gandhi was a wizened sage. But I decided to follow Attenborough and Americanize Gandhi even more. By Americanizing a man, you modernize him a bit. That was the real question. How far would Gandhi have modernized himself today?

I spent the next month hurtling through the collected works. Fortunately Raghavan Iyer had made it easier culling Gandhi into three volumes. I read N.K. Bose, Bhikhu Parekh, Fulton Sheen, the Kumarappas, Lanzo Vastc, Paul Ricouer, Erik Erikson, Ashis Nandy, and Pyarelal, folios of *Gandhi Marg*, and also looked through hundreds of photographs seeking a point of entry. It was then that I saw in Robert Payne's book a photograph of Gandhi in a loin cloth peering through a microscope. It had a shattering impact on me. It reminded me of a picture I saw in a museum once. It was a Dali-like shot of a fried egg, a yellow sun at the centre, with a crisp petticoat of white around it. At the centre of the yolk is an eye looking back at you. I felt that the Gandhi photograph was telling me something.

For a while I was toying with the safer option, a comparative study of three texts, *Hind Swaraj*, *The Communist Manifesto*, and Tom Paine's *Rights of Man*. I felt that the three texts were like a *mandala*. But then I found the bibliography formidable. Commentaries are by necessity scholastic. They demand enormous reading. However, inventions permit and are in fact only possible with illiteracy. To invent you have to know less.

II

I began dreamily with simple word associations. Mention the name Gandhi and people would say pacifist, satyagrahi, nationalist, anti-colonial, Luddite, Hindu, vegetarian, and Congressman. All these descriptions are right and yet strangely inadequate because Gandhi went beyond the official or dictionary definition of each word. Gandhi was a nationalist who fought the nation-state, an anti-colonialist who wished to redeem the British, a Hindu who happily bypassed the shastras. He was a Congress leader who wanted to preside over the dismantling of the Indian National Congress transforming it into a series of *seva sanghs*. He was a Luddite but the word Luddite embraces too many different people from Ned Ludd to Blake to the Shakers and may be even the inventor of the computer virus. One word is missing in this list and that is the noun, 'scientist'. Gandhi was one of the great scientists of the swadeshi era. Of this period, three scientists are talked about and celebrated: Ramanujan, the mystic mathematician; J.C. Bose, the

legendary plant botanist; and Prafulla Chandra Ray, the chemist-entrepre-
neur. But this list is not complete without Gandhi and, Gandhi I believe was
the most inventive of them all.

Today Gandhi would have studied science rather than law in a large
midwestern university, not unlike mine. His shyness, quite normal in a
scientist would still have bothered him. Instead of entering into the confines
of vegetarian and feminist groups, he would have joined a radical science
group. But it would not be the Mahesh Yogi variety or like Fritjof Capra's
splicing cultures in instant books but something more anti-nuclear and
ecological. He would have initially liked groups like John Todds, The New
Alchemists, or the Amory Lovins Institute for Soft Energy Paths or may be
the Gaia network comprising of scientists like Lynne Margolis and James
Lovelock. These would have been the equivalents of Ruskin, Thoreau,
Tolstoy, Edward Carpenter, the dissenting sages of Gandhi's own time. He
would have wondered how his Hindu background and its hypotheses would
have blended with these western critiques of science, still unnecessarily
pop-orientalist like Capra or bull-doggedly scientific like James Lovelock.
He would have realized that physics was an inadequate basis for science and
would have discarded the innumerable physical metaphors scattered defensively throughout his earlier works. He would have agreed with Aldo
Leopold's claims that ecology functioned at right angles to science, that it
was a liminal threshold to a new niche of sciences.

In his encounter with the west today, Gandhi would have looked for a
Christian critique of theology and technology. He would have been disappointed by the Billy Grahams of technology. Probably Jacques Ellul is the
only one who would satisfy him both as a Christian and critic of technology.
Marshall Mcluhan would have sounded too facile. Lewis Mumford like his
old master Patrick Geddes would have fascinated him. Ivan Illich would
have been closest to him but he would have been troubled by finding Illich
more Gandhian than he was. Two other formidable figures would have
bothered him. He would have been impressed by Solzhenitsyn but repelled
by his Christianity. Foucault, despite his homosexuality, he would have
loved but felt a need to combat in practice. Deep questions there, especially
about how moves for reform merely become another set of disciplinary
practices, networks of technology that embed power further.

For Gandhi, technology umbilicalized man and the blood that
flowed through the new cord was not love or tenderness but only the
corpuscles of dependence. He would have loved Mumford's description of
the space capsule as an umbilicalizing environment and seen some of the

same power-dependence syndrome in the *rathyatra*s of the VHP/BJP across India.

The combination of technology and revivalism resident in it would have intrigued him. In ancient times it was a king's horse that was sent as a symbol of power, now it is the white Toyota van, symbol of borrowed technology. The Toyota rath is dependence hidden in the trappings of Hindu revivalism. Symbolically embodying both in his person is Lal Krishna Advani, the BJP leader. While rushing through Hindu Hindi India, Advani, according to newspaper reports, found the ride bumpy. Drinking tea or any other beverage became difficult. His inventive wife, may be with a touch of unconscious irony, fits a glass bottle with a plastic nipple. It worked perfectly. No more embarrassment of dripping, slopping tea, and suckling it, Advani rides to conquer India. One wishes somebody had video-taped Bonny India.

Gandhi would have admitted now that too much of Tolstoy had blunted his sense of aesthetics, of the purpose of art and literature in modern society. Tolstoy's question, 'What good is Shakespeare?' was too instrumental. It expected literature to perform a technological function. He would admit today that play and play alone could redeem technology.

In the America of today Gandhi would have steered clear of the world of occult and vegetarianism. These are faddist now. Once at the time of Anne Kingsford and Annie Beasant they were Archimedean points of entry into the world of the West. Bypassing even official theologians, he would have realized that it is the writers who are the true theologians. Maybe I am imposing my biases but I feel Gandhi would respond today to Ray Bradbury and Norman Mailer. Bradbury in his stories creates a world of innocence, of the blessedness of the meek. Two stories in particular would have touched Gandhi. First *Fahrenheit 451* the little novella, about a world which has banned books making it a crime to possess them. *Fahrenheit 451* is the temperature at which paper burns. A small group of dissenters decide to memorize the great books and each person is known by the title or author of the book. One is Hamlet, another Hans Andersen, the third knows Tom Wolfe by heart. It is this sense of and commitment to memory that would have moved Gandhi. By heart is such a beautiful word.

Gandhi, the satyagrahi, loved to walk and celebrated walking. He would have loved Bradbury's *The Pedestrian*, about a man walking, breathing in the pleasures of walking, alone in a city where every citizen is glued to the TV screen. The story ends when an electronically driven car arrests him as a dangerous dissenter. If you walk and walk alone, you might think and act alone.

But it is Norman Mailer who has shades of the Old Testament prophet today. He is sensuous, angry, aware of the body and yet is strangely respectful and rigorous about it. Do you remember his *Pontifications*, a collection of interviews where he talks about plastic?

He called plastic the perfect material example, the technological signature of the twentieth century, 'a material without any grain, any organic substance, any natural colour or predictability. Plastic cracks in two for no reasons whatsoever. It bears up under killing punishments and then explodes in the night. A fibreglass hull can go through storms which would spring a leak in a wooden hull. Then one day in a modest squall, the fibreglass splits completely. Or abruptly capsizes. That is because it is a material which is not even divorced from nature but indeed has not been part of nature.'

Gandhi would have realized that technology had made power into a spectacle. The map of the world is no longer the cartographic division of countries, but divided according to TV channels and TV time. It is the TV screen as spectacle, as the new polis that grants identity. Without the bureaucratic trappings of an information society, a man seems nothing. Even charisma appears a function of TV. The sheer humour and charm of this came out in an incident which would have done a Heidegger or Alfred Schutz proud.

It is the report of an incident between an eight-year-old school boy and the American President, George Bush. The incident, a truly phenomenological encounter recounts that Bush goes to a small school, meets a normal child. The President introduces himself as George Bush, king of kings, President of USA. The school boy looks at the ex-CIA official and is unimpressed. How do I know, he says. Bush takes out his identity card, 'George Bush, President, USA'. The young boy is unconvinced. Anyone can get a card. If you can enter a computer or sell the Eiffel Tower, identity cards of the President should be a dime a dozen. Pointing to the athletic secret agents around him does not help either. They could be rising executives of a new mafia don. Bush points to the residential limousine outside. No impact. Any Hertz car rental agency could do better on a phone call. What Saddam Hussein couldn't do, the young school boy did. Reduced a president to sheer helplessness. Bush, President Bush, is left feeling nude outside TV. It is the idiot box that provides the trappings of Empire. Gandhi would have loved the story, a modern version of the Emperor's New Clothes. It would have reminded him of Churchill's label of him as the naked *fakir*, or his own comments after meeting George V, 'that the King was wearing enough for both of us.'

Power is the real con. It is the power of the powerless that needs to be understood. Power disempowers by splitting. It is dualism that maintains power in position. In the west you can conquer the head or the heart; you are scientific or religious. For instance, Dalai Lama and Mother Teresa represent compassion, Norman Borlaug or Kissinger power and science. There is no place for compassionate power. Machiavelli and St Francis stand across a divide. Gandhi would have remembered Tolstoy's magnificent question 'why can't the Sermon on the Mount have the same law-like status as Pythagoras' Law?'

I confess writing about power, after Foucault and especially Hannah Arendt, is difficult. That damned woman sipping coffee and smoking away understood power better than any man. I could happily steal a few lines from each but Gandhi would smoothly go beyond them into a world these Europeans are afraid to touch—science. Even if not a black box, science for them was a privileged order of discourse. In fact, Europe and even the west would regard itself as barbaric or at least medieval without modern western science. If Gandhi wanted to escape the modern West, he had to subvert or transform science, playfully, laughingly, and politically but a degree in science is a bad way to begin.

III

Modern science like Anglo-Saxon law encodes a western view. With law, all the little graces, the idiosyncracies of colonialism become part of you. Similarly with years of biochemistry, you feel Crick and Monod are gods and you believe the double helix to be more mystical and sacred than any eucharist. But India, durable India, has a way of curing such an attitude. It makes nonsense of any world, it domesticates any conqueror. All it needs is time to weave its magic.

Imagine Mohandas Karamchand Gandhi armed with a PhD in science, returning to be a CSIR pool officer. American PhDs in India are a dime a dozen. Fortunately Gandhi found a job in a small agricultural institute in Madhya Pradesh. There is nothing more emasculating than being a professional scientist in India. The magical world of science is in the west. CERN (European Organization for Nuclear Research) and Brookhaven are the new Vaticans or Disneylands. Our scientists need to keep visiting the west like Aeneus touching the earth. Too long an exile from the west and your charm wears off. Even the most radical scientist needs a certificate from a second rate American. A young scientist told me 'if you don't go abroad, don't write in a foreign journal, you cease to exist. Have you seen M.G.K. Menon going abroad? He maintains all the foreign stickers on his suitcase, an off-hand representation of his power.' It is the west that certifies one as a scientist. For the new Gandhi, there would be no period of experiment. There would have been no time as in South Africa, no time to become myth before he entered history building an uncritical reputation in Africa before he entered the Indian stage.

If he had lived today Gandhi would have felt once again the desperation of every foreign-returned intellectual. India frightens with its size, its dirt, its masses, its corruption, its fetishization of the past, its pomposity. Looking for support among fellow scientists is futile. Trade unions only want promotion. The Bernalian radicals, Marxists in all shades of pink merely want to carry science to the villages. Environmentalism is a drawing room discourse. You can talk pollution or recycling as long you leave the world view of science intact. In fact environmentalism is an invitation card to a UN conference. It is like that campus joke among Indians at my university. A young scientist rushes into a cafe saying, 'I have turned environmentalist. I just got my green card today.' There is no greater fundamentalism than science. You don't have to embody it in a figure like Khomeini, it is present in the nature of method.

I want to answer only one question now. What would be the skeletal outlines of the *Hind Swaraj* Gandhi would have written today? What would he add on science to his critiques of law and medicine? Skeletally, crudely, how would he challenge the dualism of knowledge and power in modern society?

IV

Hind Swaraj—it reads like a child's essay. When Gandhi claimed modern civilization is wrong it has the same simplicity as a child's statement that a cow has four legs. There is something clear, obvious, and crystalline about the text. But read it again; try visualizing it and the whole thing appears surreal. It is as if there is a Salvador Dali lurking in Gandhi, a trickster inside the sage. A Dali and a Dalit, a Salvador Dalit. Being a Dalit is important today. Without them, India would turn sentimentally revivalist or crassly modernist. The search for equality is a trapeze act between the two. Equality needs modern technology. There is no greater sanity than tap water. Those who talk of village wells and *lota*s haven't lived it. Water in a tap spells freedom and cleanliness. Sanitation is both sanity and freedom. Utopian

India is a clean tap in every house. I don't want to sound like Sam Pitroda with that integrated chip on his shoulder. Technology needs deeper thinking than our C-Dot guru. Critics have read *Gandhi's Experiments* generally in terms of four grids of sex, diet, politics, and technology. Linkages are made across columns as between diet and sex, politics, and technology but, strangely, there is absence of an overall connection. Gandhi's was a fluid science: integral yet full of shifts and transforms. Reading Gandhi one feels both a sense of tremendous consistency and adaptability, the langue and the parole of a new ethic for technology and life. The model allows tremendous free play for transformations, twists, ambiguities. There is also a shifting scale within Gandhi's text, like a shifting between lower and higher octaves. Consider simple examples.

Gandhi was against modern medicine. Even when desperately sick, Gandhi refused to take the wonder drug of his time, penicillin. Yet he happily got his appendix removed. Consider his objections to alcohol and tobacco. He led movements against alcoholism, made it part of his political platform and was uncompromising about it. Yet when it came to smoking, Gandhi was relaxed, contending it would be stopped through persuasion and pedagogy, through example. Consider again his attitude to technology. He was opposed to technology in many forms yet was acutely sensitive to it. He was ecstatic about the sewing machine. William Shirer observes that it is in Gandhi's public meetings that the loudspeaker first enters India. In fact Shirer admits it was the first time he himself had seen a loudspeaker used in a public gathering. Shirer adds an interesting vignette on Gandhi's trip to Manchester. Visiting the mills closed by the Indian boycott, Gandhi was surprised by the low quality of English machines and remarked that it was not surprising that England could not cope with Japanese competition. Gandhi criticized the iatrogeny of modern medicine yet this same man complained to his physician Sushila Nayyar about the lack of equivalent innovation among local *vaid*s and *hakim*s. Gandhi helped pilot a bill of fundamental rights and he also argued that caste could not be read within such a system. This was the man who ranted against the colonial city yet always operated politically from it whether it was Johannesburg, Wardha, Ahmedabad, Delhi, or Calcutta. This sense of fluid scale gets embodied in the relation of Gandhi and Nehru. The great Luddite nominated as his successor the great modernist. The lover of Ruskin and Tolstoy chose as his successor the Cartesian Fabian-Socialist, Nehru. It was not an error of judgement. India, Gandhi realized, was a Janus-faced entity. What Gandhi wanted was that the two faces should talk. He was afraid that lacking reciprocity they would become two masks confronting each other stonily. Gandhi did not deny the Nehru in him; he only wanted Nehru and his modernists to recognize the voice of Gandhi's India. I think it was in this way that Gandhi saw *Hind Swaraj*. Even in the late 1940s Gandhi offered *Hind Swaraj* to Nehru as his vision of India, contending he would still not alter one line of it. He implied that Nehruvian India needed two sacred texts—the Constitution of India and *Hind Swaraj*. Why?

For Gandhi, modernity was a movement of forgetfulness where secular, scientific urban India dismissed its roots in the village community. The Indian modernist, like any new convert, knew his catechism, but had no theological training about doubts, debates, and controversies, the costs and pain of choice. Progress meant a move away from the loincloth and the bullock cart. More particularly he had a theory for eliminating poverty but little understanding of pain and suffering. Poverty could be eliminated but pain and suffering needed to be lived out and understood. Not all pain was a disease or discomfort to be eliminated. If it were, altruism, restraint, and asceticism, in fact love would have little play in the emerging consumer society.

Hind Swaraj was an attempt to provide a creative unconscious for modern India, an attempt to make modernity in India more sensitive, less imitative, more confident. The Indian elite literally believed in Macaulay's statement that a shelf of western books—particularly scientific books—was worth the whole library of the Orient. Indian modernists, lacking an intellectual geneology, adopted uncritically the ersatz pedigree of Bacon, Locke, Newton, and Spencer. They thought that modernity like rationality or formal logic was a pellucid inheritance, with no place for pain, ambiguity, or suffering. *Hind Swaraj* was an attempt to create this equivalent of Grecian unconscious for modernity, a Gita for the modernist.

The Indian modernist viewed science and technology as a sack one carried. Instead, it should have been a kite played out or reeled back in the free play of life. *Swadeshism* was still terribly imitative. As Gandhi said India without the English was still Englishstan.

One would ask how Gandhi the scientist would have looked at tradition today. The political scientist Bhikhu Parekh provides the first of the answers. In a recent study, he stated that for Gandhi, tradition was not a blind collection of precedents, 'but a form of enquiry, a scientific adventure, an unplanned but vigorous communal science constantly tested and revised against the harsh reality of life. Far from being antithetical, tradition and science are cousins. Tradition was unplanned science and science was a tradition of unplanned enquiry'. Parekh is clear and precise in recognizing the rational and empirical nature of both exercises. One only wishes he were less restrained. Otherwise he would have immediately followed up by exploring one of the grand inversions Gandhi had performed. It is true he was a scientist in his attitude to Hinduism, playfully but rigorously bypassing the shastras, ready to gently confront the Sankaracharya's ire. But more importantly Gandhi was a Hindu in his attitude to science, denying high church status to any paradigm or bowing before cardinals of philosophy like Popper or Carnap.

V

Gandhi was a great pedagogue. He knew the dangers of rendering any document lifeless through certain forms of mechanical utterance. It is true that in 1947 he had told Nehru that he would not alter one line of *Hind Swaraj*. But today, he would have realized that *Hind Swaraj* needed to be even more dialogical than before, that his legacy had become dull and stereotyped, more alive in Europe and America, than at home. The satyagrahi abroad had been more inventive than the *satyagrahi* at home. A Lanzo Vasto or a Bayard Rustin, a Luther King, a Alan Paton, or a Vaclav Havel could understand the spirit of *Hind Swaraj* more than his museumized epigoni, mothballing khadi. It is precisely in this spirit that he would have broken the stereotypical opposition between town and country, a dualism that a litany of sociologists had helped aggravate further.

Gandhi would have innovated beyond his earlier critique of the colonial city as parasitic, realizing it was too defensive, too endemically biographical, the reflections of a second rate lawyer from a third-rate town, sour graping about London and Bombay. He would have become one of the great exponents of the city, but not the western notion of the city which treats civitas, civilization, civics, and the dreams of the polis as similar mosaics. Gandhi would have tried to revive the imagination of the Indian city. Within such a frame town and country become not impregnable fortresses but 'a complicity of opposites'.

In fact, if Gandhi had a western complement, it was Francois Rabelais. Both were great scientists and great students of the philosophy of resistance. Both went beyond the crowd and the mob to celebrate the citizen in the city. Satyagraha is essentially a civics in that sense.

Both Rabelais and Gandhi were sociologists of the body. Both suggested that it was only the recovery of the body that would redeem the city.

Rabelais was the sociologist of mimicry, excess, obscenity, and the carnivalesque. Gandhi thrived on a celebration of limits but of a non-repressive kind. In Gandhi, the fool and the jester give way to the satyagrahi who unlike the puritan or the revolutionary ascetic never looses the twinkle in his eye. Both Rabelais and Gandhi linked the *polis* not only to the problems of politics but of rationality. In Rabelais, the somersaulting clown overthrows both the pompous bishop and threatens the Ptolemaic world. Gandhi's construction of the body offered a different notion of politics and science. Instead of mime, laughter, and parody, Gandhi talked about suffering, pain, and resistance. He returned the responsibility of the body back to the victim showing how it was uncontrolled desire that allowed the invasion of both disease and the expert. Gandhi seems to make suffering the site of a different kind of rationality. Pain and suffering are not merely objects to be erased or overthrown. Science has repeatedly technologized pain and has a virtually monologic attitude towards it. In fact, pain like a slum becomes something to be eradicated. For Gandhi, suffering needs languages beyond the technological. In a Heideggerian sense, it is a dwelling to be lived in and talked about. The language of resistance, of coping must go beyond the purely technological.

The satyagrahi as citizen was also challenged by a new figure who made the Gandhian theory of the city even more imperative. The guerilla in his romantic or realist incarnations also struggled with the dialectic of town and country. In the most mechanical version, he was Pol Pot dreaming of ruralizing every city through genocide. Also, was not Pol Pot only a more exaggerated version of Mao of the cultural revolution who condemned or eliminated myriads of city intellectuals? Once the revolution is over the guerilla becomes merely an intermediate technologist offering eclectic solutions regarding the city. His revolutionary politics lapses quickly into an everyday centralism. It is the satyagrahi who has to provide for the rhythm of everyday resistance, which is both scientifically and politically innovative. Gandhi would have approached this through an agricultural theory of the city. Remember there is no sentimentalism here, no environmentalism swooning over a park or a reservation.

In *Hind Swaraj* (1908), Gandhi saw the city as embodying a triangle of violence. The city was the home of vivisection, racism, and prostitution. It was also the site of the parasitic professions.

Racism violated the fundamental dignity and equality of man and the call to celebrate the diversity of bodies. Strangely, Gandhi appears weakest here. His success in Africa had a slightly hyperbolic note to it. As he himself confessed, he was uncomfortable with the kafir and even complained when he was confined in the same cell with them or when offered the same food. But Gandhi realized how city authorities could use planning as an aid to segregation and fought this with some success. His critique of the professions was more a reaction to what colonialism had done to the bureaucrat, lawyer, and doctor turning them into third-rate mimics of western knowledge. The rapacity of the professions had also created the city as an efflorescence of touts. It was in this vein that Gandhi contended that western medicine was a form of slavery and to indulge in it was sin. Gandhi's ideas on vegetarianism, his attempt to resist modern drugs, his attempts to work out a theory of fasting can be seen as celebrated attempts to work out an alternative way of looking at the body. Sometimes they border on the obsessive. Today Gandhi would have realized that all this while important was not enough. *Hind Swaraj* needed to be much more inventive and provide for a more playful vision of work, waste, and energy in the city.

For Gandhi, the modern city was a disembodied world: the home of abstractions and the modern machine. The dynamism of the city was not of a creative kind. The city as a site of perpetual mobility lacked memory. The city as the home of the intellectual was producing third-rate work. To recover the Indian sources of creativity demanded that we reclaim the Indian city. For Gandhi this could only be achieved through a threefold recovery of an agricultural view of the world, a naturopathic approach to life, and the concept of handicraft.

VI

The modern city dualized mind and body, *lexis* and *praxis*. Such a dualism was endemic to the modern university and its basic product—the professional. Professionalization was in a deep sense the disembodiment of the craft traditions. Gandhi's critique of prostitution was not, I would like to suggest, restricted to the oldest profession. The prostituting of the professions was endemic to the mind–body dualism. The disembodied mind can prostitute itself as much as the mindless body. For Gandhi, the only way to resist the commercialization of the professions was to reintegrate mind and body. It is only such an integration that allows for trusteeship. For this Gandhi would have advocated a return to handicraft. The Gandhian notion of handicraft is positively Heideggerian. In *What is Called Thinking*, Heidegger observed,

We are trying to learn thinking. Perhaps thinking too is like building a cabinet. At any rate, it is a craft, a handicraft. Craft literally means the strength and skill in our hands. The hand is a peculiar thing. In the common view, the hand is part of our bodily organism. But the hand's essence can never be determined or explained by its being on organism which can grasp. The hand is infinitely different from all grasping organs— paws, claws or fangs—different by an abyss of essence. Only a being who can speak, that is think, can have hands and can be handy in achieving works of handicraft. But the craft of the hand is richer than we commonly imagine. The hand does not only grasp and catch, or push and pull. The hand reaches and extends, receives and welcomes—and not just things; the hand reaches itself and receives its own welcome in the hand of others. The hand holds. The hand carries. The hand designs and signs, presumably because man is a sign. Two hands fold into one, a gesture meant to carry one into the great oneness. The hand is all this and this is handicraft.

Heidegger adds that, 'every notion of the hand in every one of its works carries itself through the element of thinking, every bearing of the hand bears itself in that element. All the work of the hand is rooted in thinking. Therefore thinking itself is man's simplest and for that reason, hardest handiwork.' Modern professionalism is the perspective of an abstract mind that handles equations, files, and formulae as disembodied entities. To redeem professionalism one needs to recover this pious union of language, body, and thought. It is such a piety of thinking that is embodied in the charkha and khadi.

Round the *charkha*, that is amidst the people who have shed their idleness and who have understood the value of cooperation, a national servant would build up an anti-malaria campaign, improved sanitation, settlement of village disputes, conservation and breeding of cattle and a hundred other beneficial activities.

We have frozen khadi today and converted Gandhi's writings into an irrevocable shastra. But khadi and satyagraha were not irrevocable symbols, or abstract signs, but part of an evolving grammar of resistance in the concrete. Remember Gandhi was fortunate. He entered the realm of technology as cook, nurse, and weaver not as a high-brow engineer. His theory of technology was a part of ethics and thus had a beautiful everydayness to it, a superb sense of the concrete and its interrelationships. For him, technology could only remain technology by reactivating communitas. It is only such a notion of handicraft that can resist obsolescence. An attitude of obsolescence is endemic to the modern professional who handless equations, files, and formulae as disembodied entities and who can easily ignore bodies and contexts. Obsolescence is unthinkable in a handicraft community. In fact, the much praised Schumpetarian innovator who rules by disruption, is a classic idiot in this context.

VII

Hind Swaraj was a major critique of the professions. But the one profession that Gandhi ignored would become central in any rethinking of the book. Today, a Gandhian epistemology of science would be necessary. Such an essay is beyond the abilities of the author. What we will explore, however, is how Gandhi would have altered the organization of science.

Gandhi was a sage and Gandhi was a Baniya. It is precisely these avatars of his that would become a scissors pruning science to size. It is as a Baniya that Gandhi's critique of science would have been more devastating. No Baniya stifles work but every Baniya is ruthless about flabbiness and waste. He has a bloodhound's nose for it. And in criticizing science, Gandhi would have felt like Rachel Carson that 'science had grown fat, lazy and corrupt and like an *obese athero-selerotic* man imagines more rich food will cure his condition.' When money is a vocation, one husbands it. Also one is inventive with it. Gandhi would have realized that what science needs least is money. What it requires is a more playful asceticism, a catalytic shift whereby science from being a career returns to being a vocation.

Gandhi would have added with that other great Baniya, James Lovelock that 'no annual report ever asks how many students enjoyed work, how many children visited a laboratory, how many students functioned as willing apprentices.' Transforming this playful asceticism to an Indian context, Gandhi would have asked for ashrams and *gurukul*s in science. It is the *gharana*s and gurukuls that can encourage scientific genius, give the scientist the tacit knowledge that makes for creativity. In fact only one modern Indian scientist, C.V. Raman, successfully created a nursery of Indian scientists. Raman was cantankerous authoritarian, unbearable but he eventually encouraged more creative scientists than the entire CSIR which he dubbed as 'tombs for the burial of scientific instruments'. But what Raman grumbled about or ranted against, Gandhi would have formulated more systematically.

His suggestion in a Lovelockian fashion would be for dismantling of all large laboratories. He would demand that the scientist work at home, like the housewife. Based on the political economy of research he would make four other arguments. Gandhi would contend that science like medicine was becoming increasingly iatrogenic. Iatrogeny is any state of malaise or disease introduced by an expert. Gandhi would add that to practice western agriculture like western medicine was slavery and that the peasant was as responsible as the agricultural scientist for the ecological havoc of the green revolution. He would add further that the solution to the problems of science was not more investment in science. Science in its present form was subject to diminishing returns. This was not a procession in the Piercian sense of *a fin-de-siecle* physics where once a paradigm gets entrenched one needs more and more investment to solve problems of diminishing intellectual viability. Gandhi's idea would have stemmed more from medical research. Here every cycle of drugs invented tends to be more cost intensive and less effective than its predecessor. Hence cost-effectiveness, namely, prudence necessitates that the patient (or the farmer) accept responsibility for the illness and strengthen the body (or the soil) against the need for drugs (or fertilizers). The political economy of modern science demands that every man become a scientist and every village or city a science academy.

Gandhi was not a philistine. His calipers for measuring science were not the blinders of relevance or productivity, the obsessions of the science policy expert and the mission-oriented laboratory. He would have met science at its own level by contending that the goal of science was creativity and then contended that modern organizations showed little evidence of it. A community should be judged 'by the number of cranks, eccentrics, mystics, inventors it has.' A mission-oriented laboratory is hardly the place for ensuring the survival of such a species. But at the same time Gandhi would have suggested that the scientific credo of idle curiosity as an abstraction would not do. The solution to the dangers of idle curiosity is not abstract, ivory tower science. It is to return science to the community, where one interacts with everyday questions from the mundane to the esoteric. Theories like khadi would be spun at home, and science would not be just abstract problem solving. Nor would relevance be ordained by the bureaucrat. The scientist would, like the housewife, care, heal, preserve, nurse, and realize that there is an inventiveness to maintaining, preserving, and preventing. The community of science would vary from city to city, village to village studying plants, sky, forests, wood, seasons, stone, houses, flowers, soil, tools. Yet each community would not be an ocean of alternatives. Gandhi would have loved a passage from James Lovelock's John Preedy lecture, of a vision of science as 'lean and fit, as though in mind and heart as the nurses of Florence Nightingale's time.'

But a science pruned by the baniya's eye alone will not do. The sage in Gandhi would see it as incomplete. An accountant's book does not exhaust the cosmos. Prudence as budgeting is not enough. What one needs is the notion of a sacramental science which can save nature. Gandhi would suggest that the sage becomes an intrinsic part of the experiment. After all he took his experiments on himself seriously. He would have realized that every sage is a laboratory, that his experiments on himself can provide valuable insights for other people. Here the notion of the sage is closer to the shaman than the doctor. The sage, because of his discipline, is trained to amplify his consciousness. His forays into the body can provide new insights and medicines more delicately attuned to it. It is this process of self-testing that would have appealed to Gandhi, where the initiate rather than an innocent guinea pig becomes the source of insight. By doing so the sage adds two new elements to science. Firstly the ethical and cognitive dictum that the physician as sage should experiment on himself. Secondly by relying on his dreams, his subjective experiences, the sage adds to empiricist testing, the idea of revelation. The scientist becomes part shaman in his search for understanding. Despite or may be because of the Jain elements in his philosophy, Gandhi was never sentimental about nature. He would have realized that most forms of work involve some violence to nature but one must seek to minimize it. If the theory of handicraft constitutes one aim of this, his naturopathic perspective constitutes the other. Possibly because of the influence of Kuhne, his experiments in vegetarianism, and the experience with theosophy, *Hind Swaraj* is written as an intensely naturopathic document. Essential to naturopathy is the idea of harmony. For Gandhi, the body was a microcosm of the universe and he sought a harmony of two kinds. Firstly the harmony of the body and its constituent parts, and secondly between the body and its environment particularly with earth, water, light, and air. All disease is a violation of harmony. In naturopathy, one strengthens the body to resist disease. The healer is one who recognizes the wisdom of the body rather than relying on the all conquering drug. For naturopathy there is no greater violation than the body on clock time. The modern city and the modern idea of work adds to the stresses that disrupt the harmony of the body, the soil and the cosmos. One uses natural rhythms of life and death to strengthen the soil and so avoids synthetic fertilizers. One uses the idea of organicity to redeem the mechanomorphic city. One limits desire to restrict technological rapacity. Naturopathy like traditional agriculture and handicraft builds into the system a sense of limits, of what one can do and do no further. It is this sense of limits, of responsibility, which no modern system of knowledge possesses at the epistemic and ethical level.

Gandhi had shades of the Zen master. In that peculiar twist, he would
have claimed that what the sacramental requires is a grasp of the excremen-
tal. Gandhi's writings repeatedly emphasize his preoccupation with cleanliness. He claimed that one's toilet should be so sparklingly clean that one
could eat one's food there. In another instance, he stated that the only thing
India needed from the West is a drainage system. It is the sewer and the flush
tank that made the modern city possible. But today Gandhi would realize
that the modern flush tank is one of the most wasteful and retrograde
machines known to man. It is symptomatic of modern industrial life where
waste is an externality.

It is interesting to note how the *Oxford English Dictionary* defines waste.
Waste is a term used to refer to any space which is barren, uncultivated,
untouched; all these are wastelands. Waste is also used to refer to any object
which has been overutilized, to describe anything which has been sucked
out and abandoned. Here what has been destroyed by overuse is then
labelled as irrelevant. The term waste also refers to decaying or dying
objects. So the concept of waste falls at opposite ends of the spectrum of
'normal' life, between the underutilized and the overextracted, between the
untouched and the untouchable.

Gandhi would seek to redeem an agricultural view of life by restoring
waste as the central category in any system. Waste is not only a life form, it
conceals under that general rubric various forms of life. In fact one has to
show that there is no such thing as waste in nature, that what is called waste
is part of a phenomenally complex food chain. Secondly, it forces us to look
at the cultural construction of waste and the forms of violence it might hide.
Once the category of waste is unravelled we discover the multiple forms of
life present in it. It includes shit, rubbish, dirt, snot, sweat, junk, refuse,
garbage, scum, pollution, obsolescence. Modern economics which is constructed around the axes of scarcity and waste, condemns whole life worlds
with this glossary.

Gandhi would seek to redeem both modernity and tradition by focusing
on waste. He would make the scavenger the paradigmatic figure of modern
India. Automatically, the brahminic world of Indian science would receive
a shock. But the threat is not only to the status hierarchies of the system. For
Gandhi argued that waste has not been fully thought through by city science.

Modern science by over-focusing on production has not celebrated
decomposition, the reduction of manufactured goods to their original materials. If the notion of biodegradability had been celebrated, we would not
have cars in junkyards and abandoned plastic containers, let alone nuclear

waste. The modern consumer too is a big mouth who forgets his even bigger anus. It is in this context that sewage rather than becoming a source of pollution would become a source of life and work. The classic example of city sewage use is Calcutta. This much maligned city uses its sewage to grow its finest vegetables.

It is in this context also that fermentation, the great folk science of Asia, central to food as to garbage, must recapture the imagination of any third world science. The idea of bio-conversion also provides a pluralist touch. It is modest, local, culture specific yet it does not preclude sophistication of analysis or thought. By focusing on waste, the city sciences of today can recover an agricultural view of the world.

Probably the way to understand Gandhi today is to ask how we would have looked at the Narmada struggle.

VIII

More than Chipko and Bhopal, it is Narmada that could represent one of the great moral struggles of our time. Chipko emphasized the importance of seeing green but somehow lost its importance by becoming a rorschach for environmentalists who saw in it everything from subaltern politics to alternative science. Bhopal had possibilities as it raised questions of a peoples' science movement but stopped there, enmeshed in the labyrinth of litigation. But Narmada can link issues of cognition, survival, and democracy. Yet strangely, the struggle is seen as primarily a local problem today.

Within the media, the struggle against the proposed dam centres around two figures. The first is the stark figure of Baba Amte. Recipient of the Magsaysay Award, Amte is a legend for his work among lepers. Baba Amte seems to have subconsciously realized that dam oustees are among the lepers of development, stuck in limbo between land and market, between a world they have lost and a world they may not enter. Their rehabilitation is never in the same place. Even when land is offered for land, it is either degraded forest land or worse. If the compensation is paid in money, the aftermath is as traumatic. The no-dam position is not extremist; it is the logical position of a people driven to extremes by a state that has never systematically rehabilitated oustees.

The second figure is Medha Patkar, who represents a slightly different position. Patkar captures the limits and possibilities of voluntary group politics. If Amte's is an ethical position (he has built his hut on the territory to be submerged and has sworn to die there), Medha's is a more political stand. Besides these two remarkable individuals, the accompanying bevy of environmentalists, journalists, human rights activists do not really spark the imagination. They appear less convincing than even Sanat Mehta, who General Motors style virtually contends that what is good for the Narmada dam is good for Gujarat and India. Despite the international concern, despite the media attention, the anti-dam struggle has failed to move India as a whole, splitting up into a series of eclectic or esoteric debates. The fate of the oustees has left the nation indifferent.

For Gandhi, this failure would have been a twofold one. Firstly it is the failure of the ethical to be convincingly political. The Narmada protest seems amateurish or ineffective. The tribals resisting the dam appear like a bit show staged by the Indian National Trust for Art and Cultural Heritage (INTACH). There seems to be a lack of rhythm between the leaders and the various voluntary groups. The protests in Delhi appear a ten-to-five affair. Short of Medha Patkar's fast, the use of the fast as a political weapon seems woefully inadequate. What is worse Narmada rarely seems to bother the scientific or middle class imagination. It seems a throwback, an antiquarian piece of resistance. Basically, neither the cognitive nor the ethical levels of the debate have entered into and transformed the political imagination.

Mahatma Gandhi would have seen in the Narmada struggle perfect possibilities of theatre. But the language of such theatre must capture the pain and the voice of the victim. This is lost in the language of modernity, secularism, progress, and cost-benefit. An accountant's ledger or a consultant's report cannot be a mourning ritual.

Gandhi would alter the language of such a debate. The damning of the Narmada would be an act of sacrilege and undoubtedly ecocidal and geno-cidal. What adds to the obscenity is that murder is justified as an act of consumerism. The plaintive comment 'what about electricity?' is the moral equivalent of the defence of the Emergency because the trains ran on time.

Gandhi would have rescued religion from the fundamentalists, contend-ing that the real sources of the sacred are forests, mountains, and rivers rather than the Ram Janmabhoomi. Conversely, to think that the Narmada or the Ganga can be saved by an environmental board or a hobby-time INTACH (Indian National Trust for Art and Cultural Heritage) is also inadequate. It is Narmada as a river that captures the unity of India, of cultures—Hindu, Buddhist, Muslim, and of ecologies that have existed side by side. All this is living memory. But it fades when Narmada merely becomes a fragment of a dam project, a piece of ersatz history called 'development', it becomes a victim of what Mumford has called 'the myth of the machine'.

Maybe like bad magic there is bad myth, that is myth that is not life-giving, whose rites are not festival, whose violence conflates vivisection and sacrifice. For such a regime you need the machine and the ideology of progress; its calendars don't celebrate life-cycles and seasons. All it marks are conquests and revolutions. What a strange word revolution. It does not connote a full circle, a return, or a rebirth. A revolution in history does not revive. It erases. A dam promises a revolution. Once a river is 'developed' it is no longer memory. It is merely power for irrigation, it is cusecs of water. A dam desacralizes and desemanticizes a river. The Nile was never *the* Nile after Aswan. A dam is an act of reductionism. The river as watts or cusecs is no longer nature or part of the sacred cosmos. The river no longer flows, it is harnessed and 'made to work'.

A river is not only a physical resource. Like tradition, it is commons of memory, a weave of different forms of life. Seeing the river as only a resource disembeds it, abstracts it, and instead of worshipping the river, we worship the dam on it. The sadness began with Nehru. Long after the ersatz religion of Comte had been abandoned, Nehru revived it by calling dams and laboratories the temples of modern India.

To recover Narmada we need myth and sacred geography. Gandhi would not have argued merely from statistics and survey maps. Body counts of development can be as pathetic as body counts of war. Gandhi would have become a pilgrim doing a *parikrama* of the river. By retracing its course, one remembers the worlds existing side by side. It is this sense of the river that Nehruvian development has destroyed. Nationalist theories of development desemanticized the river. The story of the river shrinks to the moment of the dam. Sacred geography, tradition, and myth yielded to secular spaces and the economic map. Even the map becomes abbreviated to the tourist folder, and the citizen instead of becoming a pilgrim becomes a tourist. Destroying the river at the level of production, he consumes what remains, through leisure.

Gandhi would have ignored the consultant's report or the World Bank assessments and interpreted the Narmada struggle like a new Mahabharata. It is here that town and country, Gandhi and Nehru, critical tradition and progressive modernity come to battle. It is around Narmada that Gandhi would have restarted his struggles against modernity. His tract on the Narmada, as the centrepiece of a transcreated *Hind Swaraj*, would literally be a Gita of anti-development.

For Gandhi, a dam was only a reified expression of modern economics and modern science. Remember his notion of economics was radically different from the experts variant. He confessed he had not read Ricardo and Adam Smith and added that he was not bothered about it. Unlike Nehru he would not need to import consultants from the first world, be they Blacketts, Bernals, Kaldors, or Joan Robinsons. Nor would he require short courses at the World Bank or Harvard to run the economy. (Not that he was averse to foreigners. Only he would encompass them within his dream. After all, he collaborated with C.F. Andrews, and the Polish engineer Maurice Frydman did design his spinning wheels.) Being a shrewd sage, he realized that modern economics was either *ego-nomics* or *ergo-nomics*. It dealt with the obsessions of the bloated individual self called the maximizing individual or the gargantuan collective self called the corporation or the state. Or it was the idolatory of efficiency which repeatedly invented scarcity to justify expansionism.

Central to any alternative manifesto would be his attempt to recover the moral economy of waste, work, and energy.

For Gandhi, modern work was no longer about livelihood and living. It is seen as abstracted and separate from man, measurable as output, analysable as a science. What is even more pathetic is that nature is seen either not doing work or working badly. In fact, the consultant's reports on the Narmada see the river and the surrounding forests as lazy workers producing wood and some minor forest produce.

There are shades of Victorian discourse in these technocratic texts. It is not the usual observation of nature as a resource to be mined or a woman to be raped. It is a more disturbing sense of nature itself. Nature, especially tropical nature, is constituted as excess. There is a sexual corsetting that needs to be touched upon. For the economist, nature as river, nature as water, needs to be 'harnessed'. Mere flow is excess. It is the indecency of spillover. Excess pollutes or wastes and therefore it must be bound. So nature as seed, as forest, as river is bound and stored in banks, in reserves, in dams. There is a disciplining of nature here. Nature as a reproductive process is being forced into a productive discourse.

But it is a myth that nature does not work. One constantly hears that it is the dam that is going to produce but nature is always working and nature is playfully efficient. Gandhi might have quoted Felix Paturi's fascinating table.

Every year terrestrial plants store 17,200 million tons of carbon, marine plants as much as 25,000 million tons. This total of 42,200 million tons of carbon is contained in 105,500 million tons of glucose which corresponds to a goods train 30 million miles long filled to the brim with glucose. It would be long enough to cover the entire railway network of the world 40 times without break. It would be 130 times as long as the distance from earth to moon. This train would contain the glucose production of one single year.

Imagine if this were the production of our public sector plants or of a multinational or a collective farm. It would be on the news, touted with the modesty of newspaper supplements on Lenin or Kim-Il-Sung. But when 40,000 hectares of forest land gets submerged at Narmada, the experts do not mourn. They see it merely as loss of timber and minor forest produce to be written off.

Nature's economy can never be caught in the present categories of political economy or market economics. The work of nature and the economists notion of work are incommensurable. The work of a large dam and the life world called the forest are incommensurable domains. It is in 'accounting' for the latter that the sage and the baniya in Gandhi would have striven for.

Gandhi would have simply stated that all work is a form of caring. Nursing, cooking, weaving: these are forms of caring. You tend, you cultivate, you grow, you weave, you spin. All these are forms of touching and touching gently. Today, work has lost its gentle metaphors. We mine, we excavate, we bulldoze, we dam, we harness, we exploit. Work has become a form of disciplined violence organized within the framework of brute machismo, Puritanism, or abstract technique.

Partly this is disguised by the western idea of energy. The modern thesaurus of energy is short and bleak because energy like the western concept of God is monotheistic. It is incarnate in the calorific notion of work and efficiency. This notion of energy provides for a simple but gigantic idea of power. When energy becomes an index of progress (the new sign of grace), the state becomes a big machine for the control of energy. A mechanistic notion of energy seems statist, while biology generally seems on the side of civil society. All attempts at returning to small scale have been biologistic.

Unfortunately the age old relation between energy and state is present in Narmada. In fact Gandhi would show that the challenge to the dam is a challenge to the state. Otherwise why prescribe protest at the Narmada under the Defence of India Rules. If the dam goes, the state or at least the current model of the state, may go too. When we cease to worship dams, the cult of the state may itself disappear. Smaller dams or tanks might mean a less powerful state or a more revitalized civil society. What Gandhi would have challenged through the Narmada is the fundamentalism of state power embodied in rituals like large dams and reactors. And it is precisely in this context that he would show that what was missing in the Narmada protest was the politics of knowledge. He would have added to the Patkars and the Amtes, someone like the scientist C.V. Seshadri.

Seshadri, like a playful Gandhian, would show that the western notion of energy, its concept of efficiency and power, is based on mechanical work done at high temperatures and gaseous states. It is modelled on the heat engine, the harbinger of modern industry. The question such a frame asks is how to obtain work at high temperatures. Secondly its focus is on a special kind of work that can be harnessed by market and the state. It is anchored on a parochiality that does not realize that many important processes in the world take place at ordinary temperatures and in liquid and solid states. However, once we accept the official scientific notion of energy, certain decisions follow.

Agriculture will only be improved through high-yielding seeds and synthetic fertilizers produced by the high temperature Haber-Bosch process. Such a notion of efficiency shifts the control of seed and fertilizer to the corporation and the state. Similarly, once a forest is visualized in terms of modern energy markers, its multiple uses as food, fodder, medicines, dwellings, play, is lost or devalued. The forest becomes a raw material for the energy guzzling paper industry. Simultaneously, the notion of the forest itself changes, as monocultural strands of eucalyptus plantations are regarded as moral equivalents of a traditional forest. With such a notion of work, renewability also becomes a problem as emphasis shifts to fossil fuels which require millions of years. So too with a dam. When a river is seen purely as cusecs of water, of electricity and irrigation, the traditional notion of the river as a great chain of being, as a dwelling, as a source of food or work disappears altogether. What Seshadri through his concept of *shakti* suggests is that the modern concept of energy like money dissolves ecologies, and destroys wealth as other cultures see it. What Gandhi might add is that the notion of energy which is so monolithic needs to be reworked into a pantheon of concepts, by breaking energy into a parole of meanings. From the one universal *energetika* or the abstract energy index of planners and economists, it must break into a polyphonic sense of energy symbols. Energy must become carnivalesque as pidgin energy, mixed metaphor energy, misspelt energy. Such a notion of energy is present in Seshadri's search for an alternative idea of energy, shakti, but the search is not merely to replace one God with another. It is to multiply energy into a number of village deities, with innumerable concrete powers varying from niche to niche.

Gandhi would show that the Indian state itself had thought of such a move. In the era of Indira Gandhi, two outstanding scientists, Hussain Zaheer and A.N. Lahiri, of the Central Fuel Research Institute of Dhanbad had advocated that India shift its industrial base away from petroleum. Zaheer had suggested gasification of coal as an alternative. Gandhi would suggest that the entire civil society must participate in this project through acts of prudence, through bits of local inventiveness, through restricting want, and multiplying the renewable sources of energy. Within such an effervescence, the somnolent indifference to the Narmada project would not be possible. Years ago, just prior to the Emergency, Jayaprakash Narayan asked the police not to participate in the atrocities of the state. Today Gandhi would ask the scientists not to participate in projects devoted to petrol and nuclear energy. He would in fact articulate a call for a civil disobedience movement in science, where scientists join the Amtes and Medha Patkars in showing that the proposed Narmada dam is scientifically and politically obscene. The first of these dissenting groups should be sustained by local communities. Years ago, during the national movement, it was money collected during the Ganapati festivals under the leadership of Tilak that helped the Paisa Glass fund, which pioneered the glass industry in India. Today this same spirit of Swadeshism should sustain the Satish Dhawans, the Jayant Narlikars, the Siddiquis, the Seshagiris, the Kalams, the Amulya Reddys, the Visvamitras, the innumerable younger scientists if they choose to move out of the laboratories.

In fact, Narmada should become the equivalent of the Salt March, dissolving the new empire built around the state–science nexus. It is around the protest against the dam that a whole series of new cooperative programmes must begin; a new model of decentralization, a revival of traditional forms of irrigation and their improvement, community action to resist soil erosion, the possibility of making forests into autonomous communities, of creating new ways of doing science outside the corporation and the laboratory. Such an effort would also break the undialogical nature of the current struggle.

Any struggle while emphasizing resistance must never loose its dialogic power, a dialogicity which appeals, embarrasses, questions, offers alternatives and eventually redeems those in power. Such a struggle disables the cliches of the Indian middle class which sees science as god's truth and the bureaucratic file as divinely ordained. The alternative is there, the vision is being lived out and the struggle begins not at Harsud, the town doomed to die because of the dam, but within everyone. Gandhiji once said 'they say that control over the hidden forces of nature enables every American to have

33 slaves. Repeat the process in India and every Indian will be 33 times a slave.' The struggle against the dam is not an appeal to preserve and museumize; it is a call to invent, maintain, adapt, create a new forest and riverine science, new ways of looking at energy, waste, new suggestions for sustaining diversity, for new critiques of power, and the possibilities of resistance. There is no need to fetishize the charkha. If khadi symbolizes cooperation and communitas and if it can be built around another symbol, so be it. It is around the Narmada that the new festivals of politics and science can begin. But one must realize that effervescence alone is not enough. The everydayness of resistance must continue till a new culture emerges and words like World Bank, transfer of technology, nuclear waste sound like distant echoes of a lost or forgotten civilization.

8

Mahatma Gandhi and the Environmental Movement[*]

RAMACHANDRA GUHA

I

In this essay I ask and seek to answer the question: was Mahatma Gandhi an early environmentalist? The life and work of Gandhi have had a considerable influence on the contemporary environmental movement in India. This movement truly began with the Chipko Andolan in April 1973; in one of the first printed accounts of Chipko, a breathless journalist announced that Gandhi's ghost had saved the Himalayan trees. Ever since Mahatma Gandhi has been the usually acknowledged and occasionally unacknowledged patron saint of the environmental movement. From the Chipko Andolan to the Narmada Bachao Andolan, environmental activists have relied heavily on Gandhian techniques of non-violent protest, and have drawn abundantly on Gandhi's polemic against heavy industrialization. Again, some of the movement's better-known figures, for example, Chandi Prasad Bhatt, Sunderlal Bahuguna, Baba Amte, and Medha Patkar, have repeatedly underlined their own debt of Gandhi.

One must, of course, not deny other influences; for under the broad umbrella of the Indian environmental movement are many groups with little connection with Gandhi. Think, for example, of an organization like the Kerala Sastra Sahitya Parishad; a group coming from a background of

* Ramachandra Guha, 'Mahatma Gandhi and the Environmental Movement', in Ramashray Roy (ed.), *Gandhi and the Present Global Crisis*, Shimla: Indian Institute of Advanced Study, 1996, pp. 113–29.

Marxism, but whose contribution to the environmental movement is second
to none. Other voluntary groups in the environment field are variously
influenced by socialism, liberation theology, and traditions of selfhood. All
the same, it is probably fair to say that the life and practice of Gandhi are the
single most important influence on the environmental movement.

However, the environmentalists of today do not merely claim that they
are following the example of Gandhi; they go on to argue that the Mahatma
himself foresaw the ecological crisis of modern industrial society. This
question whether Gandhi was indeed an 'early environmentalist' is usually
answered in the affirmative by his admirers, but rarely with supporting
evidence. That is, it is taken for granted that Gandhi anticipated our environmental concerns, but without demonstrating precisely where and in what
ways he did so. If at all his writings are invoked for the purpose, it is almost
always his work *Hind Swaraj* (published in 1909), which a distinguished
Gandhian of the present day has claimed, gives us an 'alternate perspective'
on development while explaining how 'the current mode of development is
exploitative of man by man and of Nature by man'. Rereading *Hind Swaraj*
recently, I found myself unable to agree with this verdict. Despite its
eloquent denunciation of modern Western culture, the book has nothing to
say about man's relationship with nature: still less does it offer an alternate
perspective.

II

But perhaps *Hind Swaraj* is not the place to look. That book was, of course,
written while Gandhi was still in South Africa. On his return to India in
1914, Gandhi immediately began to acquaint himself first hand with economic
and social conditions in the village. Through his travels in the Indian
countryside and the organization of those early satyagrahas among the
peasants of Champaran and Kheda (1917 and 1918), Gandhi was to come
face to face with colonialism as a system of economic exploitation, not
merely—as had been his experience in South Africa—of racial discrimination.

Through his immersion in village India and his deeper understanding of
colonialism, Gandhi came to see that it would be impossible for India to
emulate Western patterns of industrial development. It must be acknowledged at once that he does not anywhere offer an alternate model of
development for India—for one thing, he was not a systematic thinker; for
another, he was preoccupied with more pressing questions of political
mobilization and social reform. All the same, scattered through his writings

of the 1920s, 1930s, and 1940s are clues to such an alternate path. It is to these writings that I now turn.

Gandhi's reservations about the wholesale industrialization of India are usually ascribed to moral grounds—namely the selfishness and competitiveness of modern society—but they also had markedly ecological undertones. Take this remarkable passage, from *Young India* of 20 December 1928: 'God forbid that India should ever take to industrialization after the manner of the West. The economic imperialism of a single tiny island kingdom (England) is today keeping the world in chains. If an entire nation of 300 million took to similar economic exploitation, it would strip the world bare like locusts'.

Two years earlier, Gandhi had claimed that to 'make India like England and America is to find some other races and places of the earth for exploitation'. As it appeared that the Western nations had already 'divided all the known races outside Europe for exploitation and there are no new worlds to discover', he pointedly asked: 'What can be the fate of India trying to ape the West?' (*Young India*, 7 October 1926.)

The answer to his question is by now painfully obvious. For in the last few decades, we have attempted precisely to 'make India like England and America'. Without the access to resources and markets enjoyed by those two nations when they began to industrialize, India has had perforce to rely on the exploitation of its own people and environment. The natural resources of the countryside have been increasingly channelized to meet the needs of the urban-industrial sector; the diversion of forests, water, etc., to the elite having accelerated processes of environmental degradation even as it has deprived rural and tribal communities of their traditional rights of access and use. Meanwhile, the modern sector has moved aggressively into the remaining resource frontiers of India: the North-East and the Andaman and Nicobar islands.

Perhaps Gandhi would not have been surprised as he had recognized that the bias towards urban-industrial development could result only in a one-sided exploitation of the hinterland. In 1946, he had expressed this with characteristic lucidity: 'The blood of the villages is the cement with which the edifice of the cities is built,' (*Harijan*, 23 June 1946.) On an earlier occasion, Gandhi had, in his characteristically gentle yet forceful manner, alerted a gathering in Indore to the concentration of resources on which city life has come to rest. 'We are sitting in this fine *pandal* under a blaze of electric lights,' he remarked, 'but we do not know we are burning these lights at the expense of the poor,' (*Harijan*, 11 May 1955.)

From this diagnosis of the ills of industrialism flowed Gandhi's preferred solution, wherein economic development would be centred on the village. He wished, above all, to see that 'the blood that is today inflating the arteries of the cities run once again in the blood vessels of the villages'. Pre-eminent here was the decentralization of political and economic power, so that villages could resume control over their own affairs. When he was accused of turning his back on the great scientific inventions, including electricity, Gandhi remarked (in words to inspire all proponents of decentralized energy systems): 'If we could have electricity in every village home, I should not mind villagers plying their implements and tools with the help of electricity. But then the village communities or the State would own power houses, just as they have their grazing pastures.' (*Harijan*, 22 June 1935.)

In 1937, some years after he had moved to Wardha to devote himself to rural reconstruction, Gandhi defined his ideal Indian village:

It will have cottages with sufficient light and ventilation, built of a material obtainable within a radius of five miles of it. The cottages will have courtyards enabling householders to plant vegetables for domestic use and to house their cattle. The village lanes and streets will be free of all avoidable dust. It will have wells according to its needs and accessible to all. It will have houses of worship for all, also a common meeting place, a village common for grazing its cattle, a co-operative dairy, primary and secondary schools in which industrial [i.e. vocational] education will be the central fact, and it will have Panchayats for settling disputes. It will produce its own grains, vegetables and fruit, and its own Khadi. This is roughly my idea of a model village ... (*Harijan*, 9 January 1937.)

There are many elements here that would fit nicely into the utopia of the environmentalist: local self-reliance, a clean and hygienic environment, the collective management and use of those gifts of nature so necessary for human life, water and pasture. But Gandhi himself had an uncanny knack of combining a Utopian vision with shrewdly 'practical means'. Notable in this connection is the attention he paid to the crucial problem of soil fertility. Towards the end of his life, he warned the proponents of the rapid mechanization of agriculture that 'trading in soil fertility for the sake of quick returns would prove to be a disastrous, shortsighted policy. It would result in virtual depletion of the soil.' (*Harijan*, 25 August 1946.) He was an enthusiastic supporter of organic manure, which enriched the soil, improved village hygiene through the effective disposal of waste, saved foreign exchange, and enhanced crop yields—all this, as we now know, without the attendant pollution and resource exhaustion caused by modern chemical techniques. He greatly admired the work of Albert Howard, who had pioneered methods of organic agriculture at his Institute of Plant Industry in Indore. In his own journal, *Harijan*, Gandhi described approvingly and in great detail, the methods developed by Howard and his associates to convert a mixture of cowdung, farm wastes, wood ash, and urine into invaluable fertilizer (*Harijan*, 17 August and 24 August 1935).

Finally, Gandhi's philosophical critique of modern civilization has profound implications for the way we live and relate to the environment today. For him, 'the distinguishing characteristic of modern civilization is an indefinite multiplicity of wants'; whereas ancient civilizations were marked by an 'imperative restriction upon, and a strict regulating of, these wants'. (*Young India*, 2 June 1927). In uncharacteristically intemperate tones, he spoke of his 'wholeheartedly detest[ing] this mad desire to destroy distance and time, to increase animal appetites, and go to the ends of the earth in search of their satisfaction. If modern civilization stands for all this, and I have understood it to do so, I call it satanic' (*Young India*, 17 March 1927).

At an individual level, Gandhi's code of voluntary simplicity offers a sustainable alternative to modern lifestyles. One of his best known aphorisms, that the 'world has enough for everybody's need, but not enough for everybody's greed', is, in effect, an exquisitely phrased one line environmental ethic. This was an ethic he himself practised; for resource recycling, and the minimization of wants were integral to his life.

His analysis of macro processes of economic development, his prescriptions for rural reconstruction, and his ethics for living; at all these levels Gandhi's writings, when reinterpreted in contemporary terms, offer acute insights into the environmental crisis. During his lifetime, this economic philosophy was liberated and fleshed out by one of the Mahatma's close disciples, J. C. Kumarappa. Kumarappa has strong claims to being considered the first Gandhian environmentalist; as his work is largely unhonoured and forgotten today, a brief assessment is perhaps not out of place here.

Kumarappa was a Tamil Christian who had been trained in accountancy in London. He had a flourishing practice as an auditor in Bombay, which he left temporarily to take a master's degree at Columbia University in New York. There he embarked on a study of public finance, in the course of which he systematically uncovered the colonial exploitation of the Indian economy. He returned home in 1929, now a nationalist, and soon came into contact with Gandhi. His thesis on public finance was serialized in *Young India*, and Kumarappa himself abandoned his practice to join the ashram at Sabarmati. He was put in charge of Gandhi's schemes of village reconstruction, and over the next decade conducted important surveys of the agrarian

economy and helped run two key Gandhian institutions, the All India
Spinners Association and the All India Village Industries Association.

In a number of books written in the 1930s and 1940s, J.C. Kumarappa
attempted to formalize Gandhian economics. As with his mentor, strewn
through his writings are observations with profound ecological implications. This remark, for instance, could well serve as a basic condition for
ecological responsibility: 'If we produce everything we want from within a
limited area, we are in a position to supervise the methods of production;
while if we draw our requirements from the ends of the earth it becomes
impossible for us to guarantee the conditions of production in such places'.

Like his teacher, J.C. Kumarappa powerfully denounced industrial civilization. 'There can be no industrialization without predation', he observes,
whereas agriculture is, and ought to be, 'the greatest among occupations', in
which 'man attempts to control nature and his own environment in such a
way as to produce the best result.' Notably, he expressed this contrast
between agriculture and industry in terms of their impact on the natural
world. As he put it:

In the case of an agricultural civilization, the system ordained by nature is not
interfered with to any great extent. If there is a variation at all, it follows a natural
mutation. The agriculturist only aids nature or intensifies in a short time what takes
place in nature in a long period.... Under the economic system of [industrial society]
... we find that variations from nature are very violent in that a large supply of goods
is produced irrespective of demand, and then a demand is artificially created for
goods by means of clever advertisements.

Like most Gandhians of his generation; Kumarappa was primarily interested not in theoretical reflection but in ameliorating the lot of the Indian
peasant and artisan. A theme that runs through much of his work is the
careful husbanding of natural resources in the agrarian economy. Thus he
stressed the need to use night soil as manure, asking for subsidies to be given
to individuals, as a means of overcoming caste prohibitions, for converting
human excreta and village waste into organic fertilizer. At the same time,
Kumarappa also dwelled on the importance of maintaining soil quality by
checking erosion and water logging.

Water and forests are perhaps the two resource sectors that have most
exercised the Indian environmental movement in recent years and Kumarappa
was not slow to criticize the poor maintenance of irrigation tanks under
British rule, or to urge the conservation of water to augment the water table
and reduce brackishness. In a pithy comment on actual and preferred models
of forest management, he says:

The government will have to radically revise its policy of maintaining forests. Forest management should be guided, not by consideration of revenue but by the needs of the people.... Forest planning must be based on the requirements of the villagers around. Forests should be divided into two main classes: (1) those supplying timber to be planned from the long range point of view, and (2) those supplying fuel and grasses, to be made available to the public either free of cost or at nominal rates. There are village industries such as palm gur, paper making, pottery, etc. which can flourish only if fuel and grass can be supplied to them at cheap rates.

Equally foresighted are Kumarappa's remarks on potential biomass shortages in the rural economy. He was particularly concerned about fodder availability, pointing out that cash crops like jute, tobacco, and sugar cane reduce food availability for men and his domestic animals. He also noted the widespread complaint of peasants that there was not enough grazing land, taking the colonial government to task for its reluctance to allow grazing on waste land without payment of a fee.

Soil maintenance and fertility, water conservation, recycling, village forest rights, biomass budgets—this is an agenda of rural environmental problems that are still very much with us. In setting agriculture so firmly in its natural setting, Kumarappa could be said to have begun the task of building an ecological programme on Gandhian lines. Although they are for the most part unaware of his work, the environmentalists of today are only taking up where he left off.

Another associate of Mahatma Gandhi with environmental ideas far in advance of her time was Mira Behn (Madeline Slade), the daughter of an English Admiral who joined the Sabarmati Ashram in 1925. Mira Behn, like J.C. Kumarappa, was part of the Mahatma's inner circle, the core group of his followers, and like the Tamil economist, she too spent many years working for rural reconstruction, elaborating in practice the precepts of her teacher. In 1947 she set up an ashram near Rishikesh, at the foot of the Himalayas, shifting her base several years later to the Bhilangna valley in the interior hills. Mira Behn, through her writings, drew the attention of the public and of policy makers to the intimate links between Himalayan deforestation, soil erosion, and floods. Years before the Chipko Andolan was to give popular force to these criticisms, she identified the lacunae of forest management as being, first, the lack of involvement of villagers; and second, the replacement in many areas of oak with pine, a species with much less capacity to absorb and retain rain water. She sent detailed reports with photographs to the prime minister, Jawaharlal Nehru; he passed them on to the forest officials concerned, but (as Mira Behn wryly noted many years

later) the 'necessary changes were too fundamental' for the forest department to make.

In her years in rural Uttar Pradesh, Mira Behn also made some percipient
comments on the chief ecological problems of Indian agriculture, problems
that remain with us. These included the large-scale waterlogging that appears
to be an almost inescapable feature of canal irrigation; the ploughing up of
lands more suitable for growing pasture for cattle (this adversely affecting
the quality of livestock); and rampant soil erosion. For Mira Behn, the
rapidity of ecological change and disturbance was a distinguishing feature
of modern life. While ancient civilizations in North Africa and the Middle
East had collapsed due to their abuse of the natural environment, she wrote
in the *Hindustan Times* of 5 June 1950 'in those days it took centuries and
centuries to reach complete destruction, but in these days of modern
machinery and science, what took a thousand years or more in the past may
be accomplished in a paltry hundred years today!'

In common with Gandhi and Kumarappa, Mira Behn's primary concern
was rehabilitating the village economy of India. Yet her interest in the
natural environment was not merely instrumental: at times she expresses a
spiritual affinity with nature of a Wordsworthian kind, straight out of the
European romantic tradition. She called herself a 'devotee of the great
primeval Mother Earth'. As she wrote in April 1949:

The tragedy today is that educated and moneyed classes are altogether out of touch
with the vital fundamentals of existence—our Mother Earth, and the animal and
vegetable population which she sustains. This world of Nature's planning is ruthlessly plundered, despoiled and disorganized by man whenever he gets the chance.
By his science and machinery he may get huge returns for a time, but ultimately will
come desolation. We have got to study Nature's balance, and develop our lives,
within her laws, if we are to survive as a physically healthy and morally decent
species.

III

I began this paper by recognizing and commenting upon the visible influence of Mahatma Gandhi on the Indian environmental movement. I then
went back in time to investigate to what extent Gandhi himself had anticipated the distinctive ecological problems of the present day. The evidence in
this respect does confirm that the ideas of Gandhi, as also of his followers
—J.C. Kumarappa and Mira Behn—do constitute an eminently usable past
for the environmental movement.

It is time now to turn our attention to one widely prevalent myth that has its origins in the environmental movement's reclamation of Mahatma Gandhi. It is an unfortunate tendency, prevalent especially among the radical fringe of the movement, to identify good and evil with particular individuals. For the radical environmentalist, Gandhi is good in almost exact proportion to which Nehru is bad. While celebrating Gandhi as a model to honour and follow, he wishes simultaneously to demonize Jawaharlal Nehru, at whose feet he lays the blame for the ecological crisis of Indian society. Many environmentalists even believe that Gandhi had himself outlined a model of ecological sound development; and that this Gandhian alternative was cast into the dustbin by Nehru, who then imposed, on independent India, his own model of capital-intensive, environmentally destructive, economic development. A tale to illustrate this was recently told by an expatriate Indian environmentalist now based in Britain. Apparently Gandhi was staying with Nehru in the latter's family house at Allahabad, and asked for a bucket of water to wash up in the morning. Nehru sent two buckets, whereupon Gandhi sent one back. 'Why Gandhiji', protested Jawaharlal, 'this is the city where the Ganga and Yamuna meet; there can be no shortage of water here.'

This incident is meant to exemplify the prudence of Gandhi, and the profligate ways of his host; ways which after 1947 are believed to have found expression in the path of destructive development followed by the new nation. No source is given for the story, which is almost certainly a figment of the environmentalist's imagination. Yet the beliefs underlying his tale are widely held by the Gandhian environmentalists of today. In an essay published some years ago, a prominent Indian environmental writer and activist claimed that Mahatma Gandhi 'tried in vain to persuade Jawaharlal Nehru not to take India down the path of over consumption'. This statement expresses in succinct fashion the two core elements of the myth: first, that ecologically speaking Nehru was as profligate as Gandhi was prudent; and second, that Gandhi had his own, alternate plan of development for India, which Nehru, in his arrogance, rejected out of hand. It is in this manner that the environmental debates of today have brought Gandhi and Nehru into fierce, if posthumous, public competition; violating in spirit and letter the intimate relationship that actually existed between the two.

The environmentalists' opposition of Gandhi to Nehru stems, in part, from the need to explain a self-evident puzzle: that the development experience of independent India has been marked by a profound insensitivity to ecological considerations—and this despite what we have just demonstrated, namely that the 'Father of the Nation' was, in our terms, emphatically an 'early environmentalist'. The puzzle can be most conveniently explained by contrasting the prudent Gandhi with the profligate Nehru, and by putting forth a conspiracy theory whereby the younger man first took over the Congress in some kind of palace coup, then swiftly rid it of its Gandhian heritage.

That the puzzle exists I do not dispute; but I do wish to qualify, perhaps even challenge, the way it is usually explained by my friends in the environmental movement. To challenge their black and white portraits of Nehru and Gandhi is not, of course, to ignore the profound philosophical differences between the two. Gandhi's vision of free India centred on village renewal; Nehru's vision, just as firmly, on rapid industrial development. The older man preferred stability to change; the restless Nehru, change to stability. These differences come out clearly in an exchange of letters between the two in October 1945. Following a working committee meeting on social and economic objectives after independence, Gandhi wrote to Nehru of his belief that India could 'realize truth and non-violence only in the simplicity of village life'. He went on to liken industrial society to the moth that whirls faster and faster around the light, only to perish in it. In his reply, Nehru disputed that the village, for him a milieu backward both intellectually and culturally, could ever embody the principles of truth and non-violence. He identified, as the chief goal of economic planning, not 'over consumption' (as the environmentalist quoted earlier would have us believe) but rather, 'a sufficiency of food, clothing, housing, education, sanitation, etc.', for every Indian. This was a goal on which both Nehru and Gandhi agreed, but the younger man, in common with other intellectuals of the time, was convinced that it could be achieved only through rapid industrialization and the use of modern technology.

These differences notwithstanding, we must also recognize the deep and abiding love between Gandhi and Nehru. 'I cannot think of myself as a rival to Jawaharlal or him to me', wrote Gandhi in July 1936. He continued: 'Or if we are, we are rivals in making love to each other in the pursuit of the common goal. And if, in the joint work for reaching the goal, we at times seem to be taking different routes, I hope the world will find that we had lost sight of each other only for the moment, and only to meet again with greater mutual attraction and affections'.

I do not know how environmentalists reconcile this with the Gandhi/ Nehru polarity they so fervently uphold; or indeed how they ignore the Mahatma's public anointing of Nehru as his heir in the early 1930s, a succession Gandhi repeatedly confirmed in later years. More substantively, the environmentalists' interpretation of the crucial years before independence fails to recognize that by 1940 or thereabouts, Gandhi's own economic ideas had been decisively rejected by the national movement. There had come about an overwhelming consensus, among politicians and intellectuals, that rapid industrialization was the only viable economic strategy in independent India—a strategy its proponents believed would go a long way in reducing poverty and unemployment, and in making for a strong, self-reliant, genuinely independent society. Nehru expressed this consensus in a particularly eloquent fashion; but behind him stood a solid phalanx of utterly sincere and deeply patriotic men.

Indeed, if the Gandhian model had been adopted as the basis for an economic policy in 1947, that would have been an undemocratic imposition in the face of strong, majority opinion to the contrary. The actual marginalization of the 'Gandhian alternative', such as it was, is well expressed in the career of J.C. Kumarappa. In 1937, he was appointed to the National Planning Committee of the Congress as a representative of the All India Village Industries Association, but resigned when his fellow members of the NPC did not agree to put the village at the centre of planning. After independence, Kumarappa was deputed by the Sarva Seva Sangh to represent it in the Planning Commission's Advisory Body. Again, the Gandhian economist quickly sensed that he was in a minority of one, and left the committee.

From our own vantage point, it is possible to celebrate the Mahatma and his disciple as environmentalists before the age of environmentalism. By contrast, India's first prime minister represented the majority intellectual opinion within the national movement, namely, that the revitalization of India could only come about through massive industrialization. One may justly honour Gandhi and Kumarappa for being ahead of their time; but it is grossly unhistorical, as well as unfair, to condemn Nehru for being, merely, a man of his time.

The great British socialist Edward Carpenter once remarked that the Outcast of one age is the Hero of another. Perhaps the converse, that the Hero of one age is the Outcast of another, is equally true. For no man was as greatly adored during his lifetime as Jawaharlal Nehru, yet no man has been more villified since his death. It appears that Nehru was responsible for all that is wrong with India today. Thus the Right holds Nehru's policies of pseudo-secularism and state planning squarely responsible for communal conflict and economic stagnation, while the Left, just as effortlessly, traces the roots of economic inequality and environmental degradation to the same man's practice of pseudo-socialism and ecological arrogance.

This demonization of Nehru, within and outside the environmental movement, fails to allow for the possibility that times change, and so do men and ideas with them. Take, for instance, the controversy around the Sardar Sarovar project, which environmentalists have found easy to represent in terms of the Gandhi/Nehru opposition. Thus a critic of the project wrote recently of a historic old temple being submerged by the rising waters of the dam characterized by him as 'one of Jawaharlal Nehru's temples of modern India'. Here a man who died thirty years ago was being held guilty for the construction of a dam today, on account only of a phrase he had used to describe another dam built in the early years of independence. But how can one be so sure that a man as generous and open-minded as Nehru would have held steadfast to a viewpoint, despite mounting evidence to the contrary? For myself, I have little doubt that were both Nehru and Gandhi alive today, on the Sardar Sarovar controversy they would have found themselves on the same side.

IV

The urge to demonize Nehru comes from a Cowboys and Indians vision of history, wherein the world is effortlessly divided up into good and bad guys. These black and white portraits are especially congenial to social activities: they were once characteristic of the Marxist, and they now, sadly, appear to be characteristic of the radical environmentalist. But the ideas and actions of individuals must be set in context: that is the task of the historian, in doing which he might find himself qualifying, to lesser or greater degree, the beliefs of the activist. It is in this spirit that I have contested the environmentalists' portrayal of Nehru in uniformly dark colours, and it is in the same spirit that I now wish to qualify their portrayal of Gandhi in uniformly light ones. The historical figure of Gandhi provides a body of ideas, and a vocabulary of protest against unjust laws, that have proved critical to the environmental movement. This much is indisputable—but perhaps it is now time to ask: are there ways in which the heritage of Gandhi might actually limit the movement? Or put more plainly, does Gandhi provide all the answers to those working for environmental and social renewal today? Some environmentalists are emphatic that he does, indeed—thus one friend recently claimed that 'for each and every environmental event or crisis or challenge one can find inspiration and guidance in Gandhi'. This most emphatic statement notwithstanding, I think that Gandhi does not provide all the answers, sometimes he does not even ask the right questions.

Let me clarify. I believe that the heritage of Mahatma Gandhi has limited the vision of the environmental movement in two crucial respects. First, it is striking how heavily focused on the countryside are the horizons of most environmentalists. Like Gandhi, his present-day followers appear to have little understanding of the urban context and its distinctive social and environmental problems. In their angry denunciations of the urban-industrial way of life, Indian environmentalists, by and large, have yet to come to terms with the fact that by the turn of the century India shall have the largest urban population in the world. I do not have to belabour the ecological problems associated with such rapid and unregulated urbanization: massive pollution, overcrowding and the diseases associated with it, acute water shortages, grossly inadequate housing and sanitation, and a system of transportation that is highly inefficient from an energy conservation and environmental point of view. In actively engaging with these problems, and in trying to make our cities and towns habitable, environmentalists can find no help from Gandhi, who in his own life and work simply turned his back on the city.

Like the city, the wilderness has no attraction for Gandhi. It is true that his practice of vegetarianism and non-violence oriented Gandhi towards a respect for all life, yet by all accounts he was hardly moved by the glories of unspoilt nature. This might, perhaps be attributed to his severely practical temperament, for there was nothing of the romantic in Gandhi. Intriguingly, Nehru, by far the more romantic of the two men, was deeply appreciative of the natural beauty of India. There is a near mystical quality to Nehru's invocation, in his last will and testament, of his affinity with the soil, the mountains, the rivers of India.

An anecdote to illustrate this contrast is told by Edward Thompson, the British educationist and writer who was a close friend of both Gandhi and Nehru. When the Congress ministries were formed in different provinces of British India in 1937, Thompson tried hard to interest the nationalist leaders in the cause of saving India's disappearing wildlife, with (as he noted) 'animal after animal ... either extinct or on the danger list'. When he confronted Gandhi with the problem, the Mahatma merely joked, saying, 'we shall always have the British lion'. But then, noting Thompson's disappointment, Gandhi asked him to speak to Jawaharlal, as one who might show more interest. Nehru did, indeed—he went on to speak of the issue to the Prime Ministers (as they were then called) of Congress-ruled states.

Later, Nehru was able to report to Thompson, with some pride, that
C. Rajagopalachari's last act, as Premier of Madras, was to put through the
Periyar Nature Reserve.

Nature lovers and those with a focus on the urban environment would,
therefore, find little direct help from Mahatma Gandhi. But between the
wilderness and the city lies a vast terrain, home to the seven hundred
thousand villages Gandhi spoke of so often, and so eloquently. It is here that
his life and message admit of more direct application, in the resistance to
environmental destructive projects or in the restoration of the relationship
between the agrarian economy and its natural environment. And all of us
without exception—whether living in the city, the country or the wild—can
try and simplify our lifestyles to the extent compatible with individual
circumstances, taking our lead from a man who, in his own life, made
remarkably few demands on the earth. And so it is that the environmental
movement must perennially return to Mahatma Gandhi, while at the same
time going beyond him.

A Note on the Sources

The Collected Works of Mahatma Gandhi, which run to more than ninety volumes,
are the basic sources for all scholarly studies of Gandhi. For my own limited
purposes, namely, the reassessment of Gandhi as an 'environmentalist', I have relied
heavily on three invaluable thematic anthologies of his writings: *Industrialize—And
Perish!*, compiled by R.K. Prabhu, Ahmedabad: Navjivan, 1966; *Village Swaraj*,
compiled by H.M. Vyas, Ahmedabad: Navjivan, 1962; and *My Picture of Free
India*, compiled by Anand T. Hingorani, Bombay: Pearl Publications, 1965. However
the citations in my text, identifying date and journal, can be followed by the
interested reader to the *Collected Works*.

J.C. Kumarappa's important works include *Why the Village Movement?*, second
edn, New Delhi: Hindusthan Publishing, 1938 and *The Economy of Permanence*,
second edn, New Delhi: All India Village Industries Association, 1948. Kumarappa's
ideas are examined in greater detail in my essay 'Prehistory of Indian Environmentalism: Intellectual Traditions', *Economic and Political Weekly*, issue of 4–11
January 1992.

Finally, a fascinating selection of Mira Behn's writings compiled by her associate Krishna Murti Gupta, which I have drawn on here, has been published in a recent
issue of the journal *Khadi Gramodyog*, Vol. 39, (2), November 1992. A fuller
selection of articles, as well as tributes to her work, can be found in Krishna Murti
Gupta (ed.), *Mira Behn: Birth Centenary Volume*, New Delhi: Himalaya Seva
Sangh, 1992.

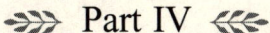 Part IV

9

*Mahatma Gandhi**

SUMIT SARKAR

The Appeal of Gandhi

The South African experience (1893–1914) contributed in a number of different ways to the foundations of Gandhi's ideology and methods, as well as to his later achievements in India. Down to 1906, Gandhi as a rising lawyer–politician had followed the usual 'Moderate' techniques of prayers and petitions in the struggle against racial discrimination affecting Indians in Natal (disenfranchisement and restrictions on landholding and trade), and his movement had essentially been one of merchants and lawyers alone. A totally new departure began with the three campaigns of passive resistance (soon redefined as satyagraha in 1907) of 1907–8, 1908–11, and 1913–14. The issues involved were the 1906 Transvaal ordinance on compulsory registration and passes for Indians, the 1913 immigration restrictions, the derecognition of non-Christian Indian marriages while deciding the cases of new entrants, and the £ 3 tax on ex-indentured labourers. The peculiar conditions of South Africa allowed the amalgamation into a successful movement of people of disparate religions, communities, and classes: Hindus, Muslims, Parsis, and Christians, Gujaratis and south Indians, upper-class merchants and lawyers, as well as Newcastle mine workers whom Gandhi led in a memorable strike and cross-country march in October 1913. It needs to be emphasized that this experience made Gandhi into potentially much more of an all-India figure from the beginning of his work in India than any

* Sumit Sarkar, 'Mahatma Gandhi', in *Modern India 1885–1947*, New Delhi: MacMillan India Limited, 1984, pp. 178–87.

other politician, all of whom (like Tilak, Lajpat, or Pal, for example) had essentially regional bases. Gandhi's lifelong recognition of the necessity and possibility of Hindu–Muslim unity certainly goes back to his South African movements in which Muslim merchants had been extremely active. South Africa also made him something of an international celebrity, while the connections which many South African Indians still had with their original homes in different parts of the country helped to spread the name of Gandhi throughout India. Thirteen out of the first 25 inmates of the Sabarmati Asrama (1915) came from Tamil Nadu—something which would have been inconceivable then for any other Indian leader.

The basic Gandhian style was worked out in South Africa after 1906. This involved careful training of disciplined cadres (in the Phoenix Settlement and the Tolstoy Farm), non-violent satyagraha involving peaceful violation of specific laws (compulsory registration, entry permits, trade licenses, etc.), mass courting of arrests, and occasional *hartal*s and spectacular marches. It included a combination of apparently quixotic methods together with meticulous attention to organizational and particularly financial details; a readiness for negotiations and compromise, at times leading to abrupt unilateral withdrawals which were by no means popular (like the January 1908 withdrawal of the first satyagraha on the strength of a verbal promise from Smuts which was soon broken—Gandhi was beaten up by a militant Pathan after this unexpected retreat); and the cultivation of what non-disciples usually considered to be the Gandhian 'fads' (vegetarianism, nature-therapy, experiments in sexual self-restraint, etc.). The net impact had a clear twofold character: drawing in the masses, while at the same time keeping mass activity strictly pegged down to certain forms predetermined by the leader, and above all to the methods of non-violence.

Non-violence or ahimsa and satyagraha to Gandhi personally constituted a deeply felt and worked-out philosophy owing something to Emerson, Thoreau, and Tolstoy but also revealing considerable originality. The search for truth was the goal of human life, and as no one could ever be sure of having attained the ultimate truth, use of violence to enforce one's own necessarily partial understanding of it was sinful. As a politician and not just a saint, Gandhi in practice sometimes settled for less than complete non-violence (as when he campaigned for military recruitment in 1918 in the hope of winning post-war political concessions), and his repeated insistence that even violence was preferable to cowardly surrender to injustice sometimes created delicate problems of interpretation. But historically much more significant than this personal philosophy (fully accepted only by a relatively small group of disciples) was the way in which the resultant perspective of controlled mass participation objectively fitted in with the interests and sentiments of socially decisive sections of the Indian people. Indian politicians before Gandhi, as we have seen, had tended to oscillate between moderate 'mendicancy' and individual terrorism basically because of their social inhibitions about uncontrolled mass movements. The Gandhian model would prove acceptable also to business groups, as well as to relatively better-off or locally dominant sections of the peasantry, all of whom stood to lose something if political struggle turned into uninhibited and violent social revolution. In more general terms, as we shall see, the doctrine of ahimsa lay at the heart of the essentially unifying, 'umbrella-type' role assumed by Gandhi and the Gandhian Congress, not only mediating internal social conflicts and contributing greatly to joint national struggle against foreign rule, but also leading to periodic retreats and some major reverses.

A third, crucial, aspect of the Gandhian appeal lay in his social ideals, put forward most unambiguously in *Hind Swaraj* (1909). The basic point made in this pamphlet is that the real enemy was not British political domination, but the whole of modern industrial civilization. Taking over and extending the Romantic critique of industrialism developed by the mid-nineteenth century English writers like Carlyle and Ruskin, (whose *Unto His Last* remained a favourite text of his), Gandhi argued that mere political Swaraj would mean 'English rule without the Englishmen', while 'It would be folly to assume that an Indian Rockefeller would be better than the American Rockefeller. Railways, lawyers and doctors have impoverished the country'—railways have spread plague and produced famines by encouraging the export of food grains, lawyers have stimulated disputes in their greed for briefs and helped to maintain British rule by manning the law courts, Western medicine is expensive and ruins natural health measures. The central passage reads: 'India's salvation consists in unlearning what she has learnt during the past 50 years or so. The railways, telegraphs, hospitals, lawyers, doctors and such like have all to go, and the so-called upper class have to learn to live consciously and religiously and deliberately the simple life of a peasant.'

The Gandhian social Utopia as outlined in *Hind Swaraj* is undoubtedly unrealistic and indeed obscurantist if considered as a final remedy for the ills of India or of the world, and it never had much appeal for sophisticated urban groups which by the 1930s and 1940s would turn increasingly to either capitalist or socialist solutions based on industrialization. But it did represent a response to the deeply alienating effects of 'modernization' particularly under colonial conditions. For the artisan ruined by factory industries, the peasant to whom law courts were a disastrous trap and going to a city hospital usually an expensive death sentence, as well as to the rural or small-town intelligentsia for whom education had brought few material benefits, the anti-industrial theme had a real attraction, at least for some time. After his return to India, Gandhi concretized his message through programmes of khadi, village reconstruction, and (somewhat later) Harijan welfare. Once again, none of these really solved problems in the sense of changing social or economic relations, but, when tried out with sincerity and patience by devoted Gandhian constructive workers, they could improve, to some limited extent, the lot of the rural people. The message of self-reliance and self-help of the Swadeshi period thus acquired wider dimensions. It must be added that the peasant appeal of Gandhi was greatly helped also by his political style: travelling third-class, speaking in simple Hindustani, wearing a loin-cloth only from 1921 onwards, using the imagery of Tulsidas' Ramayana so deep-rooted in the popular religion of the north Indian Hindu rural masses. (Such use had its problems so far as Muslims were concerned, but more of that later on.)

THE ROLE OF RUMOUR

Yet the tremendous breadth of Gandhian movements cannot be explained purely by what Gandhi as a personality thought, stood for, or actually did. What we have to understand also is the role of rumour in a predominantly illiterate society going through a period of acute strain and tensions. From out of their misery and hope, varied sections of the Indian people seem to have fashioned their own images of Gandhi, particularly in the earlier days when he was, at the time, to most people a distant, vaguely-glimpsed or heard-of tale of a holy man with miracle-working powers. Thus peasants could imagine that Gandhi would end zamindari exploitation, agricultural labourers of UP believed that he would 'provide holdings for them' (Viceroy Reading to the Secretary of State, 13 October 1921—*Reading Collection*), and Assam tea coolies left the plantations en masse in May 1921 saying that they were obeying Gandhi's orders. A CID report on the *kisan* movement in Allahabad district in January 1921 makes the same point in vivid detail:

The currency which Mr Gandhi's name has acquired even in the remotest villages is astonishing. No one seems to know quite who or what he is, but it is an accepted fact that what he says is so, and he orders must be done. He is a Mahatma or sadhu, a

Pundit, a Brahman who lives at Allahabad, even at Deota ... the real power of his name is perhaps to be traced back to the idea that it was he who got *bedakhli* (illegal eviction) stopped in Pratapgarh ... as a general rule, Gandhi is not thought of as being antagonistic to Government, but only to the zamindars ... We are for Gandhiji and the Sarkar (*Home Political Deposit*, February 1921, No. 13).

That a Gandhi-type leadership with strong religious overtones was something like a historical necessity in this period is indicated, as we shall see, by the emergence of a number of somewhat similar regional or local leaders in the early 1920s: Swami Viswananda and Swami Darshanananda among Bengal and Bihar miners, Swami Vidyananda in north Bihar, Baba Ramchandra in Pratapgarh, Swami Kumarananda in Rajasthan, Ananda Swami in Maharashtra, Alluri Sitarama Raju among the 'Rampa' tribals of Andhra. The dual nature of this process of image-building needs to be emphasized. As the Allahabad CID report indicates, peasants were giving the vague rumours about Gandhi a radical, anti-zamindar twist. But at the same time they were attributing their own achievements to him—for, if bedakhli had been restricted in Pratapgarh, it was due to peasant struggle under local leaders like Baba Ramchandra; Gandhi or the leadership, as we shall see, had little or nothing to do with it directly. If, as would happen repeatedly from 1922 onwards, the Mahatma categorically ordered a retreat, the bulk of the masses would obey. The peasants still needed to be represented by a saviour from above—a crucial limitation which is perhaps at times underestimated by some recent scholar who reacting against elite historiography, tends to somewhat romanticize the spontaneous revolutionary potential of the rural masses.

The millenarian vision faded in course of time, and was in fact curbed by the very growth of Gandhian Congress organization and discipline. Thus, a recurrent pattern in Gandhian movements would be a kind of inverse relationship between organizational power and the strength of elemental, often violent and radical, popular outbursts.

Champaran, Kheda, Ahmedabad

Gandhi returned from South Africa in 1915 having won a partial victory there. Smuts' Indian Relief Act of June 1914 abolished the £ 3 tax and recognized Indian marriages, though discrimination certainly did not end and the broader question of white racist exploitation of Africans and Indians alike had hardly been touched upon as yet. During the next three years, Gandhi acquired the reputation of a man who would take up local wrongs (of Champaran indigo cultivators, Ahmedabad textile workers, and Kheda peasants) and usually manage to do something concrete about them—a political style in sharp contrast to the established Congress (and Home Rule League) pattern of starting with somewhat abstract all-India issues or programmes and proceeding from top downwards. Judith Brown has argued that the main importance of these early movements lay in the recruitment of 'sub-contractors' who would serve as his life-long lieutenants—like Rajendra Prasad, Anugraha Narayan Sinha, and J.B. Kripalani in Champaran, or Vallabhbhai Patel, Mahadev Desai, Indulal Yajnik, and Shankarlal Banker in the two Gujarat movements. But her own and other available accounts reveal other important dimensions, too: the existence in every case of pressures from below, a note of millenarian appeal at times, and the first indications also of a restraining role.

Champaran, as we have seen, had a long history of anti-planter discontent and agitation. Jacques Pouchepadass's detailed analysis makes clear that the crucial mediating role in peasant mobilization was played not so much by Gandhian converts from the small-town intelligentsia (*vakil*s like Rajendra Prasad, A.N. Sinha, or Braj Kishore Prasad, or the Muzaffarpur College teacher J.B. Kripalani—the 'subcontractors' of Judith Brown) but by a somewhat lower stratum of rich and middle peasants (Rajkumar Shukla who had gone to Lucknow to invite Gandhi, Sant Raut, Khenddar Rai), local *mahajan*s and traders who resented planter competition in moneylending and trade, and a few village *mukhtar*s (attorneys) and school teachers (Pir Muhammad, Harbans Sahai). Gandhi's own role was at first sight confined to instituting an open enquiry in July 1917 (after a local ban on his entry had been rescinded by higher authorities in face of a satyagraha threat), and giving all-India publicity to the grievances of the Champaran indigo cultivators—an enquiry and a publicity which led to the abolition of *tinkathia*. Yet the psychological impact far surpassed the concrete activities: Gandhi 'is daily transfiguring the imaginations of masses of ignorant men with visions of an early millennium', reported the Bettiah SDO on 29 April 1917. A *raiyat* compared Gandhi to Ramchandra, and declared before the enquiry committee that 'tenants would not fear the Rakhshasa—planters now that Gandhi was there'. Rumours were current that Gandhi had been sent by the Viceroy or the King to overrule all local officials and planters; and even that the British would leave Champaran in a few months There were some signs of militancy going beyond Gandhian limits—a few attacks on indigo factories and cases of incendiarism, for instance. By late 1917, peasants were at times refusing to pay even the reduced *sharahbeshi* which had been accepted by the Gandhian settlement. Gandhi left behind him a group of fifteen volunteers who tried to start constructive village work, and told Rajendra Prasad that the only real solution 'was the education of raiyats and a constant process of mediation between them and the planters'—but such efforts do not seem to have been particularly successful at Champaran, where only three village-level workers were still active by May 1918.

The Gandhian intervention proved much more of a permanent success at Kheda district of Gujarat, a land of relatively prosperous Kanbi-Patidar peasant proprietors producing food grains, cotton, and tobacco for nearby Ahmedabad (and not of big zamindars, planters, and extremely impoverished petty tenants, as Champaran was). Many Patidars had gone to South Africa as traders, and primary education was fairly widespread among them. As David Hardiman has pointed out in a recent micro-study of Kheda, a late-nineteenth century 'golden age' here was succeeded by repeated famine and plague after 1899, making revenue payments (which were seldom reduced) very difficult. The 'lesser Patidars', living in villages occupying a lower position in the marriage network within the caste were the worst affected, for the superior Patidars could accumulate extra wealth through dowries and often also got employment in the civil service of nearby Baroda state—and it was the former group which was to provide the most permanent support to Gandhian nationalism. In 1917–18, a poor harvest coincided with high prices of kerosene, ironware, cloth, and salt, while the low-caste Baraiyas whom the Kheda Patidars employed as farm labour had successfully forced up wages. 'We have to pay six annas for labour which we used to get for three', a Patidar complained in April 1918, The initiative for no-revenue (to press the case for remissions in the context of the poor harvest) really came not from Gandhi or Ahmedabad politicians, but from local village leaders like Mohanlal Pandya of Kapadvanj taluka in Kheda in November 1917; it was taken up by Gandhi after a lot of hesitation only on 22 March 1918. The delay proved unwise, as by that time the poorer peasants had already been coerced to pay up revenue, and a good rabi crop had weakened the case for remissions. Kheda, the first real Gandhian peasant satyagraha in India, consequently proved a rather patchy affair, affecting only seventy villages out of 559, and having to be called off in June after no more than a token concession. But sustained village work would build up over the years a solid Gandhian base in Gujarat, particularly in the Anand and Borsad talukas of the rich tobacco and dairy-farming Charotar tract of Kheda, and Bardoli taluka of Surat (where Gandhians linked up with the constructive work already started by Kunvarji Mehta's Patidar Yuvak Mandal). The deep

Patidar faith in Gandhian non-violence followed not just from traditional
Vaishnava-bhakti influences, but from the fact that 'as property-owners
they did not want violent revolution'. The Kheda satyagraha had been
followed in fact by a spate of dacoities in Patidar houses by Baraiyas who
apparently felt that British law and order was collapsing. That the Gujarat
peasants had a mind of their own, and were not simply responding to strings
pulled by Gandhi's 'sub-contractors' as Judith Brown likes to assume, is
proved by the extremely poor response that Gandhi and his followers
obtained in Kheda for their war recruitment campaign in the summer of
1918—'villagers who had met them previously with garlands, now refused
them food' (quotations from Hardiman, *Peasant Agitations in Kheda District, Gujarat,* 1917–34, Sussex thesis, 1975, pp. 113, 158, 151).

   Unlike the Champaran and Kheda movements against white planters and
revenue authorities, Gandhi's intervention in Ahmedabad in February–March
1918 was in a situation of purely internal conflict between Gujarat mill-
owners and their workers. The textile magnate Ambalal Sarabhai had been
an early contributor to the Sabarmati Ashrama finances, while his sister
Anasuya Behn had become a Gandhian disciple, visiting Kheda during the
satyagraha and starting nightschools among mill-workers. The mill-owners'
attempt to end the 'plague bonus' of 1917 in a period of rising prices led to
a confrontation despite Gandhi's mediation attempts, with the workers
demanding a 50 per cent wage hike: in lieu of the plague bonus (later
reduced under Gandhi's advice to 35 per cent) and the owners offering only
20 per cent. The Ahmedabad strike of March 1918 under Gandhi's leadership was notable for the Mahatma's first use of the weapon of the hunger-
strike (from 15 March). Conventionally this is described as a successful
attempt to rally the flagging spirit of the workers, an alternative to militant
picketing which Gandhi strictly forbade. The District Magistrate's report
quoted by Judith Brown gives an interestingly different version: the workers, we are told, had 'assailed him (Gandhi) bitterly for being a friend of the
mill-owners, riding in their motorcars and eating sumptuously with them,
while the weavers were starving', and Gandhi allegedly began his fast
'stung by these taunts'. Whatever its motives, the hunger-strike successfully
won for the workers a 33 per cent wage increase. The Gandhian hold on the
Ahmedabad workers was consolidated through the Textile Labour Association of 1920, grounded on the philosophy of peaceful arbitration of disputes,
interdependence of capital and labour, and the concept of owners being
'trustees' for the workers. Gandhi's excellent personal contacts with
Ahmedabad mill-owners and workers alike made such methods a success

here. It is significant, however, that this Gandhian model, which rejected not only politicization along 'class-war' lines but also militant economic struggles, never spread beyond Ahmedabad. Gandhi himself, unlike many other nationalist leaders, kept strictly aloof from the AITUC right from the beginning, long before the communists became important within it. The message of class peace and mutual adjustment had much greater success among the peasantry than with the proletariat, for in the countryside exploitation at times took on a 'paternalistic' colour and issues like land revenue or the salt tax provided unifying grievances.

Down to early 1919, Gandhi's interventions in matters of all-India politics had been relatively minimal, being mainly confined to protests against the internment of Annie Besant and repeated pleas for the release of the Ali brothers (through which he had already started developing important contacts with Muslim religious leaders like Abdul Bari of Lucknow). He showed little interest in the reform proposals, which were engrossing the attention of most other politicians. The provocative enactment of the Rowlatt Act in February 1919 made him turn to an all-India satyagraha campaign for the first time.

10

Gandhi's Integrity[*]
The Philosophy behind the Politics[1]

AKEEL BILGRAMI

I

I was once asked by a literary magazine to write a review essay on Nehru. Some weeks later, I was asked by the editor if I would throw in Gandhi as well. As it happened I never wrote the piece, but I remember thinking that it was like being asked while climbing the Western Ghats whether I would take a detour and climb Mount Everest as well. I am not now trying to scale any great peak or to give a defining interpretation to Gandhi. Its generally foolhardy to write about Gandhi, not only because you are never certain you've got him right, but because you are almost sure to have him wrong. There is a lack of plain argument in his writing and there is an insouciance about fundamental objections, which he himself raises, to his own intuitive ideas. The truth of his claims seem to him so instinctive and certain that mere arguments seem frivolous even to readers who disagree with them. Being trained in a discipline of philosophy of a quite different temperament, I will try to not get distracted by the irritation I sometimes feel about this.

In reading Gandhi recently I have been struck by the integrity of his ideas. I don't mean simply that he was a man of integrity in the sense that he tried to make his actions live up to his ideals, though perhaps in fact he tried more than most to do so. I mean something more abstract: that his thought

* Akeel Bilgrami, 'Gandhi's Integrity: The Philosophy behind the Politics', *Postcolonial Studies*, Vol. 5(1), 2002, pp. 79–93.

itself was highly integrated, his ideas about very specific political strategies in specific contexts flowed (and in his mind necessarily flowed) from ideas that were very remote from politics. They flowed from the most abstract epistemological and methodological commitments. This quality of his thought sometimes gets lost because, on the one hand, the popular interest in him has been keen to find a man of great spirituality and uniqueness and, on the other, the social scientist's and historian's interest in him has sought out a nationalist leader with a strikingly effective method of non-violent political action. It has been common for some decades now to swing from a senti-mental perception of him as a 'Mahatma' to a cooler assessment of Gandhi as 'the shrewd politician'. I will steer past this oscillation because it hides the very qualities of his thought I want to uncover. The essay is not so much (in fact hardly at all) inspired by the plausibility of the philosophy that emerges as by the stunning intellectual ambition and originality that this 'integrity' displays.

II

Non-violence is a good place to get a *first* glimpse of what I have in mind. Violence has many sides. It can be spontaneous or planned, it can be individual or institutional, it can be physical or psychological, it can be delinquent or adult, it can be revolutionary or authoritarian. A great deal has been written on violence: on its psychology, on its possible philosophical justifications under certain circumstances, and of course on its long career in military history. *Non*-violence has no sides at all. Being negatively defined, it is indivisible. It began to be a subject of study much more recently and there is much less written on it, not merely because it is defined in negative terms but because until it became a self-conscious instrument in politics in this century, it was really constituted *as* or *in* something else. It was studied under different names, first usually as part of religious or contemplative ways of life remote from the public affairs of men and state, and later with the coming of romantic thought in Europe, under the rubric of critiques of industrial civilization.

For Gandhi, both these contexts were absolutely essential to his conception of non-violence. Non-violence was central in his nationalist mobilization against British rule in India. But the concept is also situated in an essentially religious temperament as well as in a thorough-going critique of ideas and ideologies of the Enlightenment and of an intellectual paradigm of perhaps a century earlier than the Enlightenment. This is a paradigm in which science became set on a path, which seemed destined to lead to *cumulative* results, building to a *progressively* complete understanding of the world in which we lived, a world which we could as a result control. It is a familiar point that there is no understanding Gandhi, the anti-colonial nationalist, without situating him in these larger trajectories of his thought.

The strategy of non-violent resistance was first introduced by him so as to bring into the nationalist efforts against the British, an element beyond making only constitutional demands. On the face of it, for those reared on western political ideas, this seemed very odd. Constitutional demands, as they are understood in liberal political theory, are the essence of non-violent politics; as is well known, the great early propounders of liberal democratic thought conceived and still conceive of constitutions and their constraints on human public action as a constraint against tendencies toward violence in the form of coercion of individuals by states and other collectivities, not to mention by other individuals. So why did Gandhi, the prophet of non-violence, think that the Indian people, in their demands for greater self-determination, needed more than constitutional demands? And why did he think that this is best called 'non-violent' action? The obvious answer is the instrumental and strategic one: he knew that making demands for constitutional change had not been particularly effective or swift in the first two decades of the twentieth century, and that since the conventionally conceived alternative was violent revolutionary action—which found advocates on the fringes of nationalist sentiment in India—he instead introduced his own strategy of civil disobedience, at once a non-violent and yet a non- or extra-constitutional strategy. But, of course, he had more in mind than this obvious motive.

First, Gandhi wanted all of India to be involved in the movement, in particular the vast mass of its peasant population. He did not want the nationalist achievement to be the effort of a group of elite, legally and constitutionally trained, upper-middle class Indian men ('Macaulay's bastards'), who argued in assemblies and round-table conferences. He almost single-handedly transformed a movement conceived and promoted along those lines by the Congress party into a mass movement of enormous scale, and he did so within a few years of arriving from South Africa on Indian soil. Non-violent action was the central idea of this vast mobilization. Second, he knew that violent revolutionary action could not possibly carry the mass of people with it. Revolutionary action was mostly conceived hugger-mugger in underground cells and took the form of isolated subversive terrorist action against key focal points of government power and interest, it was not conceived as a mass movement. He was not unaware that there existed in the West ideologies of revolutionary violence which were geared to mass movements, but he was not unaware either, that these were conceived in terms of middle class leadership *vanguards* that were the fonts of authority. Peasant consciousness mattered very little to them. In Gandhi there was not a trace of this vanguard mentality of a Lenin. He did indeed think that his 'satyagrahis'—the non-violent activists whom he described, with that term, as 'seekers of truth'—would provide leadership which the masses would follow, but it was absolutely crucial to him that these were not to be the vanguard of a revolutionary party along Leninist lines. They were to be thought of along entirely different lines, they were to be *moral exemplars*, not ideologues who claimed to know history and its forward movement better than the peasants to whom they were giving the lead. Third, Gandhi chose his version of non-violent civil disobedience instead of the constitutional demands of the Congress leadership because he thought that the Indian people should not merely ask the British to leave their soil. It was important that they should do so by means that were not dependent and derivative of ideas and institutions that the British had imposed on them. Otherwise, even if the British left, the Indian populations would remain a subject people. This went very deep in Gandhi and his book *Hind Swaraj*, is full of a detailed anxiety about the *cognitive* enslavement even of the nationalist and anti-colonial Indian mind, which might, even after independence, never recover from that enslavement.

Those points are well known, and they raise the roughly political considerations which underlie his commitment to non-violence. As I said, they give only a *first* glimpse of the integrity of his ideas. There are deeper and more ambitious underlying grounds than these in his writing.

III

The idea that non-violence was of a piece with the search for truth was central to what I have called his 'integrity' and to these more ambitious and abstract considerations than the ones I have just discussed. Gandhi was explicit about this, even in the terminology he adopted, linking ahimsa (non-violence) with satyagraha (literally, 'truth-force', or more liberally, a tenacity in the pursuit of truth). There is a standard and entrenched reading of Gandhi which understands the link as follows (and I am quoting from what is perhaps the most widely read textbook of modern Indian history, Sumit Sarkar's *Modern India*):

Non-violence or ahimsa and satyagraha to Gandhi personally constituted a deeply-felt and worked-out philosophy owing something to Emerson, Thoreau and Tolstoy but also revealing considerable originality. *The search for truth was the goal of human life, and as no one could ever be sure of having attained the truth, use of violence to enforce one's own view of it was sinful* (p. 231 in this volume; the emphasis is mine).

I have no doubt that Gandhi says things that could lead to such a reading and for years, I assumed that it was, more or less uncontroversially, what he had in mind. After scrutiny of his writings, however, especially his many dispatches to *Young India*, it seems to me now a spectacular misreading. It fails to cohere with his most fundamental thinking.

Notice that according to this reading, or misreading, his view is no different from one of the most celebrated liberal arguments for tolerance—the meta-inductive argument of Mill's *On Liberty*. Mill contends that since much that we have thought to be true in the past has turned out to be wrong, this in itself suggests that what we presently think true might also be wrong. We should, therefore, tolerate, not repress dissent from our present convictions, just in case they are not true. According to Mill, and according to Gandhi in this widespread misreading of him, truth is never something we are sure we have attained. We must therefore be *made modest* in the way we hold our present opinions, and we must not impose our own conceptions of the truth on others. To do so would be a form of violence, especially if it was enforced by the apparatus of the state.

The modesty would appeal to Gandhi, but he would find something very alien in Mill's argument for it. There is no echo in Gandhi of the idea that the source of this modesty is that however much we seek truth, we *cannot attain it*, which is what Sarkar contends is the ground of his non-violence. In fact, it makes little sense to say that truth (or anything else) is something we should *seek*, even if we can never attain it. How can we intend to attain what we know we cannot attain? It would be bootless to protest that Gandhi and Mill are not saying that we can never attain the truth, only that we cannot know if we have attained it—so there is still a point in the search for truth. That does little to improve matters. What sort of a goal or search is that? On this epistemological view, our inquiry and search for truth would be analogous to sending a message in a bottle out to sea, a search that is blinded about its own possible success, making all success a sort of bonus or fluke.

In any case, there is something rather odd in Mill's argument for tolerance. There is an unsettling tension between the argument's first two premises. The first premise is that our past beliefs have often turned out to be wrong. The second is that there are grounds for thinking that our present opinions might be wrong. And the conclusion is that we should therefore be tolerant of dissent from current opinion. But the fact is that when past opinions are said to be wrong, that is a judgement made from the *present* point of view, and we cannot make that judgement unless we have the conviction in the present opinions which Mill is asking us not to have. It is all right to be asked to be diffident about our present opinions, but then we should, at least to that extent, be diffident about our judgement made on their basis, namely, that our past opinions are wrong. And if so, the first premise is shakier than he presents it as being.

The pervasive diffidence and lack of conviction in our opinions which is the character of the epistemology that Mill's argument presupposes, is entirely alien to Gandhi; and though he is all in favour of the modesty with which we should be holding our opinions, that modesty does not have its source in such an epistemology and such a conception of unattainable truth. What, then, is its source?

It is quite elsewhere than where Sarkar and everybody else who has written on Gandhi has located it; its source is to be found in his conception of the very nature of moral response and moral judgement. The 'satyagrahi' or non-violent activist has to show a certain kind of self-restraint, in which it was not enough simply not to commit violence. It is equally important not to bear hostility to others or even to criticize them; it is only required that one not follow these others, if conscience doesn't permit it. To show hostility and contempt, to speak or even to think negatively and critically, would be to give in to the spiritual flaws that underlie violence, to have the wrong conception of moral judgement. For it is not the point of moral judgement to criticize. (In the section called 'Ashram Vows' of his book *Hindu Dharma*, he says, 'Ahimsa is not the crude thing it has been made to appear. Not to hurt any living thing is no doubt part of ahimsa. But it is its least expression. It is hurt by hatred of any kind, by wishing ill of anybody, by making negative criticisms of others.') This entails the modesty with which one must hold one's moral opinions, and which Mill sought in quite a different source: in a notion of truth which we are never sure we have attained and therefore (from Gandhi's point of view) in quite an untenable epistemology; the alternative source of the modesty in Gandhi has less to do with issues about truth, and more to do with the way we must hold our moral values.

Despite the modesty, one could, of course, *resist* those with whom one disagrees, and Gandhi made an art out of refusal and resistance and disobedience. But resistance is not the same as criticism. It can be done with a 'pure heart'. Criticism reflects an impurity of heart, and is easily corrupted to breed hostility and, eventually, violence. With an impure heart you could still indulge in non-violent political activism, but that activism would be strategic, merely a means to a political end. In the long run it would, just as surely as violence, land you in a midden. Even the following sensible sounding argument for his own conclusion, often given by many of his political colleagues who found his moral attitudes obscure, did not satisfy Gandhi: 'Let us adopt non-violent and passive resistance instead of criticising the British colonial government. Because to assert a criticism of one's oppressor would usually have the effect of getting his back up, or of making him defensive, it would end up making things harder for oneself'. Gandhi himself did occasionally say things of that sort, but he thought that colleagues who wanted to *rest* with such arguments as the foundation of non-violence were viewing it too much as an instrument and they were not going deep enough into the spiritual nature of the moral sense required of the satyagrahi. One did not go deep enough until one severed the *assumed theoretical connection* between moral judgement and moral criticism, the connection which, in our analytical terms, we would describe by saying that if one judges that 'x is good', then we are obliged to find morally wrong those who in relevant circumstances, judge otherwise or fail to act on x. For Gandhi this does not follow. The right moral sense, the morally pure-hearted satyagrahi, sees no such connection between moral judgement and moral criticism. Of course, we cannot and must not cease to be moral subjects; we cannot stop judging morally about what is and is not worthy, cannot fail to have moral values. But none of that requires us to be critical of others who disagree with our values or who fail to act in accord with them. *That* is the relevant modesty which Mill sought to justify by a different argument.

This view of the moral sense might well seem frustratingly namby-pamby, now, as it certainly did to those around him at the time. Can't it be argued, then, that Gandhi is shrewdly placing a screen of piety around the highly creative political instrument he is creating, both to confuse his colonial masters and to tap the religious emotions of the Indian masses? This is the oscillating interpretation I have been inveighing against, which, finding his religiosity too remote from politics, then fails to take his philosophical ideas as being intended seriously and views him only as a crafty and effective nationalist politician. It sells short of both his moral philosophy and his politics. The fact is that his view of moral sense is of considerable philosophical interest, and is intended entirely earnestly by its author. It is given a fascinating theoretical consolidation in his writing which may be lost on his readers because it is buried in a porridge of saintly rhetoric, of 'purity of heart'.

IV

What is the assumed theoretical connection between moral judgement and moral criticism, which Gandhi seems to be denying? It has a long history in the Western tradition of moral philosophy. Our moral judgements or values are the basis of our moral choices and actions. Unlike judgements of taste which are the basis, say, for choosing a flavour of ice cream, *moral* judgements have a certain feature which is often called 'universalizability'. To chose an action on moral grounds under certain circumstances is to generate a principle which we think applies as an 'ought' or an imperative to *all* others faced with relevantly similar circumstances.

Universalizability is not to be confused with universality. Universality suggests that a moral value, whether or not someone in particular holds it, applies to all persons. Universalizability suggests merely that if someone in particular holds a moral value, then *he* must think that it applies to all others (in relevantly similar situations). Yet despite the fact that it is much weaker than universality in this sense, it still generates the *critical* power which Gandhi finds disquieting. If moral judgements are universalizable, one cannot make a judgement that something is morally worthy and then shrug off the fact that others similarly situated might not think so. They (unlike those who might differ with one on the flavour of ice cream) must be deemed *wrong* not to think so.

Gandhi repudiates this entire tradition. His integrating thought is that violence owes to something as seemingly remote from it as this assumed theoretical connection between values and criticism. Take the wrong view of moral value and judgement, and you will inevitably encourage violence in society. There is no other way to understand his insistence that the satyagrahi has not eschewed violence until he has removed criticism from his lips and heart and, mind.

But there is an interpretative challenge hidden here. If the idea of a moral value or judgement has no implication that one finds those who disagree with one's moral judgements to be wrong, then that suggests that one's moral choices and moral values are rather like one's choice of a flavour of ice cream, rather like one's judgements of taste. In other words, the worry is that these Gandhian ideas suggest that one need not find one's moral choices and the values they reflect relevant to others at all, that one's moral thinking is closed off from others. But Gandhi was avowedly a humanist, and repeatedly said things reminiscent of humanist slogans along the order of 'Nothing human is alien to me'. Far from encouraging self-enclosed moral subjects, he thought it the essence of a moral attitude that it takes in all within its concern and its relevance. How, then, to reconcile the rejection of universalisability and of a value's potential for being wielded in criticism of others with this yearning for the significance of one's choices to others? That is among the hardest questions in understanding the philosophy behind his politics, and there are some very original and striking remarks in his writing which hint at a reconciliation.

So far, I have presented the challenge of providing such a reconciliation as a philosophically motivated task. But it is more than that. It is part of the 'integrity' that I am pursuing in my interpretation of Gandhi that it also had a practical urgency in the political and cultural circumstances in which he found himself. We know very well that it was close to this man's heart to improve India in two ways which, on the face of it, were pointing in somewhat opposite directions. On the one hand there was the violence of religious intolerance, found most vividly in the relations between Hindus and Muslims. This especially wounded him. Religious intolerance is the attitude that the other must not remain other, he must become like one in belief and in way of life. It is an *inclusionary*, homogenizing attitude, usually pursued with physical and psychological violence toward the other. On the other hand, for all his traditionalism about caste, there was something offensive to Gandhi within Hinduism itself. The social psychology of the Hindu caste system consists of an *exclusionary* attitude. For each caste, there was a lower caste which constituted the other and which was to be *excluded* from one's way of life, again by the most brutal physical and psychological violence. When I think sometimes about caste in India—without a doubt the most resilient form of exclusionary social inegalitarianism in the history of the world—it's hard to avoid the conclusion that even the most alarming aspects of religious intolerance is preferable to it. To say 'You *must* be my brother', however wrong, is better than saying, 'You will *never* be my brother'. In religious intolerance there is at least a small core which is highly attractive. The intolerant person cares enough about the truth as he sees it, to want to share it with others. Of course, that he should want to use force and violence in order to make the other share in it, spoils what is attractive about this core. It was Gandhi's humanistic mission to retain the core for it showed that one's conception of the truth was not self-enclosed, that it spoke with a relevance to all others, even others who differed from one. How to prevent this relevance to others from degenerating into criticism of others who differed from one and eventually violence towards them, is just the reconciliation we are seeking.

In the philosophical tradition Gandhi is opposing, others are potential objects of criticism in the sense that one's particular choices, one's acts of moral conscience, generate moral principles or imperatives which others can potentially disobey. For him, conscience and its deliverances, though relevant to others, are not the well-spring of principles. Morals is only about conscience, not at all about principles.

There is an amusing story about two Oxford philosophers which makes this distinction vivid. In a seminar, the formidable J.L. Austin having become exasperated with Richard Hare's huffing on about how moral choices reveal principles, decided to set him up with a question. 'Hare', he asked, 'if a student came to you after an examination and offered you five pounds in return for the mark alpha, what would you say?' Predictably, Hare replied, 'I would tell him that I do not take bribes, on principle!' Austin's acid response was, 'Really? I think I would myself say, "No Thanks."' Austin was being merely deflationary in denying that an act of conscience had to have a principle underlying it. Gandhi erects the denial into a radical alternative to a (western) tradition of moral thinking. An honoured slogan of that tradition says, 'When one chooses for oneself, one chooses for everyone'. The first half of the slogan describes a particular person's act of conscience. The second half of the slogan transforms the act of conscience to a universalized principle, an imperative which others must follow or be criticized. Gandhi embraces the slogan too, but he understands the second half of it differently. He too wants one's acts of conscience to have a universal relevance, so he too thinks one chooses for everyone, but he does not see that as meaning that one generates a principle or imperative for everyone. What other interpretation can be given to the words 'One chooses for everyone' in the slogan, except the principled one?

In Gandhi's writing there is an implicit but bold proposal: 'When one chooses for oneself, *one sets an example to everyone*'. That is the role of the satyagrahi. To lead exemplary lives, to set examples to everyone by their actions. And the concept of the exemplar is intended to provide a wholesale alternative to the concept of principle in moral philosophy. It retains what is right in Mill (the importance of being modest in one's moral opinions) while rejecting what is unsatisfactory (any compromise in our conviction in them). There is no Millian diffidence conveyed by the idea that one is only setting an example by one's choices, as opposed to laying down principles. One is fully confident in the choices one wants to set up as exemplars, and in the moral values they exemplify. On the other hand, because no principle is generated, the conviction and confidence in one's opinions does not arrogate, it puts us in no position to be critical of others because there is no *generality* in their truth, of which others may fall *afoul*. Others may not follow. Our example may not set. But that is not the same as disobeying an imperative, violating a principle. As a result, the entire moral psychology of our response to others who depart from us is necessarily much weaker. At most we may be disappointed in others that they will not follow our example, and at least part of the disappointment is in ourselves that our example has not taken hold. And the crucial point is that disappointment is measurably weaker than criticism, it is not the paler shade of contempt, hostility, and eventual violence.

This is a subtle distinction, perhaps too subtle to do all the work we want from morals. But that there is a real distinction here is undeniable as is its theoretical power to claim an alternative way of thinking about morals. It is a commonplace in our understanding of the western moral tradition to think of Kant's moral philosophy as the full and *philosophical* flowering of a core of Christian thought. But Gandhi fractures that historical understanding. By stressing the deep incompatibility between categorical imperatives and universalizable maxims on the one hand, and Christian humility on the other, he makes two moral doctrines and methods out of what the tradition represents as a single historically consolidated one. And discarding one of them as lending itself ultimately to violence, he fashions a remarkable political philosophy and national movement out of the other.

I want to stress how original Gandhi is here as a philosopher and theoretician. The point is not that the idea of the 'exemplary' is missing in the intellectual history of morals before Gandhi. What is missing, and what he first brings to our attention, is how much theoretical possibility there is in that idea. It can be wielded to make the *psychology* surrounding our morals a more tolerant one. If exemplars replace principles, then it cannot any longer be the business of morals to put us in the position of moral*izing* against others in forms of behaviour (criticism) that have in them the potential to generate other psychological attitudes (resentment, hostility) which underlie interpersonal violence. Opposition to moralizing is not what is original in Gandhi either. There are many in the tradition Gandhi is opposing who recoiled from it; but if my interpretation is right, his distinction between principle and exemplar and the use he puts it to, provides a theoretical basis for that recoil, which otherwise would simply be the expression of a distaste. That distaste is a distaste for something that is itself entailed by a moral theory deeply entrenched in a tradition, and Gandhi is confronting that *theory* with a wholesale alternative.

This conception of moral judgement puzzles me, even while I find it of great interest. It has puzzled me for a long time. Before I became a teenager (when I began to find it insufferably uncool) I would sometimes go on long walks with my father in the early mornings. One day, walking on a path alongside a beach we came across a wallet with some rupees sticking visibly out of it. With a certain amount of drama, my father said: 'Akeel, why should we not take that?' Flustered at first. I then said something like, 'Gee (actually I am sure I didn't say 'gee'). I think we should take it.' My father looked most irritated, and asked, 'Why?' And I am pretty sure I remember saying words more or less amounting to the classic response: 'Because if we don't take it then I suppose someone else will.' My father, looking as if he were going to mount to great heights of denunciation, suddenly changed his expression, and he said magnificently, but without logic (or so it seemed to me then): 'If *we* don't take it, *nobody* else will'. As a boy of twelve, I thought this was a non-sequitur designed to end the conversation. In fact I had no idea what he meant, and was too nervous to ask him to explain himself. Only much later, in fact only while thinking about how to fit together the various elements in Gandhi's thought, did I see in his remark, the claims for a moral ideal of exemplary action. But notice how puzzling the idea is. Here is a wallet, abandoned, and we should not take it. This would set an example to others, though no one is around to witness it. The romance in this morality is radiant. Somehow goodness, good acts, enter the world and affect everyone else. To ask how exactly they do that is to be vulgar, to spoil the romance. Goodness is a sort of mysterious contagion.

The idea is as attractive as it is romantic. The question is, how attractive? I will leave the question hanging since all I want to do in this short essay is to present Gandhi's highly 'integrating' suggestion that there is no true non-violence until criticism is removed from the scope of morals. This is to see the ideal of non-violence as being part of a moral position in which moral principles, by the lights of which we criticize, are eschewed. Exemplary action takes the place of principles. If someone fails to follow your example, you may be disappointed but you would no longer have the conceptual basis to see them as transgressive and wrong and subject to criticism. So the integration Gandhi wishes to achieve (the integration of non-violence with total non-criticism) is as plausible as is the moral position stressing exemplars.

The plausibility of the moral position depends a great deal on the degree to which the moral action and judgement is made visible. How else would an example be set except through public visibility? Gandhi was of course fully aware of this as a political thinker and leader, which is why it is even possible to integrate the detail of his political ideas with the moral philosophy I have been sketching. He was fully aware that the smaller the community of individuals, the more likelihood there is of setting examples. In the context of family life, for example, one might see how parents by their actions may think or hope that they are setting examples to their children. Gandhi's ideal of peasant communities organized in small panchayat or village units could perhaps at least approximate the family, where examples could be visibly set. That is, in part, why Gandhi strenuously argued that flows of populations to metropoles where there was far less scope for public perception of individual action, was destructive of the moral life. Indeed, once such metropolitan tendencies had been unleashed, it is easy to understand his habit of going on publicized fasts. It was a way of making visible some moral stance that could reach a larger public in the form of example rather than principles.

V

I have been arguing that the standard view, which presents Gandhi as essentially applying Mill's argument for tolerance to an argument for non-violence, is very wide of the mark. They exhibit diverging attitudes towards the concept of truth, and the epistemology it entails. Gandhi, like Mill, wants our own opinions to be held with modesty, but, unlike him, with an accompanying epistemology that does not discourage conviction or confidence. To that end, Gandhi rejects the notion of truth that Mill seems to presuppose in his argument for tolerance. He replaces the entire argument, as I have been indicating, with another that seems to have less to do with the notion of truth per se than with the nature of moral judgement.

But now a question arises. How can this argument have less to do with truth and one's search for it, when the term 'satyagraha' with which 'ahimsa' is constantly linked in his thinking, has truth as its target?

It is in answer to this question that his final and most audacious step of theoretical integration takes place. For him, truth *is* a moral notion, and it is *exclusively* a moral notion. So there is no possibility of having misrepresented his argument in the way that I am worrying. The worry I have just expressed is that once Gandhi repudiates Mill's basis for tolerance and non-violence (that we may never be confident that we have arrived at the truth in our search for it) and once he replaces it with his own basis (the separability of moral value and judgement from moral principle and moral criticism), truth then drops out of the Gandhian picture in a way that seems un-Gandhian. It in fact does not drop out since truth in the first place is not, for Gandhi, a notion independent of what his argument rests on, the nature of our own experience of moral value.

What this means is that truth for Gandhi is not a *cognitive* notion at all. It is an experiential notion. It is not propositions purporting to describe the world of which truth is predicated, it is only our own moral experience which is capable of being true. This was of the utmost importance for him. It is what in the end underlies his opposition to the Enlightenment, despite the undeniably Enlightenment elements in his thought including his human- ism and the concern that our moral judgements be relevant to *all* people. Those who have seen him as an anti-Enlightenment thinker usually point to the fact that he is opposed to the political and technological developments which, he insists, issue inevitably from the very conception of Reason as it is understood in scientific terms. So understood, some time in the seven- teenth century, with the rise of the scientific method in Europe, all the *pre*dispositions to modern government and technology came into place. All that was needed for those predispositions to be triggered in our sustained efforts to organize and control our physical and social environment, was for the Enlightenment to articulate the idea of Reason as it affects social life and the polity. But this familiar understanding of his view of the Enlightenment does not take in what I have called his 'final and audacious integrating' philosophical move. This conception which set in sometime in the seventeenth century *itself* owes much to a more abstract element in our thinking, which is that truth is a cognitive notion, not a moral one. Only if truth is so conceived can science become the paradigmatic pursuit of our culture, without it the scientific outlook lacks its deepest theoretical source. And it is a mark of his intellectual ambition that by making it an exclusively and exhaustively moral and experiential notion instead, Gandhi was attempting to repudiate the paradigm at the deepest possible conceptual level.

What I mean by truth as a cognitive notion is that it is a property of sentences or propositions that describe the world. Thus when we have reason to think that the sentences to which we give assent exhibit this property, then we have knowledge of the world, a knowledge that can then be progressively accumulated and put to use through continuing inquiry building on past knowledge. His recoil from such a notion of truth, which intellectualizes our relations to the world, is that it views the world as the object of study—study that makes it alien to our moral experience of it, to our most everyday practical relations to it. He symbolically conveyed this by his own daily act of spinning cotton. This idea of truth, unlike our quotidian practical relations to nature, makes nature out to be the sort of distant thing to be studied by scientific methods. Reality will then not be the reality of moral experience. It will become something alien to that experience, wholly external and objectified. It is no surprise then that we will look upon reality as something to be mastered and conquered, an attitude that leads directly to the technological frame of mind that governs modern societies, and which, in turn takes us *away* from our communal localities where moral experience and our practical relations to the world flourish. It takes us *towards* increasingly abstract places and structures such as nations and eventually global economies. In such places and such forms of life, there is no scope for exemplary action to take hold, and no basis possible for a moral vision in which value is not linked to 'imperative' and 'principle', and then, inevitably, to the attitudes of criticism and the entire moral psychology which ultimately underlies violence in our social relations. To find a basis for tolerance and non-violence under circumstances such as these, we are compelled to turn to arguments of the sort Mill tried to provide in which modesty and tolerance are supposed to derive from a notion of truth (cognitively understood) which is always elusive, never something which we can be confident of having achieved because it is not given in our moral experience, but is predicated on propositions that purport to describe a reality which is distant from our own practical and moral experience of it.

All these various elements of his opposition to Mill and his own alternative conception of tolerance and non-violence were laid open by Gandhi and systematically integrated by these arguments implicit in his many scattered writings. The only other philosopher who came close to such a sustained integration of political, moral, and epistemological themes was Heidegger; whatever the fundamental differences between them, not least of which is that Gandhi presents his ideas in clear, civil, and bracing prose.

There remains the question of whether such an integrated position is at all plausible. It should be a matter of some intellectual urgency to ask whether our interests in politics, moral philosophy, and notions of truth and epistemology, are not more fragmented or more miscellaneous than his integrations propose. Is it not a wiser and more illuminating methodological stance sometimes to recognize that there is often a *lack* of connection in our ideas and our interests and that to register that lack is sometimes more important and revealing than to seek a strained connection?

I will resist answering these questions, except to say that Gandhi's idea—the idea that it is a matter of great moment, both for epistemology and for society and politics and morals, that truth is not a cognitive notion—is impeached by the worst aspects of our intellectual culture.

If Gandhi is right and if truth is an exclusively moral notion, then when we *seek* truth, we are pursuing *only a moral value*. This leaves a great deal out of our normative interest in truth, which, as we have seen, Gandhi is perfectly willing to do. He is quite happy to discard as illusory our tendency to think that apart from the moral virtues involving truth (such as that *of telling* the truth, and living by and exemplifying our moral values) there is also in some sense *a value or virtue* in getting things right about the world and discovering the general principles that explain its varied phenomena. This latter is not a moral virtue, it is a cognitive virtue, and for Gandhi, cognitive virtues are a chimera. For him truth's relationship to virtue cannot consist at all in the supposed virtue of acquiring truths of this kind; it is instead entirely to be understood in how truth surfaces in our practical and moral relations. That is why truth itself will have no value for us *other* than the value of such things as *truth-telling*, which *does* involve our practical and moral relations. To tell the truth is among other things (such as, say, generosity, or kindness, or considerateness) a way of being moral, and it was an aspect of morals that Gandhi himself was keen to stress. But the point is that truth being *only* a moral notion, there is no *other* value to truth than the value of such things as *telling* the truth, no more *abstract* value that it has. There is a palpable mistake in collapsing the cognitive value of truth into the moral value of truth-telling, a mistake evident in the fact that somebody who *fails* to *tell* the truth can, in doing so, still value *truth*. That is to say, the liar often values truth and often values it greatly, and precisely because he does so, he wants to conceal it or invent it. The liar indeed has a *moral* failing in that he disvalues truth-telling, but he still values truth, and what he values in doing so therefore cannot be a moral value. It cannot be what Gandhi (and more recently Richard Rorty) insist is the only value that attaches to truth. To put it very schematically and crudely, truth has to be a more abstract value than a moral value because both the (moral) truth-teller *and* the (immoral) liar share it.

So what is this more abstract value of truth, which even the liar shares? If there is this abstract value to truth, and if *even* the liar values it, *someone* must surely in principle be able to *fail* to value it, else how can it be a value? How can there be a value if no one can fails to value it?

This is indeed a good question and only by answering it can we come close to grasping the value of truth that is not a moral value. The answer is: yes, someone does indeed fail to value truth in this more abstract sense. But it is not the liar. It is the equally common sort of person in our midst: the bullshitter. This is the person who merely sounds off on public occasions or who gets published in some academic journals simply because he is prepared to speak or write in the requisite jargon, *without any goal of getting things right* nor even (like the liar) concealing the right things which he thinks he knows.

The so-called Sokal hoax[2] on which so much has been written, allows this lesson to be sharply drawn. I don't want to get into a long discussion about this incident both because it is remote from Gandhi's interests but also because I think that it has become a mildly distasteful site for people making careers out of its propagandist and polemical potential. Everything that I have read on the subject of this hoax, including Sokal's own contribution, takes up the issue of how Sokal exposed the rampant and uncritical relativism of postmodern literary disciplines. I don't doubt that literary people in the academy have recently shown a relativist tendency, and yet I wonder if that is really what is at stake. The point is analogous to the one I just made about the liar. The relativist also does value truth in the abstract sense I have in mind, even if he has a somewhat different gloss on it from his opponents. In fact, it is because he does value truth in this sense that he wishes to urgently put this different gloss on it. I believe it quite likely that the journal in which Sokal propagated his hoax would have been happy (at least before the controversy began) to publish a similarly dissimulating hoax reply to his paper in which all kinds of utterly ridiculous arguments were given, this time for an anti-relativist and objective notion of truth, so long as these arguments were presented in the glamorous jargon and with the familiar dialectical moves that command currency in the discipline. If so, the lesson to be learnt from the hoax is not that relativism is rampant in those disciplines but that very often bullshit is quite acceptable, if presented in the requisite way. To set oneself against that is to endorse the value of truth in our culture, truth *over and above* truth-telling, for a bullshitter is not a liar.

Living and working in the context in which I do—contemporary American academic culture—I feel almost as strongly about the value of truth in this sense as I do about moral values surrounding truth, such as telling the truth or indeed many of the other moral values one can think of. That it might have mattered less to Gandhi is of course a matter of context, a matter of the quite different and much more impressive political concerns and interests of the Indian nationalist movement. But the philosophical lesson is a perfectly general one, and the very fact that he himself had gathered the strands of his political concerns and interests and tied them into 'integral' relations with these more abstract issues about truth and epistemology, make it impossible for us to dismiss the lesson as being irrelevant to him. So I must conclude by saying that I don't think that Gandhi should have denied this cognitive value of truth. He should in fact have allowed that it defines the very possibility of his own philosophical undertakings and that it underlies his own yearning to find for his philosophical ideas the highest levels of what I have called 'integrity'. These undertakings and yearnings are all signs of a commitment to the very notion of truth which he wishes to repudiate. Whether allowing it will in the end have unravelled that integrity must remain a question for another occasion.

But I will end by saying that what that question will turn on is really the underlying question of this essay: How much integrity can these themes tolerate? It is Gandhi's essentially religious temperament that motivates the extraordinary ambitions of his integrations of these themes. What I mean here is that for all his romanticism about the power of exemplary actions to generate a moral community, Gandhi like many religious people is deeply pessimistic in one sense. He is convinced of the inherent corruptibility of our moral psyches. It surfaces in two crucial places which drive his 'integrity'. It is what lies behind his fear that criticism will descend inevitably into violence, and it is also what underlies his fear that the intellectualization of the notion of truth to include a cognitive value, will descend inevitably into an elevation of science into the paradigmatic intellectual pursuit of our culture, and thus descend further in turn to our alienation from nature with the wish to conquer and control it without forgiveness with the most destructive technologies. The modern secular habits of thinking on these themes simply do not share this pessimism. Neither descent is inevitable, we will say. We can block the rise of bad technologies by good politics. There is no reason to see it as inevitable once we think of truth in cognitive terms, not even inevitable if we value scientific inquiry. So also we can block violence with good constitutional politics and the rule of law, and there is no reason to think it inevitable just because we think of values as entailing the exercise of our critical capacities towards one another. This modernist faith in *politics* to control and via this control to instil cognitive and moral habits in us which distract us from what might otherwise be seen as our corruptible nature is the real achievement, if that is what it is, of the Enlightenment. It is only this faith that convinces us that the integrations which Gandhi's pessimism force on him are not compulsory.

It needs a large and elaborate stocktaking of modernity to figure out whether the faith is justified, one in which philosophy and moral psychology will play as large a part as history and political economy. I have only raised the issue at stake at the highest level of generality. It is in the details, however, that it will be decided, and those really must await another occasion.

NOTES

1. This is a modified version of an article first published in *The Raritan Quarterly*. Fall 2001. My thanks to Raritan for permission lo republish here.

2. This was a hoax perpetrated by Alan Sokal, who wrote a paper making the most deliberately incoherent and ridiculous arguments for the cultural relativity of certain mathematical notions, and submitted it to a well-known journal of literary and cultural studies. The paper was published, and then Sokal publicly announced that the paper was a hoax intended to expose the charlatanism of postmodern tendencies in literary and cultural studies.

Part V

11

Gandhi on Women*

MADHU KISHWAR

'When woman, whom we call *abala* becomes *sabala*, all those who
are helpless will become powerful.'[1]

This message of Gandhi to the All India Women's Conference in 1936
reflects the crucial importance Gandhi gave to the issue of women's freedom and strength in the struggle to build a humane and exploitation-free
society. Gandhi saw women not as objects of reform and humanitarianism
but as self-conscious subjects who could, if they choose, become arbiters of
their own destiny. In this way, Gandhi represents a crucial break from the
attitude of many of the leaders of the reform movements of the late nineteenth century, who tended to see women as passive recipients of more
humane treatment through the initiative of enlightened male effort.

Any approach to understanding Gandhi on women must include: (a) an
evaluation of Gandhi's general understanding of the nature of women's
oppression in India and his views on the role of women in society; (b) an
evaluation of Gandhi's role in bringing a large number of women into the
mainstream of the national movement and of politics, and the quality of
women's participation under the leadership of Gandhi (this is the most
important aspect because, more than anything else, this has had the most

* Madhu Kishwar, 'Gandhi on Women,' *Economic and Political Weekly*, Vol. XX(40), 5
October 1985, pp.1691–702 and Vol. XX(41), 12 October 1985, pp. 1753–8. Later published
as a book entitled, *Gandhi and Women*. Delhi: Manushi Prakashan, 1986.

(This is a revised version of a paper I wrote in 1977. I am indebted to my friends Berny and
Ruth for their suggestions and help in revising the paper.)

lasting impact on the situation of women even in free India); and (c) the place that women found in his life, the experimental nature of these relationships as embodiments of his attitudes towards women, and of his views of an ideal man–woman relationship as these views themselves went through an arduous process of change.

The three aspects—social, political, and personal—are inextricably linked because it is only with Gandhi's emergence as a political leader when he confronted the problem of mass mobilization, that he became aware of women not only in terms of their problems but also as a powerful potential force in society, hitherto overlooked and kept suppressed. The image of the new woman that he wanted to help create was deeply influenced and coloured by the kind of cultural and emotional environment in which he grew up. Gandhi's responses to women are important for an understanding of his general social views on women not only because he, more than any other leader, tried to live his personal life as publicly as possible, but also because many of his experiments which most people consider eccentricities and obsessions are inextricably linked to his vision of new types of relationships between men and women.

I
GANDHI'S VIEWS ON NATURE OF WOMEN'S OPPRESSION

'It is good to swim in the waters of tradition, but to sink in them is suicide.'[2] These words of Gandhi, in a way, sum up his entire social and political philosophy and technique of mass action. It is nowhere more apparent than in the use that he made of traditional Indian symbols to convey a contemporary social-political message. Sita, Damyanti, and Draupadi were the three ideals of Indian womanhood that Gandhi repeatedly invoked as inspirations for the downtrodden women of India. But the Sita or Draupadi of Gandhi was not the commonly accepted lifeless stereotype of subservience. They were symbols versatile enough to incorporate the qualities that he chose to endow them with. In fact, sometimes, he tended to overburden the symbols with meanings they were ill equipped to carry. For example, Sita was used as a symbol of Swadeshi, to convey an anti-imperialist message. Sita only wore 'cloth made in India' or home-spun, and thus kept her heart and body pure.[3] Furthermore, 'Sita was no slave of Rama'.[4] She was portrayed as being able to say 'No' even to her husband if he approached her carnally against her will. Gandhi's Sita was no helpless creature. Even the great physical might of Ravana dwindled when pitched against her superior moral courage. This is the ideal he presented for Indian women to emulate. They were not to consider themselves *abala*s but rather to be like Draupadi, a symbol of 'robust independence' who could bend even 'mighty Bhima himself to her imperious will'.[5] From Sita, who was 'gentleness incarnate ... a delicate flower', to Draupadi, 'a giant oak' in her strength and resoluteness, to Olive Doke (a young girl who had worked among the unclad primitive negro tribes of Africa), a symbol of absolute fearlessness, courage, and will to serve a cause Gandhi saw no contradiction in the transition.

If women were to be 'free' they had to be 'fearless'. Gandhi rightly realized that it was more a matter of psychological fear and helplessness, culturally imposed upon women by society, than physical weakness which kept women crippled. His constant message to them was that bravery and courage were not the monopoly of men. Even if all women could not become Ranis of Jhansi they could emulate the still better example of Sita who even the mighty Ravana dared not touch. 'Let no one dismiss the example of Sita as legendary ... It was that higher type of valour which he wanted Indian womanhood to cultivate ... women in our country was [sic] brought up to think that she was well only with her husband or on the funeral pyre. He would far rather see India's women trained to wield arms ... than that they should feel helpless.'[6] But arms, for Gandhi, were a symbol of one's weakness. The real strength of a woman was her consciousness of her 'purity' and 'chastity'. This 'dazzling purity' could disarm even the most beastly of men.[7] Woman's virtue was to be her defence. In any case, she should prefer to give up her life rather than her virtue. This equation of rape with loss of virtue reflects the age-old patriarchal bias. This was Gandhi's standard advice to women for defence against male aggression. Even though he admitted that he was himself incapable of this kind of courage, he felt sure that a truly chaste and brave woman would not find it difficult to kill herself at the altar of her chastity. Women should be as 'self-reliant' as Draupadi was. 'Who will call Draupadi dependent, Draupadi who, when the Pandavas failed to protect her, saved herself by an appeal to Lord Krishna?'[8] Krishna here represents no physical man but as in the Bhagvad Gita the voice of one's conscience and resolute will to follow one's chosen path.

It is significant that Gandhi repeatedly dismissed the more situationally relevant Rani of Jhansi symbol in favour of a combination Sita–Draupadi symbol whereby answers were sought not primarily in a woman's individual strength and the way to cultivate it but in the realm of women's spiritual and moral courage. His choice of a certain kind of feminine courage in preference to other kinds of strength and heroism reflects his vision which was one of women acting primarily as the best exemplars of a certain moral force in society. This vision stressed the superiority of women's suffering and self-sacrifice rather than aggressive assertion and forceful intervention to protect their interests and to gain political power.

Rules of social conduct had to be framed by 'mutual co-operation and consultation', not forcibly imposed on women from outside. But men had reduced women somewhat to the position 'of the slave of old who did not know that he could or ever had to be free'.[9] Since 'legislation has been mostly the handiwork of men ... man has not always been fair and discriminate in performing that self-appointed task.[10] Therefore, if women were to get justice, scriptures needed to be revised and all religious texts biased against the rights and dignity of women should be expurgated.[11] For this, Indian women had to produce from amongst themselves new Sitas, Draupadis, and Damyantis 'pure, firm and self-controlled'. Their 'words will have the same authority as the *Shastras*' and command the same respect as those of their 'prototypes of yore'.[12]

If most Indian women had lost 'the spirit of strength and courage, the power of independent thinking and initiative, which actuated the women of ancient India, such as Maitreyi, Gargi and Savitri' this was 'the result of social tyranny'. The liberation of women, therefore, was set as a fundamental task before Congressmen: 'Let Congressmen begin with their own homes'.[13] They should begin by imparting education to their own wives, mothers, and daughters. If they believed that 'freedom is the birthright of every nation and individual' and if they were determined to achieve it, then they should 'first liberate their women from the evil customs and conventions that restrict their all-round healthy growth'.[14] To those who argued that the political struggle ought to have primacy over everything else, he answered: 'To postpone social reform, till after the attainment of Swaraj, is not to know the meaning of Swaraj.'[15]

The fact that women had been for so long 'caged and confined in their houses and little courtyards' had had a ruinous effect on their personality, narrowing their vision and stunting their interests to petty things. At the various meetings where Gandhi addressed women, he felt that at times they created an unbearable din, and it was difficult to interest them in problems larger than their immediate lives, because 'they know nothing of them having been never allowed to breathe the fresh air of freedom'.[16] This kind of denial of freedom to women leading to their infantilization had to be put an end to, notwithstanding the religious scriptures that legitimize such denial since they are 'repugnant to the moral sense'.[17] In fact, according to Gandhi,

Hinduism's essential postulate was the absolute freedom of every individual, man or woman, to do whatever he or she liked for the sake of self-realization, for which alone every human being was born. But then, this absolute freedom, even according to Gandhi, functioned within relatively narrow parameters and well-defined boundaries.

However, the main contribution of Gandhi to the cause of women lay in his absolute and unequivocal insistence on their personal dignity and autonomy in the family and in society. Personal and social experience had convinced him that hitherto 'Man has regarded woman as his tool. She has learnt to be his tool and in the end found it easy and pleasurable to be such, because when one drags another in his fall the descent is easy ...'[18] While he agreed with those who felt that 'there is no power of resistance left' in the women of India 'to fight against any evil whatever', yet he emphasized that women needed to take the task of their upliftment into their own hands: 'No doubt man is primarily responsible for this state of things. But many women always throw the blame on men and salve their consciences? Do the enlightened among them not owe it to their sex, as also to men whose mothers they are, to take up the burden of reform? ... But where are the brave women who work among the girl-wives and girl-widows, and who would take no rest and leave none for men, till girl marriages become an impossibility, and till every girl feels in herself strength enough to refuse to be married except when she is of full age and to the person about whom she is given the final choice?'[19] Though men owed it to themselves to help in the cause of women, 'ultimately women will have to determine with authority what she needs'.[20]

But if women were to assert themselves in family life 'wives should not be dolls and objects of indulgence, but should be treated, as honoured comrades in common service'.[21] Women must protest against being treated as sex objects: 'If you want to play your part in the world's affairs, you must refuse to deck yourselves for pleasing man' and revolt against 'any pretension on the part of man that woman is born to be his plaything'.[22] Again, the ever versatile image of Sita is evoked for he could not imagine Sita ever 'wasting a single moment on pleasing Rama by physical charms'.[23] He equated the purity and nobility of womanhood with absolute sexlessness—a negation of the sexuality of women.

Gandhi insists on the inviolability of the personal dignity and autonomy of women. She had the right to say 'No' even to her husband. 'I want woman to learn the primary right of resistance. She thinks now that she has not got it'.[24] The woman has the right to her own body which she does not surrender for a lifetime with marriage. However, this view is intimately linked with his view of a noble woman as a sexless being and legitimate sex as only that which is meant for the purpose of procreation.

Despite his obsession with sexual chastity, in response to an attempt to justify pre-puberty marriages on the basis that the sexual drive of women could lead them to indulgence and sexual malpractices before marriage, Gandhi indignantly retored:

'And why is there all this morbid anxiety about female purity? Have women any say in the matter of male purity? ... Why should men arrogate to themselves the right to regulate female purity?'[25]

In Gandhi's view, one of the glaring abuses of Indian womanhood was the custom of child marriage. He saw this evil as intimately related to that of child widowhood. 'It is irreligion, not religion, to give religious sanction to a brutal custom' and by countenancing them 'we recede from God as well as Swaraj'.[26] Thus the question of women's oppression was linked to social and national health. When the Sarada Act sought to raise the age of consent to 14, Gandhi felt it should have been raised to 16 or even 18. He was perfectly willing to overlook and disregard, in this matter, religious texts of 'doubtful authority' which sanctified an immoral practice which he believed to be ruinous for the health of the nation. Legislation alone would be a 'mere palliative' and 'may be good for bringing a minority to book'. 'A popular evil' could be curbed only by 'enlightened public opinion'.[27] Parents who committed the sin of ' "marrying" their daughters of tender age should expiate for the sin by remarrying these daughters, should they become widowed while, they are yet in their teens'.[28] A woman should have the same freedom to remarry 'without incurring any odium' as men had.[29] Gandhi felt that the presence of thousands of such widows in any society was a serious menace. It was like 'sitting on a mine which may explode at any moment'.[30] In the increasing number of child widows, he saw a very destructive force, especially since, 'men have ordained perpetual widowhood for women and conferred on themselves the right to fix marriage with another partner, on the cremation-ground itself'.[31]

But his advocacy of remarriage was not based on seeing ascetic widowhood as an inherent part of the patriarchal ideology for women's repression. Remarriage was advocated more in the interest of social health. It is 'better that [a widow] married openly than that she should sin secretly'.[32] Thus every sexual relationship outside of marriage was seen as sinful. That is why while in the case of child widows, Gandhi was emphatically in favour of remarriage, in the case of grown-up widows, the stand taken was equivocal. Enforced widowhood was seen as a curse. Even a grown-up widow who 'cannot restrain herself, ... should have the freedom to remarry without incurring any odium'.[33]

However, Gandhi favoured a repressive asceticism to a healthy assertion of life. He saw 'voluntary enlightened widowhood' as a great social asset and believed that 'a real Hindu widow is a treasure. She is one of the gifts of Hinduism to humanity.'[34] This was because a Hindu widow had 'learnt to find happiness in suffering, has accepted suffering as sacred'.[35] 'May chaste and, virtuous women ever cling to their suffering. Their suffering is not suffering but is happiness'.[36] However, it is significant that however repressive this may seem, Gandhi wanted men to emulate the same ideal: 'Hinduism will remain imperfect as long as men do not accept suffering', as some of these widows did, and, like them, 'withdraw their interest from the pleasures of this life'.[37]

Gandhi emphasized the potential of widows as servants of the nation: 'It is worth considering carefully in what way the country can avail itself of the services of hundreds of widows, young and old ...'[38] Likewise, Gandhi was convinced that most Hindu divorced women would 'not want to be remarried' after one bad experience. So 'friends, and relatives in such cases [should not] be satisfied with the mere negative result of isolating the victim from the zone of tyranny. She should be induced to qualify herself for public service. This kind of training would be more than enough compensation for the doubtful privilege of a husband's bed'.[39]

He believed that a wife had the right to live separately, if a husband was unjust: 'If divorce was the only alternative' he would not 'hesitate to accept it'. It was better than interrupting one's 'moral progress'. However, even while he agreed that 'divorce should be granted within well-defined limits' he could 'never think of carrying on propaganda in favour of it'.[40]

The oppressive custom of dowry too came under fire from Gandhi. He preferred girls to remain unmarried all their lives than to be humiliated and dishonoured by marrying men who demanded dowry. If women wanted to resist these evil customs some of them 'will have to begin by remaining maidens either for life, or at least for a number of years'.[41] He found dowry marriages 'heartless'. '... the system has to go. Marriage must cease to be a matter of arrangement made by parents for money. The system is intimately connected with caste. So long as the choice is restricted to a few hundred young men or young women of a particular caste, the system will persist no matter what is said against it. The girls or boys or their parents will have to break the bonds of caste if the evil is to be eradicated. Then the age for marrying has also to be raised and the girls have to dare to remain spinsters, if need be, i.e., if they do not get a suitable match.'[42] According to him, 'the only honourable terms in marriage are mutual love and mutual consent'.[43]

The impact of Gandhi's message was felt in the movement. Especially during high points of the movement, Congress activists in different parts of the country began to propagate simple, ritual-free weddings which came to be known as *Gandhi lagan*. This type of wedding involved simply the exchange of garlands by the bride and groom while their friends and relatives blessed it by clapping their hands. Many such marriages are reported to have taken place even in rural India.[44]

Gandhi saw education as an essential means for 'enabling women to uphold [their] natural rights', to exercise them wisely, and to work for their expansion.[45] Yet much good and useful work could be done 'without a knowledge of reading and writing' and he insisted that 'there is no justification for men to deprive women or to deny them equal rights on the ground of their illiteracy'.[46] Moreover, 'what is all the education worth if on marriage they are to become mere dolls for their husbands and prematurely engaged in the task of rearing would-be manikins?'[47]

GANDHI'S VIEWS ON PROSTITUTION

The evil of prostitution received some of his bitterest diatribes. 'The beast in man has made the detestable crime a lucrative profession'.[48] In Gandhi's view, it degraded men no less than it did women.

It is a matter of bitter shame and sorrow, of deep humiliation, that a number of women have to sell their chastity for man's lust. Man, the law-giver, will have to pay a dreadful penalty for the degration he has imposed upon the so-called weaker sex .... It is an evil which cannot last a single day, if we men of India realise our own dignity. If many of the most respectable among us were not steeped in the vice, this kind of indulgence would be regarded as, a greater crime than ... the picking of a pocket by a youngster who is in need of money ... Let me not be told that the public woman is party to the sale of her honour, but not the millionaire on the racecourse whose pocket is picked by a professional pickpocket ... Does not man, by his subtle and unscrupulous ways, first rob woman of her noblest instinct and then make her partner in the crime committed against her?[49]

But he felt that 'work among the unfortunate sisters must be left everywhere to experts', because he was not sure whether all of the Congressmen who began to take up this cause with enthusiasm were themselves inspired by the right motives, and were equipped to handle the problem. Instead, he suggested that the work among 'the visitors to these houses of ill fame', that is, the men who visited prostitutes and brought shame on society.[50]

The fight against prostitution and the rehabilitation of 'our fallen sisters' was an integral part of the programme for national reconstruction and purification which Gandhi urged women to take up. He asked them to 'form a women's volunteer league for the reclamation of the fallen women'.[51] There are quite a few instances of prostitutes, young and old, having given up their calling and taken to charkha as a means of livelihood, in response to Gandhi's call. This happened at Madaripur and Noakhali in Bengal. But beyond khadi and charkha, Gandhi's panacea for all evils, he had no clear programme for these women and their rehabilitation nor did he put forth any ideas about how to combat the institution. Therefore, he could only ask the women to give up their 'unworthy profession' and become '*sannyasinis*' of India.[52] Most of his concern, though genuine, remained at the level of pleas to men to restrain and purify themselves, and cease to be beasts.

On the other hand, Gandhi displayed an insufferable kind of self-righteousness, quite out of character, when he heard the form and shape the movement for the reclamation of 'fallen sisters' was taking at Barisal. These women had been organized there under the banner of Congress to undertake social work like helping the poor, nursing the sick, spreading education among themselves, promoting spinning and weaving, and helping other organizations involved in satyagraha. Gandhi lashed out at the organization's documents as an 'obscene manifesto' which 'advised [these women] to do humanitarian work before reforming themselves'.[53] Even though he admitted that they were 'intelligent, modest and dignified' and that their 'determination was as firm as that of any satyagrahi', he declined to accept them as Congress members or even to accept their donations unless they gave up being prostitutes. The prostitutes were told that 'None could officiate at the altar of Swaraj who did not approach it with pure hands and a pure heart!' He was alarmed that the 'corporate activity' of these women was tending to make them 'unhealthily forward'. He declared: 'We will not incorporate an association of known thieves for the purpose for which these women have formed their association!'[54] Yet he considered them even worse than thieves because while thieves stole material possessions, these women 'steal virtue'.[55] The comparison of these women with thieves gives an interesting psychological insight. It is significant that Gandhi never displayed this kind of self-righteousness vis-à-vis better known exploiters of society. The doors of the Congress were not closed to even the most tyrannical of landlords or the most corrupt of businessmen.

GANDHI'S IDEAL OF WOMANHOOD

Gandhi's ideal of womanhood was Sita but his message to Indian women was to rise above wifehood and become 'sisters'. He felt a wife could never become a sister in the full sense of the word. 'A sister is such to all the world, while a wife hands herself over to one man. Wifehood is needed, but has not to be cultivated, as it includes the possibility of satisfaction of passion.' He lamented that our women 'know how to be wives, not sisters'. It was possible to become the world's sister only by making *Brahmacharya* 'a natural condition' and being fired by the spirit of service'.[56]

Again, even though Gandhi's 'ideal of a wife is Sita' he was willing to concede that every husband was not likely to be an ideal man. Therefore, in response to a question on how a wife could defy her husband to undertake national service, Gandhi denied that a wife need suppress herself or believe in her husband's absolute claim over her. In this regard, he felt the famous sixteenth century saint—poet Mirabai—had 'shown the way'. He saw her as one who had the courage to reject the confining role of wife and mother, and to remain undaunted by the persecution which she had to suffer at the hands of her husband and his powerful family. By sheer dint of her moral courage and determination to continue on her chosen path in defiance of all norms of social behaviour, she was even able to convert her husband into a devotee. Likewise, every wife 'has a perfect right to take her own course and meekly brave the consequences when she knows herself to be in the right and when her resistance is for a nobler purpose'.[57]

He wanted women to become 'sisters of Mercy' by serving the poor and unfortunate. Women were asked to relate the movement for their own emancipation with that of all the oppressed people and to make common cause with them. Thus, by directly linking women's aspirations with national aspirations, he gave the movement a wider perspective, and a greater legitimacy.

Women were not to confine their concerns only to what are normally seen as women's issues but have a say in the rebuilding of the whole society. For that, he insisted that 'the few educated women we have in India will have to descend from their western heights and come down to India's plains ... This question of liberation of women, liberation of India, removal of untouchability, amelioration of the economic condition of the masses and the like resolve themselves into penetration into the villages, reconstruction or rather reformation of the village life'.[58]

In any case, he did not see marriage and motherhood as the only mission in life for every young woman. Any woman who chose to remain unmarried for the nobler purpose of serving society was a much more preferable ideal for self-realization. He repeatedly lamented that 'a vast majority of girls disappear from public life as soon as they are discharged from schools and colleges'. He would rather they were inspired by better examples: 'Every Indian girl, is not born to marry. I can show many girls who are today dedicating themselves to service, instead of servicing one man.'[59] However, in Gandhi's view, dispensing with marriage and motherhood would necessarily involve dispensing with sexual relations altogether.

On the one hand, Gandhi encouraged those who wanted to live a socially useful life to stay unmarried. One strain in his thinking emphasizes that setting up one's own home and family narrows down one's interests and channelizes one's altruism towards a few select individuals rather than letting it flow freely to all humanity. On the other hand, however, he did not altogether reject the institution of marriage. Because he realized that sexuality could not be eliminated, no matter how much he propagandized in favour of conquering it altogether, he saw marriage as the only existing, though inadequate, restraint on sexuality. He advocated a minimization of sexual contact within marriage and a complete repression of it outside marriage: 'Marriage is a fence that protects religion. If the fence were to be destroyed, religion would go to pieces. The foundation of religion is restraint and marriage is nothing but restraint.'[60]

This dichotomy in his attitude towards marriage overlooked the fact that restraint, to be meaningful, should be self-defined, whereas the restraint in marriage is socially imposed and any violations of this restraint, especially by women, are cruelly punished. It also overlooks the fact that marriage of the kind that exists institutionalizes double standards that arise out of a situation of unequal power relations. Therefore, the institution restrains women in a very oppressive way while allowing much greater freedom to men.

IMPACT OF GANDHI'S VIEWS ON INDIVIDUAL WOMEN

However, Gandhi seems to have been very influential in moulding the personal aspirations of many a woman, who came into the national movement, away from marriage. His Sita obsession notwithstanding, the message that emerges most forcefully from his speeches, conversations, and writings is that while marriage has to be tolerated as a social necessity, it is neither desirable nor ennobling. He held up many of those women as role models who stepped out of the confines of marriage, like Mirabai, to devote themselves to a higher cause. He evoked the idea of woman by and in herself, woman as sage and social regenerator. The idea that singleness can be a more exalted form of existence than marriage, and celibacy than procreation, worked as a liberating idea for many women who were active in the movement. Many among them chose to remain unmarried and were able to enjoy an unusual amount of freedom and mobility, interacting and working with men as co-servers of the cause.

Yet, the number of women who were able to exercise this option remained very limited. The social and economic situation of women did not allow this to become a real option for women on a large scale. But the few who exercised this option, did so in the atmosphere of social respect generated by the movement and left behind them a legacy which is visible even today. It seems to me that there were a larger number of women who remained unmarried by choice amongst the national movement generation than there are today.

In terms of his general views on the need to uplift women, there is not too much to distinguish Gandhi from the early nineteenth century reformers. Often, his attempts to explain the causes of women's inequality are not only inadequate but also remain confined to some of the outward symptoms of the problem. For instance, speaking on the occasion of the passing of the Sarda Act, Gandhi described 'mutual lust' as the 'root of the evil' of inequality between the sexes.[61] That this had 'played an important part in bringing about the disqualifications of the fair sex hardly any demonstration'.[62] Likewise, the institution of *parda* was attributed to the 'period of Hindu decline'.[63] The origin of the practice of Sati was found in 'superstitious ignorance and the blind egotism of man'.[64] If men molest women, Gandhi's 'diagnosis of the disease' is that 'the modern girl loves to be Juliet to half a dozen Romeos. She loves adventure.'[65] Likewise, the evil of child marriage was attributed to the 'sheer lust' of man.[66] His solutions, therefore, were sometimes equally off the mark. Women were advised to leave cities and go and work in villages where, Gandhi felt, they would not only be treated much better but their virtue would also be safer.

Gandhi is one of the few leaders whose practice was far more radical than the words he used for describing it. However, where Gandhi remains unsurpassed in terms of impact and influence even today is in the fact that he helped women find a new dignity in public life, a new place in the national mainstream, a new confidence, a new self-view, and a consciousness that they could themselves act against oppression. From passive objects, women could become active subjects or agents of reform not only of their own predicament but of the whole society.

II
Women's Role in the Struggle for Swaraj

Gandhi's first encounter with woman-power took place in Africa. There he realized how women could 'become the leader in *satyagraha* which does not require the learning that books give but does require the stout heart that comes from suffering and faith'.[67] This was during the agitation against the Black Act in 1913 when, instead of eliminating the disabilities already imposed on Indians, a new Supreme Court ruling, in a test case, declared all Hindu, Muslim, and Parsee marriages invalid. Gandhi 'suddenly found himself heading, or rather swept along by, a cohort of furious and exalted maenads'.[68] The long-delayed entry of women in the satyagraha gave the movement a new force. Women went to prison willingly, underwent hard labour, and were not demoralized even when some of them lost their children as a result of the privations suffered in the struggle. Their impassioned appeals instantly brought out thousands of miners in a protest strike. The success of this satyagraha was in no small measure due to the new moral force that women's entry brought into the movement. Gandhi was quick to learn this lesson: 'Many of our movements stop halfway because of the condition of our women. Much of our work does not yield appropriate results; our lot is like that of the penny-wise and pound-foolish trader who does not employ enough capital in his business.'[69] In India, Gandhi would make this new investment pay rich dividends for the cause that he had undertaken.

In the first non-cooperation movement of 1921, Gandhi consciously involved women in an attempt to link their struggle with the struggle for national independence. But the programme for women was devised in a way that they could remain at home and still contribute to the movement. As a part of non-cooperation, Congressmen were asked to boycott government educational institutions, law courts and legislatures, and to defy the government and its unjust laws in a peaceful manner. But the constructive programme of Swadeshi hinged around boycott of British goods, and the spinning and wearing of khadi. Both these were eminently suited to the limitations imposed upon the contribution of women by their roles in the household with which Gandhi had no serious quarrel. His programme for women in fact complemented their household role and yet seemed to give them a sense of mission within their prosaic existence. 'The restoration of spinning to its central place in India's peaceful campaign for deliverance from the imperial yoke gives her women a special status. In spinning they have a natural advantage over men ... Spinning is essentially a slow and comparatively silent process. Woman is the embodiment of sacrifice and therefore, non-violence. Her occupations must therefore be, as they are, more conducive to peace than war.'[70]

It was with a remarkable insight that Gandhi, without challenging their traditional role in society, could make women an important social base for the movement. As with the other important groups such as the students and the peasantry, he told them they had to take the responsibility not just for changing their own situation, but that of the society at large. 'The economic and the moral salvation of India thus rests mainly with you.'[71] Because khadi was seen as a symbol of self-reliance and regeneration, it seemed to provide solutions to various problems. 'I swear by this form of Swadeshi, because through it I can provide work to the semi-starved, semi-employed women of India. My idea is to get these women to spin yarn, and to clothe the people of India with khadi woven out of it.'[72] With the destruction of India's village craft, especially the textile industry, due to the impact of colonialism, millions of women lost their means of subsistence. They responded to Gandhi's appeal: 'Today, the Charkha Sangha covers over one hundred thousand women against less than 10,000 men.'[73]

Addressing the Gujarat Hindu Stri Mandal, Gandhi said that spinning and weaving were for women 'the first lesson in the school of Industry.'[74] While for the middle class women the charkha would supplement the income of the family, for poor women it was a means of livelihood. Further, 'the spinning-wheel should be, as it was, the widows' loving companion'. But for the educated, well-to-do women, Gandhi's appeal presented spinning—'as a duty, as dharma'—a means by which to relate their lives with those of their poor countrywomen.[75]

Khadi, therefore, became a common bond uniting women from different walks of life. While for the mass of women it meant spinning and weaving, the well-to-do women were exhorted not only to give up their foreign finery but also to don khadi, which purified both the body and soul. Large bonfires of foreign cloth took place during 1921. Sarla Devi Chaudharani became a trendsetter by going even to parties in her khadi sari. She toured many parts of north India enlisting support for khadi.[76] She and many such others became the symbols of modern womanhood that Gandhi held up as models—self-sacrificing, resolute, and willing to throw themselves heart and soul into the movement.

Gandhi's relentless propaganda in favour of charkha spinning and wearing of khadi was designed to bring the spirit of nationalism and freedom into every home, even in the remotest village. In this way, abstract political ideas, such as struggle against colonial rule assumed concrete form for ordinary people. This was a very remarkable way of reaching out to women and bridging the gap between their private lives and the economic-political life of the country. The decision of what to wear or not to wear is one of the decisions likely to be more in the control of a woman and Gandhi was able to imbue this seemingly mundane sphere of life with a new political and moral significance. The choice of spin-and-wear khadi was at once the simplest, least dramatic of choices, calling for no obvious heroism. At the same time, it symbolized each individual's conscious choice of a philosophy, a way of life. To wear khadi came to mean many things—opposition to colonial rule, identification with the poor and the exploited, and an assertion of the spirit of self-reliance, of freedom.[77] It is important to remember that khadi could not really compete with foreign mill cloth in terms of durability, comfort, and cheapness. That is why its use became a way of making a personal statement that the person concerned was willing to pay a personal price for freedom and voluntarily chose discomfort in order to contribute to the struggle for freedom.

The involvement of women in Swadeshi was necessary for certain pragmatic reasons too. Gandhi knew that 'the Swadeshi vow, too, cannot be kept fully if women do not help. Men alone will be able to do nothing in the matter. They have no control over the children; that is the woman's sphere. To look after children, to dress them, is the mother's duty and, therefore, it is necessary that women should be fired with the spirit of Swadeshi. So long as that does not happen, men will not be in a position to take the vow'.[78] Hence the realization of the need to mobilize the household or the family as a unit—the citadel of conservation—without, however, throwing a challenge to the social conservative function that it was supposed to fulfil. He knew that no movement could succeed if one half of the population remained indifferent and passive.[79]

Another sphere in which the women seemed to have an important role to play was the removal of untouchability. 'If the Hindu heart is to be cured of the taint of untouchability, women must do the lion's share of the work.'[80] It was the greatest movement for 'self-purification' in which women with their superior capacity for 'renunciation and penance' were asked to rise to the occasion. Gandhi addressed women on 'Our Duty Towards the Depressed Classes' during his Harijan tour. After this, various women's organizations on their own initiative took up the issue. Again, the appeal made was one that related at once to their personal lives: 'If you consider harijans untouchables because they perform sanitary service, what mother has not performed such service for her children?'[81]

Gandhi knew from the experience of his personal household that as long as the womenfolk resisted, not much of a breakthrough could be made in removing untouchability. His autobiography makes it clear that he had to face a great deal of resistance from his wife on the question of untouchability. Kasturba fought a silent but long, drawn-out battle before she finally came to accept the presence of untouchables living as part of the family in the ashram.[82]

On his Harijan tour, in 1933, and on other occasions when he addressed meetings of women, there are many touching scenes narrated about how Gandhi would make simple appeals to women to give him 'most, if not all, of the jewellery they wear'. Little girls and young and old women would walk up to him and offer their gold and silver for the cause of the harijans and Swadeshi. Gandhi's invariable condition was that 'on no account should the jewellery donated be replaced'.[83] This was indeed a remarkable way of ensuring their personal involvement as individuals because, as Gandhi remarked, 'a woman in India has rarely any cash which she can call her own. But the jewellery she wears does belong to her, though even that she will not, dare give away, without the consent of her lord and master. It ennobles her to part with, for a good cause, something she calls her own'.[84] The real ornaments for any woman were her virtues. These gold and silver ornaments only 'enslaved' womanhood. Moreover, 'In this country of semi-starvation of millions and insufficient nutrition of practically eighty per cent of the people, the wearing of jewellery is an offence to the eye ... a distinct loss of the country. It is so much capital locked up or, worse still, allowed to wear away.'[85] The giving up of jewellery would not only liberate women from their shackles but also help the poorest of the country.

Women had an important role to play in combating communalism and in helping the process of national integration by making every household the battlefield of individual Satyagraha. 'If you are convinced that the Hindu–Muslim unity is a *sine qua non*, I ask you to use against your own countrymen the same weapon of satyagraha that you used so effectively against the government.'[86] He asked women not to cooperate with their menfolk. They should refuse to cook for them and should starve themselves in protest so long as their men 'do not wash their hands of these dirty communal squabbles'.[87] Gandhi was thus seeking to extend the power of women as wives and mothers. 'If Kaikeyi could obtain all that she wanted from Dashrath by dint of *duragraha*, what could they not achieve with the help of satyagraha?'[88] This new weapon of Gandhi was thus effective even for the isolated battle of every woman in the household.

The salt satyagraha marked a new high watermark of women's participation in the movement. Gandhi's choice of salt as a symbol of protest had amused many. The British had laughed while the Congress intellectuals were bewildered by the strange idea. This, once again, proved Gandhi's genius for seizing the significance of the seemingly trivial but essential details of daily living which are relegated to the woman's sphere. Salt is one of the cheapest of commodities which every woman buys and uses as a matter of routine, almost without thought.

In the past, people could pan their own salt or pick it up out of natural deposits. The Britishers tried to acquire a monopoly over this item of everyday consumption. The only legal salt was government salt from guarded depots. The price had a built-in levy. Thus the government was able to tax everyone, even the poorest of the poor.

To manufacture salt in defiance of British laws prohibiting such manufacture, became a way of declaring one's independence in one's own daily life and also of revolutionizing one's perception of the kitchen as linked to the nation, the personal as linked to the political. This was another campaign in which women in large numbers were galvanized into action, precisely because the action, though simple, appealed to the imagination. Its symbolic value was such as to touch the everyday life of women.

On the famous Dandi march through the villages of Gujarat, Gandhi originally started off with 79 satyagrahis. People from the villages on route and around spontaneously joined the march. When the procession neared Dandi, there were thousands of people walking with Gandhi. Among them were many women. Some of them were wealthy women from cities but a majority were ordinary village women.

Kasturba initiated women's participation by leading 37 women volunteers from the ashram at Sabarmati to offer satyagraha and to demand abolition of the salt tax. Sarojini Naidu, with Manilal Gandhi, led the raid on Dharasana Salt Works in the course of which the police force went berserk trying to crush the non-violent satyagrahis.[89] Kamaladevi led a procession of 15,000 to 'raid' the Wadala Salt Works.[90] Women's associations played an active role in violating the salt laws. Women volunteers carried *lota*s of water from the Chowpatty beach to make salt at home, and many others went out onto the streets selling this contraband salt at fancy prices.

While the salt satyagraha and the civil disobedience movement encouraged and brought about greater participation of women, they also clearly brought out the fact that Gandhi, for the time being, could only envisage a supportive role for women in the movement. By now, some women were getting impatient of playing an auxiliary role, and they urged Gandhi to let them join the famous Dandi march, as volunteers in the core group that was selected to accompany Gandhi all the way. They wanted to fight for freedom like men, and not extend the traditional division of labour between men and women to the movement as well. Up to this point, women had been mainly assigned tasks which they could do while remaining at home such as practising Swadeshi and spinning, and men were primarily responsible for political organizing and public protest actions. Now they were demanding a more active political role. Gandhi saw this impatience as 'healthy sign' but refused to allow them to join the salt march on the plea that they had a 'greater' role to play than merely breaking salt laws. Although women were not permitted to join the march, it was clear that every man and woman was expected to break the salt laws all over the country.

However, according to Gandhi, the job even more suited to women's genius was the picketing of liquor and foreign cloth shops. 'Who can make a more effective appeal to the heart than women?' He chose women for this job because of their 'inherent' capacity for non-violence. He felt that the non-cooperation movement of 1921 had partially failed because men had been entrusted with picketing and violence had crept in. 'Drink and drugs sap the moral well-being of those who are given to the habit. Foreign cloth undermines the economic foundations of the nation and throws millions out of employment. The distress in each case is felt in the home and, therefore, by the women'.[91] Again, their personal lives and problems were shown to them as being linked with the national cause. Moreover, this agitation of picketing was to be 'initiated and controlled exclusively by women. They may take and should get as much assistance as they need from men, but the men should be in strict subordination to them'.[92]

Gandhi was not very wrong when he said that if women would 'take up these two activities, specialise in them; they would contribute more than man to national freedom. They would have an access of power and self-confidence to which they have hitherto been strangers'.[93] Nor could the government 'long remain supine to an agitation so peaceful and so resistless'.[94] This was an agitation likely to hit as much the Indian traders and merchants who dealt in foreign goods. The use of women as pickets would help prevent uncalled-for provocation from both sides. It was a brilliant tactical move on the part of Gandhi inasmuch as it prevented the blatant hostility of this trading class from splitting the ranks of Indians. In fact, there is hardly any evidence of their having resisted women pickets.

Further, the merit of the movement lay in the fact that 'In this agitation thousands of women, literate and illiterate, can take part'. Highly educated women had an 'opportunity of actively identifying themselves with the masses and helping them both morally and materially'. The job was no less an 'adventure' for being non-violent, Gandhi warned them. 'They might even find themselves in prison ... be insulted and even injured bodily' but 'to suffer such insult and injury would be their pride.'[95]

This programme of picketing did manage to fire the imagination of women participants for some time, at least. Hansa Mehta saw it as an effort towards 'Purna Swaraj'. From mere spinning to picketing marked a definite transition. The market now became the sphere of women's activity. For instance, the provincial Committee for Prevention of Liquor Consumption issued an appeal for 2500 volunteers in Bombay. Women dressed in orange khadi saris picketed shops. Hundreds went to prison. '... and always more women emerged from seclusion to take their places'.[96]

Though this movement too petered out in the wake of the general disenchantment with the civil disobedience movement, what Gandhi had done was to liberate the minds of Indian men and women, give them a backbone and teach them how to look straight in the eyes of their oppressors. Women from extremely traditional and conservative families, who had never been out of parda, 'faced the barefacedness of walking unveiled in public processions and all that was afterwards involved in prison life'.[97] They gave up their religious and caste prejudices in the process. 'The cause of Swaraj swept all taboos and old customs before it.'[98] They willingly accepted food from untouchables in the prison. Cousins cites an instance when even orthodox Brahmin women prisoners gave absolutely comradely treatment to a *devdasi* who had come to prison in response to Gandhi's call for civil disobedience.[99] Another case is cited of a family in which the grandmother was in prison at the same time as her three teenaged granddaughters.[100] In all, about 3000 women served prison sentences. As Brailsford observes, the movement would have been worthwhile even 'if it had done nothing more than emancipating women'.[101] It gave women a new sense of power, a new self-view. From this point on, there was no going back.

Gandhi succeeded in galvanizing the traditional housebound woman as a powerful instrument of political action. The incidental impact of this phenomenon was no less significant for not being immediately visible. By opening the gates to women's political participation, Gandhi facilitated the acceptance of the women's cause by the nationalists.

Sarojini Naidu was Gandhi's choice for Congress presidentship in 1925, much before the emergence of a women's lobby within the party. Even more significant was the way women came to be represented in legislatures in the 1920s. When Montague and Chelmsford came to India in 1917 to work out some reforms towards self-government, Sarojini Naidu and Annie Besant led a small delegation of women to demand that the same rights of representation in legislatures be granted to women as well. The British government tried to evade the issue by suggesting that the new legislatures they were creating, which included Indian representatives, should be allowed to decide for themselves on this issue. This was said on the assumption that Indians, being more 'backward', would never be able to accept the idea of equal political rights for women. But within a few years of Gandhi's entry into politics and his attempts to integrate women's issues into the movement, there had developed an unusual kind of sympathetic awareness within large sections of the Congress towards the idea of equal rights for women. Thus, beginning with the Madras legislature, between 1922 and 1928, each one of the legislatures voted to make it possible for women to be represented in them.

The sudden and massive entry of women into salt satyagraha in 1930 opened up for women further opportunities which could not be denied again. Participation in public and political life brought with it a new prestige and status vis-à-vis their male counterparts. This was the major reason why as early as 1931, the Congress party passed a resolution at its annual session in Karachi committing itself to the political equality of women, regardless of their status and qualifications. It is significant that at that time, women in most European countries had not yet won the right to vote, despite a much longer history of struggle on this issue.

However, as independence drew nearer, Gandhi kept emphasizing with more vigour: 'Women must have votes and an equal legal status. But the problem does not end there. It only commences at the point where women begin to affect the political deliberations of the nation.'[102]

NON-VIOLENCE AND WOMEN'S LEADERSHIP

The participation of women in the movement should not be seen as one of the peripheral gains of the movement. Gandhi had designed his strategy and chosen his particular forms of struggle very consciously and deliberately so as to encourage this: 'My contribution to the great problem [of women's role in society] lies in my presenting for acceptance of truth and ahimsa in every walk of life, whether for individuals or nations. I have hugged the hope that in this woman will be the unquestioned leader and, having thus found her place in human evolution, will shed her inferiority complex.'[103]

This was undoubtedly a remarkable insight because in any social situation where violence and brute force reign supreme or when social conflicts are sought to be resolved through the use of weapons, women tend to be pushed into more and more peripheral roles, and all the positive qualities of women tend to be looked upon with contempt. Thus women are compelled to prove themselves 'as good as men' in the use of force instead of exploring their own strengths, which only a few individual women can do. By and large, women end up as victims of violence.

Gandhi's insistence on non-violence as a revolutionary weapon contributed to creating favourable conditions for mass participation of people, especially women. More and more people felt encouraged to come out of their homes, instead of hiding in fear, as they tend to do when movements encourage the use of violence. The programmes of action undertaken as part of non-violent satyagraha were such that women would not feel limited or unequal to men, as they inevitably do when sheer muscle power or capacity for inflicting violence are to determine the outcome of a struggle. Thus women's traditional qualities, such as their lesser capacity for organized violence, were not downgraded but were held up as models of superior courage. When used consciously and collectively, this form of non-violence could put the mightiest weapons to shame.

Women's entry into the movement was seen as a life-preserving and humanizing force which would prevent the movement from getting dissipated by senseless and self-destructive violence. Since, in Gandhi's view, the aim of the movement was not just to gain political independence, but to restructure society in a way that no place would be left for coercion and violence, 'in the war against war women of the world will and should lead. It is their special vocation and privilege.'[104]

It is significant that Gandhi admitted to having learnt the technique of non-violent passive resistance from women, especially from his wife and his mother. He tells us that even when he managed to bulldoze his way with Kasturba, her passive resistance to what she saw as his unreasonable actions and attitudes, compelled him to change his bearing from that of a dominating husband to that of a person who believed in the spirit of equality and acted on the principle of mutual consideration.

Moreover, time and again, he cited Mirabai as a symbol of successful passive resistance or satyagraha. In a letter to Esther Falring in 1917, Gandhi wrote:

For me truth and love are interchangeable terms. You may not know that the Gujarati for passive resistance is truth-force. I have variously defined it as truth-force, love-force or soul-force ... What one has to do is to live a life of love in the midst of the hate we see everywhere ... A great queen named Mirabai lived two or three hundred years ago. She forsook her husband and everything and lived a life of absolute love. Her husband at last became her devotee. We often sing in the Ashram some fine hymns composed by her.[105]

WOMEN IN THE FREEDOM MOVEMENT: SOME CONTRADICTIONS

Hitherto all struggles of the people of the earth have been so moulded that the women have only agonised over the death and destruction of their fathers and husbands and sons and brothers far from the plains of slaughter. Mahatma Gandhi, with the help of the ancient land, is creating today new values for all mankind ... let women of all countries and above all our sisters in India realise that this one act of a mind that scales the steeps of air has liberated all womankind for equal service to humanity side by side with men.[106]

These are the words in which women of the Rashtriya Stree Sabha chose to pay tribute to Gandhi. This kind of exaggerated eulogization states as much of the truth as it tries to overlook. The participation of women in the freedom movement was limited, both quantitatively and qualitatively. Active and consistent participation was confined to a small number of urban, middle class women. Rural women joined protest activity during certain phases, and their participation brought a new vigour and militancy into the movement. Raja Rao's novel, *Kanthapura*, written in the 1930s, presents a very perspective picture of how, such mobilizing of women took place, and also indicates its limitations. In this novel, Moorthy, a young man from Kanthapura, a village in Karnataka, is sent by his mother to study in the city. There, he comes into contact with the growing freedom struggle. After he hears Gandhi speak at a public meeting, he decides to dedicate himself to the cause. At Gandhi's behest, he gives up wearing foreign cloth, stops his university studies, and goes back to his village, to devote all his time and energy to political organizational work.

Gradually, the villagers come to see him as their Gandhi. He makes a special effort to organize Harijans and women, especially widows, because of the emphasis Gandhi laid on the special oppression of these two groups, and the need to organize them. Thus the initiative to organize women of the village is taken by a man, but soon, the women, in spite of family opposition, become increasingly active. They form a women's volunteer squad and take to regular spinning and collective physical exercising. They play a prominent role in picketing toddy booths and demonstrating against owners of toddy groves. They face police *lathi*s, molestation, and many other hardships. However, Raja Rao shows how the enormous burden of domestic and fieldwork, coupled with restrictions on their mobility prevent most women from acquiring leadership roles. Most of the women are illiterate and have less than limited contact with the outside world. It is almost impossible for them to establish independent political contacts with the outside world. Thus they are dependent on men to provide a link with the larger movement. Several women also encounter active hostility and violence from men of their families who think that women's involvement in the movement will lead to neglect of household duties. The leaders intervene to reassure the men that this will not happen and to instruct the women that political activity is not to be undertaken to the detriment of domestic activity. In addition, women's lack of confidence, lack of experience, and of exposure to public collective activity of any kind acts as a hurdle. Even the two childless widows, Rangamma and Ratna, who are the most active women because they have fewer household responsibilities, are more mobile and are also literate, come to lead the other villagers only when the front rank male leaders are arrested and put in prison. Before that, these womens' diffidence and deeply ingrained habit of deference and devotion to men prevents them from coming to the fore.

When the male leaders are imprisoned, these two widows begin to take a more active initiative and assume the leadership role. The social status of women, especially of these widows, improves perceptibly, as a result of their involvement in the movement. Towards the end of the novel, when the villagers refuse to pay land revenue, government repression uproots them from their village, and they are scattered far and wide. Moorthy switches his allegiance from Gandhi to the socialist wing within the Congress which is headed by Nehru. With this switch, he gives up working in villages. Even though the local women leaders declare their abiding faith in Gandhi, yet they, and the other villagers, are left as though in a vacuum, with only memories and faith to sustain them. As the narrator, a woman, poignantly remarks, the reader is not likely to 'have heard of Kanthapura'. The heroic contribution and sacrifices of such village women are, by and large, left unrecorded by history. *Kanthapura* is one of the very few attempts made to show us what the movement looked like and meant to ordinary rural women.

As a very sensitive and insightful account by a contemporary of the situation in his own region, the novel suggests why rural women did not come to acquire leadership of the kind that could have influenced the direction of the movement.

Gandhi continually emphasized that if Swaraj was to be more meaningful than a mere transfer of power, Congress members must go and work for a radical reconstruction of the economy and polity in villages. He laid particular stress on the duty of educated urban women to work with their rural sisters. While he himself travelled widely in rural areas, establishing independent and direct communication with the people, not enough Congressmen followed his example. Few dedicated themselves to consistent work in villages. Of these few, very few were women.

Most of the urban women activists and leaders came to be involved through the involvement of their male relatives. When a household was mobilized, the extent of women's involvement was likely to be decided by that of the men. And the fervour of even leading nationalist leaders did not go so far as to encourage wives, mothers, daughters to abandon health and home, and go off to work in villages. To respond to Gandhi's call could well mean a break with one's family, and a very few women did make that break. But the large majority of even the middle class women could not have taken such a step forward in defiance of the wishes of their families. A major cause for this inability was that women were not likely to have independent means of their own, either by way of jobs or property. The small handful of women, like Kamaladevi, who made efforts to live and work in villages, remained individual exceptions, so their efforts yielded limited results. Apart from this paucity of urban women activists going to work in rural areas, there was also a dearth of rural women who could develop into full-time workers. Many rural young men who went to nearby towns to study, would get exposed to, and drawn into nationalist activity, and would then return to their villages, motivated to spread the message there. Rural women had relatively much less access to education, much less mobility and contact with urban areas. Thus, existing differences in the social possibilities open to men and to women inevitably led by a chain reaction to the development of fewer women activists and consequently, lesser mobilization of women.

Even for the mass of middle class women in cities, participation remained at a very rudimentary level such as picketing during certain phases, distributing nationalist literature, attempting meetings, and occasionally joining demonstrations. The activity of women was even more sporadic and fitful than the movement as a whole. Active involvement in Congress activities was confined to a few outstanding women such as Sarojini Naidu, Kamaladevi, and Hansa Mehta. The debates within the National Congress and the different points of view of different groups were not reflected in the discussions of the women's associations. The policy programme of the All India Women's Conference for the 1930s spells out this policy of maintaining a certain apolitical stance. 'The All India Women's Conference shall not belong to any political organisation nor take an active part in party politics, but shall be free to discuss and contribute to all questions and matters that affect the welfare of the people of India, with particular reference to women and children.'[107]

Women's activity and discussion focused on spinning, hawking khadi, fund raising, enrolling new members, picketing, and fitfully working for removal of untouchability and for promotion of Hindu–Muslim unity. The role of the women in the national movement thus remained auxiliary and supportive. They did not come out for direct action as women had in South Africa. This despite the fact that Gandhi thought satyagraha, as a new weapon of agitation, was eminently suited to the non-violent temperament of women. Gandhi's tribute to 'a woman's sacrifice' puts forward clearly the role that women came to play, which had much in common with the role played by women in many other movements. Gandhi quotes the letter of a young Congressman who had been staying for a while in the home of a woman whose son, also a Congress worker, had just been imprisoned: 'During the great awakening that took place last year amongst women there were heroines whose mute work the nation will never know. Now and then however one gets information of such village work. Here is one such sample ... when our Congress camp was declared illegal and locked up by the police we shifted to the hut of a poor Mahishya woman—Habu's mother of Baradongal. We have read of Gorki's mother. We saw her incarnate in Habu's mother.'[108] Night and day, she used to cook for them, nurse the sick among them, and look after all of them out of her meagre resources with great sacrifice and devotion. Here was the ideal 'mother' in the service of the motherland. But unlike Gorki's mother, women, by and large, could not emerge as important political leaders in the movement. They continued to play a supportive and nurturant role for the men in the movement.

Women and Harijans were rightly seen by Gandhi as the two most depressed groups in Indian society since their disabilities had certain specificities which needed special attention. Yet neither women as a body nor the mass of Harijans have lost their disabilities. Neither group had won an equal place in the national mainstream. What Gandhi ensured for both these groups by the manner in which he took up their cause was a twofold achievement. First, he contributed greatly to loosening the traditional biases to such an extent that the rare exceptions among these groups could indeed stand on an equal footing vis-à-vis the rest of society and could reach high positions. Sarojini Naidu, Gandhi's choice for Congress presidentship, in 1925 is a case in point. Speaking after the resolution on fundamental rights and economic policy, drafted by Nehru in consultation with Gandhi in 1931, had been passed, Gandhi said: 'Then there is the abolition of all disabilities attaching to the women, in regard to the public employment, office of power or honour, etc. The moment this is done, many of the disabilities to which the women are subjected will cease. So far as the Congress is concerned, we have admitted no such disability. We have had Mrs Annie Besant and Sarojini Devi as our presidents, and in the future free state of India it will open to us to have the women presidents.'[109] However, Gandhi realized that this kind of advanced legislation could benefit only the exceptional woman who had the means to make use of these opportunities.

Second, even though Gandhi failed to evolve a concrete programme for materially altering the socio-economic condition of the mass of women, he succeeded in raising the question of their depressed condition as a moral question for society to reckon with. He made a major contribution towards creating a general climate of sympathetic awareness of women's situation. Though he had a personal predilection for idealizing certain roles played by women, yet he did not shrink from accepting the logical consequences of his insistence on absolute equality between men and women. For instance, when someone suggested that if women were given equal property rights, it would lead to 'immorality' amongst them, Gandhi's reply was categorically in favour of women having such rights: 'Has not independence of man and his holding property led to the spread of immorality among men? If you answer "Yes", then let it be so also with women. And when women have rights of ownership and the rest like men, it would be found that the enjoyment of such rights is not responsible for their vices or the virtues. Morality which depends upon the helplessness of a man or woman has not much to recommend it.'[110]

However, the necessity for independent control over economic resources was not integrated into the struggle for women's rights. Gandhi did advocate spinning of khadi as a means of livelihood for women and a way of combating the declining employment of women, especially in rural areas where such decline followed the destruction of traditional crafts and occupations. However, spinning on the charkha could not, at that juncture, become a viable means of livelihood for most women. Khadi was not and could not be a real alternative to mill-made cloth for the mass of people, because khadi works out to be more expensive and far less durable than most mill-made cloth. The disappearance of British textiles from the Indian market did not mean a victory for khadi but a victory for Indian-owned textile mills.

Thus Gandhi cannot be said to have evolved a concrete programme to tackle one of the basic causes of women's powerlessness—their total economic dependence and lack of control over the resources of the family. In the absence of a programme for the economic empowerment of women or the material betterment of their condition, the moral concern for them soon degenerated in the post-Gandhian era into the payment of lip service to the cause of women on public platforms and in party manifestos, while the life condition of most women continued to deteriorate unchecked, and everyday attitudes towards women remain obscurantist and insulting.

One of the limitations of Gandhi's thinking, then, was that he sought to change not so much the material condition of women as their 'moral' condition. He sought a similar direction of change for harijans too. He failed to put an economic content into his concept for emanicipation. Gandhi failed to realize that, among other things, oppression is not an abstract moral condition, but a social and historical experience related to production relations. He tried changing women's position without either transforming their relation to the outer world of production or the inner world of family, sexuality, and reproduction.

For Gandhi, equality of the sexes did not mean equality of occupations nor did it mean equality in the realm of work and power. He was in favour of maintaining a 'harmonious' division of labour between men and women which had been operative since the time of Adam and persists to the present day. 'Adam wove and Eve span.'[111] He did not believe in women working for wages or undertaking commercial enterprises. Gandhi did not envisage any fundamental change in the traditional role-relationship of women. Whilst both men and women were seen as fundamentally one, at some point there was a vital difference between the two. Hence the vocations of the two must also be different. Gandhi could go on dogmatically asserting this in spite of the fact that in several other contexts, he challenged the idea of a rigid division of labour between the sexes. For instance, in reply to a professor's charge that he was wasting the energies of the nation by asking 'able bodied men to sit for spinning like women' instead of letting them fight for freedom with 'manlier weapons', Gandhi put forward in defence of his spinning programme the following arguments:

It is contrary to experience to say that any vocation is exclusively reserved for one sex only ... Whilst women *naturally* (emphasis mine) cook for the household, organised cooking on a large scale is universally done by men throughout the world. Fighting is predominantly men's occupation, but Arab women fought like heroines side-by-side with their husbands in the early struggles of Islam ... And today in Europe we find women shining as lawyers, doctors and administrators.[112]

Even the fact that in rural India, women among the agricultural labourers and small peasants are equally, if not more, involved in the actual production process could not shake Gandhi's belief that the woman might 'supplement the meagre resources of the family, but man remains the main breadwinner'. This he saw as 'the most natural division of spheres of work'.[113] The duty of motherhood was seen as requiring qualities which men need not possess. 'She is passive, he is active. She is essentially mistress of the house. He is the bread winner, he is the keeper and distributor of the bread.'[114] In his opinion, it was 'degrading both for men and woman that women should be called upon or induced to foresake the hearth and shoulder the rifle for the protection of that hearth. It is a reversion to barbarity.'[115]

Thus he saw male and female in terms of the 'active–passive' complimentary which has been an important ideological device for denying women any chance to acquire power and decision-making ability in the family and in society. The unjust domination of woman by man that Gandhi thought he opposed is something inherent in the very role relationship that he envisaged for her—that of being a 'complement' to man. He felt that since man is supreme in the outward life, therefore, it is appropriate that he should have a greater knowledge of that world. On the other hand, home life is entirely the sphere of woman and, therefore, in domestic affairs women ought to have more control, 'True they are equals in life, but their functions differ.'[116]

Furthermore, 'as Nature has made men and women different, it is necessary to maintain a difference between the education of the two.'[117] So, he concluded, 'it is a woman's right to rule the home. Man is master outside it.'[118] In his view, 'The woman who knows and fulfils her duty realises her dignified status. She is the queen, not the slave, of the household over which she presides.'[119]

Gandhi could not envisage 'the wife, as a rule, following an avocation independently of her husband. The care of the children and the upkeep of the household are quite enough to fully engage all her energy.'[120] He felt that 'in a well-ordered society the additional burden of maintaining the family ought not to fall on her. The man should look to the maintenance of the family, the woman to household management, the two thus supplementing and complementing each other's labours.'[121] 'In trying to ride the horse that man rides, she brings herself and him down.'[122] In the new order of Gandhi's imagination, 'all will work according to their capacity for an adequate return for their labour'. But where women's capacity is concerned, he has already arbitrarily drawn the limit: 'Women in the new order will be, part-time workers, their primary function being to look after the home.'[123]

When Gandhi was asked whether the wheel was to be a revolutionary weapon in the hands of women as he said it was in the hands of a Jawaharlal, he said: 'How could it be such in the hands of an ignorant woman? But if every woman in India span, then a silent revolution would certainly be created of which a Jawaharlal could make full use.'[124]

What Gandhi opposed was the 'excessive subordination of the wife to the husband', not the fact of women generally playing a subordinate role. For instance, Gandhi always dismissed as 'hysterical exaggeration' any outright attack on the institution of the family. From many instances, I quote one. In response to an angry letter from a young man, narrating the pathetic plight of his sister who was married to a pervert and a debauch, and describing her helplessness as 'one of the most shameful aspects of Hinduism, where woman is left entirely at the mercy of man', Gandhi insisted that this kind of rabid condemnation was 'based on a hysterical generalisation from an isolated instance. For millions of Hindu wives live in perfect peace and are queens in their own homes. They exercise an authority over their husbands which any woman would envy.'[125]

He could envisage women being 'free' even while playing a socially subordinate role. This contradiction is related to the entire Gandhian world view and his concept of 'trusteeship' in society, which represents his dual attitude of simultaneous acquiescence in and revolt against authority. As a good patriarch, the maximum he could bring himself to do was to rationalize authority, make it 'just' and 'humane'. He would not acknowledge the inherent interconnection between most forms of authority and injustice, or between the enslavement of women and the denial of economic independence to them by keeping them confined to the household as their main sphere of activity. He advocated 'harmony', not 'tyranny' in the social division of labour.[126] Coexisting with this thinking was a complex vision of a society based on anarchist principles of local self-determination and the freedom of the people in their own communities to determine their own destinies without the interference of any hierarchical authority. The essence of self-rule or Swaraj, according to Gandhi, was the realization by each individual, that unjust laws should and must be disobeyed. The refusal to be tyrannized would mean the end of tyranny.

Gandhi's dual attitude of obedience to and rebellion against authority is evident in every single movement or campaign he led, and in the very philosophy of non-violent satyagraha. The attempt of the satyagrahi was not only to try to transform and win over the oppressor into being more 'just', but also meticulously to accept the general jurisdiction of the authority and its laws, even while protesting against the 'unjust' aspect of those laws. The line was each time arbitrarily drawn by Gandhi. Therefore, it was not only the women's movement that he tried to contain and fit into a supplementary role vis-à-vis the national movement. He did likewise with the independent self-activity of all other oppressed groups—the poor peasants, the landless labourers, the industrial workers, and the Harijans. It was partly a matter of political farsightedness in anticipating the threat of movements parallel or rival to the national movement. It was also partly due to his deep-rooted, never successfully implemented conception that authority could be made to act in benevolent 'trust'—whether it was the authority of husband over wife or that of mill owner over labour.

While Gandhi could see that the self-view imposed on women with regard to their inferiority was part of the 'self-interested teaching of man' and the age-old 'subordination of women', he failed to revise his concept of the 'natural division of labour' between the sexes, nor could he see this division as part of the same 'self-interested teaching of man' which had resulted in the confinement and subordination of woman. While he could be critical of women who 'delight in being ladies this and what not, simply for the fact of being the wives of particular lords'[127] servilely cling to the privileges bestowed on them by their husband's status, he could not go on to see that the very division of labour he upheld made a vicarious existence inevitable for women. The dichotomy does not end here. He laments that 'a vast majority of girls disappear from public life' as soon as they leave school and college because they are married off.[128] Therefore, 'it is high time that Hindu girls produce or reproduce ... a glorified edition, of Parvati and Sita.'[129] In other words, though he might insist that every girl 'is not born to marry', the symbols put forward to draw them into public life are those of ideal wives whose chief qualification was that they spent their lives in selfless service of and unending devotion to husbands. These women had followed their husbands to the end of the world, and helped them to fulfil 'their' duty.

CREATING A FAVOURABLE ATMOSPHERE

Gandhi helped ensure the entry of women into public life without their having to assume a competitive posture vis-à-vis men. The way their participation in these initial years was patronized by Gandhi set a trend for sponsored, patronized participation of urban, middle class women in the political life of the country. It is due partly to the Gandhian legacy that every political party tends to reserve a few seats for women in each election without women having to organize themselves as a pressure group to make such a demand. Thus womens' entry into social and political life came not only without sufficient pressure from below, but was also characterized by the marked absence of the kind of hostility from men that womens' movements in some other parts of the world had to face. This perhaps accounts for the lack of sufficient militancy in the women's movement on women's own issues in India, and the fact that the movement constantly tried to accommodate its demands within a male dominated power structure. The same pattern characterizes most of the movement today.

Gandhi realized that even if Congressmen manifested no blatant hostility, they tended to shelve this issue, so he kept reminding them: 'It is the privilege of Congressmen to give the women of India a lifting hand' because 'women are in the position somewhat of the slave of old, who did not know that he could or ever had to be free. And when freedom came, for the moment, he felt helpless ... It is upto Congressmen to see that they enable the women to realise their full status and play their part as equals of men.'[130]

This attitude helped create an atmosphere of benevolent patronage which has left a deep mark on the political climate of India. The testimony of Margaret Cousins, an Irish feminist who played a major role in women's organizations in India as well as in Britain, brings out this feature very well:

Perhaps only women like myself who had suffered from the cruelties, the injustices of the men politicians, the man-controlled Press, the man in the street, in England and Ireland while we waged our militant campaign for eight years there after all peaceful and constitutional means had been tried for fifty previous years, could fully appreciate the wisdom, nobility and the passing of fundamental tests in self-government of these Indian legislators ... between the Madras Legislature Council in 1921 and Bihar Council in 1929 all the legislative areas of India had conferred the symbol and instrument of equal citizenship with men on women who possessed equal qualifications—a certain amount of literacy, property, age, payment of taxes, length of residence.[131]

However, Gandhi constantly warned women against depending on patronage. For example, he did not favour reservations for women of the kind that Dalits were beginning to demand. 'Merit should be the only test ... It would be a dangerous thing to insist on membership on the ground merely of sex. Women and for thát matter any group should disdain patronage. They should seek justice, never favours.'[132] Yet even while he thought women's primary work ought to be care of the home, he vigorously asserted the need to give a special weightage to women: 'Seeing however that it has been the custom to decry women, the contrary custom should be to prefer women, merit being equal, to men even if the preference should result in men being entirely displaced by women.'[133]

Gandhi envisioned women entering public life as selfless, devoted social workers. As he began to see more and more clearly that many Congressmen inclined towards self-seeking and power-grabbing, he saw in women the potential force that would selflessly undertake the task of social reconstruction that was to be hallmark of Swaraj. 'The work before them was to make women fit to take their place in society.'[134]

In 1946, a woman wrote to Gandhi complaining that Congress did not put up enough women as candidates for elections nor did they select enough women for official posts. She asked how the interests of women would be safeguarded in a situation where considerations of caste, community, and province outweighed those of merit. Gandhi replied:

So long as considerations of caste and community continue to weigh with us and rule our choice, women will be well-advised to remain aloof and thereby build up their prestige. The question is as to how best this can be done. Today few women take part in politics and most of these do not do independent thinking. They are content to carry out their parents' or their husband's behests. Realising their dependence, they cry out for women's rights ... Women workers should enroll women as voters, impart or have imparted to them practical education, teach them to think independently, release them from the chains of caste that bind them so as to bring about a change in them which will compel men to realise women's strength and capacity for sacrifice and give her places of honour. If they will do this, they will purify the present unclean atmosphere.[135]

Women are advised to focus their work in villages. 'Where better can you find yourselves than by being true to the highest traditions of Indian women, by serving your unhappy sisters today?'[136] They were to work for ensuring basic health services and to take up the task of providing sanitation and hygiene. Speaking to women workers of Kasturba Memorial Trust in 1946 at Uruli, he placed before them 'the good example of Kanu Gandhi who had said that in his camp ... it would be his aim to teach the students how to battle against famine by tilling the ground, scavenging, cooking, bringing their own expenses with them, so that they need not be a liability on anyone. Women have to work in famine areas with this ideal.'[137]

Gandhi saw 'woman [as] the embodiment of sacrifice and suffering' and felt that 'her advent to public life should therefore result in purifying it, in restraining unbridled ambition and accumulation of property'.[138] It was given to women to 'teach the art of peace to the warring world thirsting for that nectar'.[139] But politics and professions were to be, by and large, exclusively male domains: 'And you sisters, what would you do by going to Parliament? Do you aspire after the collectorships, commissionerships or even the viceroyalty? ... I know that you would not care to, for the Viceroy has got to order executions and hangings, a thing that you would heartily detest.'[140] Gandhi's long-suffering, selfless, and self-effacing woman was the product of a culture. The capacity for silent suffering which Gandhi idealized was in fact one of the key symptoms of her subordination. But Gandhi made some of these symptoms of subordination a glorified cult of eternal womanhood.

The kind of activity the Kasturba Memorial Trust was involved in was Gandhi's ideal of women in public life. His comments, at the time of the Educational Conference in 1937, on Basic Education, throw further light on this:

Here is, no doubt, an opportunity for patriotic women with leisure to offer their services to a cause which ranks amongst the noblest of all causes. But, if they come forward, they will have to go through a sound preliminary training. Needy women in search of a living will serve no useful purpose by thinking of joining the movement as a career. If they approach the scheme, they should do so in a spirit of pure service and make it a life mission. They will fail and will be severely disappointed if they approach it in a selfish spirit. If the cultured women of India will make common cause with the villagers, and that too through their children, they will produce a silent and grand revolution in the village life of India.[141]

In other words, the role of the educated, middle class woman in public life was to be an extension of her domestic role of selfless service. Women were to enter public life as 'sisters' and 'mothers' in the same garb of pseudo-veneration which had hitherto masked their exploitation in the family where their relation to social and public life was strictly mediated through men. Gandhi's very vocabulary, in its exaggerated idealization of women as 'sisters of mercy' and 'mothers of entire humanity' reveals the bias of a benevolent patriarch. Gandhi wanted women to act as moral guardians of society, as social workers, and do-gooders without competing with men in the sphere of power and politics because that would be a 'reversion to barbarity'.[142] Was this a wilful attempt to put the clock back? Or was it that even though actively patronizing such leading women politicians and professionals as Sarojini Naidu, Sucheta Kripalani, and Sushila Nayyar, Gandhi could not thoroughly reconstruct and renovate his ideas? He is one of those few leaders whose practice was at times far ahead of his theory and his stated ideas. Just as in his early years he kept insisting that he was a loyal citizen of the British Empire even while objectively cutting at the roots of British imperialism, so also he could keep on harping on women's real sphere of activity being the home even while actively creating conditions, which could help her break the shackles of domesticity.

III
Gandhi's Personal Relations with Women

Gandhi's relationship with Gangabehn is typical of the way he raised simple, ordinary women to the status of fellow workers for a common cause. 'Out of a plain, ignorant Gujarati woman' he made 'a pioneer in a new era. Through her, a tiny craft, a miniature industry was ... born.'[143] He spotted her at a meeting, and was struck by her air of alertness and independence. This woman not only 'discovered' the spinning wheel for Gandhi but became the first organizer of the khadi movement in India. To her, as to other women such as Kamaladevi, Mirabehn, Vijayalakshmi Pandit, Anasuyabehn, Gandhi was one who followed an ideal, expecting others to be equal to working with him for his ideal. 'From each alike he received in response a deep, responding devotion, a devotion not only for his purposes, but to himself ...'[144] It was mainly as a result of his influence that Sarojini Naidu and others like her were made to shed much of their elitism and to identify themselves with the mass of the country's women.

Even prominent Muslim leaders like the Ali brothers had to address meetings of Muslim women blindfolded but Gandhi had no problem having direct access to these women. He insisted on, and succeeded remarkably well, in talking to his 'Muslim sisters' unveiled. 'Gandhi', they said, 'was pure enough to go anywhere and everywhere.'[145]

However, though his attempt was to create equality among men and women workers in the movement, most of the women who came in close contact with him ended up functioning primarily as his devotees. He tried to channelize this devotion into commitment to the cause that he stood for. As he wrote to Mira in one of his very touching letters: 'You will truly serve me by joyously serving the cause.'[146] He tried his best not to permit her to 'cling' to him personally: 'All the time you were squandering your love on me personally, I felt guilty of misappropriation. And I exploded on the slightest pretext.'[147] He wanted her to learn to identify herself with the cause alone. His work alone should be dear to her. He sternly kept her apart because of her fierce attachment to him. As long as she persisted in her emotional dependence on him, he remained very uneasy about her presence in the ashram, and kept ordering her to go and work in other villages, away from him. Mirabehn may have been an extreme case, and therefore have made Gandhi uneasy. However, most of the women who came into close contact with him functioned primarily as his devotees.

A somewhat unusual relationship was the one with Sarladevi Chaudhrani. She was the wife of Pandit Rambhoj Dutt Chaudhuri, one of the nationalist leaders of Punjab. Gandhi first came into close contact with her some time in 1919. She was a very talented woman, a good singer, and an active worker for the cause of Swadeshi. However, like many others, men and women, who came into close contact with Gandhi, she was not a mere political co-worker. He seems to have become deeply attached to her as a person and he took care of her son's education in his ashram. In one his very moving letters to her he explains that what he aspired to with her was a relationship of a 'spiritual wife' which he described as follows:

It is a partnership between two persons of the opposite sex where the physical is wholly absent ... It is possible only between two brahmacharis in thought, word and deed ... It is a meeting between two kindred spirits ... Are you spiritual wife to me of that description? Have we that exquisite purity, that perfect coincidence, that perfect meeting, that identity of ideals, that self-forgetfulness, that fixity of purpose, that trustfulness? For me I can answer plainly that it is only an aspiration ...

The emotional attachment caused some raised eyebrows among Gandhi's other colleagues and Sarladevi seems to have protested. Despite all the personal attachment and fondness Gandhi was clear that this relationship like many others had to fit into the mould of the ideal man–woman relationship that he propagated. Therefore, he would give due consideration to the objections raised by his colleagues however unwarranted: 'They are jealous of their ideal which is my character. I and you ... must give everything to retain or deserve their due affection ... They are my sheet-anchor as I am theirs.'[148]

Thus we see that Gandhi was willing to sacrifice everything which, in his view, might come in the way of the ideal man–woman relationship. For him, this meant a relationship of fellow workers who were untainted by sexual feeling. He felt that he must practice in his own life what he held as an ideal for others.

Gandhi's autobiography and various other accounts of his life bring out clearly how he moved a long way from his early possessiveness and tyrannical disposition towards Kasturba to a healthy respect for her autonomy. In his autobiography he remarks that he learnt his 'first lesson in satyagraha' from his wife's capacity for silent but firm resistance to any attempt by him to impose on her. This reveals his gradual break away from the overbearing attitude of a traditional husband as he came to realize that he had no 'prescriptive rights' over her. For example, in response to questions as to what a Congressman should do if his wife refused to wear khadi or refused to fight untouchability, he answered that even for a good cause no man has the right to compel his wife: 'Remember, your wife is not your property any more than you are hers' and, therefore, a wife ought never to be compelled even to do 'the right thing'.[149] In case the wife refused to allow harijans into the house, she could have 'a separate kitchen for herself and, if she likes, also a separate room'.[150] However, this kind of freedom was never granted to Kasturba. As a leader of his people, he felt he could not allow untouchability in his own house, even if it meant that his wife was denied the kind of autonomy that he advocated other men should grant their wives. In spite of Kasturba's deep-seated resistance on several important issues, he slowly steered her into becoming a kind of junior working partner instead of letting her remain outside his work in her private domestic world. She began by offering stiff resistance to his various experiments but slowly forced herself to cooperate actively on almost every one of those issues, somewhat in the tradition of Sita, who chose to follow her husband in whatever his dharma called him to do.

BAPU—THE MOTHER

Just as in his politics, Gandhi refused to fight with 'manly' weapons, so in his personal relations he gave full vent to what are generally disowned by men as 'womanly' qualities. This 'father of the nation' is also remembered by those who came in personal contact with him as one who bestowed 'motherly' care and concern on them. Kaka Kalelkar narrates an incident which well illustrates this aspect of Gandhi's personality. A number of ex-residents of Phoenix Farm had returned to India with Gandhi and were staying at Shanti Niketan. Kaka Kalelkar was one of them. Early each morning, the group used to go to perform an hour of manual labour. One day, 'when Bapu came, we sat up till late at night, talking with him. In the morning, after prayers, we went to perform our labour. When we came back, what did we see? Our breakfast, fruit and all, was carefully prepared and kept ready in plates for us. We had all gone to work. Who had performed this motherlike labour of love?' On discovering that it was Gandhi who had done this, Kaka Kalelkar says he felt very embarrassed, but Gandhi laughed and reassured him, saying that anyone who serves, deserves to be served.[151]

Gandhi took a deep personal interest not only in the political development of all those who came in close contact with him but also in the most intimate, private details of their life in the same way that a mother does. His correspondence with hundreds of people is full of this kind of concern. He remembered the personal situation and problems of each one, and showed particular concern for their health. Even in the midst of major political storms, he never forgot to recommend, in his letters, diet changes, long walks, and various nature cure methods whenever he got to know about someone's ill-health. In his ashram and also at different places he visited, he nursed hundreds of people, personally administering nature cures to them. Even when caught up in what he considered the most serious political crisis of his life—the Hindu–Muslim riots preceding partition—he found time to nurse sick people as he walked through the villages of Noakhali in East Bengal.

In *Young India* and *Harijan*, he regularly published articles on diet reform. In these columns he emphasized the urgency of changing to healthier food habits. He also presented, for the readers' benefit, his own tried-out recipes for cheap and nutritious meals that did not require elaborate preparation.

His interest in food sprang partly from a deep concern for the individuals around him, and partly from his involvement with the question of how even the poorest person in the country was to be well fed. From the time he took to public life, he always had a group of followers and their children living with him. He held himself responsible for their well being and tended to their needs with typical motherly concern.

In his ashrams, he incessantly carried on experiments in healthy and cheap diet. He experimented with ovens, cooking vessels, quantity of water to be used, steaming, boiling, baking, determining what ingredients are to be used or avoided in cooking, various ways of making bread, preparing various dishes from nutritious but neglected food items such as oil cakes and soyabeans, manufacturing jams and murabbas out of fruits and orange peels that might otherwise be wasted or thrown away. He also spent much thought and energy on making up suitable dishes for invalids and convalescents, and on devising nature cure remedies for them. The weight of every ashramite used to be recorded regularly, and Gandhi carefully observed the effects on them of changes introduced in their diet. He spent a good deal of time devising suitable diet for Congress workers in villages. He wanted such diet to be 'nourishing and yet within the means of an average villager and within the possibility of an eight hours minimum wage' which the Congress had in those days fixed at three annas per day.[152]

Thus his experiments were conducted with a view to finding out the most wholesome food and the most sensible way of preparing it, keeping in mind the conditions of poverty in which a majority of people lived. Equally touching is his deep concern for eliminating the drudgery of women as far as possible. For instance, in reporting on his experiments with uncooked, raw foods, Gandhi tells his readers: 'I publish the facts of this experiment because I attach the greatest importance to it. If it succeeds it enables serious men and women to make revolutionary changes in their mode of living. It frees women from a drudgery which brings no happiness but which brings disease in its train.'[153]

Similarly, when he argued in favour of eating unpolished rice, that is, rice which is hand pounded rather than polished in mills, Gandhi emphasized not just the nutritional advantages but also that 'If rice can be pounded in the villages after the old fashion the wages will fill the pockets of the rice pounding sisters ...',[154] since hand pounding of rice is traditionally considered a woman's occupation.

It is important to point out that Gandhi never recommended any diet reform which he had not tried on himself over a period of time. This area of Gandhi's activity reveals him at his scientific and rational best. It also throws light on his essential humaneness which led him to try and approximate most closely to what has been defined as a 'womanly' ideal—that of being nurturant, life-giving, and healing. Towards the end of his life, he seems to have taken on the maternal role more consciously. In her aptly titled book *Bapu, My Mother*, his grandniece Manu Gandhi recalls how Bapu often said to her that though he had been a father to many, he was a mother to her. On another occasion, when replying to some workers of the Kasturba Memorial Trust who wanted the whole programme to be run by women, Gandhi endorsed their point of view, but said that he counted himself as a woman. He made such statements on several other occasions as well.

For an overall understanding of Gandhi's views on women, it is important to take into account his views on sex and man–woman relationships. These views are rooted in his personal experiences in childhood and early youth. There are obsessive and repeated references to 'lust' in his autobiography. His vow of sexual abstinence, taken in South Africa and continued to the end of his life, his later experiments to test the extent of his freedom from sexual impulses, indicate that sexuality continued to occupy a crucial place in his thinking, and also to affect his views on women. What he calls his 'juvenile excess' in the early years of his married life seem to have left a permanent mark.[155] Any form of sexual contact with his wife came to embody a threat to higher loyalties. He could never, throughout his life, forgive himself for the fact that, while his father lay dying, he was indulging in sexual intimacy with his wife who was in an advanced stage of pregnancy.[156] The fact of the death of the child, a few days before it was supposed to be born, only confirmed for him the 'latent mischief in the sexual nature of man.'[157]

The fact that he came to see in sexuality a fatal danger is perhaps also related to the vow of abstinence that he had to give his mother before he was allowed to go to England. As Gandhi himself admits, it was only 'the hand of God' that saved him from 'disaster' on many an occasion. In his autobiography he narrates how providence saved him from breaking his vow in spite of himself. The first occasion was when his friend Mehtab took him to a brothel. On another occasion, in Portsmouth, during a card session, some women made advances to which Gandhi nearly responded, but suddenly recalling his vow, he walked off. Being aware of how little resistance he had to the temptation, he was convinced that God had saved him! Likewise, at Zanzibar, the ship's captain took him to a brothel where Gandhi again experienced his lack of sufficient self-restraint and was assisted in keeping his vow only by the 'hand of God'. During his stay in Europe, despite 'grave temptations' he was able to keep his vow to his mother. His experiences, however, seem to have reinforced his growing mistrust of sexuality.

Gandhi viewed celibacy as an important component of living a higher form of life. He was aware that celibacy would not work for everyone so he recommended it only for those few who wished to live more than an ordinary life. It was a precondition for those who wished to become ashram inmates:

The conquest of lust is the highest endeavour of a man's or a woman's existence. And without overcoming lust, man cannot hope to rule over self; without rule over self, there can be no Swaraj ... No worker who has not overcome lust, can hope to render any genuine service to the cause of the harijans, communal unity, khadi, cow protection or village reconstruction. Great causes like these cannot be served by intellectual equipment alone, they call for spiritual effort or soul force. Soul force comes only through God's grace and never descends upon a man who is a slave to lust.[158]

Even between married couples, he felt that sexual restraint was vitally necessary. That is why he was firmly opposed to any form of birth control except abstinence. Margaret Sanger tried desperately to convince him of the urgent need for birth control methods as a necessary precondition for the liberation of women. He remained untouched, unmoved by her impassioned arguments based on her experience of the miserable condition of working-class women in England who suffered due to the lack of dissemination of scientific birth control methods. Gandhi insisted that 'self control or *Brahmacharya*' was the only healthy method. 'Artificial methods are like putting a premium upon vice ... [and] must result in imbecility and nervous prostration.'[159] The sexual urge in man or woman was seen by him as 'animal passion' or 'bestial lust'. He saw it as 'an insult to the fair sex to put up her case in support of birth control by artificial methods ... [which] will still further degrade her'.[160] For him, 'the difference between a prostitute and a woman using contraceptives is only this—that the former sells her body to several men, while the latter sells it to one man'.[161] Gandhi condemned 'the use of contraceptives in every conceivable circumstances' because he felt it was 'not necessary for man or woman to satisfy the sexual instinct except when the act is meant for race reproduction'.[162] Any sexual contact between a husband and wife, except when they both wanted a child, was sinful, immoral, and bestial. Gandhi insisted that there would be no birth control problem in India if the women could be taught to say 'No' to their husbands, when they 'approach them carnally'.[163] When Margaret Sanger cued cases of nervous and mental breakdowns as a result of the practice of self-control, Gandhi dismissed the evidence as 'based on examination of imbeciles'.[164] Free love was, for him, 'dog's love' which is what contraceptives would bring about. 'If people want to multiply like rabbits, they will also have to die like rabbits. If we become licentious, there will undoubtedly be Nature's punishment descending upon us.'[165]

According to Gandhi, women, to preserve their integrity and self-respect, should not allow even their husband to 'enjoy' any physical relation with them. He insisted that true love could flower between man and woman, as in his own case, only when the two voluntarily renounced all sexual or 'lustful' contact. It was only then that they could rise above 'the selfish purpose of begetting children and running a house hold'.[166] It is significant that from here he did not go on to attack the institution of marriage and the family as coming in the way of selfless humanity. His solution to the problem was that married people 'can behave [even while continuing to stay married] as if they were not married ... If the married couple can think of each other as brother and sister, they are freed for universal service.' Their love becomes free from the impurity of lust and so grows stronger.[167] His blessing to a young couple upon their marriage was 'May you have no children.'[168]

A Sati would, in Gandhi's view, regard marriage not as a means of satisfying the animal appetite but 'as a means of realising the ideal of selfless and self-effacing service ...'[169] Selflessness here equals sex-lessness and anybody wanting to perform social service or have a glimpse of religious life must lead a celibate existence, whether married or unmarried.[170] In Gandhi's ashram, even married couples had to vow to live a life of celibacy. In love and companionship between man and woman, there was no room for sexual satisfaction. That satisfaction was seen as a denial of true friendship. Gandhi tells us that he and his wife tasted the real bliss of married life when they renounced all sexual contact and that in the heyday of youth.[171] Even though he liked to believe that this self-denial was born out of their great desire for service, we know, from his own account, that he took the decision unilaterally and Kasturba acquiesced in it, as she silently acquiesced in many other things which she did not really agree with.

Gandhi's experiments with changing key aspects of the usual power relationship between men and women always included a healthy respect and consideration for every human being, allowing them to obey the dictates of their own conscience. All this mutual respect and consideration was, however, circumscribed in a benevolent and enlightened patriarchal mould. Gandhi, the patriarch, was confident that he would never abuse the authority and trust vested in him. The relationship he envisaged did not, however, provide real equality to women. Though Kasturba remained publicly silent on these issues, even Gandhi's own version of his relationship with her, despite all the respect he claimed to have for her, bears this out. In everything, he decided and she acquiesced, whether it was Gandhi unilaterally givin up all sexual contact between them, or his opting for an ashram life instead of a private householder's life, or his insisting on her cleaning latrines along with him. Whether or not she really felt convinced of all these things, Gandhi seldom questioned his right to impose them on her, because he was convinced that he could confidently decide for her what she needed to do when actions to promote a 'higher cause' were involved. The framework within which he worked may have had inbuilt safeguards against vile abuse of power for purely selfish ends but in the way it functioned, it did not provide an alternative to the traditional power hierarchy that prevails in most families between men and women and between young and old.

Though sometimes bordering on crankiness and perverseness, Gandhi's obsession and experiment with sexual abstinence should not be dismissed as mere products of personal eccentricity. His 'self control' and brahmacharya were not mere claptrap of life denying asceticism with a moralistic facade. In the hands of a reactionary moralist, sexual abstinence invariably comes to represent a repressive and life-denying ideology. But Gandhi tried literally to transcend his sexuality and to make it contribute to forging the powerful, modern political weapon of satyagraha. He experimented with these ideas as part of his social revolution and vision of a new man–woman relationship. Since there used to be many letters on sex problems written to him, he began to discuss them in a regular column in the *Harijan*. It is noteworthy that almost all his advocacy of sexual restraint was addressed to men. He saw male sexuality as almost synonymous with aggression towards and humiliation of women. In his view, women, by and large, were passive objects of male sexual urge.

His ideas on control of sexuality served to create a favourable social atmosphere for women to come out of their homes and participate in social and political struggles, to be able to live away from home without fear, shame, or exploitation. His upholding celibacy as a higher ideal than marriage also made it possible for many women to live unmarried and yet be respected in society. Just as Mirabai had opted out of marriage by embracing a new religious trend which allowed such an option, so many women during the national movement were helped to exercise this option, because of the active encouragement given by Gandhi.

Gandhi tried to ensure that his model of an ideal relationship between men and women was practised not only in the ashram but also in the national movement generally. His insistence on making the love of ashramites a love of brothers and sisters served an important purpose in bringing about a 'freer' social interaction between the sexes. The kind of innovations he tried in ashram life bear witness to this:

My brahmacharya knew nothing of the orthodox laws governing its observance. I framed my own rules, as occasion necessitated. But I have never believed that all contact with women was to be shunned for the due observance of brahmacharya. That restraint which demands the abstention from all contact, no matter how innocent, with the opposite sex, is a forced growth, having little or no vital value ... I sleep in the Ashram surrounded by women, for they feel safe with me in every respect. It should be remembered that there is no privacy in the Segaon Ashram.[172]

Sometimes, he even received visitors while bathing, and had his massage administered by young women. Besides keeping his own clothes to a minimum, he inveighed against the muffling up and false modesty imposed on women: 'Chastity ... must be a very poor thing [if] it cannot stand the gaze of men.' So he asked women to 'tear [down] the purdah.'[173]

Gandhi's conception of brahmacharya differed in one important respect from the conception that had come down through the mainstream tradition of sages and ascetics who practised and preached celibacy as a precondition to the achievement of self-realization. In the ancient ascetic tradition, woman was consistently seen as the embodiment of temptation, the seductress who lured the sage away from his high pursuits. Therefore, a *tapasvi* who had taken the vow of brahmacharya was always warned to stay far away from women and to shun them like the plague. Many of them went to the ridiculous extent of vowing never to set eyes on women lest their tapasya be shattered. Gandhi took a far more rational view of the phenomenon of lust, and temptation, in that he blamed the lustful eye rather than the object viewed by that eye. His writings on sexuality are free of that misogynist taint which is so visible in much theology and mythology of the ascetic traditions, Christian, Hindu, and Islamic. Gandhi, by and large, saw man as the perpetrator of lust and woman as its victim rather than as temptress or agent. His life at the ashram, surrounded by women, was an acknowledgment that woman in herself is not an embodiment of evil sexuality but that such evil must be cleansed from the mind wherein it may exist.

In the ashram, there was no segregation. Men and women slept, ate, and worked together. Taking the cue from Gandhi, ashramites of opposite sex nursed each other in illness without the usual restraints. This was indeed a radical experiment for evolving a new framework and a new concept of a working relationship between men and women. Uninhibited by each other's sex, the common bond between man and woman was to be their common ideal and their common work.

Moreover, under the prevalent social circumstances, brahmacharya had a very liberating potential for women. In the existing social structures, this was perhaps the only way women could free themselves from household drudgery and the burden of childcare to an extent sufficient for them to become active participants in social change. Even married couples were asked to practise sexual abstinence and direct their energies to constructive work.

However, Gandhi recommended sexual abstinence even more strongly for men than for women. These experiments with brahmacharya as a way of life were part of a much larger effort for finding newer and healthier ways of relating with the opposite sex and moving out of the framework of power relations based on sex.

The experiments with abstinence are also part of an old Indian tradition wherein ascetics were believed to acquire extraordinary powers, even greater than those of the gods, by years of hard tapasya. Gandhi's sexual abstinence was part of a larger tapasya through which he attempted to discipline his life for devotion to a high cause. His rigorous austerity, various fasts and dietary experiments, vows of silence, living barebodied except for a loin-cloth, and travelling as far as possible in the manner of ordinary poor people, all were essential components of his rigorous tapasya. While most of this seemed to come relatively easily and naturally to Gandhi, he seems to have been bothered by sexual unrest till the very end of his life. Could it be that he saw himself as similar to the prominent rishis and *munis* who, after acquiring extraordinary powers through their tapasya, lost all their accumulated power because they failed to resist sexual lust? Gandhi not only deliberately surrounded himself with 'temptation', living in close proximity with a number of young women and staying in close physical contact with them. He also kept testing himself in more and more ultimate ways, especially towards the end of his life, when he was facing a serious moral and political crisis.

A very fundamental part of his philosophy and world view was the idea of the responsibility of each human being for everyone else. He believed that the spiritual force of even one fully formed satyagrahi could set right the world's wrongs. At the end of his life it was clear that many things had gone terribly wrong. He and the India of his dreams had been pushed aside. Millions were being slaughtered in communal riots. The Congress party was assuming power as the inheritor of the British Raj, not as the regenerator of India. Day after day, he sought an explanation as to why his ideals and hopes had ended in such a shamble. He no longer spoke of living a hundred years but spoke of the sadness of continuing to live at all. To one who believed so firmly in the connection between personal purity and the force of truth and fearlessness, some explanation had to be forthcoming for the ruin that had ensued.

This constant preoccupied brooding led him to make one of his final major, practical experiments with truth. He thought that perhaps his own commitment was flawed and hypocritical, and that flaw was responsible for the whole disaster. Considering the profound faith he had in the unity of theory and practice, could he in all sincerity be sure that his sexual lust was a thing of the past and that he saw women who were close to him only as sisters and daughters united in a common faith? He began to test himself, as always hiding nothing and increasing the stakes day by day. His final experiments were with Manu, his cousin's 19-year-old granddaughter. They slept together without any clothes, holding each other. In this way, Gandhi felt he could find out whether any remnants of his formerly active sexual urges remained in him to be revealed.

An important component of his views was also the belief that loss of semen leads to serious loss of physical and spiritual energy of men. Sexual responsiveness to women was to be banned as an evil temptation, not by shunning women but by acquiring total control over one's own sexuality. In this part of his attempt to transform himself, where Gandhi as a man is concerned with self-realization and disciplining himself to attain what he believed to be a higher moral and spiritual force, his attention seems to lie with his own struggle with no apparent attention paid to how his actions might affect the woman who became participants in his experiments. Just as he seems to have shown no concern for Kasturba's opinion when he first decided to launch his sexual experiments with abstinence, so he seems to overlook the possible effects of his experiment on the 19-year-old Manu.[174]

Gandhi's revulsion against sex and sensuality often led him to practise a kind of inner violence on those under his charge. Certain autobiographical instances narrated by him highlight a streak of perverse self-righteous arbitrariness. For example, at Tolstoy Farm, as part of an experiment, he used to send young boys and girls 'to bathe in the same spot at the same time' after having fully introduced them to the necessity of 'self-restraint'. He tells us that his eye 'always followed the girls as a mother's eye would follow a daughter'. One day, he got to know that one of the boys had 'made fun of two girls'. He then forced the girls to 'cut off their fine, long hair so that they would have some sign on their persons to 'sterilise the sinner's eye'. He reports with satisfaction that he never heard of a joke again.[175] Later on, at Phoenix, a girl of 20 was made to chop off her hair because of having sinned with two boys. Much later, he had Mirabehn also shave off her hair to make her fit for ashram life.

While it is true that Gandhi gave up sexual intimacy for a wider communal intimacy, and for disciplining himself as a servant of a higher cause, yet there is also some sign of a streak of vindictiveness towards woman as the temptress that can be detected in his views and actions. While some of his diatribes against promiscuous male sexuality have humane aspects, Gandhi made one most uncharacteristic and shocking statement which betrayed his violent revulsion against any sexual contact outside marriage. When criticizing the work of orphanages, one of his points among several others, was that they admit 'foundlings', that is, infants who have been abandoned because they were born out of wedlock:

I am not yet convinced that providing for such admissions is ethically sound. I have a kind of feeling that such facilities lead to increase in indulgence. It can in no way be proved that keeping alive every creature that is born, no matter how, is a part of humanitarianism. It is indeed futile to make such an effort ... Humanitarianism does not mean saving a definite number of lives ... Unclean flour is infested with numberless lives. To preserve such flour is no humanitarianism. It lies rather in covering up the flour with earth or destroying it, though either way the vermin in the flour perish. Numberless vermin perish even in the process of keeping our bodies clean.

Therefore he concludes that humanitarianism 'will not encourage and shield laxity by accepting the burden of such admissions.'[176] The fact that one as devoted to non-violence as was Gandhi, should see innocent children born out of marriage as vermin who deserved to be left to perish is another reflection of his moralistic self-righteousness and vindictive revulsion against what he saw as irresponsible sex for the sake of sensual enjoyment. Even if one makes allowance for the statement by acknowledging that it was made in 1917 when Gandhi was only beginning to evolve his philosophy of non-violence and love for every human being including an enemy, it is hard to comprehend the violence of thought underlying this sentiment considering that he never used similar language or expressed such sentiments against well-known exploiters of society, and would not have condoned violence against them as he does against little babies who could not by any stretch of imagination be held responsible for being born of people who refused to take responsibility for them.

PRACTICE IN ADVANCE OF PRECEPT

While in many ways, Gandhi's views on women and their role in society are not very different from those of the 19th century reformers, in some other important ways he marks a crucial break from that tradition. The most crucial difference is that he does not see women as objects of reform, as helpless creatures deserving charitable concern. Instead, he sees them as active, self-conscious agents of social change. His concern is not limited to bringing about change in selected areas of social life such as education and marriage as a way of regenerating Indian society, as was that of most 19th century social reformers. He is primarily concerned with bringing about radical social reconstruction. The political movement for national liberation was a means, a weapon to achieve that end. And he saw women playing a major role in the task of social reconstruction. He thought that in the process of reconstructing society, they would also free themselves from the specific forms of bondage that affected them as women.

Yet, while the new society that he envisions is a radical departure from the past, and is based on anarchist principles of local self-determination, the role that he envisages and advocates for women is based on the ideology of division of labour between the sexes which has been historically an important tool for the oppression and exploitation of women.

Gandhi saw the home as the main sphere of activity of most women, barring the exceptional woman who devotes herself to serving humanity as an extension of the domestic role of selfless service. Gandhi believes in the equal dignity of both men and women and in women's absolute freedom for self-realization. But his notion of equality does not extend to equality in employment, or in economic and political power. He wanted, first and foremost, to change the moral condition of women's lives, and to do away with the vile abuses of power by men, but not so much to alter the basic relationship from which that power was derived. He attempted to extend the power of women as wives, mothers, and sisters within the household rather than to have women acquire political power in their own right. Gandhi did not envisage a radical change in their social role even though he was in favour of removing all legal and juridical disabilities against them.

One of the most lasting contributions of Gandhi to the women's cause was that he gave it a moral legitimacy. He helped create a tradition and a social-political atmosphere in which even today, hardly anyone will publicly stand up and. explicitly oppose women's fundamental rights or will deny them participation in politics. Such was the moral legitimacy that leaders like Gandhi created for the cause of women that women's entry into politics as 'equal' partners came without much overt resistance and opposition. The tradition was set for patronized entry of a handful of urban middle class women into politics and for tailoring the movement in such a way that some women's issues could easily be accommodated within the parameters of male domination and supremacy without throwing a serious challenge to it.

Slowly, this legitimacy had degenerated into token representation of women, with a handful of urban, educated, middle class women being the beneficiaries while the mass of women remain voiceless with no access whatsoever to political power at any level, especially no access to power at the village level.

Women's representation in Parliament has never exceeded 5 per cent of total seats and has been on a decline, recently settling down to about 3 per cent. In most parts of the country, women are not allowed to participate in whatever exists by way of panchayats and other more informal institutions of political power at the village level. Gandhi's legacy in the contemporary political culture has been distorted to mean encouraging 'tokenism' at the very top without bringing about any real changes at the bottom. Thus the myth has come to acquire a powerful hold that Indian women have equal rights in every sphere and that if things are wrong, it is because women choose not to make use of their rights.

Despite great concern for women's rights. Gandhi did not encourage women to organize as a political force in their own right around their own issues. They were to seek their liberation by serving the national cause, in the tradition of selfless social workers. As a result, women never came to acquire any real political power within the Congress. Even the most prominent of women leaders remained peripheral to the hard-core decision-making within the Congress because they were not seen as representing any organized constituency of women.

Even as women's participation grew numerically in the national movement, women did not come to play a greater role at decision-making levels. Women were more prominent in running the ashram on a day-to-day basis by their unremitting services. They were involved in decision-making only at rare and exceptional moments.

This is partly because Gandhi saw an important role for women not in political decision-making but in those parts of the movement which addressed themselves to the task of transforming people's ideas and lives as, for instance, participants in demonstrations, satyagrahis, boycott organizers. Moreover, even within the movement, women were encouraged to be more active in the 'constructive' programme, which had to do with social transformation and social service. Gandhi saw the world of politics and power as too ruthless and corrupt for women. They were to be the moral force in the movement by staying away from the struggle for power and by transforming people's hearts through their quiet, non-violent strength.

The very presence of women was seen as a disciplining force in agitations and struggles. Women were frequently preferred as leaders of picketing squads because Gandhi was afraid that it would be far more difficult to restrain men picketers from using violence. Also, he felt that those against whom picketing was being practised would be less likely to retaliate with violence against women picketers. Thus, on the one hand, emphasis on women's participation in satyagraha sought to ensure that the movement stayed non-violent, while on the other hand, emphasis on non-violence made it possible for larger numbers of women to participate. It fact, Gandhi's non-violence was a powerful revolutionary weapon because it created a favourable atmosphere for participation of very large numbers of people, especially women, giving them all a meaningful place in the struggle. It is easier for women to prove their courage and strength without resort to violence while in wielding weapons and using physical violence, men usually have the upper hand. Historically, men have come to acquire an almost exclusive monopoly over weapons of destruction and over organized social violence. Therefore, it was out of that faculty which was hitherto considered the source of women's powerlessness that Gandhi forged an effective weapon for political action. In this kind of satyagraha, women in large numbers could participate and even lead, more naturally than men. Again, however, Gandhi's idealizing the image of woman as the 'embodiment of sacrifice' and extolling the strength that comes from suffering helped strengthen the prevailing oppressive stereotype of woman as selfless companions and contributors to a social cause defined by men, in the tradition of Sita.

Integral to the image of women as the moral force in society, as the 'embodiment of sacrifice' was the idea of woman having to transcend her sexual needs so that she need not be as a 'slave to any man'. Gandhi did not see the sexual life of women as very important. In his mind, women's needs seem to exist in response only to men's needs. Women are to say 'no' to men when the latter behave 'carnally' like 'beasts'. This is to help men become better human beings. It is best if women renounce sexual contact altogether in order to set free men's energies for higher goals. In all this, there is no place for women's own sexual expression.

Despite insisting on the stereotype of women as running the household while men dominate the affairs of the outside world, in practice Gandhi encouraged a breaking away from these stereotypes. This is most evident in his belief in the superiority of non-violent satyagraha as a weapon of struggle. He learnt this from his wife and it is a form of resistance more often practised by women. So far, this kind of resistance used to be considered 'unmanly'. Gandhi realized that the identification of 'manliness' with violence was likely to lead humanity to destruction. Men needed to emulate women's quiet strength and their resistance of injustice without resorting to violence.

Similarly, Gandhi insisted on every Congressman taking to spinning, hitherto considered a women's occupation, as a necessary qualification. This despite resistance from within the Congress on the ground that this amounted to wasting the energies of men. This was indeed a radical step in breaking the hold of oppressive stereotypes and in weaning men away from aggressive 'manliness'. It was an essential step in purging violence out of society.

Gandhi's action, in bringing women dignity in social life, in breaking down some of the prejudices against their participation in social and political life, in promoting an atmosphere of sympathetic awareness of their issues, goes far beyond his own views and pronouncements of women's role and place in society.

NOTES AND REFERENCES

1. *The Collected Works of Mahatma Gandhi*, Vol. LXIV, 1936–7, p. 165. Ahmedabad: Navajivan Trust, 1982. Message to the All India Women's Conference, sent before 23 December 1936.

2. *Navajivan*, 28 June 1925. *CW*, Vol. XXVII, p. 308.

3. *CW*, Vol. XXVII, p. 126, Speech at women's meeting, Mymensingh, 19 May 1925.

4. *Young India*, 21 October 1926, *CW*, Vol. XXXI, p. 511.

5. *Young India*, 24 March 1927, cited in 'To the Women', Gandhi Series, Vol. II, A. Hingorani (ed.), Karachi, 2nd edn, 1943, p. 24.

6. *Harijan*, 27 October 1946. Speech reported by Pyarelal. *Harijan*, Vol. X, p. 375.

7. *Harijan*, 1 March 1942, *CW*, Vol. LXXV, p. 338.

8. *CW*, Vol. XXVII, page 99. Reply to women's address in Noakhali, 14 May 1925.

9. M.K. Gandhi, *The Role of Women*, Anand Hingorani (ed.), Bombay: Bharatiya Vidya Bhawan, 1964, p. 1.

10. Cited in 'To the Women', op. cit, p. 19.

11. 'Woman in the Smritis', *CW*, Vol. LXIV, 1936–7, pp. 84–5.

12. *The Role of Women*, op. cit, p. 3.

13. Cited in D.G. Tendulkar, 'Mahatma', New Delhi: Publications Division, Vol. 6, p. 24.

14. *CW*, Vol. XL, pp. 416–17, 23 May 1929.

15. *Young India*, 28 June 1928, cited in 'To the Women', op. cit, p. 217.

16. 3 February 1927, cited in 'To the Women', op. cit, pp. 213–14.

17. Ibid., pp. 7–8.

18. *Harijan*, 25 January 1936, *CW*, Vol. LXII, p. 157.

19. *Young India*, 7 October 1926. *CW*, Vol. XXXI, 1926, p. 480.

20. *Harijan*, 24 February 1940, *CW*, Vol. LXXI, p. 207.

21. Cited in *The Role of Women*, op. cit, p. 1.

22. 'Gandhiji in Ceylon', cited in 'To the Women', op. cit, p. 195.

23. Cited in 'To the Women', op. cit, p. 17, *Young India*, 21 July 1921.

24. *Harijan*, 25 January 1936. *CW*, Vol. LXII, p. 158.

25. *Young India*, 25 November 1926. *CW*, Vol. XXXII, pp. 89–90.

26. *Young India*, 26 August 1926. *CW*, Vol. XXXI, pp. 329–30.

27. Ibid., p. 330.

28. *Young India*, 14 October 1926. *CW*, Vol. XXXI, p. 493.

29. *Young India*, 23 September 1926. *CW*, Vol. XXXI, p. 443.

30. *Young India*, 5 August 1926. *CW*, Vol. XXXI, p. 264.

31. *Navajivan*, 28 June 1925. *CW*, Vol. XXVII, p. 309.

32. *Young India*, 23 September 1926. *CW*, Vol. XXXI, p. 443.

33. Ibid.

34. *Young India*, 19 August 1926. *CW*, Vol. XXXI, p. 314.

35. *Navajivan*, 28 June 1925. *CW*, Vol. XXVII, p. 307.

36. *CW*, Vol. XXVII, p. 309.

37. Ibid., p. 309.

38. *CW*, Vol. XIV, p. 87. Message to Gujarati Hindu Stree Mandal on or before 14 November 1917.

39. *Young India*, 3 October 1929. *CW*, Vol. XLI, p. 495.

40. Cited in *The Role of Women*, op. cit, p. 63, from 'The Diary of Mahadev Desai', p. 172.

41. 'Advice to Girl Students', cited in 'To the Women', op. cit, p. 120, 29 November 1927.

42. *Harijan*, 23 May 1936. *CW*, Vol. LXII, pp. 435–6.

43. *Young India*, 27 December 1928, in *The Role of Women*, op. cit, p. 48.

44. Interview with Indumati Patankar, a freedom fighter from Maharashtra, in *Manushi*, issue No. 20, 1984, pp. 2–8.

45. 20 February 1918, 'To the Women', op. cit, p. 20.

46. Ibid., p. 20.

47. 'Women and Social Injustice', p. 39, cited from *Young India*, 7 October 1926.

48. *Young India*, 18 August 1927, cited in *The Role of Women*, op. cit, p. 103.

49. *Young India*, 16 April 1925. 'Our Unfortunate Sisters', cited in 'To the Women', op. cit, pp. 166–7.

50. Ibid., p. 167.

51. Tendulkar, op. cit, Vol. II, p. 187.

52. *Navajivan*, 11 September 1921. *CW*, Vol. XXI, p. 94.
53. *CW*, Vol. XXVII, pp. 290–1, 25 June 1925.
54. Ibid., p. 291.
55. Ibid.
56. 'The Role of Women', op. cit, pp. 65–6.
57. *Young India*, 21 October 1926. *CW*, Vol. XXXI, p. 512.
58. *Young India*, 23 May 1929. *CW*, Vol. XL, pp. 417–18.
59. 'Advice to Girl Students', 29 November 1927, cited in 'To the Women', op. cit, p. 120.
60. M.K. Gandhi, 'To the Women', op. cit, p. 153.
61. *Young India*, 17 October 1929. *CW*, Vol. XLII, p. 5.
62. Ibid., p. 5.
63. *Young India*, 24 March 1927, cited in *The Role of Women*, op. cit, p. 37.
64. *Young India*, 21 May 1931. *CW*, Vol. XLVI, p. 75.
65. *Harijan*, 31 December 1938. *CW*, Vol. LXVIII.
66. 20 February 1918, in 'Women and Social Injustice', Ahmedabad: Navjivan Press, p. 7.
67. *Harijan*, 24 February 1940. *CW*, Vol. LXXI, p. 209.
68. Geoffrey Ashe, *Gandhi: A Study in Revolution*, London: Heinemann, 1968, p. 122.
69. 20 February 1918, in 'To the Women', op. cit, p. 20.
70. *Harijan*, 2 December 1939. *CW*, Vol. LXX, p. 381.
71. *Young India*, 11 August 1921. *CW*, Vol. XX, p. 497.
72. M.K. Gandhi, *Autobiography*, p. 413.
73. 'To the Women', op. cit, p. 37.
74. *CW*, Vol. XIV, p. 87. Message to Gujarati Hindu Stree Mandal, 14 November 1917.
75. *Young India*, 11 August 1921. *CW*, Vol. XX, pp. 496–7.
76. Tendulkar, op. cit, Vol. I, p. 292.
77. *Bombay Chronicle*, 27 March 1925. *CW*, Vol. XXVI, pp. 419–20.
78. *CW*, Vol. XV, p. 291. Speech at women's meeting, Bombay, 8 May 1919.
79. *CW*, Vol. XV, p. 189. Speech at meeting of ladies at China Baug, 6 April 1919.
80. *Harijan*, 9 March 1934, cited in *The Role of Women*, op. cit, p. 76.
81. *CW*, Vol. LVI, p. 332, Speech at women's meeting while on Harijan tour.
82. Geoffrey Ashe, op. cit, p. 90.
83. *Harijan*, 22 December 1933. *CW*, Vol. LVI, p. 369.
84. 22 December 1933. *CW*, Vol. LVI, p. 368.

85. Ibid., pp. 368–9.
86. Cited in Tendulkar, op. cit, Vol. III, p. 60.
87. Ibid.
88. Cited in Tendulkar, Vol. II, p. 347.
89. Geoffrey Ashe, op. cit, pp. 290–2.
90. Ibid., p. 292.
91. *Young India*, 10 April 1930. *CW*, Vol. XLIII, p. 220.
92. Ibid., p. 220.
93. Ibid.
94. Ibid.
95. *Young India*, 10 April 1930. *CW*, Vol. XLIII, pp. 220–1.
96. Geoffrey Ashe, op. cit, p. 295.
97. Margaret E. Cousins, *Indian Womanhood Today*, Allahabad: Kitabistan, Series No. 5, 1937, p. 64.
98. Ibid., p. 63.
99. Ibid., p. 65.
100. Ibid., p. 64.
101. Geoffrey Ashe, op. cit, p. 298.
102. *Young India*, 21 July 1921. *CW*, Vol. XX, p. 410.
103. *Harijan*, 24 February 1940. *CW*, Vol. LXXI, p. 208.
104. *Harijan*, 4 August 1940. *CW*, Vol. LXXII, p. 326.
105. 11 June 1917. *CW*, Vol. XIII, p. 442.
106. *Bombay Chronicle*, 28 March 1930, Rashtriya Stree Sabha Appeal.
107. Cited in Margaret E. Cousins, op. cit, pp. 41–2.
108. *Young India*, 21 May 1931. *CW*, Vol. XLVI, p. 189.
109. Cited in Tendulkar, op. cit, Vol. III, p. 89.
110. *CW*, Vol. LXXII, p. 137.
111. *Harijan*, 2 December 1939. *CW*, Vol. LXX, p. 381,
112. *Young India*, 11 June 1925. *CW*, Vol. XXVII, pp. 219–20.
113. *Harijan*, 24 February 1940. *CW*, Vol. LXXI, p. 208.
114. Ibid., p. 207.
115. Ibid., pp. 207–8.
116. *CW*, Vol. XIV, p. 31.
117. 20 October 1917. *CW*, Vol. XIV, p. 31.
118. Ibid., p. 31.
119. *CW*, Vol. LIX, p. 147.
120. *Harijan*, 12 October 1934. *CW*, Vol. LIX, p. 147.
121. Ibid., p. 147.

122. *Harijan*, 24 February 1940. *CW*, Vol. LXXI, p. 208.

123. *Harijan*, 16 March 1940. *CW*, Vol. LXXI, p. 324.

124. Cited in Tendulkar, op. cit, Vol. VII, p. 87.

125. *Young India*, 3 October 1929. *CW*, Vol. XLI, pp. 493–4.

126. Geoffrey Ashe, op. cit, p. 242.

127. *CW*, Vol. LXII, p. 5.

128. *CW*, Vol. XXXV, p. 346.

129. Ibid., p. 346.

130. Cited in Tendulkar, op. cit, Vol. VI, p. 24.

131. Margaret E. Cousins, op. cit, pp. 32–3.

132. *Harijan*, Vol. X, No. 9, 7 April 1946, p. 67.

133. Ibid., p. 67.

134. *CW*, Vol. LXXXIII, pp. 331–2.

135. *Harijan*, 21 April 1946, 'What About Women?', *CW*, Vol. LXXXIII, p. 398.

136. Tendulkar, op. cit, Vol. VII, p. 87.

137. *CW*, Vol. LXXXIII, p. 332.

138. *Young India*, 17 October 1929. *CW*, Vol. XLII, p. 5.

139. *Harijan*, 24 February 1940. *CW*, Vol. LXXI, p. 209.

140. Cited in Tendulkar, op. cit, Vol. III, p. 61.

141. Tendulkar, op. cit, Vol. IV, p. 200.

142. *Harijan*, 24 February 1940. *CW*, Vol. LXXI, pp. 207–8.

143. Eleanor Morton, *Women Behind Mahatma Gandhi*, London: Max Reinhardt, 1954, p. 107.

144. Ibid., p. 108.

145. Cited in Tendulkar, op. cit, Vol. II, p. 34, Vol. V, p. 196.

146. *Bapu's Letters To Mira*, Ahmedabad: Navajivan Publishing House, 1949, p. 152. Letter dated 24 June 1931.

147. Ibid., p. 152.

148. Martin Green, *Tolstoy and Gandhi*, New York: Basic Books, 1983, pp. 163–5.

149. *Harijan*, 9 March 1940. *CW*, Vol. LXX1 p. 302.

150. *Harijan*, 13 April 1940, in M.K. Gandhi, *Women*, Ahmedabad: Navajivan Prakashan, 1958.

151. Kaka Saheb Karlekar, *'Bapuki Jhankiart'*, Ahmedabad: Navajivan Prakashan, 1948, p. 6.

152. M.K. Gandhi, *Diet and Diet Reform*, Ahmedabad: Navajivan Prakashan, 1949, p. 30.

153. Ibid., p. 16.

154. M.K. Gandhi, *Diet and Diet Reform*, op. cit, p. 41.

155. Eric Erikson, *Gandhi's Truth*, London: Faber and Faber, 1970, p. 120.

156. M.K. Gandhi, *An Autobiography*, The Navajivan Trust, 1983, pp. 24–6.

157. Geoffrey Ashe, op. cit, pp. 11–12.

158. Tendulkar, op. cit, Vol. IV, p. 63.

159. M.K. Gandhi, 'Birth Control', Anand T. Hingorani (ed.), Bombay: Bharatiya Vidya Bhawan, 1962, pp. 1–2.

160. Ibid., p. 4.

161. Ibid., pp. 52–3.

162. Ibid., pp. 8–9.

163. Ibid., p. 65.

164. Ibid., pp. 65–6.

165. Ibid., p. 60.

166. Ibid.

167. Ibid.

168. Eleanor Morton, *The Women in Gandhi's Life*, New York: Dodd, Mead and Co., 1953, p. 148.

169. *CW*, Vol. XLVI, 21 May 1931, pp. 73–4.

170. Ibid., p. 74.

171. M.K. Gandhi, *The Role of Women*, op. cit, p. 64. See also *CW*, Vol. LXV p. 111.

172. Cited in Tendulkar, op. cit, Vol. V, p. 196.

173. Ibid., Vol. II, p. 249.

174. N.K. Bose, *My Days with Gandhi*, Calcutta: Nishana, pp. 174–5.

175. M.K. Gandhi, *Satyagraha in South Africa*, Ahmedabad: Navajivan Publishing House, 1928, p. 245.

176. *CW*, Vol. XIII, p. 471.

12

Construction and Reconstruction of Woman in Gandhi*

SUJATA PATEL

I
INTRODUCTION

The last few years has seen a renewal of interest in Gandhi. This renewal of interest has not been restricted to the disciplines of history and political science but has stretched into new interdisciplinary areas like peasant studies, labour studies, women studies, and peace studies. These new interventions have drawn their theoretical and epistemological roots from diverse traditions, as varied as the first world liberal perspective, now gripped by concern of growing militarization; the third world anti-imperialist radical theories in search of a messiah; and Marxist ideological and scientific theories rooted in the analysis of the specific Indian experience. The application of this scholarship has led to a new evaluation and understanding of Gandhi, his ideology and his role in the national movement, and as well as a statement on the promise he thus holds out, for the liberation of various oppressed strata, in the world today.

* Sujata Patel, 'Construction and reconstruction of woman in Gandhi', *Economic and Political Weekly*, Vol. XXIII(8), 20 February 1988, pp. 377–87.

This is a revised version of a paper presented at Nehru Memorial Museum and Library, New Delhi and prepared during the year of fellowship held at NMML. I would like to thank the participants at the seminar, Ravinder Kumar and KumKum Sanghari for comments on the earlier version of this paper.

Within women's studies the interest in Gandhi has led to a perception of him which is intrinsically related to an analysis of the relationship between his ideology and the subsequent participation of women in the national movement. This position was most clearly outlined in the mid-1970s by Veena Mazumdar (1976) who stated that Gandhi's greatest contribution towards the raising of women's status 'lay in his revolutionary approach to women in society'. He respected their 'personal dignity' without 'belittling their roles as mothers and wives' and gave women with men 'equal tasks to perform in the achievement of freedom'. Gandhi's ideas on women, she concludes, are 'remarkably similar to those voiced by the women's liberation movement all over the world'. Both of them propagate equality in the family and society, dignity of a women's personality, the opening up of wider opportunities for women for her self-development, and 'refusal to be regarded as sex symbols'.[1] These ideas find reflection in other articles and papers such as those written by Geraldine Forbes (1979), Karuna Ahmed (1984) and, recently, Devaki Jain (1986). According to Devaki Jain, because the freedom struggle 'was the struggle to build self-reliance from the individual level right up to the nation', it became the means also of the liberation of women. Gandhi, according to Jain, made a stringent criticism of those roles that cloistered women into ignorance. He made propaganda for self-reliance of women by postulating their economic independence, advocating social practices that emphasized simplicity and identification with the poor, 'while encouraging the discipline of mind and body'. She concludes that Gandhi was 'methodologically' a feminist, because for him 'the means were as important as the ends'.[2]

One of the more comprehensive and sophisticated critiques of Gandhi has come from Madhu Kishwar (1985). A lengthy and detailed analysis of Gandhi's writings convince her of the fact that Gandhi used constructively the traditional symbols, highlighting their positive characteristics, to effectively push women into participating in the political movement. His ideology, according to Kishwar, is both liberationist and revolutionary.

It is difficult to summarize Madhu Kishwar's reading of Gandhi in a few sentences as her critique is based on detailed analysis of Gandhi's ideas and flows over a number of issues including his personal relationships with women. Yet, it is possible to state that her evaluation of Gandhian ideology on women attest simultaneously two major ideas. One, that Gandhi's entrance into the national movement signalled a break in the perception of women in nationalist thought. The reform movement leaders saw women as recipients of a more humane treatment through the initiative of enlightened male effort. Gandhi, on the other hand, saw women 'not as objects of reform and humanitarianism, but as self-conscious arbiters of their own destiny'.[3]

Secondly, Madhu Kishwar also acknowledges the existence of some inherent contradictions within Gandhi relating to his ideas on women. She accepts that the fruits of his ideology were not scale-neutral and were specially used by those women who came from the middle class family and whose male members were involved in the national movement.[4] She also accepts that Gandhi failed to put an economic content in his conception of women. However, she does not use this admission to understand the social basis of Gandhi's ideology of human, instead she records it as limitation or at best a contradiction within Gandhi. She accepts that Gandhi sought change 'not so much in the material condition of women as their "moral" condition'.[5] Instead of making a critical estimation of the social and historical basis of Gandhi's morality she moves on to examine other issues in Gandhi, in spite of agreeing that Gandhi tried changing the women's position without transforming that relation to the outer world of production and the inner world of family, sexuality or reproduction.[6]

It is, as mentioned before, difficult to do full justice to Madhu Kishwar's reading of Gandhi, in a few sentences. She is asserting simultaneously two positions on Gandhi; one who perceives his ideology and liberationist, which empowers women as subjects fighting oppression and another, that criticizes its inherent limitations and contradictions. If the 'economic content' is distilled in Gandhi, she does not ask why, and thus evaluates the social roots of this 'absence'. Yet, her reading of Gandhi is important, not only because it is the first detailed account of his ideology, but also because she provokes her readers to ask questions of her own interpretations and thus extend her arguments.

To a large extent, the above mentioned contributors on 'Gandhi and Women' have been influenced by an important historical fact: Gandhi's entrance into the national arena did lead to mass participation of women in the national movement. As Veena Mazumdar puts it, 'Gandhi facilitated the acceptance of the woman's cause by the nationalists, particularly in the public life'.[7] This assumption has guided the interpretations and commentaries on him. As a result an attempt has been made to 'look' for the liberationist aspects inherent in his ideology. It has led to a construction of one perception of Gandhi and his ideology, where women appear as homogeneous category, undifferentiated in terms of class, caste, religion, or region.

Participation of any group of people in political activity cannot simply be understood in terms of the way in which a particular leader perceived this group and attempted to integrate them into the movement which also contained other groups. Because participation deals with actions, it is necessary to understand the context in which action is possible. In the case of women and the national movement, equal, if not primary importance has to be given to the role played by caste associations, the family, the school, the college, the peer group, and especially the mother. And to make a comprehensive study of such participation, it is important not only to examine the way in which categories like class, caste, and region operate to differentially integrate individuals into movements, but also to analyse the mediatory roles played by local political and ideological leaders. At best, an ideology can create a climate for action. The action itself is determined by other factors, not necessarily only ideology. In case of women and their participation in the national movement, to reduce the Gandhian ideology to this purpose is both to de-historicize a figure and trivialize the context in which momentous steps have been taken.

Also, Gandhi was not only a politician par excellence, but also an individual, integrated within his social milieu and aware of his internal contradictions and the need to transcend them. If he was the national leader who could put forward an ideological and political perspective that could successfully mobilize the class, caste, community, and gender divided Indian society into a single cohesive political force, he was also a self-conscious individual, commenting on his society from a perspective extracted and extended from his social strata and who simultaneously was also attempting to resolve his personal conflicts through a well thought-off theory of personality.

One of the critical and crucial issues that had gripped his entire self-conscious life was his relationship with women. In no other aspect have the personal traumas and anxieties so coloured his ideas as in the case of women. If Gandhi's views on women are intrinsically interwoven with these tensions, his personal resolution of these are rooted in the social patterns and ideologies of the historical moment in which he lived. Any analysis of his ideology has to understand the social roots of his perceptions, if it has to make a critical evaluation of Gandhi and understand the relevance of his ideas today.

Madhu Kishwar, among all the above mentioned writers, has been able to perceive this homogenizing tendency in the perception of women in Gandhi. She admits that Gandhi failed to understand that 'oppression is not an abstract moral condition but a social and historical relation, related to production relations'.[8] Yet, her analysis does not examine in any comprehensive manner the reasons for Gandhi's failure to understand this oppression. Though she accepts that there was a differential level of involvement of women of different classes into the movement, she fails to relate that to his construct of women. Instead, she emphasizes the use of traditional symbols by Gandhi for contemporary contexts. This use, she insists, conveys a political message for the 'inspirations of the downtrodden women of India'.[9] She almost believes that these are universal symbols and does not perceive them also as ideologically rooted in the social context. She does not question why only certain roles of certain historical and mythological heroines are highlighted by Gandhi and not others. Or that they are used to give meaning only to certain social contexts but not others. There is a social frame in which Gandhi articulates his perception of women. Madhu Kishwar is not able to layout the contours of this frame.

This chapter attempts to take up this task by making an analysis of the Gandhian ideology as a set of ideas on, of, and about woman. These ideas incorporate assumptions and notions regarding the origin and nature of gender differences on whose basis Gandhi models out the social roles, the possible cultural and political choices and actions, and the kind of involvement in certain activities that women can undertake in contemporary society. By affirming certain roles and negating others, Gandhi is extracting and reformulating from the received ensemble of ideas on women in a given historical moment a construct of contemporary womanhood; the reformulation, itself being mediated by his class, caste, and religious ideologies. Gandhi is thus not only making an attempt on woman but also on what she should be. For, interlaced with these assumptions are a set of legitimizers that define the concepts of femininity and womanhood which act as prescriptive frames of reference in his construction of women.

It is argued that though these assumptions are rooted in the socially given set of received ideas on woman, Gandhi's ideology relating to women developed over time and was contingent to his involvement in the political events occurring in the country and his response to them. Gandhi is the figure of that historical moment and his ideas on women show very clearly his intense involvement in the making of the history and design for that time. Thus, if this chapter attempts to answer the question, how is gender created in Gandhi, it also attempts to do so diachronically. It locates the growth and development of his ideas over the years in which he self-consciously and actively contemplates and debates on the problem of women, understands his own contradictions and attempts to resolve them. In the process he constructs and reconstructs various aspects that define the woman in India in the early twentieth century.

The Gandhian ideology assumes the following about women:

1. Men and women have distinct qualities whose roots are biological. Both of them have separate spheres in societies and specific roles in the making of the Indian nation, for they are essentially complementary to each other.

2. Women are not 'playthings' but creative individuals who have a specific space for the construction of this creativity. This is mainly in the arena of the household and the domestic space. They play important roles as mothers and as wives.

3. In the domestic space, that is as wife and mother, women manifest feminine qualities unsurpassable and sometimes superior to the masculine ones. These are self-reliance, courage, patience, purity, and a capacity to undergo suffering.

4. To be able to be a good mother, a woman has to be given different education which gives her a training in not only basic domestic needs but also home economics and basic information about the world in which she is living.

5. Existing Hindu social customs do not allow women to grow into her new role. Child marriage, sati, and dowry exploit women and reduce her dignity. Women's organizations should be formed which not only fight against these social evils but also build awareness in women of her new role in free India. These organizations should be run only by women as their distinctiveness is only understood by women.

6. The most distinct and precious quality of a woman is her purity. To retain this purity, she should not do economic work; by doing economic work her purity and honour are violated.

7. Men and women have political rights, that is, the right to vote. Woman also have an important role in politics—as a mother, she instils national consciousness in the children and participates in the programmes. However, it is important that separate and different programmes that involve women in participation be evolved. During the non-cooperation movement, spinning, and in the civil disobedience movement, picketing of liquor and foreign cloth shops were introduced and became special women's programmes.

8. If she is forced to enter the public sphere where she is not 'honoured' or

'respected' and if her purity is violated she has to kill herself through sheer will force.

9. Marriage is only for reproduction. Sex without reproduction is abnormal.

10. A woman can achieve a higher moral and spiritual role if she rejects her sexuality, reproduction, and family life and devotes herself to the welfare of the people.

Every construct draws its elements from a particular context. In Gandhi, I am arguing, that his construct is drawn from a space inhabited by an urbanized middle class upper-caste Hindu male's perception of what a woman should be. In a significant way, there is a sense of continuity in Gandhian ideas on woman and those formulated by the reformers of late nineteenth century. Though Gandhi did introduce a dynamic concept, that of politics, in his model of social role for woman, he did not revolutionize the assumptions on which these middle class reformers perceived woman. In Gandhi, politics was redefined to find its space in the 'home'. The reformers of the 19th century believed in the doctrine of 'the separate spheres' whose roots were in biology. The differences between sexes was explained in terms of 'natural differences' which legitimized different social and cultural roles for men and women in society and on whose basis, moral prescriptions underlying their behaviours and interaction with each other were built. Marriage was the social institution in which the two spheres got articulated. The male was the 'bread winner', the 'provider', and the 'protector' and thus 'superior'; woman was the 'mother', the 'nurturer', the 'giver', and the 'inferior'. There were slight variations in the various forms that this ideology articulated itself: the male could be 'selfish', or 'independent', or 'possessive', yet lacking in 'intuition' and 'strength', the woman on the other hand could be 'selfless', 'patient', 'dependent', 'full of courage and humility'. We will see that this theme runs as a leitmotif in Gandhi's ideology of woman.

In the mid-19th century, when the reformist articulated some of these perceptions, he was confronting a society undergoing rapid social change. On one hand colonization had led to the slow growth of an industrial working class and urbanism had become a sign and symbol of 'modern progress', on the other, the traditional system based on agriculture and structured hierarchical interrelationships was slowly disintegrating, tearing apart the rubric of family and kin relationships. The establishment of educational institutions had led many upper-caste Hindu males to gravitate to urban areas in search of a place in the new system. As a result, they were confronted with received modern ideas of women in their roles as spiritual and moral repositaries of the 'home', the 'shibboleth of the Victorian era',[10] now divorced from its activities concerning production, education, and health.

The 19th century ideas relating to 'home' were reintegrated into the Indian situation by the modern Indian, who traumatized by the modern world, yet fascinated by it, created his own ideal woman in the sanctuary of his inner sanctum, the 'home', which preserved both the traditional division of society, as well as prepared them for their and the future generations' entrance into the modern world. One of the various forms in which patriarchy recreated itself was through the formulation of a morally superior ideal woman, who was the embodiment of all the best and goodness of human life and the world, the conscience of the male and the society. Gandhi, not only accepted these assumptions but he extended them to fit his own perspective relating to the participation of women in politics. The introduction of spinning wheel as a political symbol becomes an instrument for the woman-in-the-home to participate in political life from within the home. The morally superior woman of the 'home' created by the reformist was now given another attribute via the spinning wheel. In Gandhi, the spinning of khadi was turned into a political message which was reposed onto the morally superior woman, who in turn became the symbol and conscience of the new nation-in-the-making. The woman as 'mother' who had 'innate', 'natural' capacities for 'wiseness', 'strength', 'courage', 'patience', and 'intuition' now becomes the symbol of the new political message and its strategy of non-violence. Only her involvement could free the nation from the clutches of the colonial power.

It is important to note, that if the reformers were writing at a time when industrial development was slow, Gandhi was engaged in his construction of woman when there was a sizeable formation of the working class. By 1921, the census reports that out of 33 per cent women workers, nearly 11 per cent were in industry. Also, the reformers with their class and caste insularity had constructed an image of women mainly based on their experiences. The pre-colonial upper caste Hindu woman had always remained within the four walls of the house. Gandhi, on the other hand, was writing at a time when urban India had many visible women workers who did not remain at home. He was also extremely familiar with rural areas, where women workers have been part of its visible reality and had toured the country before setting up the Sabarmati ashram. Yet, his image of woman is enclosed and confined within that articulated by the middle class reformers.[11] Not only does Gandhi see woman as the repository of all that is morally and spiritually good within the 'home', he gives this woman-in-the-home a specific space in his political ideology, thereby legitimizing this space.

On the other hand, it is important to note that if he extracts and extends the urban middle class image of woman to reformulate it as a design for the new woman of India, he also reconstructs in the process her space-in-the-home. He gives more power to her within the home and a legitimate space with her husband in the struggle for nationhood. If he does not free her from the bondage of biology and 'naturalness', he also does not confine her role only to motherhood, though it remains that of primary importance.

But this very extension of her activities and specially her involvement in politics creates within the Gandhian ideology an unresolvable tension. For politics cannot be restricted necessarily to the home. The spinning wheel did become the political symbol of woman's participation in the 1920s. However, in the 1930s the women came out in large numbers in the streets to perform satyagraha. The sanctity of home was brought into question. This act did not lead Gandhi to break and dismiss the assumptions of 'separate spheres'. Rather, he reconstructs a new model of woman extracted from the received image of a Hindu widow living on the periphery of the society. Adding new dimensions to it, that of charity and social welfare, he builds a new model of an Indian woman, dedicated to the service of the nation. However, she can perform this role only if she turns her back on sex, reproduction, and family life. In this way, Gandhi retains the superior position of marriage as the only social institution guiding the sexual repro- ductive and social aspects of relationship between male and female which define their 'separate spheres' in modern Indian life and yet creates a space for a woman involved in public life after rejecting the Gandhian notions of femininity and womanhood. On one hand is the construction of a morally superior woman, a loving wife, and a dedicated mother, involved actively in the making-of-the-nation, spinning khadi, sharing equal tasks in the house with the male, and on the other a reconstruction of a de-sexed woman, who has 'sacrificed' her reproductive aspects, her family life, and has dedicated herself to the service of the nation.[12]

II

FORMULATION OF BASIC POSTULATES, 1917–22

It will not be a surprise for readers to note that Gandhi's ideas on women crystallized in a coherent fashion in the period between 1917 and 1922. This is not only the first phase of active participation of the Indian people in the national struggle, but it also saw the emergence of Gandhi as the leader directing this struggle. Given that this phase is characterized by the spontaneous and later organized expression of protest against the British and participation of both men and women in this struggle, it is difficult to separate analytically which proceeded first: women's participation or Gandhi's advocacy of this. However, what is of significance is that Gandhi did not show any displeasure at this participation of women. Rather, some of his own earlier writings show his fascination for the potentiality that such participation can have in a moment of struggle.

Gandhi's writings till 1916, on women, have been couched in a framework common to the reformists. Gandhi specially seems to have close affinity with Ishwar Chandra Vidyasagar and his ideas on women's education with which he agreed and whose cause he advocates. Only once, in 1906–7, does he strike a different note whilst commenting on the struggle being waged by the upper class suffragettes for their political rights in England. He notes with 'awe' the 'manly strength' that they have shown in their confrontation with the police, specially, given the fact that they were not from the 'working class'. Gandhi does not make any disparaging remarks on their confrontation with the police or their fight for political equality, but he also does not draw out any implications for this movement for the women of India.[13] He only feels that the entire Indian population should draw a lesson from them. As yet, in Gandhi there does seem to be any consciousness of the distinct place of women in the national awakening.

The first explicit connection between women and their role in nation building appears in Gandhi in the context of the recruitment of Indians in the army during the first world war, specifically in 1916. At that time, on his tour around India, he asks wives, mothers, and sisters to involve 'their men' in military service, because voluntary recruitment will lead to Swaraj.[14] Henceforth, we see Gandhi addressing himself more and more to the question of women in India, first, by questioning existing Hindu practices that limit the involvement of women in the national awakening, like purdah,[15] and later by affirming and establishing for himself the distinct role that women can play in the national movement. It is a slow process that builds his ideas and makes the necessary mediations that link women to the national movement through the spinning wheel, a process in which if he moves forward he also moves backwards, until by the 1920s he is able to crystallize his thoughts on this problem in a coherent fashion. However, what seems clearly articulated, even in the period of uncertainty, is his belief in the complementarity and indivisibility of the two sexes rooted in their distinctive biological and reproductive features and socially manifested in a romantic togetherness.

In a foreword to a book published on women by Bhagini Samaj in late 1917 Gandhi condemns Hindu practices like child marriage and the legitimation it has received in contemporary Hindu shastras. Even Tulsidas' famous couplet: 'The drum, the fool, the sudra, the animal and the woman—all these need beating' comes in for Gandhi's wrath and he insists that the older Smritis did not have these interpretations.[16] These have been introduced recently by contemporary commentators who have through such interventions degraded the image and the status of women.

However, his ire is directed not only against these commentators, but also against men, who perceive women as 'play things' or 'beautiful dolls to be adored as many goddesses and decorate them with ornaments'.[17] Rather, he asserts man can receive salvation only when 'our women become to us what Uma was to Shanker, Sita to Ram, and Damayanti to Nala, joining us in our deliberations, arguing with us, appreciating us, and nourishing our aspirations, understanding us with their marvellous intuition the unspoken anxieties of our outward life and sharing in them, bringing us the peace that soothes'.[18]

In the next year, 1917–18, Gandhi continues to write in this vein in the context of women. He is affirming their place as thinkers and actors in modern family which in his opinion, had earlier secluded women in participating in society and perceived them only as sexual objects. Women are, he asserts, something more than mere objects. They are subjects and people of importance.

A series of articles indicates the trends his mind is working on. In a speech to All India Service Conference, he shows clearly his differences from the early nationalist thinkers by inverting the equation that they had posed between education and the upliftment of the status of women. He says that for the real 'reformer ... the way to women's freedom is not through education but through the change of attitude on the part of men and corresponding action'. He continues 'we dare not wait for literary education to restore our womanhood to its proper state. Even without literary education our women are cultured as any ...'[19] No longer is education considered a means for the development for women. Women already have their strengths and according to Gandhi, they can intervene and act in contemporary issues.

But as yet, concern for the national situation and the ferment in the country continues to dominate his mind. His first immediate response is to ask the upper class women's organizations to work on spreading the nationalist message. A large number of men and women are ignorant of the awakening in the nation, he asserts. He, therefore, asks the women's organizations not only to spread this message, but to link the social evils of contemporary society to the national problem—that of immense poverty and the strangulation of indigenous production systems both of which were part of the colonial process. At this stage, he makes the first crucial connection between the macro problems affecting the country and women when he asks the women's organizations to involve widows in spinning as a start of the process to counter the trend that has led to the destruction of the handicrafts.[20]

Soon this becomes his message for all women. From early 1919 onwards, Gandhi advocates the use of the spinning wheel in a series of writings mainly meant for women, wherein he has given his new message for the women of India: spin for the upliftment of the country. This was indeed a very shrewd intervention by Gandhi. It was not only an effective strategy for increasing the involvement of women in the national struggle, but it also made possible their involvement, without shifting the terrain of the movement and struggle from the household. He knew that the successful implementation of the vow of Swadeshi was only possible if women were involved in the movement', for they 'look after the children' and 'take decisions regarding dress'.[21] If the women could now show their national consciousness and their strength by taking decisions on wearing Indian clothes, they could make Swadeshi a success.

From the above, it seems that Gandhi has indeed travelled a lot, in his understanding of the role women could play in the nation's resurgence. Starting with the idea that they have a place in the family as a creative subject, he evolved to believe in their definite role in the national movement. In the course of one year, Gandhi was able to develop his ideas in such a way, a significant part of the movement of non-cooperation, specially its symbolic and spiritual sustenance now lay vested in the hands of women. There are, he said, two meanings to Satyagraha: civilly disobeying law and actively disobeying law. If the campaign against the Rowlatt Act is the manifestation of the latter, the Swadeshi vow was the manifestation of the former.[22]

The fight for Swadeshi now became the ideal for women, her dharma. As he says, 'if you wish a prosperous future for your children you should leave them as legacy the idea that is a dharma to obtain our needs by imports'.[23] Today, he continues, the dharma of the country reposes in your hands. And for this dharma, the higher moral good, 'the women have the right to even question her [sic] husband's authority, if he does not let her take the Swadeshi vow.'[24] The nation now takes precedence over the household.

It is important to note that there are two dimensions to these prescriptions. Gandhi is not only bringing the nationalist programme within the four walls of the household but he is also redefining political participation. Participation for the women in the nationalist awakening means spinning at home. In this process he is creating a new interpretation of women's role in the household and is simultaneously asserting her significance in the political world. Gandhi, it seems, has a very clear idea of the characteristics that define public and private space. The private is the domestic sphere, the household, a sphere where he seems to be affirming the complete legitimacy of the woman by creating a new role for her in it. He asserts that the decision regarding the household lies only with women. When some women complain to him that their husbands do not let them take such decisions, he states very clearly: 'In my home, I take a second place to my wife' and gives the example of Doodhabhai, a Harijan whom his wife had not allowed to enter her home.[25]

Gandhi is now creating a new arena of domination for women and that is in the domestic sphere. He is at once demolishing her seclusion and her image as a sexual object and simultaneously asserting her power in all household decisions. He does this by introducing nationalist politics into the household without breaking the domestic space which defines women. That he wishes to affirm and emphasize the crucial role of the women in the household as against her activity outside comes out very clearly in his writings on women and work.

In September 1919 he writes in *Young India* about a letter he has received from Dohad (a town, south-east of Ahmedabad) which mentions that the Dhedh women go out to labour in the field and thus become open for abuse by men. (Dhedhs are a sub-caste of the Scheduled Castes who have traditionally been weavers and are also called Wankers.) Gandhi is outraged and writes: 'The male members of these women's family—craven creatures—know this fact, but are sleeping over it.' What he finds difficult to accept is the fact that these women when they go out to work 'have to put up with all sort [sic] of indecent jokes and abuse ...'. Hundreds of years ago our 'mothers', he points out, were 'protected' by spinning cloth at home. Thus, he says to the wealthy and educated sisters of India, if you wish to protect the chastity of the poor sisters, you must take a prominent part in the movement for hand-spinning and hand-weaving.[26]

Gandhi's belief that within the household the women are 'protected' leads him to state this theme to the workers of the Ahmedabad textile industry in whose trade union movement he participates. He says in a speech at the meeting of the workers in Ahmedabad:[27]

If the workers find it necessary today to send their wives and children to work in factories, it is our duty to see that they do not have to. There ought to be no need for women, children to go to work at the cost of their education for the sake of an extra income of three to four rupees. Work is not for children. Nor is it for women to work in factories. They have plenty of work in their own homes. They should attend to bringing up their children. They may give peace to the husband when he returns home tiredly, minister to him, soothe him if angry and do any other work they can staying at home. It is not for our women to go out and work as men do. If we send them to the factories, who will look after our domestic and social affairs? If women go out to work, our social life will be ruined and moral standards will decline ... I feel convinced that for men and women to go out for work together will mean the fall of both. Do not, therefore, send your women out to work, protect their honour, if you have any manliness in you, it is for you to see that no one casts an evil eye on them ...

Gandhi, when confronted with what appears to him a problem of 'honour' 'purity', and 'chastity' which is mediated by his own middle class patriarchal attitudes, reasserts with more directness, the need for women to remain in the house and fight for Swadeshi from the house. The vow of Swadeshi is thus transformed from its political roots into religious and moral ones. To practice Swadeshi now means to protect Indian womanhood. The protection of this honour becomes in turn Ishwarbhakti.[28] The fight for the country's freedom, the protection of her wealth, and of the honour of her women becomes in Gandhi the programme for the future. Purity, the attribute of Sita, is now transformed into a fight for freedom. Sita's purity made possible Ramarajya,[29] the fight for Swadeshi will give purity to India.[30] As he says, 'the spinning wheel is the symbol of the chastity of womanhood of India. In the absence of the spinning wheel, I give you my testimony, that thousands of our poor sisters are giving themselves to a life of shame and degradation.'[31]

That in Gandhi the notion of purity is connected to the women's place within the household is clear from an extract from another speech to the Ahmedabad textile workers. The male and female, he argues, are partners in life, complementary to each other.

They become good householders only by dividing their labour and a wise mother only finds her time fully occupied in looking after her household and children. But when both husband and wife have to labour for mere maintenance, the nation becomes degraded. It is like a bankrupt living on his capital.[32]

After his travels in Punjab to propagate spinning in 1920 he comes back, convinced that:[33]

They [the women of Punjab] felt that Swadeshi is not merely a means of protecting India's wealth, but it makes a means of protecting women's honour, it is a form of Ishwarbhakti and in it lies the country's best freedom.

Honour and respect, concepts evolved to legitimate sexual exclusivity and re-establish women's place in the household are now given political legitimacy. What we now see is that Gandhi is constructing a new image of women extracted from his own perceptions of what a woman should be. In this formulation the role is played by his belief that a woman's biological features, mainly her reproductive aspects, distinguish her from the male. He thus creates for her a distinct role in society—as a mother and wife and gives her the prime role of actor in the household. In and through his experience, in Gandhi's perception, a woman develops qualities and attributes such as courage, patience, purity, and suffering which are exclusive to her and superior to the male. These attributes he extracts from his own reading or from the role that historical and mythological heroines have played, and these are then interwoven and reframed into the prescriptions for the role that contemporary women involved in the national struggle, have to play from within their domestic space. In this process of transformation and of reconstruction, these attributes are given a qualitatively new place and superiority in the hierarchy of the attributes that define both male and female. But that it reposes on key distinctions made between male and female should not be underemphasized. As Gandhi states:[34]

Men and women are of equal rank, but they are not identical. They are a peerless pair, being supplementary to one another; each helps the other so that without the one, the existence of the other cannot be conceived ... Man is supreme in the outward activities of a married pair and, therefore, it is in the fitness of things that he should have a greater knowledge there of. On the other hand, home life is entirely in the sphere of women, and, therefore, in domestic affairs, in the upbringing and education of children, women ought to have more knowledge.

And these very biological characteristics, of having reproductive capacities and of being mother, give women:[35]

The power, denied to men, of creating new ideals and translating them into action. By comparison, man is thoughtless, impatient and given to the pursuit of novelty. Women, it is observed, are serious-minded, patient and inclined generally to cling to old ways. When, therefore, she has a new idea, it seems to have its birth in the tender depths of her heart. An idea born in this manner commands her unshakeable faith and for that reason it is capable of being rapidly propagated.

The process of extraction, transformation, and glorification of 'negative' attributes made positive can be seen in the way he treats suffering, the most superior of all the rights of women:[36]

Women have to suffer more than the men. Men and women are, of course, equal in authority. I myself believe in the idea, or rather in the matter of suffering, women have a greater right than men. In this world men have not suffered more than women, nor displayed the gentleness that she has done ...

Thus, now this morally superior woman assumes a force of strength in Gandhi. Women cannot think of themselves as 'weak creatures'. 'Sita, Draupadi and other women (have) filled the wicked with awe', he states.[37] They cannot be weak if they have been 'mothers of sons, like Hanuman'. A woman might have convinced herself that she is weak 'to impress the male of his duty towards her'. Men being physically stronger should not become a monster and oppress woman, but on the contrary, 'he must do her service by protecting her and providing her with the means through which she may cultivate strength of soul'.[38]

In Gandhi, women's weakness is now turned into strength. This construction does not seem surprising, given that the entire repertoire of Gandhi's concepts rests on this philosophical and moral notion. Satyagraha is indeed the weapon of the weak against the strong. The fight by the Indians against the British, of weak against the strong, is only possible when the weak perceive their weakness as strength and as a strategy to overpower their enemy. Gandhi links his understanding of women's weakness and its transformation into strength as part of the same strategy and as embodied in the conceptions of satyagraha and ahimsa.[39] 'The non-violent movement', he asserts, 'is to enable the weakest human beings to vindicate their dignity'. Woman is the weakness personified. Yet, 'she may be weak in body, but she can be as strong in soul'.[39] The spinning wheel with all its implications is the weapon in India at least for the strong in soul.

A reading of Gandhi's text shows Gandhi's inability to understand the reasons for the weakness of the woman as he does in the case of the Indian people in context of colonialism. Thus, it seems, that while he has been able to creatively use this understanding as a strategy to confront colonial domination, in case of the women's question, because he has not understood the nature of women's oppression, he merely has seen the women's problem as an extension of the national question.

What we do see, however, in Gandhi is an extraction and reformulation of received social ideas in moral terms. The social roots of this extraction are very clear. The emphasis on reproductive attributes of women, her complementarity with male on her roles as mother and wife and revulsion to work, indicate Gandhi's middle class urban leanings. And it is women from this class who attend his meetings and to whom he is addressing as can be deduced from the adjectives, adverbs, and phrases he uses to describe them. They are 'lazy',[40] 'idlers',[41] 'only-doing cooking',[42] 'sleeping',[43] 'going to the temple',[44] 'prone to gossiping'[45] and 'quarreling',[46] and 'leisure seeking'.[47]

Yet, in spite of a clear structuration of the problem and thus ideology on women in Gandhi, by the late 1920s one still gets evidence of his ambiguity to the question relating to women. Two instances attest to this point. The first are his commentaries on his encounter in the late 1920s with the dancing girls of Barisal. The second relates to his reactions to the arrest of C.R. Das's wife and sister in 1922.

In the first instance Gandhi's commentaries on this issue show his agitation and anger at the situation faced by these women. He says that he feels 'ashamed of his sex' at what they have done in Barisal though such treatment of women is 'common enough in one shape or another in the rest of India'. As in the case of women who work outside the household, he considers these women, 'impure'. However, he relates this 'impurity' to the 'nation's impurity'.[48] And if 'spinning' is the symbol of the 'movement of purity' for the nation, and if 'Swaraj' is possible only 'through self-purification',[49] he asks males not to 'make women a prey to our lust'. He continues:[50]

The law of the protection of the weak applied here with peculiar force. To me the meaning of cow protection includes the protection of chastity of our women. We will not regenerate India unless we learn to respect our women as we respect our mothers, sisters and daughters.

That he has couched this problem in essentially patriarchal terms, outlined above is of no doubt. Women 'like this' cannot get married.[51] Yet, he accepts the fact that, if they do not live in 'sin', they have a role to play in the movement, as Sanyasins. For in a self-respecting India a woman's virtue is as much 'every man's concern'. 'Swaraj' means the ability to regard every inhabitant of India as our own brother and sister. He thus asks these women to do social work, start spinning activities, and lead a movement against this institution, an endeavour to which he and his sympathizers will help.[52] Gandhi's ideology based on sexual exclusiveness cannot permit the prostitutes to enter into the system of marriage to make it impure. But politics in Gandhi had not yet become the symbol of morality, as later he thus finds it possible to associate them in his programme of politics.

In fact, his writings in 1921–2 indicate that he seems to be quite open to the idea that women should participate in political activity outside the house, that is in his own definition, actively disobeying law, though he had not been able to so conceptualize it earlier. When he hears the news that C.R. Das's wife and sister are arrested he shows his agitation at the problem of protection of honour and chastity. But he soon reconciles himself and affirms that this step is inevitable for it is now the 'honour of their sex' to step into 'male places'. 'Honour' now is defined as that act by which women follow their husbands' footsteps. He asks the women all over India to take up this challenge and organize themselves. 'Let them be side by side with men in sharing the hardships of jail life,' he adds, 'God will protect them.'[53]

III
Redefinition of Hindu Marriage and Family, 1923–32

The basic tenets of Gandhi's ideology on women have been laid down in the earlier phase in which Gandhi extends the concept of 'separate spheres' to assert a crucial relationship between women and politics. The woman who is the repository of the spiritual and moral goodness of society now becomes the conscience of the national movement. The spinning wheel and the protection of women's honour together became the symbols of Swaraj. In this way Gandhi is able to bring politics inside the household, if not introduce it within the household. It is important to emphasize that this extension of politics to the household made possible a radical review of women's role in her domestic space and gave her a new status and legitimacy in this space. Simultaneously, Gandhi extracted and reformulated a notion of an ideal Hindu women, converting the attributes commonly perceived as that signifying weakness into that of strength. Notwithstanding the radical departure he was making, the paper has argued that this set of ideas was related to middle class urbanized understanding of women and their role in society. It was also argued that some of these ideas remained ambiguously stated specially those relating to women's active involvement in politics outside the household.

What we see in this period is not a resolution of these ambiguities. In this period, Gandhi is actively involved in confronting and redefining the contours of Hinduism. His campaign for Harijan entry into temples makes him seriously challenge contemporary orthodox Hindu interpretations and redefine for himself both Hindu religion and its conscience keeper—the Hindu women. As a result, he attacks the conservative and orthodox elements that constrict Hindu women in society as well as inhibit them in their political work. By commenting on child marriage, widow marriage, dowry, sati, he exposes and challenges the Hindu orthodoxy while simultaneously reformulating and, thus, emphasizing marriage as the only regulator of man–woman relationships in society. In this process of reformulation, Gandhi comments on romantic love and its role in marriage, on legislation relating to women's rights, and on division of labour in the household. Gandhi is preparing a construct of modern women for the new nation. His writings in this period indicate the radical departures he is making in unravelling and questioning the existing modes of exploitation of women (no doubt of only one group of women, yet the dominant mode of understanding of women in contemporary Indian society) and the constraints of his own framework from which he cannot break out.

An examination of Gandhi's writings in the *Collected Works* indicates that after 1922–3, his interest in women tapers down to revive after 1925, when he starts commenting on issues as diverse as child marriage, widow remarriage, prostitution, and marriage.

From 1925 onwards, Gandhi starts a campaign against untouchability and writes a series of articles against the evils of Hinduism. As part of this campaign, he also introduces the problem of child widows and actively advocates the remarriage of these widows. These acts, he insists, are against Swaraj—the social, educational, moral, and political awakening of the people of India.[54]

In a stringent critique he exposes in detail the contemporary discriminatory practices that legitimize male widower's remarriage, while not allowing women to remarry. He criticizes the argument that early marriage makes possible the retention of purity in women and their adjustment into the new family.[55] Gandhi instead argues that the shastras which have affirmed the early marriage of girls are not depicting the true essence of Hinduism but are in fact 'interpolations'. It is sinful and illegal to marry off girls at a young age. 'It is', he asserts, 'a moral and physical evil and makes us recede from the fight for Swaraj'.[56] In fact, he suggests that there is causal relationship between child marriage and high proportion of child widows in our country. He therefore advocates their remarriage by their parents and also advises young men to marry such widows.[57]

It is with the same ferocity and zeal that he attacks the purdah system common in Bihar, Bengal, and the United Provinces, as well as dowry and sati. In a seminal article 'Tear Down the Purdah' he laments at the existence of the 'barbarous custom' which is doing 'harm to the country'. Purdah, he asserts, becomes an impediment in the growth of the Indian women. Because they are 'caged and confined in their houses and little courtyards' they are even unsure of what to do when they are congregated in one room to listen to a speaker. They 'create noise and din'.[58] But he does not blame the women for this 'din', for he knows that they have 'high culture' and 'can raise themselves to the same height as men', but they are not allowed to do so. If his attack in the case on child marriage had been on the Shastras, in the case of purdah it is on the contemporary denotation of chastity that enforces women to remain secluded physically in the household. Instead of asking them to breath the 'fresh air of freedom' he asserts that chastity should come from within and 'to be worth anything must be capable of withstanding every unsought temptation'. 'It must be as defiant as Sita.'[59] Chastity is now defined to become a prescriptive moral notion residing within a woman.

The same condemnation is unleashed on the custom of sati. 'How can society', he asks, 'demand allegiance and devotion from the wife when it cannot do so from the husband?' This practice, he feels, has its origin in superstitions and 'blind egotism of man'. 'The wife', he asserts, 'is not a slave of her husband, but a comrade, his better half, colleague and friend. She is a co-sharer with him of equal rights and duties. Their obligations towards each other and towards the world must therefore be the same and reciprocal.'[60] A similar argument is repeated by Gandhi in the context of dowry where 'women who are in fact *ardhangini*, the better half' are 'reduced ... to the position of mere cattle to be bought and sold'.[61]

Gandhi, no doubt is making a radical critique of contemporary social practices and simultaneously asserting a need for the reappraisal of the role of women in the context of Swaraj. However, this reappraisal is couched in ideological terms that, at best, make a partial critique of social oppression of women. It is important to note at this juncture that if he was critical of child marriage and propagated the remarriage of child-widow, he was not that enthusiastic of the remarriage of adult widows. As early as 1920 he had the following to say:[62]

Impatient reformers will merely say that remarriage is the only straight and simple remedy for this [bane of society]. I cannot say so. I too have a family of my own. There are many widows in my family, but I can never bring myself to advise them to remarry and they will not think of doing so either. The real remedy is for men to take a pledge that they will not remarry.

And when he takes up the campaign for widow remarriage of children he says:[63]

The definition of widow can have no reference to child marriages. A widow means a woman who, at the proper age, married a person of her choice or was married to him with her consent, who had relations with her husband and who has now lost her husband. A wife who has not known consummation of marriage or a girl of tender aged, sacrificed by her parents cannot and must not be included in this definition.

That the girl-children can be remarried because they have not 'loved' and consummated their marriage is a prescription intrinsically related to the new conception of marriage in Gandhi.

'Marriage', he asserts, 'is a sacrament', the union not only of bodies, 'but also of souls'. Love is possible only once in one's lifetime and only in marriage. 'It is also a fence that protects religion'. Once marriage occurs, then 'man and woman become one in soul'.[64] A child bride cannot understand this meaning of marriage and therefore she should not be married when young and if married and widowed should be remarried again. A grown-up widow who has been married comprehends this meaning of marriage and therefore should constrain herself getting married. It is only when a widow 'cannot restrain herself', that she should have the freedom to remarry for it is better 'to marry openly than to live in sin'.[65] 'If she does not feel the desire to remarry, she deserves to be revered by the whole world because she is the pillar of *dharma*'.[66] 'A real Hindu widow', he asserts, 'is a treasure. She is one of the gifts of Hinduism to humanity. Ramabai Ranade was such a gift'. 'God created nothing finer than the Hindu widow!'[67]

This theme of sacrosanctity of marriage permeates itself even in his writing on Sati. Because true marriage is not only the union of bodies, it does not get destroyed by the mere break in physical relationship. 'Self-destruction is thus futile'.[68] The dead cannot be brought to life. To be a sati means not to destroy oneself but 'to realise the ideal of selfless and self-effacing service by completely merging her individuality in her husband's'. Satihood, for Gandhi, means the realization of purity through 'renunciation, sacrifice, self-discipline and dedication to the service of her husband'. If Gandhi does not want the woman to 'mount the funeral pyre on her husband's death', he wants her 'to strive to make her husband's ideals and virtues live again in her actions in this world'.[69]

What Gandhi is attempting is to make a critique of those aspects of Hindu culture 'which has erred on the side of excessive subordination of the wife' and has resulted in the 'husband exercising authority that reduces him to the level of a brute'.[70] He highlights some practices that restrict the freedom of women to operate within this definition of marriage and thus within the household. Child marriage, purdah, dowry, and sati, he feels, need to be discarded. Also those legal codes that do not treat women and men as equal within the family need to be changed. Women, Gandhi insists, are co-sharers in their husband's power and privileges'.[71]

Thus, he even insists that the woman should not be overburdened with household chores. Food requirements should be kept simple, and it should be cooked only once so that the kitchen should not occupy all of the woman's time. He even goes on to state that 'since cooking has to be done, both (husband and wife) should take a hand in it'.[72]

Gandhi, while making a partial critique of contemporary Hindu customs, is emphasizing once again the woman's crucial role only in the household. In a seminal article entitled, 'Myself, My Spinning Wheel and Women', he states that he believes in complete equality for women. They are and should be considered co-workers. In India, women have never been subordinated.[73]

Only those who were wealthy and who had thus become objects, have let themselves be subordinated and thus have become prey to fine clothes and ornaments. Women's ancient prerogative was to be the 'queen in the household'. From this position she should never be dethroned. It would indeed be a dreary home of which a woman was not a centre ... who would look after the children, the brightest jewels of the poorest household? Man, he insists, 'is the bread winner' and works better because 'he has a happy home'. It is women's work to bring the little ones and mould their character' ... 'whatever the race, family life is the first and greatest thing. Its sanctity must remain. Upon it rests the welfare of the nation ... no state can survive unless the sacred security of the home life is preserved'.[74]

We thus see that Gandhi is giving marriage and the home a religious and moral sanctity within the contours of a national ideology. If he is accepting formal legal equality between partners in marriage and redistributing to some extern duties within the household, he is not changing the basic precepts under which, in his perception, the institution of marriage is based; that is complementarity of the two sexes. As he asserts, men and women should not be regarded as superior or inferior. The place and functions of both are 'different'.[75]

Gandhi does not even question the other institutional practices of contemporary Hindu marriage like the rules governing choice of marriage partners whose base is the caste system. In fact, he affirms his belief that marriage should only take place within particular varnas and condemns intercommunity and inter-varna marriage. That Gandhi is only partially critical of contemporary Hindu practices is accepted by Gandhi himself, who says in some revealing sentences that:[76]

Brahminism I adore. I have defended Varnaashrama Dharma. But Brahminism that can tolerate untouchability, virgin widowhood, spoliation of virgins, strikes in my nostrils. It is a parody of Brahminism. There is no knowledge of Brahman therein.

We thus not only see Gandhi making only a partial critique of social practices of Hinduism but also see him, in this phase extending ideas of and on women, developed earlier. He affirms and legitimizes once again the woman's intrinsic space within the household, simultaneously postulating their formal equality with males. Outside the household the problem of retaining her purity and honour remains a thorn in Gandhi. Gandhi has not yet been able to solve this issue in spite of his remarks on the arrest of Das's wife and sister. Yet, we see that there is in Gandhi an attempt to evolve a new definition of politics, as shown below. Gandhi is also by now convinced that sex and reproduction can only be possible within the boundaries of marriage and sex outside marriage and therefore outside the 'home' it is impure. Thus, now, contrarily to his earlier position, though he accepts that the prostitutes are victims of man's lust, when the dancing girls of Barisal are being made Congress members, he objects vehemently. The status, he says, that these women have acquired is against the moral well being of the society. Congress, he asserts, cannot incorporate an 'association of known thieves'. In fact these women are 'more dangerous than thieves'. 'The latter steal material possessions, the former steal virtue'. And though there is no legal bar against their entry, public opinion should have kept them out of this.[77] In his earlier writings, if Gandhi is protecting purity of marriage, now he is attempting to protect the purity of the Congress. Politics and the Congress party both are now perceived in moral terms.

The strong feeling of middle class sexual exclusiveness that directs the legitimation of women's role within the household continues to remain within Gandhi's ideology and it reflects itself at the time of the civil disobedience movement. Even before the Dandi march had started Kasturba had led a group of volunteers in a satyagraha. Gandhi was very disturbed by this active participation and within a few days came out with a special message for the women of India. The wearing of khadi, he says, should be their goal for khadi represents purity.[78] They have to, he insists, not join the civil disobedience movement, for 'they will be lost in the crowd' and when they are so lost, there 'would be no suffering for which they are thirsting'. Arguing that they do not have 'brute strength' but 'moral power', Gandhi asks them to picket against foreign clothes shops and liquor shops for 'who can make a more effective appeal to the heart than women?'[79] And yet he is troubled about their 'purity' in this participation for he writes 'who will cast

an evil eye on you if you walk straight on with the name of God on your lips? Be convinced at heart that purity itself is a shield.'[80]
What we thus see in the inability of Gandhi to break out of the middle class ideological moorings on women which can only posit her role within the household. If he is trapped within this framework it is also because his personal search to understand sexuality has not led him to understand the social or historical roots of sexuality. His personal solution has been denial of the sex instinct, a denial which he believes not only gives happiness but leads human beings towards the path of moksha and makes possible the growth of moral strength that can counter unlimited physical force. His belief in his personal resolution as a universal resolution of the problem of sexual attraction, which he considers a weakness, is the reason for this fascination and empathy for the role played by the Hindu widow.

Tradition, by keeping the widow away from family life, from material and physical pleasures, had condemned her to a puritanical simple life though investing her with moral superiority. In Gandhi this denial itself becomes a higher moral truth. Widows in Gandhi become representatives of not only the best in Hindu tradition but, as he evolves his ideas, also become the key to the role that Indian women can now play in society. The widow is the ideal through which Gandhi is able to transcend the limitations to which his own morality has bound him in relation to women. It is now possible for women in Gandhi to find a place in public life without being confronted with the problems of 'honour', 'chastity', and 'impurity'. They become the epitome of all ideals once they deny sex, marriage, reproduction, and family. They can now practise the love of all of humanity. It is ironical and paradoxical that when Gandhi is able to make the necessary mediations to arrive at a position of accepting the entrance and role of women outside the household, that he is at a stage when he has lost all hope in politics. Thus the image of women in his writings at this stage is that of one who is dedicated to the cause of service of the nation and humanity.

IV
WOMAN AS RENUNCIATOR, 1932–48

If what underlines the Gandhian ideology on women in the earlier period is his search for her creative role in politics, his need to free her from the bondage of contemporary images, in this phase of Gandhi's writings, we see an image of women which is constricting and all-enveloping. Gandhi is now able to solve ambiguities in his own thoughts and make a structured analysis of the problem of a woman and articulates his own particular solution for her freedom. What we see in his writings at this stage is a well-articulated understanding of woman, her physical needs, emotions, attributes, role in marriage and outside marriage, her weaknesses and her strengths, and her place in the emerging nation. What we see through these ideas is that Gandhi is unable to break out from his middle class understanding of women. Now he extends his own perceptions regarding sexuality and prescriptions relating to it in the construction of the ideology on women. The social critique and personal prescriptions now blend together in the construction of contemporary womanhood.

In a series of commentaries on marriage, self-control, and the use of contraceptives in 1936–8 Gandhi lays down his postulates on women very clearly.

Marriage he says 'is only for those who want children'.[81] The norm defining marriage is restraint. Sexual enjoyment is not an aspect of marriage. The 'very purpose of marriage is restraint' and 'sublimation of the sexual passion'.[82] The 'sexual act should only be performed for begetting children'.[83] Therefore 'marriage unites a male and a wife as friends, as comrades and co-sharers'. Each are 'the master of the other, each helpmate' and a complement to one another, 'each co-operating with the other in the performance of life'.[84] It is only then that 'true happiness pervades both the husband and wife'.

The contemporary form of marriage, he insists, bases itself on 'lust and sexual passion'. In this form, woman becomes the object of man's lust, a 'tool' for his gratification.[85] Because of social norms, a woman cannot say 'no' to her husband who by inflicting himself on her makes her a prostitute.[86] It is only when the woman learns to say 'no' that she can really become free;[87] because what she considers as her weaknesses are not weaknesses but her strengths. Woman, he says, is 'not a prey to sexual desires', it is easier for her to enforce self-restraint and thus she can refuse to become 'a doll in her husband's hands'.[88] If she does so, she will show herself not to be a slave of her husband's wishes and instead project herself as a person free from physical slavery'.[89] Marriage, he insists, is geared for the 'growth of the spiritual development of the couple' and for their service to family and social life.[90] Love that 'is intense affection without lust' is also a means through which 'marriage can become a means of service'.[91] The spirits, he insists have also justified this view of marriage, that is that the union of male and female should be permitted only, if there is a desire for children. This notion of marriage, he insists is a form of 'science' and is 'the truth'.[92] Contraceptives, he insists, will bring corruption back into marriage. The male will now force himself more on the female and thus condemn her to a 'life of excessiveness, of lust and thus of impurity'. Birth control 'is only possible through restraint and self control'.[93]

The Gandhian ideology of sexuality assembles now a very interesting set of attributes together. On one hand, the male is considered a highly sexed individual and on the other the female, it seems, does not have sexual needs and is a model of restraint. Sexual relationships are only to be initiated for the continuation of the species and marriage can become the only 'science' known to humankind for relating man and woman together.[94] In Gandhi, love and happiness is only possible through the divorce of sexual enjoyment in marriage.

No doubt this ideology has its roots with Gandhi's experience and experiment with his own sexuality, but it leads to some very negative conclusions in the case of understanding women. It denies her a sexual life and simultaneously imposes on her the role of a mother which in turn posits to her a certain role in the family organization, and thus in society. She is now the mistress of the house, the 'keeper and distributor of the bread earned by her husband' and in her resides the art of bringing up the infants of her race which is her 'special and her sole prerogative in life'.[95]

Having drawn out and extracted woman's distinctiveness on the basis of this construct of sexuality, Gandhi proceeds to give it a higher moral value and places it as the most supreme attribute in the world. It helps him thus to state very clearly that the 'women cannot ride the horse which men ride',[96] that is, be the breadwinner because by doing so she will destroy her very 'essence'. Gandhi now defines the woman's essence as the lack of 'sexual need', a sense of 'restraint', combined with 'courage', 'patience', and 'suffering'; a universal mother. This 'essence' in turn makes her 'the incarnate of Ahimsa':[97] a person who gives infinite love and 'has infinite capacity of suffering',[98] and therefore can also become 'the apostle of peace'.[99]

As he says,[100]

Who but a woman, the mother, of man, shows this capacity in the largest measure? She shows it as she carries the infant and feeds it during nine months and derives joy in the suffering involved. What can beat the suffering caused by the pangs of labour? But she forgets them in the joy of her creation ... Let her transfer that love to the whole of humanity, let her forget that she ever was or can be the object of man's lust. And she will occupy her proud position by the side of him as his mother, maker and silent leader. It is given to her to teach the art of peace to the warring nation thirsting for that nectar. She can become the leader in Satyagraha which does not require the learning that books give but does require the heart that comes from suffering and faith.

We now see in Gandhi the final stages of the reconstruction of a new image of the woman which attributes a new role for her. That he has modelled this new woman, on the basis of a received notion of the Hindu widow is also clear. As early as in 1924, he had stated that in the Hindu widow 'self control has been carried by Hinduism to its greatest heights' and in the widow's life, 'it reaches its perfection'. A widow 'does not even look at suffering as suffering. Renunciation has become a second nature to them, and to renounce it would be painful to them. They find happiness in their self denial'.[101] And he continues.[102]

This is Hinduism at its best. I regard the widow's life as a reflection of Hinduism. When I see a widow, I instinctively bow my head in reverence. A widow's blessing is to me a gift which I prize. I forget all my sorrows. Man is but a clod before her. A widow's patient suffering is impossible to rival.

Gandhi now creates a god-like woman leader fighting violence and justice. As the embodiment of the universal mother she is the repository and the symbol of all that is morally good of mankind. It is not necessary for her to involve herself in politics to fight injustice because she is now the 'personification of renunciation' and thus can now 'adorn both her sex and nation'.[103] She is no longer weak and at the mercy of men. She is *sabala*,[104] the reservoir of strength and of moral force. It is this strength that gives her power to fight any attempt made on her chastity and honour. She can use her nails and teeth to kill herself or use her tongue. And in her resides the spiritual strength of the nation. And only four months prior to independence, Gandhi has the following to say to some women workers:[105]

Have faith in God and build up your self confidence and courage. Everyone frightens the timid therefore if you continue to be timid you will not be able to make any use of the strength to cultivate courage. In order to utilise your strength, you have to realise the power inherent in you ... (It is by) building up (your) ... moral courage ... (that you can) develop immense strength. If women resolve to bring glory to the nation within a few months they can change the face of the country because the spiritual background of the Aryan women is totally different than the women of other countries.

Gandhi has created a puritanical and ascetical Kali.

V

CONCLUSION

This chapter has argued that the Gandhian ideology is no doubt taking an enormous leap by giving a significant role to women in contemporary

Indian society. It is also making a significant change on the image of women developed by the reformists. No doubt, Gandhi made women into a subject, making her realize that she had freedom, qualities, and attributes which are crucial to contemporary society. In a radical reconstruction, he gave her confidence in herself and in her essence. He made woman realize that she has a significant and a dominant role to play in the family, that both she and her husband are equal, and that within the family they both have similar rights. In a path-breaking intervention, he made possible not only the involvement of women in politics, but made them realize that the national movement could not succeed without their involvement in the struggle. Gandhi ultimately empowered woman in the family and in marriage.

But, this reconstruction of women and femininity did not make a structural analysis of the origins and nature of exploitation of women; in fact Gandhi used essentialist arguments to reaffirm her place as mother and wife in the household. He denied her sexual needs, yet emphasized her distinct social role in the family by glorifying some of her 'feminine' qualities. By giving these qualities a separateness and a justification of morality he was simultaneously able to assert a positive and a creative role for the married woman in certain situations but enclose her in those of the others that extend outside the family and the household. If he constructed a significantly new place for the married Indian woman in the household, he reconstructed another one for the unmarried one outside the household. Yet, there was an attempt thereby to invert the essentialist 'separate spheres' doctrine. Gandhi fails in this task miserably because he is only able to extend logically the doctrine rather than demolish it. If the 'separate spheres' doctrine is based on the 'giveness' of biological differences, Gandhi's new woman can now break the 'Lakshman Rekha' of the 'home' only by denying her biology. Thus the inversion and questioning can never take place and marriage remains sacrosanct and remains the 'essence' of modern Indian society. It is no wonder that the present-day women's movement is now attempting to fight this legacy through its struggle.

The revival of Gandhi is occurring at a point of time in the women's movement when the focus of analysis has shifted away from an evaluation of social and historical roots of the construction of womanhood and manhood in different countries, regions, and stratas—class, caste, ethnic, tribe, and race—towards an acceptance of essential distinctions between femininity and masculinity arising out of a concern and preoccupations with male violence, sexuality, motherhood, and peace. Gandhi's ideas fit into this stream of consciousness without difficulties. For he creates a new woman, a woman who could have strength, courage, patience, and a capacity for suffering and thus can become a symbol of non-violence and peace. However, it should not be forgotten as it is shown above, that the new image of women that he creates is drawn from one particular historical and social setting and for one particular political goal: to unite the different stratas in India against imperialism, Gandhi was a figure of that historical time and of that social milieu. He was also a political strategist par excellence who attempted to unite different, unevenly developed stratas. Any extension of his ideas to contemporary situations has to understand this fact in their evaluation of his role. This chapter was written not only to show the internal coherence in Gandhi's ideas about women as they developed over time but also to unearth and articulate the core assumptions behind his perspectives on women. It has been argued that the essentialism that guides his perspective is something that the contemporary women's movement has to understand and guard against in their search for alternative messiahs in their struggle against exploitation and oppression.

NOTES

1. Veena Mazumdar, 'The Social Reform Movement in India: From Ranade to Nehru', in B.R. Nanda (ed.), *The Indian Women: From Purdah to Modernity*, Delhi: Viking, 1976, p. 58.

2. Devaki Jain, 'Gandhian Contributions towards a Theory of Feminist Ethic' in Devaki Jain and Diana Eck (eds), *Speaking of Faith: Cross-Cultural Perspectives in Women, Religion and Social Change*, Delhi: Kali for Women, 1986, pp. 267–8.

3. Madhu Kishwar, 'Gandhi on Women', p. 258 in this volume.

4. Ibid., p. 280–1.

5. Ibid., p. 284.

6. Ibid.

7. Veena Mazumdar, op cit, p. 60.

8. Madhu Kishwar, op cit, p. 284.

9. Ibid., p. 259.

10. Sudesh Vaid, 'Ideologies on Women in Nineteenth Century Britain, 1850s-1870s'; in *Economic and Political Weekly*, Vol. XX, Review of Women's Studies, 26 October 1985, p. WS–63.

11. It is the urban middle class that Gandhi is addressing.

12. The following is based on a reading of Gandhi's writing in the *Collected Works of Mahatma Gandhi*.

13.   *Collected Works of Mahatma Gandhi* (henceforth *CW*), Vol. 7, 1907, p. 65.
14.   *CW*, Vol. 13, 1916, pp. 443, 454, 496.
15.   Ibid., p. 435.
16.   Ibid., Vol. 14, 1917, p. 32.
17.   Ibid., p. 33.
18.   Ibid.
19.   Ibid, p. 127.
20.   Ibid.
21.   Ibid., Vol. 15, pp. 290–2.
22.   Ibid., pp. 322–6.
23.   Ibid., p. 441.
24.   Ibid., pp. 322–6.
25.   Ibid., p. 325.
26.   Ibid., Vol. 16, 1919, pp. 129–30.
27.   Ibid., Vol. 17, 1920, pp. 47–51.
28.   Ibid.. Vol. 16. 1919. p. 31.
29.   Ibid., Vol. 18, 1920, p. 393.
30.   Ibid., Vol. 19, 1920, p. 389.
31.   Ibid., Vol. 21, 1921, p. 123.
32.   Ibid., Vol. 17, 1920, p. 31.
33.   Ibid., p. 326.
34.   Ibid., Vol. 14, 1918, pp. 207–8.
35.   Ibid., pp. 86–7.
36.   Ibid., Vol. 15, 1919, p. 322.
37.   Ibid., Vol. 18, 1920, pp. 57–8.
38.   Ibid., p. 393.
39.   Ibid., Vol. 23, 1922, pp. 33–7.
40.   Ibid., Vol. 15, 1919, p. 322.
41.   Ibid., p. 327.
42.   Ibid., p. 439.
43.   Ibid., Vol. 16, 1919, p. 79.
44.   Ibid., p. 129.
45.   Ibid., p. 190.
46.   Ibid., p. 286.
47.   Ibid.
48.   Ibid., Vol. 19, 1920, p. 572.
49.   Ibid., pp. 565–6.
50.   Ibid., pp. 565–6.

51. Ibid., Vol. 21, 1921, p. 123.
52. Ibid., pp. 104–6.
53. Ibid., Vol. 22, 1921, pp. 21–4.
54. Ibid., Vol. 30, 1926, p. 430.
55. Ibid., p. 430.
56. Ibid., p. 365.
57. Ibid., p. 340.
58. Ibid., Vol. 34, 1927, p. 141.
59. Ibid., Vol. 33, 1927, pp. 44–5.
60. Ibid., Vol. 46, 1931, p. 75.
61. Ibid., Vol. 39. 1928, p. 415.
62. Ibid., Vol. 18, 1920, pp. 319–21.
63. Ibid., Vol. 22, 1924, p. 527.
64. Ibid., Vol. 30, 1926, p. 364.
65. Ibid., pp. 493–4.
66. Ibid., Vol. 31, 1926, p. 443.
67. Ibid., Vol. 34, 1927, p. 141.
68. Ibid., Vol. 30, 1926, p. 314.
69. Ibid., Vol. 46, 1931, p. 75.
70. Ibid., p. 75.
71. Ibid., Vol. 42, 1929, p. 5.
72. Ibid., Vol. 34, 1927, pp. 32–3.
73. Ibid., Vol. 48, 1931, p. 19.
74. Ibid., p. 80.
75. Ibid.
76. Ibid., Vol. 34, 1927, p. 142.
77. Ibid., Vol. 27, 1925, pp. 290–1.
78. Ibid., Vol. 43, 1930, p. 189.
79. Ibid., pp. 219–20.
80. Ibid., p. 155.
81. Ibid., Vol. 55, 1937, p. 109.
82. Ibid., p. 9.
83. Ibid., Vol. 55, 1937. p. 261
84. Ibid., Vol. 55, 1937. p. 110.
85. Ibid., Vol. 52, 1935, p. 156.
86. Ibid., p. 157.
87. Ibid., p. 158.
88. Ibid., p. 157.

89.   Ibid., p. 362.
90.   Ibid.. Vol. 55, 1937, p. 202.
91.   Ibid., Vol. 52, 1936, p. 458.
92.   Ibid., p. 262.
93.   Ibid., Vol. 53, 1936, p. 310.
94.   Ibid., Vol. 71, 1940, p. 208.
95.   Ibid., p. 207.
96.   Ibid., p. 206.
97.   Ibid., p. 208.
98.   Ibid., p. 209.
99.   Ibid.. Vol. 52, 1936, p. 311.
100. Ibid., Vol. 71, 1940, p. 209.
101. Ibid., Vol. 22, 1924, p. 523.
102. Ibid., p. 524.
103. Ibid., Vol. 83, 1946, p. 398.
104. Ibid., Vol. 87, 1947, p. 293.
105. Ibid.

References

Ahmed, Karuna, 'Gandhi, Women's Role and the Freedom Movement', Occasional Paper, New Delhi: Nehru Memorial Museum and Library,1984.

Forbes, Geraldine, 'Women's Movement in India: Traditional Symbols and New Roles' in M.S.A. Rao (ed.), *Social Movement in India*, Vol. 2, Delhi: Manohar, 1979.

Gandhi, Mahatma, *Collected Works of Mahatma Gandhi*, Vol. 1 to 87, Delhi: Government of India, 1969.

Jain, Devaki, 'Gandhian Contributions towards a Theory of Feminist Ethic', in *Speaking of Faith, Cross-Cultural Perspectives on Women, Religion and Social Change*, Devaki Jain and Diana Eck (eds), Delhi: Kali for Women, 1986.

Kishwar, Madhu, 'Women in Gandhi', *Economic and Political Weekly*, Vol. 20 (40, 41), 5 and 19 October 1985.

Mazumdar, Veena, 'The Social Reform Movement in India: From Ranade to Nehru', in B.R. Nanda (ed.), *Indian Women: From Purdah to Modernity*, Delhi: Vikas, 1979.

Vaid, Sudesh, 'Ideologies on Women in Nineteenth Century Britain, 1850s–1870s', *Economic and Political Weekly*, Vol. XX(43), Review of Women's Studies, 26 October 1985.

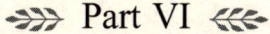 Part VI

13

Self-purification versus Self-respect
On the Roots of the Dalit Movement*

D.R. NAGARAJ

Where two principles really do meet which cannot be reconciled
with one another, then each man declares the other a fool and a
heretic.

(Wittgenstein in 'On Certainty')

I

The best way to begin this book is by a critical invocation to Babasaheb
Ambedkar. After all, the Buddhist method, taught by the Tathagatha, excels
in offering a critique of the master himself. The Dalit Movement, in ways
more than one, owes its existence to Babasaheb, and is also facing a crisis
because of his fatherhood. A critical estimate of his philosophical and
political career will both illuminate and situate the movement in a proper
context.

Irony of Ironies: To understand the nature of Babasaheb's political
career one has to place it along with Gandhiji's, for the apparent divergence
between the two will highlight the unique problems of the former. Is the
irreconcilability between the two real and fundamental? I shall try to explore
a truthful answer to this question. Since the answer will have far-reaching

* D.R. Nagaraj, 'Self-purification v/s Self-respect: On the Roots of the Dalit Movement,'
in *The Flaming Feet: A Study of the Dalit Movement*, Bangalore: South Forum Press, 1993,
pp. 1–30.

consequences for the Dalit movement, one has to proceed with care and
caution, fighting deep-rooted prejudices, and of course, wishful thinking
too. In other words, the Dalit movement was a product of the mental state
that believed in the firm rejection of the Gandhian model of tackling the
problems of untouchables, and that has shaped the contours of its themes
and patterns. But today historical circumstances have changed, and their
consequences have forced us to re-examine the origin and structure of these
forces that have conditioned the movement. Even if a nasty surprise is in
store for us, we should be able to bear it, for it could also mean the existence
of certain undiscovered affinities.

For a start, let us study the already accepted notions regarding the
Gandhiji–Ambedkar relationship. While studying this we should be extremely careful for we have become captives of the picture that has been
presented to us. Babasaheb's politics was decidedly different from the
Gandhian ideology and cultural politics that had dominated the nation till
1947. Gandhiji had become the centre of the nation's politics, and those who
disagreed with him—there were many—were considered eccentrics. Particularly, the imprint of the Gandhian model of tackling the Harijan question
merits a serious analysis. This question has been foisted on us by the
necessity of studying the Congress–Harijan leadership against which the
angry young generation of Dalits revolted in the 1960s and onwards. The
Harijan leadership created by Gandhiji was not at all like him; the politico-
psychological factors that shaped these leaders had given birth to a new kind
of nationalist political articulation, but there was a great deal of silence also
on socio-cultural questions. A paradoxical convergence of articulation and
silence. In the post-independence decades, the new generation of Dalits
interpreted the nationalist rhetoric of senior Harijan leaders as nationalist
crap which concealed structural disparities, and their cultural silence was
dubbed both as domestication and cowardice. For a change, in the history of
socio-cultural movements, it was not exactly a case of passionate misreading of the Father tradition. The case for patricide looked both genuine and
unavoidable. Was the judgement on senior Harijan leaders not too harsh and
equally guilty of being ignorant of complex historical forces which shaped
them? Well, that is the seductive charm of history; she convinces one that a
partial view is the total view and drives the passionate to act. One who waits
for the total view will never act or take a plunge into history, and here lies,
precisely, the liberative potential of history. Both Babasaheb and Bapuji
plunged into history with such creative impatience and clashed. Historical
action is the *Mahasamadhisthiti* of the creatively impatient, and having

jumped into action they cured each other's excesses; they emerged as transformed persons at the end of a very intense encounter. I am referring to the complex, yet fascinating, Gandhiji–Ambedkar encounter of the 1930s. It is true though each continued to refer to the other as a 'fool' and 'heretic' (not necessarily using these very words) till the end of their respective lives. This ferocity was more true, however, in the case of Babasaheb. But I suspect that this was only for the sake of form; it was for the consumption of those who laid a great deal of emphasis on the continuity of form. By the end of the mid-1930s both Ambedkar and Gandhiji were not the same persons they were when they had set out on a journey of profound engage-ment with each other. They were deeply affected and transformed by each other. Let us study this story closely. I shall not try to explain the story, but here is an attempt to describe its major events. As for the source of the story, I have picked a thing or two from the epic of *Harijan* weekly; in my view, particularly the issues between 1935–6 are truly a work of epic dimension with all the stunning variety of genres (not in terms of the narrow literary definition of the word), the experiences of life having transcended their limitations and become genres of literature.[1]

Untouchability was one of the central concerns of Gandhiji. In all historical fairness it must be admitted that it was Bapu who made untouch-ability one of the crucial questions of Indian politics, although there were many yogis and movements before him in the eighteenth and nineteenth centuries whose contributions require a deeper grasp and analysis. On the whole, there seems to be a general ferment in the Indian society of the nineteenth century, which created both social movements and a religious symbolism that sought to question the foundations of the caste system. The mechanisms which generated these movements and activities are not neces-sarily linked to India's problematic relationship with the West, although some were decidedly the products of this contact or encounter.[2]

In fact, historically speaking, a whole range of indigenous yogis and sadhus, for whom colonialism hardly mattered either as a transitory phase or as a source of confrontation, had tried to deny, quite forcefully, the central-ity of caste hierarchy in the scheme of things. In this regard, Shishunaala Sheriff and Kaivara Narayanappa, two yogis of Karnataka, the Satnamis and the Mahima Movement of north India come to mind immediately.

Apparently, the chief reason for their inability to influence the historical events in any significant way was that they did not either see or present the problems as a political one which was related to the larger task of regener-ating Indian society as a whole. To be precise, they did not see their society as a part of the nation-state. For these indigenous radicals the task of fighting the caste system had been one of the spiritual requirements of their tradition. Their notion of society was, basically, a cultural one consisting of smaller communities which lived intimately in terms of geographical and social space. Most of them lived and travelled, say, in a geographical boundary of 100–200 miles. They were the conscience of smaller communities. Colonial intervention—the historical experience which dominated the Indian discourse totally for more than a century—did not make them nervous. Some of them were awed by this intrusion while some maintained stoic indifference towards it. The most important reason for such a response on the part of these yogis was that their tradition had always treated temporal power as something alien on which very little or no positive influence could be exerted. According to them, state power and historical agencies are like nature; erratic and beastly at one time and friendly, generous, and benevolent at another. Many have used nature-metaphors to respond to the colonial intervention. Shishunaala Sheriff, a Muslim Veerashaiva yogi with a Brahmin advaitin guru, has described this in a beautiful poem as the birth of rainflies which descend on the fields at the onset of monsoons. He had also reacted to the setting of a ginning mill in Hubli, as the beginning of capitalist industrialization. The response made him write a poem which begins with these lines: 'Look at the vast expanse of the mill and salute it'; and proceeds further by totally spiritualizing the experience. Even the machine, with all its complex mechanical body, could provide him with a perfect metaphor to delineate the more complex yogic experience. The mill was equated with a transcendental realm of existence. To put it differently, anxiety and nervousness—the two experiences which are presented as central to colonialism by modem theorists—were never the dominant mental states in these yogis. For them the liberation of the self from the phenomenal world was the spiritual goal, and both the arrogance and humiliation of the caste system were the major obstacles in the path of moksha or nirvana. Not surprisingly, these yogis did not make use of the logical schools of Indian philosophy. The anti-caste attitude was, mostly, a product of a-Brahmanical traditions, though, many dissident Brahmins contributed to their glory and vitality. In their view, the spiritual transformation of the 'being' has the aspect of social reform built into it. It was not a deliberate position or a dogma, but simply a matter of metaphysical requirement.

That Gandhiji, not Ambedkar, had many things in common with these yogis is evident from the way he defined the problem of untouchability, though he was different from them in ways more than one. Since *desi* spiritual traditions were slight modifications of the Bhakti schools of both Shaiva and Vaishnava varieties, Gandhiji could be innovative. He drew inspiration from the Vaishnavite tradition, for instance the centrality of temple symbolism, which gave him many moments of inner torments and self-questioning, a theme to which we shall return later. As opposed to the yogis, anxiety had entered Gandhiji quite deeply; he knew the destructive power of colonialism too well to harbour any illusions about its neutrality or to pretend that it would pass away smoothly without injuring the Indian psyche. He had stubbornly refused to transcend the reality of colonial experience into something else which was the practice with some yogis. There were many other traditions in Gandhiji which had shaped his sensibility, and they were not certainly Western. When anxiety, a product of colonial experience, became unbearable, thus threatening the very integrity of existence, Indian spiritual traditions provided him with a healing touch. Gandhiji never allowed the spiritualist zeal towards the annihilation of the caste-ego to turn upside down his priorities in the larger task of the nationalist struggle. Similarly, the nationalist battle against foreign power did not reduce the importance of the struggle against the caste system. But the Gandhian view of the problem of untouchability is basically a religious and spiritual one, its models are in Indian mystical schools. Such was his position in the 1930s before the encounter with Ambedkar began.

There existed another response to the problem of the caste system, and this was wholly secular in character and thrust. This is popularly referred to as the non-Brahmin movement of the South, although it is by no means confined to the region.[3] This development is over-determined by a whole range of complex forces of which the politics of colonial intervention is the most crucial factor. It is a deliberate, organized, and conscious effort on the part of the lower castes and social groups.[4] They chose to fight the hegemony of superior castes through gradualist and constitutionalist methods that they had learnt from their white masters. The demands of the shudras were materialistic. The colonial policy of promoting collaborative elites also had played a big role in shaping the movement.[5] The social policy of the Raj combined with an intense desire for upward mobility among lower castes had generated quite a strong optimism among the shudras; but unfortunately the non-Brahmin parties and movements were not adequate enough a medium to realize their ambitions.

It is quite easy to denigrate the importance of this movement, and it has been done so by scholars of various persuasions in the past. The non-Brahmin movement, particularly in its incarnations as the Justice Party in

the Madras Presidency and as the Prajamitra Mandali in the princely Mysore
State, was lacking in larger ideals, and was given to opportunistic and anti-
nationalist political manoeuvre. To take an uncharitable view of this movement, one could describe it as a rat race to join the ranks of government
clericaldom. The leadership of the movement was drawn from the middle
castes and landed gentry, and the fact that Brahmins had cornered and
dominated both important and minor official positions in governments had
infuriated the Shudras. The internal contradictions of the movement sur-
faced in public quite often. Particularly, the condescending attitude of
middle castes was hardly sufficient to conceal the caste-Hindu prejudices.
They had internalized the Brahminical value system totally. In fact, this is
one of the major problems faced by the Dalit movement today. Whenever it
tries to build a larger base for itself by involving other castes as allies, very
soon contradictions emerge and this particularly assumes acute forms in
questions of values. Other non-Brahmin castes would not hesitate to take the
support of the Dalits when it is a question of fighting the hegemony of other
powerful social groups. In fact they are quite desperate to build this alliance.
But they usually shy away on fundamental social and cultural issues. In
other words, the Janus-faced collaborative tendencies of other castes are an
integral part of their mobility, and they are active allies of social and cultural
conservatives. This tendency was evident in the early years of the non-
Brahmin movement.

All these rightful criticisms should not make us blind towards the
complexity of those forces, which had shaped the movement, and the
legitimacy it had gained, though it was only partial. It was confined to the
justified task of securing proportional representation in jobs and education.
Here one should pause for a while and reflect on the relation between the
noble and ignoble faces of such movements. Usually, one is moved by the
lofty philosophical talk against caste, and is equally horrified by the mean
and ignoble faces of the movement. The latter are seen in the determined,
though crude at times, efforts to secure jobs and other material benefits in
the name of communal justice and positive discrimination. The beauty and
the horror stem from the source of defying the caste system. The caste
system in India is not only a structure of cultural values but also a certain
pattern of inequitable distribution of power and wealth of different kinds
along the lines of caste hierarchy. One who appreciates the spiritual beauty
of the revolt against the caste system should also accept the horror of
materialistic demands. Gandhiji could deeply respond to the spiritual beauty
of the revolt, but he recoiled in utter embarrassment when confronted with

its material form. Even to this day such a fragmented response to injustices of the caste system continues to affect the liberal supporters of the Dalit movement. They are, justly, touched by the exercises in symbolic politics, and strangely annoyed when they see the movement's involvement with concrete issues like the Mandal Commission. The origin of the Dalit movement lies in the convergence of these two forces: the transcendental aspect of fighting the caste-ego and the mundane reality of fighting for real opportunities in education and jobs. If the aspirations of the people are not translated into real and tangible terms, there is always the danger of a movement losing its wider social base. At the same time, it can also become a prisoner of the materialist and immediately realizable demands of an articulate and influential group in a class. The terrifyingly commonsensical approach to a movement can diminish its radical energy and potential. Against this background, Babasaheb had developed a pragmatic attitude towards the non-Brahmin movement which was also equally informed by more radical aims. He was in deep sympathy with its drive towards upward mobility, and simultaneously, suspicious of the statusquoist implications of such moves. In a dinner speech in 1944, when the Justice Party was trounced in the general elections in the Madras Presidency, Ambedkar deeply reflects on the decline and downfall of the party.

Then what was wrong with the party to make it fall like a pack of cards, notwithstanding the long period in office? What was it that made the party unpopular with a large majority of non-Brahmins themselves? In my view, two things were responsible.

Firstly, they had not been able to realize exactly what their differences were with Brahminical sections. Though they indulged in virulent criticism of Brahmins, could any one of them say those differences had been doctrinal? How much Brahminism had they in them? They wore namams and regarded themselves as second class Brahmins. Instead of abandoning Brahminism they had been holding on to the spirit of it as being the ideal; their anger against Brahminism was that they (the Brahmins) gave them only a second class degree.

The second reason for the downfall of the party was its very narrow political programme. One defect in the political programme of the non-Brahmin party had been that the party made it its chief concern to secure a certain number of jobs for their young men. That was perfectly legitimate. But, did the non-Brahmin young men for whom the party fought for twenty years to secure jobs in public service remember the party after they received emoluments for their jobs? During the twenty years the party had been in office, it forgot the 90% of the non-brahmins living in the villages, leading an uneconomical life and getting into the clutches of the money lenders.[6]

This speech throws up two interrelated themes that have a definite bearing on the different kinds of pulls within the Dalit movement today. First, the process of upward mobility of a certain section within the multitudes of Dalits and its induction into the middle class ethos. This process generates a powerful optimism among the class which, usually, envelops the entire community, and the basis of this optimism is both real and illusory: real in the sense that a visible section of the community gets into public services, thus presenting itself as a model to be emulated. But it is also, ultimately, illusory in the sense that the Dalits as a whole can never attain the status achieved by their own visible minority, without a structural change in the entire society. The real problem of this selective upward mobility lies elsewhere. I would describe it as the phenomenon of wilful amnesia. To be more precise, it is amnesia towards one's own past. Babasaheb was referring to the same problem when he posed this question to the Justice Party: did the non-Brahmin young men remember the party after they had received emoluments for their jobs? The working of the caste system has always tried to create mental states of self-doubt, self-denial, and self-hatred among the lower caste individuals in the modern context, and, generally these attitudes are collectivized. The birth of the modern individual in the humiliated commun- ities is not only accompanied by a painful severing of ties with the com-munity, but also a conscious effort to alter one's past is an integral part of it.

Siddalingaiah, a famous Dalit writer of Kannada, portrays this entire syndrome in his unique style full of humorous pathos, wit, and irony in his play 'Panchama' (the Fifth One). The dramatic locale of the play is an interview conducted by an Indian Administrative Service (IAS) officer, Hayavadan Rao, whose Brahminical arrogance and condescension, dwarfs and deforms all the untouchable candidates who appear before him. The first four candidates, both men and women, present different faces of the making of modern Dalit identity in all its unauthentic forms. The first four are not sure of themselves, they are awkward and clumsy, they lie and are caught in the act; one thing that is common to all is that they show an attitude of wilful amnesia towards their past. The Panchama, the Fifth One, appears and then everything is changed utterly. A terrible beauty is born. Hayavadan Rao has not seen the likes of the fifth one before in his entire life. Panchama not only refuses to forget his past, he remembers it deliberately; an aura of noble anger surrounds him. The play ends with an impassioned plea to his community to begin a new life of self-respect. To put it metaphorically, the first four ones of the play are the unavoidable baggage of the Dalit movement, the Panchama its power and glory.

Since the very moment of its inception, the Dalit movement is saddled with the first four ones of the play, and this is what distinguishes the movement from the Marxist–Leninist inspired struggles of the landless that are prevalent in rural India. But it would be culturally blind to judge the first four as beyond redemption. Such a position ignores the psychology of the caste system and the way it deforms human beings. The first four need succour, a radical atmosphere, which will accept and respect their Dalit identity, and only a strong movement could provide them. The entire Dalit movement at one level starts from the assumption that the first four will be eventually transformed as the Panchama. That is also the understanding of the play. The task of transforming its own inadequate members is central to the movement and is also a pointer to its inbuilt idealism.

To take the debate further, wilful amnesia regarding one's own past on the part of an influential group means a firm riveting of the movement to the present. In terms of actual demands, what it means is that there will be considerable pressure on the movement to act as an instrument to safeguard and promote the interests of select groups, and the struggle is subjected to a definite process of conditioning and reflects only the aspirations of the city-based groups. It is to the credit of Babasaheb that he had identified this danger in the very beginning of the movement.

The second theme that Babasaheb introduces in the speech is the problem of defining alternative cultural values not only for the individual Dalit but for the entire movement. The state of amnesia induces a state of stupor discouraging the painful effort of building a new culture along with the rejection of the old. One thing that Ambedkar could never tolerate was this cultural inertia, and his entire life can be summed up as a relentless battle against this mental state, although this landed him in a great deal of problems in terms of defining the relationship between a movement and the structure of its memories. This was one of the areas where Ambedkar clashed bitterly with Gandhiji. The latter's use of Hindu symbols is heavily dependent on mainstream Hinduism and the method he used to invest them with radical energy could hardly inspire the non-initiate. Gandhiji's method of using Hinduism required a very profound kind of inwardness towards a very imaginative way of expressing dissent against it. Not only Harijan followers of Bapu, even his caste-Hindu followers, with the possible exception of Lohia and Rajaji, could follow the double-edged use of Hindu symbolism. A majority of them understood and practised it as celebratory acts thus missing the subversive dimensions. It was only during the Temple Entry Movement that they were placed in a confrontationist situation. But the enemies of Bapu had well understood the implications of his strategies to allow them to go unchallenged. His detractors succeeded where the disciples failed.

As far as Ambedkar was concerned, the dialectical method adopted by Gandhiji appeared complicated and too ineffective a route to fight the evils of Hinduism. Developing such inwardness towards Hinduism could easily degenerate into a pious and mild grumbling about the caste hierarchy, and this is what happened with the majority of the followers of Gandhiji. Babasaheb wanted a strong bedrock foundation to build a new Church (to alter Eliot slightly), and the *Vatapi Garbha* of Hinduism allows only the occasional eruption of protest only to be re-absorbed again in the quiescence of conservatism. But for the time being, the relevant thing for us is that the impassioned and sad reference to village India by Babasaheb almost sounds Gandhian, and the reverse reading is equally true. This shall be the theme of my narrative. After their encounter with each other during the 1930s Gandhiji and Ambedkar had internalized each other. This could happen only in the midst of a series of malignant clashes. The whole story is worth recounting for the richness of its symbolism.

II

Gandhiji's take-off point was that the problem of untouchability was a problem of the self, in this case the collective Hindu self. He had transformed the notion of individual self and the necessity of clearing the cobwebs of the caste ego was shifted to the level of the larger notion of the collective self. But he always stubbornly maintained the importance of internalizing these values at the personal level too. The Untouchable is a part of the Self. He saw the movement to eradicate untouchability as a sacred ritual of self-purification. He wrote in *Harijan* (15 April 1933)—'The movement for the removal of untouchability is one of self-purification.'[7] This religious emphasis on the self has to be situated against the background of what is neutrally referred to as the Poona Pact of September 1932. The pact was seen as a decisive point in the battle between the irreconcilable positions represented by Bapu and Babasaheb. Babasaheb has defined the problem in terms of building an independent political identity for Dalits in the structures of social, economic, and political powers, whereas for Gandhiji it was purely a religious question, that too an internal one for Hinduism. He did not at all take kindly to the challenge thrown by this new position aggressively represented by Ambedkar. At the level of visible historical evidence, it was Gandhiji who had won this battle, and even today this has remained as a deep scar in the minds of Ambedkarites. As rightly guessed by Ravinder Kumar, what prompted Ambedkar to accept the pact was his fear of massive retribution upon Dalits in the eventuality of Gandhiji's death.[8] Everything, however, was in favour of the Father of the Nation. Fortunately, he was not the sort of man who would gloat over ephemeral victories in history. For Gandhiji, truth was more important, and in his heart of hearts he had realized that his victory stood on shaky grounds. The Krishna of history had lent a helping hand to humble Karna. Gandhiji had to know the truth. Raghavan Iyer in his brilliant exposition of Gandhiji's ideas locates the complex significance of the Mahabharata in his life.

Gandhiji invoked the Mahabharata in support of his view that Dharma signifies the way of truth and non-violence and not the mere observance of ritual externals. The scriptures, he said, have given us two immortal maxims — 1. Ahimsa is the supreme law of Dharma and 2. There is no other law of Dharma than Sathya or truth.[9]

The Yerawada fast was an outcome of Gandhiji's committed *Dharmik* position both in its abstract and applied forms. Gandhiji, I think, this time deeply felt the tragic separation between dharma and sathya, and that Ambedkar's way of looking at untouchability could also be truth, and thus had to be tested. Thus began one of the most fascinating encounters in Indian history. The pages of *Harijan* are a moving witness to this. In the first issue itself (11 February 1933), both Ambedkar and Gandhiji came out with their authentic views on the question. Gandhiji considered some issues deeply and wrote in his usual forthright manner without any rhetoric. The question:

Why do you restrict the movement to the removal of untouchability only? Why not do away with the caste system altogether? If there is a difference between caste and caste and caste and untouchability, is it not one only of degree?[10]

Gandhiji's answer:

Untouchability as it is practised today in Hinduism in my opinion, is a sin against God and man and is, therefore like a poison slowly eating into the very vitals of Hinduism. There are innumerable castes in India. They are a social institution and at one time they served a very useful purpose, as, perhaps, they are even doing now to a certain extent ... There is nothing sinful about them. They retard the material progress of those who are labouring under them. They are no bar to the spiritual progress. The difference, therefore, between caste system and untouchability is not one of degree, but of kind.

These views, along with Gandhiji's belief in *varnashrama* dharma have been attacked by radicals and are said to be at the core of his conservative social philosophy. In a way this can also be read as a statement about equality of castes with which majority of Hindu liberals would have no difficulty. Particularly, the upper and middle caste intelligentsia would define the positive aspects of the caste system in terms of its capacity to provide its members with a feeling of identity. These qualities would, certainly, have a positive appeal in the context of homogenizing tendencies of international capital. But from the viewpoint of Dalits the picture is radically different. Instead of offering a sense of identity and security the caste system constantly threatens them with humiliation and insult. Similarly, the problem of identity also carries a stigma, which cannot easily be erased. Against this background, any attempt to defend or show the caste system in a positive light is suspect from the viewpoint of the Dalit movement. It was this position, precisely, that Babasaheb articulated in the first issue of *Harijan*.

The out-caste is a by-product of the caste-system. There will be outcastes as there are castes. Nothing can emancipate the outcastes except the destruction of the caste-system. Nothing can help to save Hindus and ensure their survival in the coming struggle except the purging of this odious and vicious dogma...[11]

This brief statement, interestingly enough, was made in the context of differing from Gandhiji, and this has served as a manifesto of the Dalit movement over the last two decades. The tenor of this statement has carved out a distinct identity for the Dalit movement, which is different from other forms of Shudra dissent. Gandhiji's endorsement of the caste system came in for harsh criticism in the 1930s itself. He could never repudiate it totally, although he conceded the legitimacy of some attacks in the mid-1930s. Ram Manohar Lohia, the most imaginative leader of Left-Gandhians, analysed the implications of the caste system in certain categories which had more affinity with Ambedkarite terms.[12] Gandhiji in his dislike of the dehumanizing tendencies of modern civilization became somewhat soft towards the equally dangerous structures of the caste society.[13] Lohia had no such illusions about the caste system, hence he could develop a more subtle theory of injustices in traditional India and their techniques of self-perpetuation.

One could also debate the issue of differences between Gandhiji and the radicals employing different categories. The former did not find any fault with the 'constitutive rules' of the caste system, and his conviction was that something went wrong with the regulative aspects of it.[14] Only a strong movement could correct this, thus restoring its original vitality. The radicals, however, did not agree with this: the difference between constitutive and regulative rules was not tenable both ethically and philosophically. The only alternative was to define and articulate different sets of rules, which were a negation of the previous sets at all levels. Interestingly, though Ambedkar had rejected the Gandhian definition of constitutive rules of the caste system, he, nevertheless, played the game along the rules laid by Bapu.[15] This becomes clear when one studies the Temple Entry Movements led by Babasaheb and his followers. Two Temple Entry satyagrahas, the first one at the Parvati temple of 1929 and the second one at the Kalaram temple in Nasik (1930–5) deserve special attention. Although, in the Parvati temple Ambedkar was not physically present, he was the source of inspiration for it. Eleanor Zelliot sums up their importance thus.

The effort was conducted in the Gandhian style, but it was not approved by Gandhiji or Congress. Gandhiji's name was not mentioned but the technique and inspiration for the satyagraha undoubtedly were drawn from Gandhiji's teachings. Organised by Ambedkar and local Mahar leaders, the Kalaram satyagraha involved thousands of Untouchables in intermittent efforts to enter the temple and to participate in the annual temple procession. As in the case of the Parvati satyagraha of Poona the attempt was unsuccessful. The outcome of the Kalaram Satyagraha, however was not only further disillusionment with the satyagraha method and the attitude of the Congress, but also a rejection of Hinduism and a strengthening of the separatist political stance then developing among the Untouchables.[16]

Ambedkar succeeded in drawing attention towards inbuilt contradictions of the symbolic politics of the Temple Entry Movement, and a study of them would be quite relevant to the present-day Dalit movement as well, since the temple has remained at the centre of popular Hinduism.

Let us pause here a while and reflect on the symbolism of the temple and Gandhiji's relationship with it. In Hindu culture, the temple has always been both a source of spiritual joy and a symbol of material power. Basavanna, the great saint-leader of the 12th century Veerashaiva movement of Karnataka, rejected the very notion of the temple which had become an instrument of power. He saw the human body itself as a temple. But, Vaishnavites treat the issue differently, and in their symbolism the temple has a predominant place. Gandhiji had a very ambiguous attitude towards the temple signifying a deeper conflict within him, between his Vaishnavite attachment to the temple and a sort of Advaitin denial of the same.[17] In an issue of *Harijan*

(8 July 1944) Gandhiji says—'... for I have always believed God to be without form'. Coupled with this is the fact that he rarely visited temples during the period of the Temple Entry Movement. In Gandhiji there existed two personalities: the radical spiritualist of tradition who, like Basavanna, upholds the human body as a temple and the second one—a modern interventionist seeking to influence the course of historical events. He tried to achieve a synthesis of the two but not always successfully. Subtle failures in this regard often assumed fierce forms to ridicule him. Basavanna would not have presented one thing for the self, a different thing for the other. The anti-temple stand of radical spiritualists was irreconcilable with the Vaishnavite veneration of the temple. Probably Gandhiji had realized this contradiction, and tried to achieve a synthesis of both positions by using the same method positing a difference between constitutive and regulative rules. It was an effort to save the spiritual significance of the temple, simultaneously explaining its proneness to decay. Here is the difficult exercise undertaken by Gandhiji (*Harijan*, 11 March 1933).

Temples of stone and mortar are nothing else than a natural extension of these human temples and though they were in their conception undoubtedly habitations of God-like human temples they have been subject to the same law of decay as the latter.[18]

Even this attempt could not satisfy the critics. Surprisingly, it was Rabindranath Tagore who disagreed with Gandhiji's unauthentic fascination towards the temple and wrote a reply which was published in the *Harijan* 1 April 1933 issue.

Dear Mahatmaji,
   It is needless to say that I do not at all relish the idea of divinity being enclosed in a brick and mortar temple for the special purpose of exploitation by a particular group of people. I strongly believe that it is possible for the simple-hearted people to realize the presence of God in the open air, in a surrounding free from all artificial obstruction.[19]

Gandhiji, of course, did not offer to elaborate his position on temples further.

   In the way Gandhiji handled the Hindu symbolism and temple entry one could also identify the merger of two strands: the exegetical exercise of a *Pouranika* and the shrewd political interventionist who has an eye on the immediate response of the people. The *Pouranika* is always moved by an intense desire to reinterpret texts and symbols, and the mythological rigour of this exercise lies in his capacity to separate the constitutive and regulative rules in an effective manner. The origin has a different meaning in his/her constant refrain; the imposed imagination of the *Pouranika* can make texts and symbols to signify the desired meaning. And this was, undoubtedly, the Gandhian mode of engagement with Hindu symbolism. The political interventionist and realist in him had understood the deeper craving for temples among Harijans in the absence of other strong alternatives. As said earlier, temples have always been a source of spiritual joy and a symbol of material pride. Dalits, usually, assert their new identity by demanding temple entry and equal religious rights. It is intensely real to them on both these counts. When a given religious tradition is insulting to their self-respect, the Dalits assert their dignity by rejecting to perform their traditional roles. In such cases the position of the Dalit movement is fairly simple—it has to support such moves, whereas in the context of temple entry the movement faces many contradictions. By supporting the move it suffers from the guilt of supporting the very symbolic structure that it vows to fight. Stubborn refusal amounts to neglecting the important dimension of temples as a structure of material power and pride—this is apart from the fear of getting alienated from the people.

There is also another significant dimension to this problem. Right to worship the same God, although through different means and forms, has been one of the major motifs of the medieval Bhakti movement, the story of Bedara Kannappa, the hunter, which is available in both medieval Bhakti literatures of Tamil and Kannada, is a classic example of this, where he worships Shiva in a 'non-vegetarian' way much to the horror of the vegetarian upper caste priests.

Only 'believing' Gandhians could conceive of launching and sustaining the Temple Entry Movement. With others it could be an act of the bad faith. Playing along the Gandhian rule, Babasaheb soon realized both the bad faith dimension and the paradoxes involved in it, for he had already been tormented by cruel doubts about the very desirability of seeking solutions to the problems of untouchables within the framework of Hinduism. And then Ambedkar did not have the element of *Pouranika* in him. In this sense he had all the characteristics of the first generation Buddhists even before he formally became one. No tortuous hermeneutics. A simple straightforward reading of meaning has always been Ambedkar's strength. In the hands of lesser people, exegetical and interpretative exercise could easily degenerate into bad faith. Ambedkar was quick to act, and bid goodbye to Hindusim in 1935.

What made Ambedkar's position significant was not that the majority of the untouchables supported him. On the contrary there is enough evidence to show that they were on the other side. Influential leaders like M.C. Rajah were more favourably disposed towards Gandhiji on this question. But Ambedkar had no use for the *Pouranika* talent. Hinduism is the very embodiment of Avidya, and it can never be rejuvenated—this was his position.[20]

While playing along the Gandhian rule of temple entry, Babasaheb was almost simultaneously trying to articulate and build an alternative mode. In this regard the Mahad Struggle of 1927 to assert the untouchable's right to use public water demands serious discussion. There is a world of difference between temple and tank, and Ambedkar's way of leading that struggle serves as a useful guide to enter the world of difference that existed between him and Gandhiji in these years. In Ambedkar's Mahad model, the emphasis was on treating the question of untouchability as a civil rights' issue. In that case any one, Christians, Muslims, and secularists can support the struggle without feeling that they were trespassing into the private affairs of a religion. In Kerala, Vaikkam Satyagraha was about to acquire such character, but Gandhiji resisted efforts to secularize the issue. For him it was purely an internal religious affair of Hinduism. Even modern democratic methods have no role in this regard. If one treats the problem of untouchability as a civil rights' issue, naturally, other socio-economic and political forces join together to build a formidable front against the religious rights' approach. In fact, in the pages of *Harijan* itself such challenges went on increasing thus laying a great deal of emphasis on total or economic uplift of the community. Gandhiji himself records the resolution passed at Agra's Harijan Conference. This is an excerpt from the resolution in question. (*Harijan*, 2 September 1933.)

Harijan Movement lays stress on the Temple Entry problem more than on economical and educational problems. The former item of the programme is not desirable for the Harijans, since it will produce slave mentality, spirit of blind devotion and many other evils, which will go to mar the efficiency of the Harijans. The Pujari-Samaj will dominate the Harijans and they will become slaves of Pujaris. Hence it is highly necessary that great emphasis must be laid on the educational and economic aspects of the progress. Inter-caste marriage and inter-dining must be on the programme of the movement.[21]

While agreeing with the first line of the above cited resolution Gandhiji said: But uplift will not be complete without throwing open the temples. The throwing open of temples will be an admission of the religious equality of Harijans. Regarding the demand for inter-caste marriage and inter-dining, Gandhiji was not an unequivocal supporter of these. He did not want to provoke the wrath of *Sanatani*s on these issues. Even while agreeing with his own son's inter-caste marriage, he tried to play down the obvious radical implications of the event. Such vacillations on the part of Gandhiji made him suspect in the eyes of radicals.

Apart from all these things Babasaheb had more fundamental difficulties with the Gandhian model, and these can be summed up as follows. Since Gandhiji saw the movement to eradicate untouchability as a sacred ritual of self-purification, it had placed a great deal of moral responsibility on the caste-Hindu self. A profound ethical halo would envelop which would almost look spiritual. This would in turn generate awe in the minds of Harijans who were attracted towards Gandhiji and the Congress—and this was precisely what happened during the pre-independence days.

The agony of the spiritual cleansing of the Hindu self leading to self-purification had acquired tones of public grandeur, and in a subtle way though, led to the glorification of the individual self. The Gandhian tales of sacrifice, courage, and struggle against the Hindu orthodoxy almost became a household talk in those areas where nationalist struggle was popular. In other places it acquired a legendary character inviting both ridicule and veneration. The Gandhian grit and determination generated gratitude in the hearts of Harijans. Even the Sanatanis were not left untouched. Being deeply moved by the epic fast of Gandhiji for the great Harijan cause a Sanatani Brahmin in UP even cleaned the latrines of a government primary school before a big crowd of people in Dilkhuva on 18 May 1933.

The guilt-ridden Hindu self badly needed the untouchables to expiate its guilt. The heroic stature of the caste-Hindu reformer further dwarfed the Harijan personality. Literatures of our languages are full of such complex and yet moving encounters, and it can be safely said that this is one of the central themes of Indian literature which was produced during the phase of nationalism.

The grandeur, the agony, the moving romanticism of the Gandhian project of self-purification also came to be seen as its Achilles' heel, but it had succeeded in creating a leadership among Harijans who felt grateful. Interestingly, not all Harijans were moved by the Gandhian act. There were enough critics and doubters who were more than keen to present a realistic assessment of the programme. Not surprisingly *Harijan* itself (4 March 1933) carries such a critical piece, which acts as a counterpoint to Gandhian idealism. The untouchable correspondent portrays the relationship between the caste-Hindu reformer and Harijans on these lines.

All have to come to us as patrons. Hardly has anyone come as friend and equal, let alone as servant. Your provincial organisation is no exception. It is difficult for a Harijan to approach its chief man without fear and trembling.[22]

Gandhiji had agreed with the bitter tenor of the correspondent's argument and conceded that there is a tendency towards self-glorification, but in the end he upheld the correctness of the path he had advocated.

In the intensely moving romantic tragedy of self-purification (à la Martin Greene) there was scope for only one hero, that is, Gandhiji himself. Extend the metaphor further, it is the ultimate celebration of a hero's capacity to suffer spiritual isolation. But, unfortunately, the script could only be staged by caste-Hindu incarnations of Gandhiji. He himself wrote to admit that 'what mattered was not so much the entry of Harijans to temples as the conversion of the orthodox to the belief that it is wrong to prevent Harijans from entering temples'—this is that famous or notorious 'conversion of heart' theory. The radical critics accused that the heart of the caste-Hindu was scattered all over—in land, wealth, property, socio-political power, and unless you transformed these, it was difficult to effect the conversion of hearts of caste-Hindus. In the early months of 1933 Gandhiji could never agree with such a position but he reflected on it quite deeply.

Even philosophically, the Gandhian model provided the caste-Hindu self with much textured interiority, and what generated the real tensions was the way it initiated the self-conscious Hindu reformer into the sacred ritual of confrontation against the orthodoxy. There was very little scope for the Congress Harijan leader to develop interesting and useful models of praxis from within. That was the basic limitation of the text: Sugreeva, Hanumantha, and Guha can never aspire to act the major part displacing the hero in the Ramayana. Only Rama is the hero and Ambedkar could never settle for the roles of Hanumantha and Sugreeva.

It is quite difficult to say whether Gandhiji had visualized the nature of the fallout of the practice of self-purification. The Congress–Harijan leadership turned out to be quite soft and pliable—the two qualities that are quite pleasing to the hegemonic forces of traditional village society. The paradox was that Gandhiji challenged and sought to shake the very foundations of Hindu society, but the Congress Harijans did not pose any real threat to the social and cultural establishment. The awed leadership remained pious Hindus by and large. Because of this, unfortunately, many admirable qualities like for instance, their moral integrity, incorruptibility, rootedness in the community, and strong common sense of the senior generation of Gandhian

Harijans came to be disregarded. It was even satirized by the new generation of Dalits.

The tragedy of the Gandhian project of penance was that it came to mean different things to different people. For the idealist caste-Hindu it was a cross he had to inevitably bear, for the angry Dalit it was a subtle way of domesticating the radical energy of humiliated communities, and lastly for the conservative Hindu forces it eventually meant, although after a great deal of resistance, a difficult exercise in repressive tolerance.

Babasaheb had no other option but to reject the Gandhian model. He had realized that this model had successfully transformed Harijans as objects in a ritual of self-purification, the ritual being performed by those who had larger heroic notions of their individual selves. In the theatre of history, in a play of such a script, the untouchables would never become heroes in their own right, they are just mirrors for a hero to look at his own existentialist angst and despair, maybe even glory.

Gandhiji had staked his entire life on the question of untouchability, and that too for tackling it in a particular way. It is fundamentally a matter of religious right. Ambedkar opposed this, as discussed earlier, right from the beginning. In fact, Gandhiji's previous fast was undertaken to resist other modes of tackling the same question. The importance of his second epic fast in May 1933 has to be understood against this background. In the context of the first fast, the aims and objectives were clear: they were directed against the attempts to translate the problem of untouchables into the parlance of modern-day democratic processes in a colonial context. Such translation, Gandhiji seriously believed, could eventually prevent the 'natural growth' of the suppressed classes and would remove the incentive to make honourable amends from the suppressors. Such a position itself is a product of a firm belief in an organic community, which is essentially different from a modern democratic society. The very notion of an organic community—a favourite theme in the post-Enlightenment European thought—had special appeal for Gandhiji, and he thought that contradictions of this society are not irreconcilable. In the framework of an organic community there is scope for natural resistance, which leads to equally natural ways of solving a problem. Such an arrangement would not wreck the fabric of a given society. Ambedkar totally disagreed with this position and its strategies for social transformation. In his letter to A.V. Thakkar, he had clearly stated his perspective on the matter in question in 1932: civil rights and equal opportunities in economic matters and social intercourse. Gandhiji's first fast was precisely against this.

In his first statement regarding his second fast (May 1933) Gandhiji had specifically declared that it was particularly against himself. He explains the background of the tempest that was raging within him which was insistent on an unconditional and irrevocable fast for twenty-one days.

During all these months since September last, I have been studying the correspondence and literature and holding prolonged discussions with men and women, learned and ignorant, Harijans and non-Harijans. The evil is far greater than I had thought it to be. It cannot be eradicated by money, external organisation and even political power for Harijans, although all these three are necessary. But to be effective, they must follow or at least accompany inward health, inward organisation and inward power. In other words, self-purification; this can only come by fasting and prayer. We may not approach the God of Truth in the arrogance of strength, but in the meekness of the weak and the helpless.

But the mere fast of the body is nothing without the will behind it. It must be a genuine confession of the inner fast, and irrepressible longing to express truth and nothing but truth. Therefore those only are privileged to fast for the cause of truth who have worked for it and who have love in them even for opponents, who are free from animal passion and who have abjured earthly possessions and ambition.[23]

This statement is rich because of its undercurrents and the complexity of the suggested meanings. When Gandhiji says that it will not be eradicated by money, external organizations, and even political power, he is translating Ambedkar into the language of spiritualists, as they see such efforts to achieve material progress. The ideas of economic opportunities are translated as money and civil rights; and social intercourse as political power. Incidentally, these three have been defined as major priorities for Ambedkar. Translating the other viewpoint, even while debating, is usually a tricky job, and this is wherein traditional Indian opponents are mutilated beyond recognition. But here Gandhiji excels in his job as a demolition expert without resorting to subtle exercises in logic: he does it just by reducing the other viewpoint to its essentials. But in this context he doesn't use the 'reductio ad absurdum' method, for Gandhiji was never known to use *vitanda vada* to further his arguments. If B.K. Matilal were to write a history of those who used vitanda in the twentieth century he could not have found an uncontested place for Bapu in it. In any case Lenin would have topped the list, for he had acquired talents for dialectical thinking from the guru, Marx himself. (Many writers on Indian philosophy including Matilal translate vitanda as dialectical method.)

Neverthless, Gandhiji achieves the same Nagarjunian goal but by a different route; by reducing it to essentials the other viewpoint is trivialized.

The trivialization seems deadly because it denies the legitimacy of spiritual reasons that Ambedkar gave to strengthen his dissent. The point is that Gandhiji chose to ignore that dimension of Ambedkar's personality. According to Gandhiji, the materialist approach was the weakness of his adversary and for Ambedkar spirituality was the weakness of Gandhiji: apparently these exclusivist positions concealed the simultaneous existence of both materialist and spiritual viewpoints in both of them. It was quite a decisive question in defining the parameters of the conflict. The line cited below suggests both the firm conviction and willingness to learn from the encounter. In it, Gandhiji, a victor in the recently concluded battle, solemnly admits, 'one may not approach the God of truth in the arrogance of strength'; hence the long consultations with others, but the opponent is very much there although he too is to be loved.

I think this is the crucial difference between the two epoch-making fasts: in the first one Gandhiji wanted to win, in the second, he was seeking truth. Arrogance of strength had disappeared in him or the purpose of the fast was to fight it. The transformation of the external conflict into an internal one was complete. This was the moment of illumination where the distinction between inner and external worlds disappears.

One can compare this experience of Gandhiji with the brilliant poetic passages of the Marathi classic 'Jnaneshwari' which describes the state of Arjuna when confronted with *Vishwaroopadarshana* of Krishna. I am using this exaggerated analogy (*utprekshalankara*) only to highlight the complexity of the experience.

From a different angle, Renford Bambrough, in one of his Wittgensteinian essays, considers the meaning of such situations and reflects on some of the central themes they throw up.

That the philosopher who is alone in his room, meditating, confessing, engaging in criticism and self-criticism can be at the same time in contact and in conflict with others in the Academy, in the Agora, in the temple.[24]

Such conflict—is it internal or external?—is resolved by the conversion from the one side to another of the person who is the scene and the subject of the conflict. Here my purpose is to show that this was precisely what had happened with Gandhiji. At this stage let me confess to the secret of my methodology, for I have adopted the working patterns of metaphor and imagination which bring together undisclosed affinities.[25] One is forced to give up the method of natural and social sciences where the examination of verifiable evidence leads to scientific conclusions. But metaphors and metaphorical reading work differently: they don't organize material in a system-making method. They take a leap and illuminate a truth defying all worldly logic, and this meaning could not have been reached through the route of normal social sciences. The great Kannada poet Bendre describes the birth of metaphor in these lines: 'Flights of fancy rode on the back of the bee/Rhythms were borne to wings of the sharpening wind. A lightning smile flashed and vanished'. The method of the social science is like the working of the earthworm; it painstakingly prepares the earth for the farmer. Well, the bee is a different species altogether.

III

Treat the May 1933 fast like the central metaphor in a narrative poem: a whole range of images then start revolving around it. Particularly, the image of a Harijan boy who went to meet Gandhiji in the evening at 6 o'clock on 8th May, after waiting for some hours, keeps haunting. This puts the birth of the Dalit movement in a totally different light. Mahadev Desai narrates this entire story with touching sincerity.[26] The boy had come to see Gandhiji to seek his help about a scholarship; he was simply anxious to secure an assurance. The boy had to pass through much misery and it was with difficulty that he had scraped together money to purchase a pair of sandals to come to the jail. Till this point I was more or less using the sentences of Mahadev Desai to tell the story with slight modifications. Now I will let Desai himself describe the rest:

'Well are your satisfied? I give you the assurance', he (Gandhiji) said to the boy. 'No' said he covering Gandhiji's feet with the flowers he had brought 'Why should I ask others? Why I have no faith in them. I have only in you. Everyone else is insincere'.

'But if all my associates are insincere', said Gandhiji, 'then I must be the insincerest of them all. You had better not trust me either'.

The boy had with courage kept on the feigned irony upto now but he now burst into tears.

'Why then are you leaving us? You yourself say that your associates are impure. There is no purity around you and you must fast yourself to death'. He uttered these words sobbing.

'But why do you say I am leaving you? I am not'.

'How can we believe it'? He said with a fresh outburst of tears.

'I assure you, I am not going to die. Come along, we enter into a contract. On the noon of Monday 29th of May you come with an orange and I shall break my fast with its juice and then we shall talk about your scholarship. Are you satisfied?'

He beamed with joy, the tears had fled. 'Yes' he said. 'So you will keep the contract', said Gandhiji, every one including him filling the prison cell with laughter.

So ends the first part of the story. It was more than poetic justice that a Harijan boy would offer orange juice to break the epic fast, which was undertaken for the cause of the untouchables. So the day arrived for which hundreds and thousands had prayed. Mahadev Desai had been expecting the Harijan boy who had entered into a contract with Gandhiji to offer orange juice. No, the boy did not turn up. Desai did not know his address either. The orange juice was supplied not by him but by the kind hostess, Lady Thackersey who perhaps felt the luckiest woman that day. Mark it, the orange juice was supplied by Lady Thackersey. Among those present on that solemn occasion were Professor Wadia, Dr Ansari, Kaka Saheb, and Thakkar. The story is slowly abandoning its realist character and acquiring a symbolic note. It is becoming an image: to be fair to historical accuracy the doorkeeper had flung the doors open to all Harijans, and the first and only garland offered to Gandhiji before the break of the fast was that of a Harijan girl.

Well, why did the boy betray the contract? What happened? Let Desai, the truthful narrator, resume the story.

I have already told the readers that the Harijan youth who had been booked to see Gandhiji with an orange at midday, 29th May, had failed to keep the appointment. I was not quite happy about it for the simple reason that I felt in his place he should not have failed to do so. It was not without a pang that I told everyone that the newspaper story of the youth having come was false. But on the 1st of June I got a letter (postage due) in which the youth complained that he did come but that he had failed to gain admittance. I immediately asked him to come with an orange although it was too late. He came and told me that he could not come at noon on the 29th because he was employed somewhere during the college vacation, but that he came late in the evening when he was not admitted. Next day he told me the true story which should make us all think and feel the moral ruin that the cancer of untouchability has wrought. He said he had come during the fast once or twice and had followed the progress of the fast with anxious interest, but on the last day his courage had failed him. He felt that he was too humble an individual to be admitted to the function that day; he also feared that his good fortune (if he came and was advertised by the newspaper) would excite the envy of some of his fellows and he might lose the little he had. It was a strange mixture of feelings, which had overcome him. But all of them are to be traced to the brand of untouchability that he bore. He had not hesitated to come twice to the jail and send in his name to be admitted as an untouchable visitor, but on an occasion of this kind he felt that he lacked the strength to take hold of the luck that had appeared before him. It is we who are responsible for fostering this feeling of undue self-abasement (*Harijan*, 10 June 1933).

The way Mahadev Desai reads the story reveals the inability of a certain kind of sentimental Gandhians to understand the complexity of the educated Dalit pschye. What is seen as lack of strength by Desai could as well be profound uneasiness regarding the nature of the whole Gandhian enterprise. Desai talks about abstract historical forces that have shaped the Harijan boy, but the boy is responding to the concrete situation that is glaring at him in the present. Desai gets sentimental and loses his capacity to notice the existence of many subtle and crude ironies of the situation, he doesn't even see the tragic gap that exists between the master and his disciples. Right from the beginning the boy has retained his sense of irony and discrimination and he also knew that what was tragic with the master had easily degenerated into farce with his *shishyas*. By lying, the boy was trying to protect himself from the danger of becoming an object of holy pity. The guilt of the past can humiliate its own source in the present. Metaphorically speaking, the Harijan boy who took a decision not to keep the appointment with Gandhiji was reborn as a Dalit youth. In a different sense on that fateful afternoon, like Desai, he too came to the conclusion that there was no difference between Gandhiji and his followers. Ambedkar says that Gandhiji's enthusiasm for the Temple Entry Movement petered out in the 1930s itself. The book *What the Congress and Gandhiji have done to the Untouchables* has a couple of angry and ironical passages regarding this. At the level of concrete historical evidence what Ambedkar says is true and one can notice a definite shift in the orientation of the programme by Gandhians. In an issue of *Harijan* (28 December 1935), C. Rajagopalachari had even declared— 'untouchability is not yet gone. But the revolution is really over, and what remains is but the removal of the debris. The monster has been killed'. The naivete of this position is amazing, and this coming from a shrewd, intellectual politician like CR makes it more mysterious.

There is sufficient evidence to prove that Ambedkar and Gandhiji had transformed each other. The latter extended the very scope and definition of, the Harijan cause. It was no more a question of mere untouchability. It had become a larger holistic understanding of the untouchables. Because of the confrontation both of them had changed their emphasis: to put it crudely, Gandhiji had taken over economics from Babasaheb. Ambedkar had internalized the importance of religion. Gandhiji adopted the primacy of economic uplift, which was intelligently argued by non-Gandhian Dalits, and treated it as a question of rejuvenation of village India. In other words, Gandhiji sought to achieve a holistic philosophy of life having the Harijan question as the fulcrum, but the shift was construed as the conclusion of a successful revolution. Gandhiji himself explains the expansion of the scope of Harijan cause (21 December 1934).

Some readers have taken exception to the way in which the columns of 'Harijan' are being occupied with the development of the village industries scheme, and some other [sic] have welcomed the change in what they had thought was a monotony of presentation. Either opinion is probably hasty. Any problem connected with the welfare of village as a whole must be intimately related to the Harijans, who represent over a sixth part of India's population. If a village gets good rice and flour, Harijans will benefit by the change as much as the rest of the population. But there is a special sense in which Harijans will benefit. Tanning and the whole of the raw hide work is their monopoly and economically this will occupy the best part of the new scheme.[27]

Such issues have formed the basis of the Ambedkar–Gandhiji encounter. But from the viewpoint of the present, there is a compelling necessity to achieve a synthesis of the two. They clash, quite bitterly at that, at the level of major details but are complementary at a fundamental level. It is not an easy task to iron out the difference between two masters, but the necessities of the present are forcing us to see their inner commonality. This is a hermeneutical task of refuting the extremist positions, which pose themselves as mutually exclusive and even threaten to cancel out each other. To describe the situation using the Buddhist dialetic method of Nagarajuna—both Gandhian and Ambedkarite positions had hardened themselves and they could not see the true nature of reality.

In the final analysis, what do we learn from Gandhiji which is of central relevance to the Dalit movement today? The liberation of the untouchable is organically linked to the emancipation of village India, and the vice versa is equally true. In this context the Gandhian merger of the Harijan cause with the regeneration of the entire village has a great deal of relevance, but this enthusiasm has to be slightly altered from the Dalit perspective since village India is also seen virtually as holes of hell by the untouchables. But there is no other alternative. One should transform it totally as a livable and humane place. In other words, Gandhian endorsement of village India has to be whetted by the Ambedkarite scepticisim; this is particularly essential regarding certain strategies of economic empowerment of Harijans that Gandhiji suggests. The Khadi programme was taken up in an ambitious way by Gandhiji because simple weaving was almost an exclusive speciality of Harijans (*Harijan* 27 October 1933). [28] One need not take these ideas literally. The best way is to take them as a model of economic rejuvenation of the entire village economy with special emphasis on lower castes and untouchables. There are areas suggested by Gandhiji in his village recon-struction programme where his idealization of the rural society ignores the working of the caste ethos: one such programme is village tanning, and Gandhiji places a great deal of emphasis on this most useful and indispens-able industry' (*Harijan*, 7 September 1934).[29] Such ideas just cannot be accepted. The Ambedkarite insistence on the historic necessity for Dalits to give up such jobs is more realistic and radical in its implications.

In the caste-Hindu mind tanning is inerasably linked with the untouch-ables, and that is one of the major sources of cultural stigma. Harijans need not be delinked from villages. In fact one of the surest ways of empowering is to privilege them with independent means of subsistence. But achieving this end through means of tainted professions will be counterproductive from the viewpoint of Dalits. As suggested earlier, one should take the village-centred vision of Gandhiji and treat it with Ambedkarite distrust of the rural society to cure its romantic excesses. The lower castes in India have nowhere else to go, and their will to transform the existing rural society should be strengthened. Gandhiji weaved a whole complex network of political, economic, social, and spiritual ideas around the central question of Harijans; Dalit movement today is compelled to undertake an identical task. Forces of international capital will seek to destroy rural India. Along with it the lower castes are going to be maimed economically, culturally, and socially.

To conclude, in what way did Gandhiji transform Ambedkar? Babasaheb had always opposed to treat the question of untouchability as a religious question; he accepted the primacy of religion in the matter. He did to religion what Gandhiji did to the idea of economic uplift. It is a pattern of acceptance and altering the same. Religion is the crucial thing, true. Give up Hinduism itself was the Ambedkarite alteration. The 1935 Yeola Declara-tion of Ambedkar that he would not die a Hindu was an act of recognizing the legitimacy of the Gandhian mode although rejecting the choice in which the solution was sought. Economic uplift is the effective remedy, true; let us rejuvenate the entire village not the selective mobility: such was the Gandhian transformation of the Ambedkarite idea. Even regarding the caste system Gandhiji had to change his soft approval of it: in the *Harijan* issue of 16 November 1935, he simply declared that caste has to go much to the consternation of his orthodox supporters. He even criticized the cruel restrictions on inter-dining and inter-caste marriage, a refreshing change compared to his earlier vacillation regarding these.

Needless to mention at this stage that both Gandhiji and Ambedkar can and should be made complementary to each other. Surely such efforts will be met with stiff opposition from hardened ideologues and researchers, and they are bound to unearth fresh evidence to fuel the fire between the two. One way of fighting such tendencies, apart from pointing out the political necessity of such hermeneutic exercise, is to file a philosophical caveat highlighting the notion of ontological difference to distinguish between contingent details of historical fact and the truth of a deeper historical concern.[30] At the level of deeper historical truth the conflicting fact disappears to reveal the underlying unity. The theoretical project of this entire book draws its sustenance from the notion of ontological difference. In this case, accepting and examining the difference leads to the truth of dynamic unity.

Notes and References

1. For a very useful edition of *Harijan* (in nineteen volumes), see Joan Bondurant (ed.), *Harijan*: A journal of Applied Journalism, 1933–5, New York: Garland Publishing Inc, 1973. Separate references are given below for all passages cited in the text.

2. For an understanding of reform and protest movements among the lower castes, readers can refer to the following studies, and I have made allusive references to them in my study.

    For a critical survey of literature on social movements see T.K. Oommen, *Protest and Change*: *Studies in Social Movements*, New Delhi: Sage, 1991.

    M.S.A. Rao, *Social Movements in India*: *Backward Class Movements*, Vol. 1, New Delhi: Macmillan, 1979.

    M.S.A. Rao, *Social Movements and Social Transformation in India*, New Delhi, Macmillan, 1979.

    G.A. Oddie, *Social Protest in India*: *British Protestant Missionaries and Social Reform*, New Delhi: Manohar, 1979.

    Rosalind O'Hanlon, *Caste, Conflict and Ideology*: *Mahatma Joti Rao Phule and Low-Caste Protest in Nineteenth Century Western India*, Delhi: Cambridge University Press, 1985.

    John C.B. Webster, The *Dalit Christians*, Delhi: Indian Society for Promoting Christian Knowledge (ISPCK), 1992.

    Abdul Malik Mujahid, *Conversion to Islam*: *Untouchables' Strategy for' Protest in India*, Chambersburg: Anima Publications, 1989.

    Mark Juergensmeyer, *Religion as Social Vision*: *Movement against Untouchability in 20th Century*, Berkeley: University of California Press, 1982.

    Sumit Sarkar, *Modern India*, New Delhi: Macmillan, 1983.

    Robert L. Hardgrave Jr, The *Nadars of Tamil Nadu*: *the Political Culture of a Community in Change*, Berkeley: University of California Press, 1969.

V. Ramakrishna, *Social Reform in Andhra*, Delhi: Vikas Publishing House, 1983.

Saurabh Dube, *Religion, Identity and Authority Among the Satnamis in Colonial India* (unpublished). University of Cambridge 1992. I am grateful to Dr Dube for having given me an opportunity to read his thesis.

Susan Bayly, *Saints, Goddesses and Kings. Muslims and Christians in South Indian Society*, Cambridge: Cambridge University Press, 1989.

Gail Omvedt, *Cultural Revolt in a Colonial Society: The Non-Brahman Movement in Western India: 1873-1930*, Bombay: Scientific Socialist Education Trust, 1976.

Eugene Irschick, *Politics and Social Conflict in South India: The Non-Brahman Movement and Tamil Separatism*, Berkeley and Los Angeles: University of California Press, 1969.

For a detailed study of the Mahima Movement see Faninandham Dev 'Socio-Political Unrest in Nineteenth Century Orissa and Rise of Mahima Dharma', (a paper presented at a seminar on Social Dimensions of Religious Movements, 3–7 May 1993 at Indian Institute of Advanced Study, Shimla).

3. Washbrook, *Emergence of Provincial Politics—the Madras Presidency*, New Delhi: Vikas Publishing House, 1977. Particularly two chapters in this book 'The Vocabulary of Communal Politics' and 'Home Rule League, Justice Party and Congress' are of special relevance to our theme.

4. S. Chandrashekar, *Nationalism in South India*, unpublished monograph, Department of History, Bangalore University, Bangalore. This work has a detailed discussion on non-Brahmin Movements in South India.

5. Bjorn Hettne uses this concept in the context of analysing the politics of princely Mysore. See Bjorn Hettne, *The Political Economy of Indirect Rule*, New Delhi: Ambika Publications, 1978, p. 43.

    Also see for a discussion of non-Brahmin politics of Princely Mysore. James Manor, *Political Change in an Indian State, Mysore, 1917–1955*, New Delhi: Manohar, 1977, pp. 58–73.

6. Bhagvan Das (ed.), *Thus Spoke Ambedkar*, Vol. 1, Jullandar: Bheem Patrika Publications, 1963, pp. 88–9.

7. *Harijan*, Vol. 1, 1933, p. 8.

8. Ravinder Kumar, *Gandhi, Ambedkar and The Poona Pact*, New Delhi: 1985, p. 21.

9. Raghavan Iyer, *The Moral and Political Thought of Mahatma Gandhi*, Delhi: Oxford University Press, 1973, p. 226.

10. *Harijan*, Vol. 1, 1933, p. 2.

11. Ibid., p. 3.

12. Ram Manohar Lohia, *The Caste System*, Hyderabad: Samata Vidyalaya Nivas, sec. rpt. This entire book is an evidence to the theoretical affinity between Lohia and Ambedkar.

13. See for a discussion of Gandhiji's critique of modern civilization Bhiku Parekh, *Gandhiji's Political Philosophy*, London: Macmillan, 1982, pp. 11–36.

14. These concepts arose in a discussion with my friend Dr Satya Goutam of Chandigarh University on the possibility of using Wittgensteinian categories to study such situations.

15. For a study of the Temple Entry Movements in Maharashtra and Gujarat see Makarand Mehta, 'The Dalit Temple Entry Movements in Maharashtra and Gujrat 1930–48', a paper presented at the previously cited IIAS seminar.

16. Eleanor Zelliot, 'Gandhi and Ambedkar—A study in Leadership', in J. Michael Mahar (ed.), *The Untouchables in Contemporary India*, Tuscon: The University of Arizona Press, 1972, pp. 82–3.

17. See for an Advaithin reading of Gandhiji: Ramachandra Gandhi 'God is Truth', in Ramashraya Roy (ed.), *Contemporary Crisis and Gandhi*, Delhi: Discovery Publishing House, 1986, pp. 31–43.

18. *Harijan*, Vol. 1, 1933, p. 5.

19. Ibid., p. 36.

20. In fact, M.C. Rajah, the respected leader of the depressed classes in South India, clashed with C. Rajagopalachari on this question; being in power CR was more cautious, but Rajah was keen to move his private bill regarding temple entry, and it was defeated in the end. For an interesting discussion of the issue see S. Krishna Swamy, *The Role of Madras Legislature in the Freedom Struggle 1861–1947*, Delhi.

21. *Harijan*, Vol. 1, 1933, p. 4.

22. Ibid., 4 March 1933, p. 7.

23. Ibid., 6 May 1933, p. 1.

24. Renford Bambrough, 'Fools and Heretics', in A. Philip Griffiths (ed.), *Wittgenstein Centenary Essays,* Cambridge: Cambridge University Press, 1991, pp. 244–5.

25. Recently many studies using metaphor as a central methodological principle have appeared. See Bipin Indurkhya, *Metaphor and Cognition,* Dordrecht: Kluwer Academic Publishers, 1992, pp. 21–6. There is an interesting section on metaphors in non-linguistic domains, though it stops short of exploring metaphors in political discourse. Works of Paul Ricouer are of immense interest in this regard.
Donald Miller, *The Reason of Metaphor*, New Delhi: Sage, 1992.

26. If put together what Mahadev Desai has written on this untouchable boy, it will read like a short story which is pregnant with multiple meanings. See

Harijan, Vol. 1 issues from 13 May to June 1933 for the entire story I have narrated in the body of this chapter.

27.   *Harijan*, Vol. 11, 21 December 1934 p. 354.

28.   Ibid., Vol. 1, 27 October 1933, p. 4.

29.   Ibid., Vol. 11, 7 September 1934, p. 236.

30.   Lacoue-Labarthe uses this concept of ontological difference while defending Heidegger against attacks launched by many writers including Adomo who argued that the much celebrated German philosopher's thought is 'fascist right down to its inner most components', see Philip Lacoue-Labarthe, *Heidegger, Art and Politics*, Chris Turner (trs.), Oxford: Basil Blackwell, 1990. Clarification of a point will be in order here: I am more interested in using this particular notion of 'ontological difference' rather than endorsing the author's defence of Heidegger. I am equally fascinated by Lacoue-Labarthe's ideas regarding the quite complex relation between politics, aesthetic categories, and philosophy. See Lacoue-Labarthe, *Typography: Mimesis Philosophy, Politics*, Christopher Fynsk (ed.), Cambridge, Mass: Harvard University Press, 1989.

Contributors

A.L. BASHAM (1914–1986) was Professor of Oriental Civilizations at Australian National University, Canberra, Australia.

AKEEL BILGRAMI is Johnsonian Professor of Philosophy at Columbia University, USA.

PARTHA CHATTERJEE is Director at the Centre for Studies in Social Sciences, Calcutta, India and Visiting Professor of Anthropology at Columbia University, USA.

RAMACHANDRA GUHA is a full-time writer, based in Bangalore, India.

MADHU KISHWAR is Senior Fellow at the Centre for the Study of Developing Societies, Delhi, India.

D.R. NAGARAJ (1954–1998) was Senior Fellow at the Centre for the Study of Developing Societies, Delhi, India.

ASHIS NANDY is Senior Fellow at the Centre for the Study of Developing Societies, Delhi, India.

BHIKHU PAREKH is Professor of Political Theory at the University of Hull, UK.

SUJATA PATEL is Professor of Sociology at the University of Pune, India.

SUNIL SAHASRABUDHEY is Faculty, Gandhian Institute of Studies, Varanasi, India.

A.K. SARAN was Professor of Sociology at Jodhpur University, Rajasthan, India.

SUMIT SARKAR was Professor of History at the University of Delhi, India.

SHIV VISVANATHAN is Professor at Dhirubhai Ambani Institute of Information and Communication Technology, Gujarat, India.